ON DECK

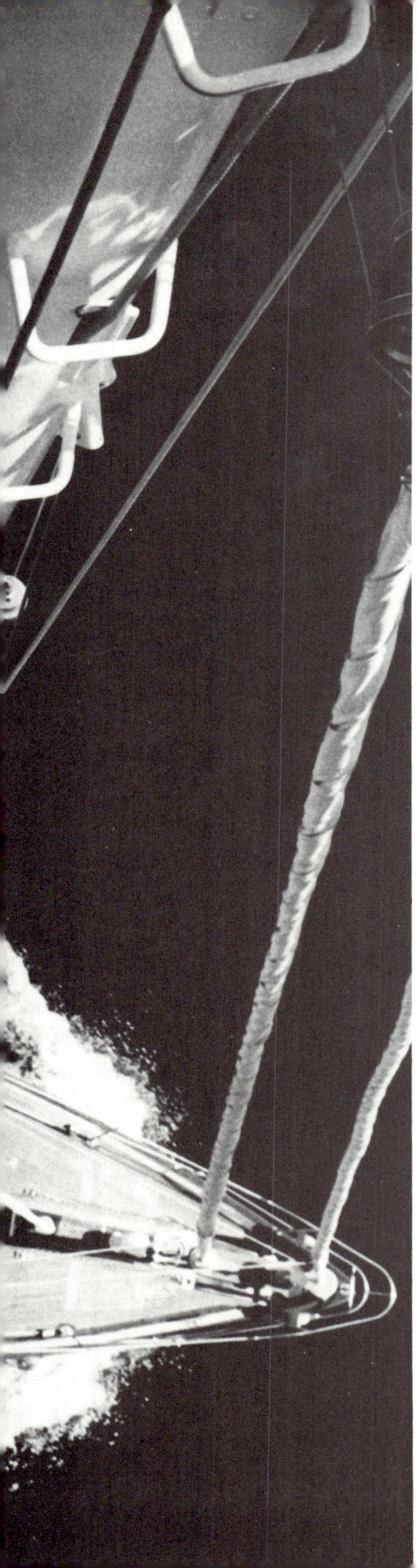

ON DECK

The Illustrated Manual of New-Tech Seamanship

JOHN R. WHITING

Drawings by Philip G. Wright
Photographs by John R. Whiting

HEARST MARINE BOOKS
NEW YORK

Library of Congress Cataloging in Publication Data

Whiting, John R.
On deck.

1. Seamanship. I. Title.
VK541.W45 1985 623.88 85-7680
ISBN 0-688-05688-1

Printed in the United States of America

First Edition

1 2 3 4 5 6 7 8 9 10

BOOK DESIGN BY ARLENE GOLDBERG
WITH JOHN R. WHITING

Philip G. Wright is the co-illustrator of this book and helped plan the voyage of its writing. As many readers know, Phil did the drawings for the author's earlier book, *You Can Sail.* He has contributed many nautical drawings to *Motor Boating & Sailing* magazine.

Mr. Wright earns his living as an architect. He received his B.S. in architecture from the University of Texas at Arlington. He is a member of the American Institute of Architects.

Phil lives—and sails—in Texas, with his wife, Roberta, and a nine-year-old daughter, Molly. The Wrights all enjoy sailing, mostly on Galveston Bay. As you might guess, Phil has been sailing for twenty years, and has a special liking for the prefiberglass days. He currently owns a thirty-four-foot ketch designed by Thomas Colvin and named *Isis.* He is a member of the Houston Yacht Club.

Acknowledgments

Many persons, organizations, and companies helped with this book by furnishing information, assisting with illustrations, and providing technical data. Among them are:

Aamstrand Ropes, Chicago, IL; Paul Brown, Advanced Mooring Systems, Camden, ME; F. E. Rothwell, Allied Fibers and Plastics, Petersburg, VA; The Aluminum Association; Amco of Windsor, ONT; James Lippmann, American Boat & Yacht Council, Amityville, NY; American Manufacturing Company, Honesdale, PA; Barney Gordon, American Marine Supply Co., Highland Park, MI; American Water Ski Association, Winter Park, FL; Jeffrey Holland and Jerry Wood, Annapolis Sailing School; Baltic Marine Products, Inc., Chicago, IL; Michael Sciulla and Richard Schwartz, Boat Owners Association of the U.S., Alexandria, VA; Campbell Chain Division, McGraw-Edison Co.; Andrew Vavolotis, Cape Dory Yachts, East Taunton, MA; Charles H. Vilas, Cruising Club of America; Klara Dallas; Detroit Diesel; Henry R. Keene, The Edson Corp., New Bedford, MA; James McGrew of Fid-O McGrew Splicing Tool Co., Elverta, CA; Edward Quest, Florida Wire and Rigging Works, Miami, FL; Forespar, Fores Manufacturing Co., Tustin, CA; George Gleistein & Sohn, GMBH, Bremen, Germany; Jay Stuart Haft, Bradenton, FL; Harken Yacht Fittings, Pewaukee, WI; David Parker and Bryant Phillips, Hatteras Yachts, High Point, NC; Herbert Hild, Hild Sails, City Island, NY; Howe & Bainbridge, Inc., Boston, MA; Irwin Yacht & Marine Corp., Clearwater, FL; Johnson Yacht Hardware, East Haddam, CT; MacLear & Harris, New York, NY; MacWhyte Wire Rope Co., Kenosha, WI; Carl Spiegel, Marine Development & Research, Freeport, NY; Marlow Ropes, Medford, MA; Merriman Yacht Specialties, Grand River, OH; Dan Fales and Peter Janssen, *Motor Boating & Sailing* magazine; Fred McKaig, Mooring Products Corp., Pompano Beach, FL; Dan Murray, Riverhead, NY; Jeff Napier, George Rounds, and Frank Scalpone of the National Marine Manufacturers Association; Navtech, Inc., Littleton, MA; Sohei Hohri, librarian and curator, New York Yacht Club; Norman S. Wright, Jr., Nicro Corp.; Robert Ogg, Kentfield, CA; Petersen Manufacturing Co., Dewitt, NE; Powerwinch, Shelton, CT; Otto Riemer, Clearwater, FL; Ronstan Marine, Inc., Clearwater, FL; Stanley Rosenfeld; Bruce Rubin Associates, Coral Gables, FL; Chris Wenz, Sailspar Design, Inc., Port Chester, NY; Samson Ocean Systems, Waltham, MA; Schaefer Marine, Inc., New Bedford, MA; Shaw & Tenney, Orono, ME; Sparkman & Stephens; Kelsey Burr, Survival Technologies Group, St. Petersburg, FL; Tubbs Cordage Company, Orange, CA; Universal Wire Products, Inc., North Haven, CT; Wall Rope Works, Elkin, NC; Wellington-Puritan, Madison, GA; Jules Fleder, Westlawn School of Yacht Design, Stamford, CT; Fred Strasser, Wilcox-Crittenden, Middleton, CT; John N. Wolbarst, Boston, MA; Yacht Rigging Systems, Manchester, MA; and Yale Cordage, Yarmouth, ME.

Credits

The drawings on pages 147, 156, 157, 160, and 185 are from Niro-Fico, courtesy of Mr. Norman Wright, Jr.

The photographs on pages 8, 182, 183, and 246 are by Chip Gamertsfelder.

The photograph on page 118 is by Mr. Peter Barlow.

The jacket photograph is from Hatteras Yachts, and was made by Sid Stapleton.

The deck plan on pages 50 and 51 is courtesy of Sparkman and Stephens.

The photograph on page 64 is courtesy of Detroit Diesel.

The stanchion detail drawing on page 56 is courtesy of Irwin Yachts.

The photographs on pages 18, 21, 22, 148, and 216 are from Samson Ocean Systems, courtesy of Mr. Gale P. Foster.

The frontispiece photograph and those on pages 144 and 158 are from MacLear and Harris, courtesy of Mr. Frank MacLear.

The photographs on pages 141, 169, and 181 are by Mr. Marion Warren, made with the cooperation of the Annapolis Sailing School.

The photograph on page 175 is by Mr. Stanley Rosenfeld.

The photograph of the lover's knot on page 216 is from Marlinespike of Clearwater, courtesy of Mr. Otto Reimer.

The photographs of Gary Jobson on pages 178, 218, and 242 are from Sebago, makers of Docksider shoes.

The illustrations on pages 153 and 186 are from Hild Sails, courtesy of Mr. Herb Hild.

The photograph on page 239 is courtesy of the U.S. Coast Guard.

The illustration on page 155 is courtesy of Arthur Bandy and Forespar.

The illustration on page 164 is from Harken, makers of rigging hardware.

The drawing on page 116 is from Shaw and Tenney of Orono, Maine.

The illustration on page 166 is courtesy of MacWhyte Wire Rope Company.

The photograph on page 191 was made with the cooperation of Florida Wire and Rigging Company and Mr. Edward Quest.

The photographs on pages 236, 237, 243, and 244 are from Survival Technology Systems.

Mr. William Transue of Block Island Marine furnished many of the backgrounds for photographs by the author.

Contents

134

Introduction

There are those who believe they can buy a boat, turn on the ignition key, and drive away from the parking space, scarcely looking in the glove compartment for the map. There are others who are so awed they think it takes computer literacy to handle a modern sailboat.

The sea changes hardly at all and the gear changes slowly, so it might be a good idea to look at what really has been happening to seamanship. Joshua Slocum, that redoubtable captain who sailed alone around the world in 1898, would have little trouble sailing today's equivalent of his thirty-seven-foot yawl *Spray*. Yet if Slocum had awakened this year from a long nap, like Rip Van Winkle, he might have done some head scratching over transparent Mylar windows in sails, electric hot knives cutting nylon rope, double-braid halyards made of Kevlar and Dacron, or a magic box with its ball-bearing blocks taking care of the downhaul or the center boom vang.

As the technology of boats has moved into exotic materials and advanced electronics, the sailor has had to learn new skills and a few variations in the old arts of the seaman. There have been more changes in the past six or seven decades than in the previous six centuries.

Consider these points: Synthetic fibers, almost entirely replacing cotton and manila for sails and rope, have required some changes in the way knots and splices are used and have made possible improvements in the geometrical design of rope, after fifty centuries of that most excellent and beautiful artifact of man,

◀
A sailboat ready to dock, with fenders rigged and crew members holding lines at bow and stern.

three-strand laid rope. Nylon and polyester, or Dacron, sails alter the rigging requirements of modern sailboats.

Other exotic or everyday materials—the stainless steels, titanium, anodized aluminum, Delrin, Kevlar, carbon fibers, plastic-reinforced fiberglass, hard nylon and synthetic rubber, new-tech lubricants—have given designers and manufacturers the opportunity to make extensive improvements to the hardware for all types of boats. Innovators have created new geometry for anchors and new devices for handling halyards and sheets. Hydraulic systems are part of the rigging controls in even medium-tech racing sailboats.

In this book, if you are starting out on the adventure of boating, you may find the beauty of the double carrick bend as it is drawn, because that beauty is part of the fun, but be aware: You may never need to tie a carrick bend. You will perhaps feel a little bit cheated to find out there are about seven basic knots and seven advanced knots—and all the rest are just useful variations or amusements for readers of clipper-ship sagas and those devoted hobbyists who take up macrame and sennet. There are also a couple of fun knots scattered around this book, like the thief knot and the lovers' knot.

You are one of four persons, sometimes one, sometimes another:

A boat owner, large or small, power or sail. You have the re-

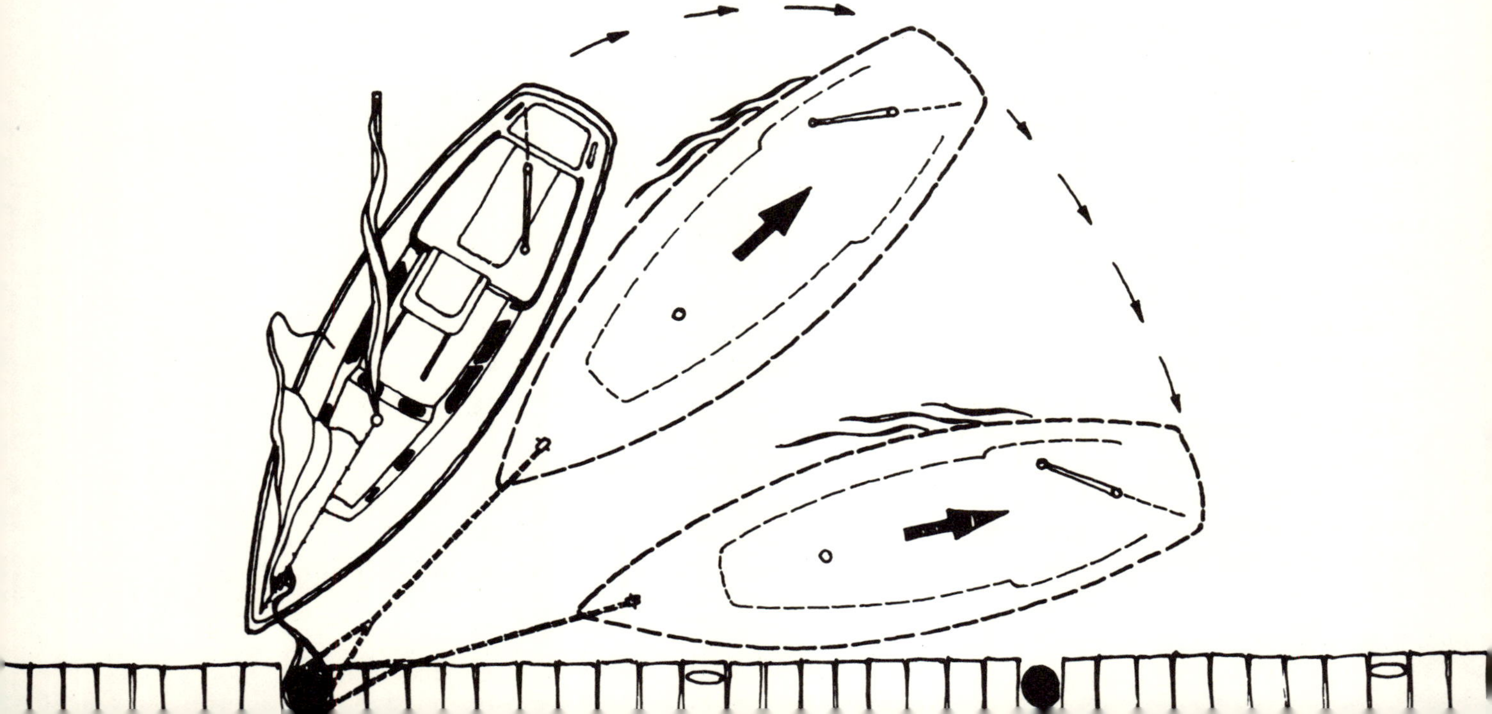

sponsibility for the boat and the people. You pay the costs. You are "the skipper."

A crew member, someone who goes boating on other people's boats. Actually, all of us do this at times, so you may be crew, guest, one who charters a strange boat for a week while on vacation in the islands, or an owner who is "between boats." For you, there is information here on "other boats."

A customer. In the world of boating there are things to make and things to buy. Knowing what to ask for, how to be an intelligent customer at a marine dealer, a chandlery, or a sailmaker's loft is often important.

An observer, one who notices unusual rigs, watches how the commercial fisherman rigs his nets, or enjoys and understands old-time sea stories. You may never sail on a square-rigger, but when you read a Hornblower novel, you want to know the differences between a brace, a sheet, and a guy. A special point: There is more to operating a boat than just the mechanics of it. If you have followed the writings of Carleton Mitchell, one of the eminently successful sailors in the two worlds of racing and cruising, you may have picked up some of his appreciation for the traditions of the sea. These matters are not just literary, they are to do with person-to-person, person-to-boat, and person-to-nature relationships. Mitch doesn't think of himself as one of the philosophers of sailing—but he is.

If you know Samuel Eliot Morrison's *Spring Tides* or Al Stanford's *The Pleasures of Sailing*, you may have caught the meaning and the beauty of small boats on the water in your own mind's eye. When you know Erskine Childers's *The Riddle of the Sands* or Slocum's *Sailing Alone Around the World*, still another part of your boating life begins.

The practical side of craftsmanship, at a certain point, becomes the elegance of perfection. My admiration for the rigging skills of Sam Barclay, a professional at Yacht Haven in Connecticut, or those of Art Northrop, one of the splendid amateurs whose beamy yet graceful *Calynda* plied New England waters for thirty-five years, must surely show in these pages. The quiet knowledge of Dr. Henry Wharton, whose *Many Moons* shone upon the waters of Long Island Sound, is reflected here, as is the inventiveness of John Van Sant, whose *Nobbin Blue* showed that a converted ship's lifeboat with a Star rig could be the start of a great sailing life. Another area of nautical thinking, for me, was what aviation has added to boating, which I first picked up visiting Gordon Groene, a pilot, aboard the little sloop, *Sans Souci*, he and Janet called home for many years. The relationship between naval architecture and aeronautical engineering is not often perceived, but it is there. Frank MacLear, a solid innovator, was once a senior production designer for United Aircraft. The MacWhyte Wire Rope Co. makes aircraft cables as well as sailboat rigging, and one adds to the other.

There are many horizons in the world of boating. Some extend only across a mountain lake, some across the Pacific. Some are conversational horizons. I remember yarning with Chris and Lew Vogler, looking out on San Francisco Bay, and learning about the commercial fishermen's boatmanship skills. Another time I was searching the London Boat Show for new ideas and discovered that the boat show swimming pool, with boats afloat and an authentic naked model (girl, not boat), is the British way. I had previously thought of Lord Nelson, I guess.

It takes beautiful memories of moonlight: going down Long Island Sound, bound for Block Island, aboard Don McGraw's *Interloper*, or watching the start of a race—a spinnaker start in the moonlight—off Lloyds' Harbor as a guest aboard Paul Hoffman's *Thunderhead*, to add up all the values of sailing.

It also takes just plain sitting in the cockpit with Ralph Naranjo aboard *Wind Shadow*, in the fogbound Salt Pond at Block Island, after he brought her three-quarters of the way around the world. Ralph was planning his charming book, *Wind Shadow West.* I watched the skill with which his two young children, Eric and Tara, handled the dinghy, and realized anew still another side to seamanship: what practicing it can do for self-reliance.

Once Charles F. Chapman, the noted author and editor who created *Piloting, Seamanship & Small Boat Handling,* talked with me about boats and the young sailor as we sat on his terrace at *Landorsea,* his home at Essex, overlooking the Connecticut River. Chap understood well what boating did for people and was one of the organizers of the largest boating group in the world, the U.S. Power Squadrons.

As a reader, you may look at your own boating confidence, at a given time, from the standpoint of one particular boat: a sixteen-foot outboard, a nineteen-foot sloop, a thirty-foot power cruiser, or a forty-foot cruising-racing sailboat. But as a typical consumer in the world of pleasure boats, you always have your eye on a larger boat, a better boat, and perhaps even another type of boat. Each maritime skill you acquire builds confidence.

This book concerns itself with small boats from the size of a dinghy up to, let's say, a sixty-five-foot sailing auxiliary like the Hatteras Sail Yacht.

You may be a beginner or you may have had one kind of experience, such as sailing on a small lake or chartering at some resort. So you may very well know one part of the subject matter but not another. As with every field of knowledge, when an author addresses the reader there is the thought: The reader knows part of this, he is interested in the subject, or he wouldn't be here. But he doesn't have all this information, or he wouldn't have picked up the book.

Because the techniques of docking or anchoring a vessel are similar whether it is power or sail, you will find this is covered as deckmanship. Of course knots are the same for power or sail. For that matter, the basics of rope and knots are the same on the farm, in rigging a circus tent, and when climbing a mountain.

A word about a word: *Wrinkles.* At the end of the nineteenth century, a Captain Leckey wrote a book about navigation. It's a great book, and it is called *Wrinkles in Practical Navigation.* I have

borrowed that name for the paragraphs of "extra ideas" at the end of each chapter.

There is a special language of the sea. It would have been easier to write this book if readers already knew that language. But don't expect to cope with *futtock shrouds, gantlines,* and *Stockholm tar* in these pages. The language of the sea is not always that exotic. After all, you know part of it already. If the meaning of a word does not come through from the context, look in the Glossary.

You may have heard that there is a right way and a wrong way to do many things. Someone may have told you ". . . and the navy way." But as Bill Rosenfeld reminded me, there is also an old saying: "Different ships, different splices." There are so many types of boats that standardization in seamanship is impossible. Even so, some ways are wrong because they can get you into trouble. As a form of emphasis, this book has a number of illustrations showing dos and don'ts . . . right and wrong. They are clearly marked.

Those who go down to the sea in small boats like to feel that they are braving the winds and the age-old dangers of the waves in modern safety, and perhaps they are. But the new technology brings new risks. If one benefit of the advanced engineering and modern materials is a potential increase in safety, it still takes thinking ahead to stay out of harm's way. This subject—thinking ahead—comes up many times in these pages.

I do not anticipate that every reader will master every one of today's advanced skills. In thirty-five years of weekend and vacation sailing, owning four sailboats, I have learned some things, such as that the wind can be dangerous, but I have left some kinds of learning to others. I decided I didn't need to learn how to make a wire-to-rope splice, for example, because a professional rigger can do it better. There are times when it is best to go to the professionals, and there are times when it is best to stay at anchor in a safe harbor while the storm blows itself out.

Our family's first boat was a twenty-six-foot cutter designed by Ellwood Sprague, who also designed Ed Raymond's famous *Chanteyman*. Our *Merrywend* was a wooden boat, with galvanized plow steel rigging, forged steel turnbuckles, cotton sails, manila lines, and a Bluejacket Twin motor. Except for the motor, she

might have been built right after the American Civil War. Our second *Merrywend* was a Sparkman & Stephens sloop, a Pilot. She too was built of wood, but she had stainless steel rigging, Dacron sails, a nylon anchor rode, Formica counters in the galley, and was as modern as her time. Our third, designed by Bill Tripp, had a fiberglass hull, vinyl-covered stainless steel lifelines, an aluminum mast, and stainless steel sheet winches. It could be said of *Merrywend III* that the oldest thing about her was the motor—for hulls, rigging, and sails had made far more progress than the gasoline engine.

As a beginner, especially, I had the advantage of occasional lessons from persons more experienced than I could ever be. There was old Eddie Quest at the City Island Yacht Club, a friendly man who had gone around Cape Horn under sail. There was Carleton Mitchell, who early on in my boating days once sailed with me for a happy weekend aboard my little cutter *Merrywend*, showing me the importance of tuning rigging and of trimming sails properly. Two years later, in his *Finisterre,* Mitch won the Bermuda race for the first of three consecutive times. The crew of *Merrywend* celebrated!

As this book has been on its own shakedown cruise, various persons have answered questions and provided information in areas where their special knowledge helped fill gaps. Two men especially have always been the "great explainers" of naval architecture for me and for many others: Rod Stephens, Jr. and Frank MacLear.

So much of this book relates to "marlinespike seamanship" that I must especially mention Gale P. Foster, of Samson Cordage, who untied for me many mysteries about rope. He is another good sailor, as is Ms. Queene Hooper, whose yawl *Moonfleet* is as good an example of boatkeeping as she is an example of friendkeeping.

The acknowledgments, preceding the Contents page, lists a crew big enough—and certainly capable enough—to sail a ship around the world. In a way, since I have drawn upon these many experts for their knowledge and experience, you sail with them in these pages. Many companies, of course, provided technical information; they are identified in the credits.

Another kind of help—pictorial and photographic—has been given by Peter Barlow, Chip Gamertsfelder, John Livingston, Marion Warren, Harry Amdur of Modernage Photographic Services, Stanley Rosenfeld of *the* Rosenfelds, and my artist and sailor friend Philip Wright. The most creative contribution of all was made by my wife, Helen, who always asks the questions, makes sure the answers are as clear as possible—and had the patience to bring to the seagoing world my daughters Wendy, Merry, and Robin.

John R. Whiting
Aboard Bayberry,
Block Island, R.I.

Everything needs tying down—awnings, rigging gear, spare lines. Eyes, cleats, and even lifelines are used.

Chapter 1

Rope . . . Is Called Line

A commercial on TV shows a barge under tow breaking loose when a frayed hawser parts. The crew of a nearby towboat swings into action. Two men leap aboard the drifting barge; lines are thrown and quickly made fast to giant cleats; the skipper of the towboat maneuvers expertly, and in less than a minute all is under control again. The skipper and the deckhands, deservedly, relax with a beer, perhaps knowing that much of the essence of seamanship is summed up in that sixty seconds.

Here's another scene you may have seen, live, not on the TV screen at all: A sailboat enters a harbor, the black cloud of an approaching squall behind it. The skipper rounds up into the wind, the crew quickly drop the sails and let go the anchor, get all sails furled and covered—and are snug and comfortable in the four minutes before the squall hits.

All this, of course, is part of deckmanship, of "marlinespike seamanship," this business of *using* line, as well as making knots and splices and thus controlling the vessel correctly and effectively.

Marlinespike seamanship can be said to have three aspects:

1) Understanding the rope and the language of rope, the equipment, the hardware, the gear, and the rig.
2) Learning certain hand skills, involving a feel for rope and knots.
3) Acquiring a sense of timing. This is partly thinking ahead, partly knowing how long certain boating procedures will take, and mostly knowing what to do when.

◄
Rope transmits power, sometimes in a straight line, around a corner, or reversing the direction. Here a halyard winch is used for control as well as power.

For centuries three-strand rope was used on land and at sea, with crude but sturdy devices, such as deadeyes, used to tighten rigging.

Rope is a hold-down, a handle, and even an art object in the hands of a skilled craftsman.

Two typical observations involving timing tell it. The skipper of a power cruiser on a river might well notice that a sailboat is tacking across the channel half a mile ahead of him and decide to slow his own speed because he knows that a boat with a keel, under sail, has constraints on its maneuverability. Or any crew member, aboard a boat about to leave its slip, might note a big sportsfisherman coming into the marina and suggest waiting a minute before taking in the dock lines and backing out of the slip.

WHAT ROPE DOES

In this introductory chapter, we will take a brief look at what rope does. We'll look at some of the kinds of rope and hardware as well as at basic hand skills. A note or two about some of the boating procedures that almost everyone must use will remind us of the timing.

First, a look at what rope basically is and does.

Rope transmits power in a straight line and around a corner, even changing the direction of force. It exchanges speed for power when used with blocks or pulleys and is, with various other kinds of cordage, the great hold-down at sea. There are a few ingenious variations: "small stuff," plus woven straps and webbing, the seemingly sticky stuff called Velcro, shock cord, and wire rope. In a general way all these products are referred to as **cordage**.

The story of rope starts with the basic three-strand form that was an excellent product twenty-five centuries ago. (It still is, of course.) For hundreds of years, rope made from various natural fibers such as hemp was the key to seagoing accomplishment. The nations with the best sources of "naval stores," lumber for ships, and fibers for rope and sails dominated the seas. Eventually, a high-quality rope, made from the fiber of the wild banana plant in the Philippines and therefore called manila, became recognized as the best for its time. Manila did not need to be tarred to protect it from rot. In its usual three-strand twisted or "laid" form it was easily spliced, and the many scores of shipboard knots invented by sailors came naturally to hand with manila.

MAN-MADE ROPE FIBERS

The synthetic fibers changed many things, beginning with the nylon first used in World War II. The inventors, the chemical engineers, developed half a dozen synthetic or man-made fibers with superior characteristics and made possible the important variations in the "geometry" and other characteristics of cordage that are part of today's marlinespike seamanship.

The first important synthetic fiber to be used in rope and for sailcloth was a polyamide plastic, generally referred to as nylon. Nylon rope is about three times as strong, size for size, as fine manila. It has a certain stretch or elasticity, which is good for some uses but undesirable for others. For anchor lines or dock lines, nylon is ideal. Similarly, nylon sailcloth is fine for spinnakers, where some elasticity is desirable. Note that nylon is not a trade name. Although the DuPont company was prominently involved in the original development and introduction of nylon, a number of manufacturers now make nylon.

For running rigging, where a minimum of stretch is wanted, polyester rope is used most often. The rope manufacturers have also developed methods of prestretching special ropes for halyards. In the United States, several brand names are popular, including Dacron (pronounced day-cron), the DuPont brand.

The most-used British trade name for polyester fibers used in manufacturing rope and sailcloth is Terylene. Other trade names used in various countries are Diolen, Duron, Lavsan, Polyant, Tergal, Terital, Terlenka, Tetoron, Trevira, and Vestan.

Although the two kinds of rope that are most familiar are nylon and Dacron (polyester), several other new kinds of materials are useful for special purposes and are coming to the fore in the world of high-tech racing.

Polypropylene rope is somewhat stronger than old-fashioned manila; it deteriorates in sunlight—but it floats. So it is frequently used for water-ski tow ropes and dinghy painters.

Kevlar, one of the newest synthetics, has the least stretch and is strong; its chief drawback is that these very qualities lead to internal breakdowns when the rope goes over a sheave. The aramid fibers break a little as they are stressed and bent, since they have little stretch. The useful life of Kevlar at maximum strength is thus decreased. Special low-stretch ropes are made by combining Kevlar with polyester or Spectra-900, the olefin high-strength fiber introduced by Allied in 1985, with polyester.

A few other kinds of rope are used on boats, usually for reasons of economy. You may see polyethylene and other kinds of plastic-based fibers, as well as some of the older natural fibers, but more usually in noncritical applications.

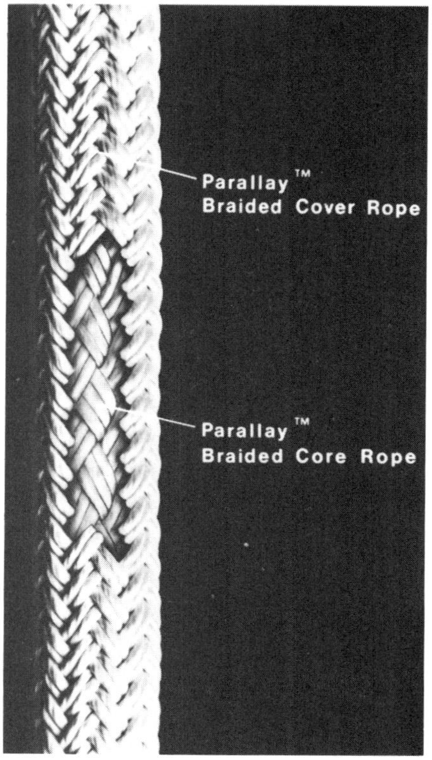

This Samson Nystron rope is a composite, with a nylon core (with some stretch) and a polyester cover for increased resistance to abrasion.

Rope-making is a changing technology, with new synthetic materials and construction forms that can be engineered.

The synthetics have other general characteristics—they don't rot as natural fibers do; in some forms they tend to be a little more slippery, which changes knot-tying and splicing techniques; and they are self-lubricating. The rope can be made with various textures and varying degrees of stiffness. Sunlight and heat, sand, friction, and chemicals are the chief enemies of synthetic ropes.

NEW SHAPES FOR ROPE

New ways of making rope, ranging from important details like controlling the length and texture of fibers and yarns to important configurations such as double braid, have been just as significant as the new materials in the development of the new kinds of cordage.

Laid rope is the traditional kind. Look first at a length of three-strand rope, for centuries the most common kind. As you hold it in your hand, it can be seen to twist to the right; most rope is right-hand lay, or Z-twist to the ropemakers. Think of the crossbar of the Z as you look at the rope.

Now, start unlaying the rope, looking at how each of the three strands is made. Each strand, made of yarns, is twisted, in the opposite direction, or to the left. Most of the "stability" in laid rope is built in by the way the yarns are twisted one way as the strands are formed, and the strands are then twisted the other way as the rope is laid.

As you might guess, small amounts of rope are made with a left-hand lay, or an S-twist, for special purposes, and a little four-strand rope is also made. Wire rope, to be discussed later, has more strands and is more complex.

Braided rope, with a number of special configurations, has so many advantages that it is fast replacing laid rope in most pleasure boating. Unlike laid rope, braided rope does not kink or hockle. It handles smoothly, knots well, and is both strong and durable. Splicing braided rope seems more difficult, but only at first.

Various forms of braiding and plaiting are used. These will be examined in detail in this and later chapters.

As every sailor knows, the standing rigging—wire rope, turnbuckles or bottle screws, tangs and shackles—is really part of the *structure* of a vessel. The running rigging, on the other hand, may be considered part of the *power system.*

The many ways rope is used: Think of a rope—a line—as a device to transfer power. A block changes the direction of the force.

A combination of blocks does approximately the same thing as gears in a transmission or other machine—they "change speeds," in most cases increasing the power while decreasing the speed. Blocks provide a "low gear."

Double braid, with a hollow core inside a hollow cover, makes a strong rope, able to resist abrasion (the cover takes the wear). Knots are the same but new splicing techniques are required.

COILS: ROPE READY TO USE

Coiling: Lines, when they are not in use, still must be ready for use. One way or another, they must be coiled or flaked down. A lesson in coiling rope, at one time, meant that you were shown how to start with the line in your left hand. Then, using the right hand to make the coils, you went *clockwise* as you coiled, taking care to make even coils that could be tied up, hung up, or laid down "ready to run." Because of the twist or lay of the rope, all standard or right-hand lay line was coiled this way. Your hand can feel it take its coils naturally.

If you are going to throw a dock line a short distance to a helping hand shoreside, as you come into a pier or float, you can hold a small part of the coil in your throwing (right) hand and the other coils in your left, releasing these coils as the line snakes out to the dock.

Coiling a halyard, to hang it on the cleat under the winch, is done in its own special way, with a quick loop through the tops of the coils to hang over the cleat. There are a number of other specific coils.

A main sheet, hanging under the end of the boom, is best made up in a seamanlike manner, so that it will be ready the next time it is needed.

Coiling braided line: One thing has changed. Today, with more than half or all the running rigging of a modern sailboat likely to be braided line and with many dock lines and anchor lines made of double braid, there's a new twist to the coiling. The braided line is not under torsion; it has no built-in twist, and it is therefore difficult to make into more than a few neat coils. Instead, the seaman goes through similar motions but probably ends up with figure eights.

As you work with line, you learn to look ahead. If you want to get an anchor line ready on deck you may very well make a better arrangement than coils: You can flake it down.

Overhauling a line is a way of making sure it will work. If you are about to drop the jib, it is good to overhaul the halyard first. At

Special braids can be made up in special ways, as this line on an inflatable boat, led through itself to make a secure fastening on a ring.

the very least you take the coil from the cleat, make sure it is completely free and untangled, and make the bitter end fast. As you know, this means you make a quick hitch with the end, a temporary half hitch would do, around a handy place, perhaps the lifeline. If the coiled halyard has become tangled or looks as though it might not run free, you recoil it, turn by turn. *Then* you go forward to pull the jib down and gather it on the foredeck, knowing that the halyard won't snag when the jib is halfway down.

The Flemish coil is a variation that may be less practical, even ritualistic in some ways. The Flemish coil is flat, however, so it is not a tripping hazard. It is sometimes used under a lazy block (one that is in place but not under strain at the moment) to keep the block from clattering on the deck. In most cases, Flemishing is an ornamental flourish—a good thing to know about if someday a visiting dignitary will be coming aboard your boat. It's a neat way to take care of the excess end of a dock line, on deck or on the pier. But if it's left on deck all week, you may have a circular set of marks on the deck to show for it.

Hanging ready for use are a line prerigged as a tackle, another with a monkey's fist (a weighted knot) attached so that a light line can be thrown, then used to haul a heavy hawser, and odd lines, ready for special jobs.

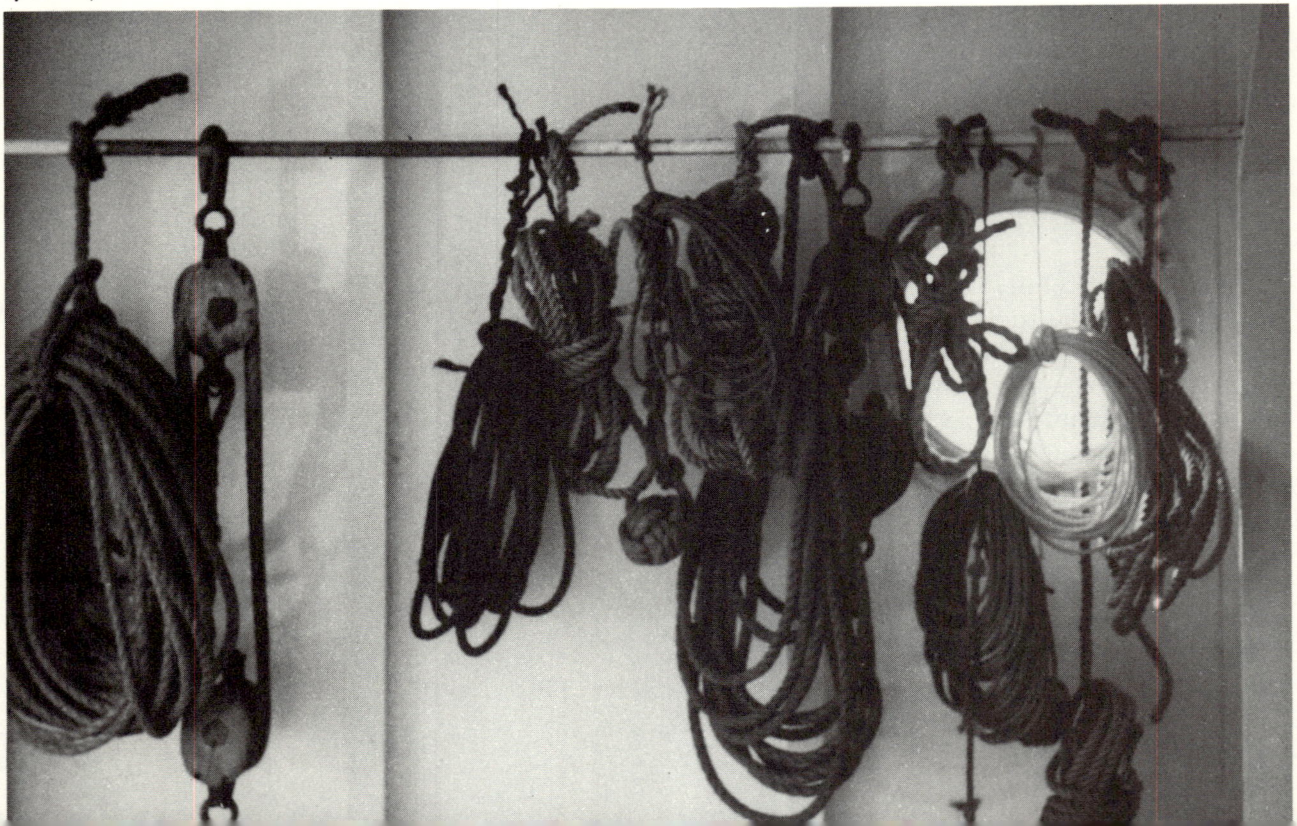

The Flemish coil is a neat way to get extra line out of the way—more useful at the dock than in rough-water conditions.

THE LANGUAGE OF ROPE

The language of rope is not only colorful, it's useful to know.

Here are the highlights: If you're working with line, the long length, the working length, is called the **standing part**. Make a half loop with your hands and what you have is called a **bight**. If the bight is around a post or ring, for example, it's a turn, and if it completely encircles the ring, it's a **round turn**, which is sometimes part of a knot. You can turn the loop into an **eye,** with a splice or a knot.

The other end of the line, which might run right out of your hands if it weren't **made fast**, is called the **bitter end**, probably because it might well be made fast to the bitts, the twin posts on the foredeck of some vessels, where the anchor line or a towline is fastened.

If a line has been taking some wear in one spot, one solution is to **freshen the nip**, to let it out or take it in a few inches, so that a fresh place takes the wear.

Handsomely is a word seldom heard today, but its meaning is important. It does not mean "with style," or "with alacrity"; it means "slowly, with care," and that's the right way to **ease** a sheet, adjust a dock line or towline, or bring a dinghy up to the boarding ladder.

When you stop a rope from running out by taking a turn around the horn of a **cleat** or the bitts, you're **snubbing** it. When you finish fastening the line, you have **belayed** it, or **made fast.** If it's a dock line and passes through a sort of metal slot to hold it in place, that's a **chock.** If the line is in active use, such as a jib sheet, a somewhat similar fixture that holds the line and perhaps makes a small adjustment in its direction is a **fairlead.**

If the turn is at a greater angle, the sheet runs through what landsmen sometimes call a pulley but on a boat is called a **block.** The grooved "wheel" on which the line runs inside the block is a **sheave.** (Actually, a pulley is the wheel itself.)

When you put a line through a block, setting up some item of rigging, you **reeve** the line. If the line is rigged so that there are two blocks, with one of them perhaps having two sheaves, you have a special way of applying power, called a **block-and-tackle** in general terms. Such an arrangement might have a specific name such as **downhaul.** Another name for such a device to apply power is a **purchase,** and the measure of its ability is called the **mechanical advantage,** generally expressed as a ratio, as we will see later.

If an alternate method of fastening a rope is used, called a **splice,** the strands are interwoven in the case of laid rope, or the core of double-braided rope is tucked inside the cover in a most ingenious fashion. A splice may be used to make an **eye** in the end of a rope or to join two ropes; there are fancier kinds of splices too. A splice is usually stronger and in many cases neater than a knot, but it has disadvantages, as we will see. One is that it cannot conveniently be undone when changes are to be made.

Friction, from blocks, fairleads, chocks, and even cleats, cuts down the power of a rope and eventually wears its surfaces. This is more of a problem with stranded rope than with the braided types.

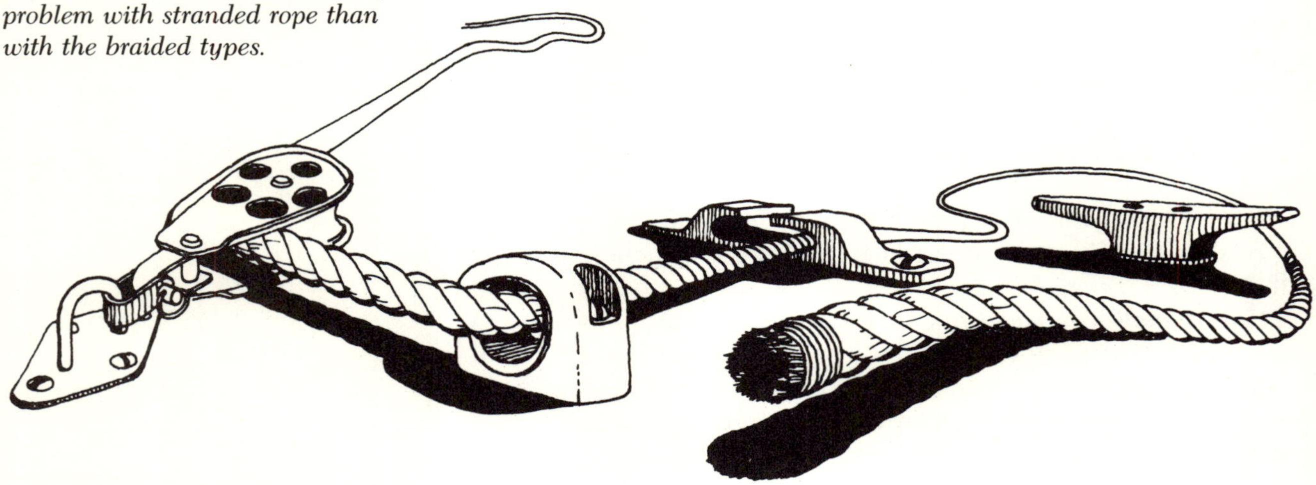

A century and a half ago, the standing rigging of a ship was made of rope and had to be tightened with clever but awkward arrangements of **deadeyes** and **lanyards.** Today's boats, yachts, and ships use wire rope rigging that is tightened by an arrangement of screw-threads called **turnbuckles** or **bottle-screws,** or by still another metal device with rows of holes and pins, called a **shroud adjuster.** A short length of line, which might also be used to fasten a sailor's knife to his belt, is still called a lanyard, and indeed, when there are no spare turnbuckles left after an accident, a sailor might still rig something resembling dead-eyes and lanyards. The nautical world of stainless steel and plastics can sometimes fall back on the past.

Rope ends are important. To make the end of a line neat and prevent it from coming untwisted or unbraided, there are a number of finishing tricks. Heat will melt and seal the ends; a **whipping** can be applied by winding waxed twine around the line in any number of ways, and the chemical people have even dreamed up a way to dip the end in a plastic that will harden.

Wrapping a section of a line with twine is a good way to prevent wear; it's called **serving.** If you bind two ropes together with a similar lashing, it's called a **seizing.** If you were to make a fancier kind of serving, using tape as well as line, the operation would be called **worm-and-parcel.**

The language of boating has its accents and variations, as we note. This is also true when it comes to **knots.** In general terms, a knot is a way of making rope hold, so a splice is also a knot. To an old-time sailor, who might have a touch of the purist about language, a **bend** is used to fasten two lines together, a **hitch** fastens a rope to a spar, a sail, or another rope—and there are a lot of exceptions.

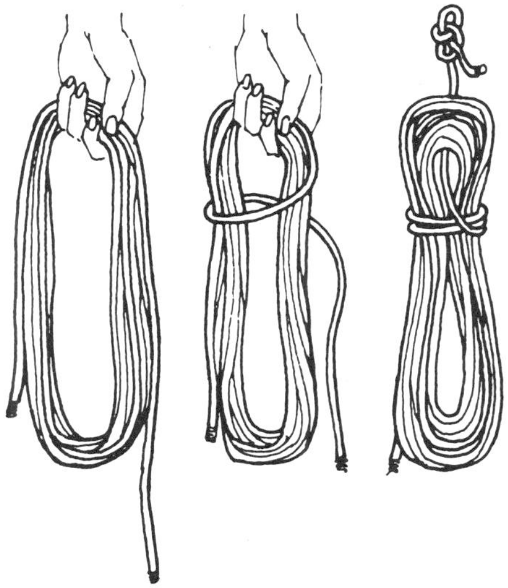

It takes practice, but coiling a line is a hand skill that uses the natural feel of the twisted rope. Braided line is more difficult to coil.

WRINKLES

Rubber or plastic water hose is difficult to stow or even coil for stowage aboard a boat. Many cruising boats need hose aboard, for taking on water at transient docks or for hosing off the decks. One workable solution: a new type of hose that coils flat on its own reel when not in use.

Coiling an electric extension wire, such as is used for shoreside power: Start in the middle of the wire and double-coil it, working toward the ends.

Chapter 2

Seven Basic Knots

Most persons who are interested in boats already know some knots and have a smattering of sailor's skills . . . but we don't all know the same things, and some of the knots many of us "know" may not work quite as well aboard a boat.

A good case can be made that just about all the knots you'll use can be counted on the fingers of one hand. One or two more also help you learn how knots work, and one variation is the right knot for the laces of your deck shoes. That brings the count to something like seven basic knots.

Let's look at the simplest knot—the **overhand knot.** It makes a bump on a piece of thread; perhaps you remember seeing your aunt tie an overhand knot when starting to sew on a button. It kept the thread from pulling through the cloth. The overhand knot is a simple "stopper knot." It is often thought of as a useless knot, yet it is a part of other knots and has several practical uses.

A slight variation is a **figure-eight knot.** This makes an even better **stopper knot** than the overhand knot, because it is larger and relatively easy to undo. Its chief place at sea is in the end of a line, to keep the line from escaping through a block or fairlead.

Now, there is another variation: If you make almost the same round turn as the overhand knot and then catch the rope or line under itself, when tying onto a ring or a pole, you have a **half hitch.** It's useful for a very temporary hold, and as you can guess, it is also the first part of **two half hitches.** In a slightly different form it is the **cleat hitch.**

There are several ways to turn even a half hitch into a useful

The slippery half hitch (you know it as part of a bow knot) is a useful temporary knot.

◄

A cleat hitch is made by taking successive half hitches around the horns. Here the extra line has been made into a Flemish coil.

knot. If you add a little bulk by doubling the second half hitch back, you have a **slippery half hitch**—a little more secure, yet easy to undo. It's still a temporary hitch, good for tying down the corner of an awning while you adjust the other corner; a minute later you give a pull and free it, readjust, and then make the longer lasting two half hitches.

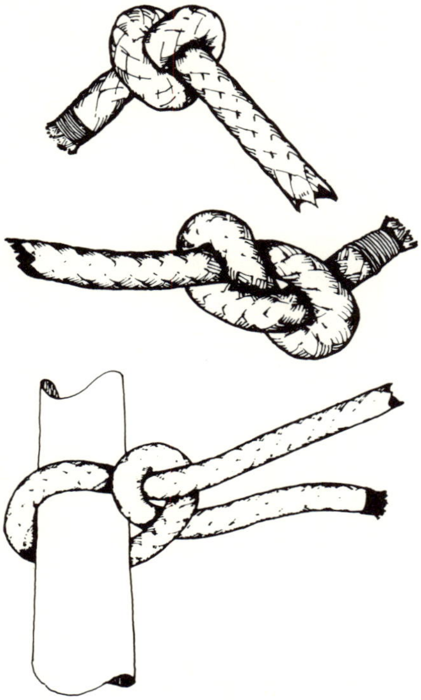

The overhand knot is so simple that it is often overlooked. Its variations include the figure eight and the half hitch.

DEFINITIONS

While we're rambling through ordinary knots, discovering small variations with even the simplest, this is a good time to remember once again that there are knots, bends, and hitches. Sometimes the name tells you which is which. A hitch is likely to be more "temporary" than a bend. *Knot* is a broader term, taking in both bends and hitches as well as some special configurations: splices or the several ways of fastening a line to a cleat or a bollard.

Working with rope turns up some small variations. Take two half hitches, for instance, tied by bringing the two binding turns around a piece of the original line. The second hitch holds the first. But make the same two binding turns around a pole or a piling (instead of around the rope itself) and you have a knot with another name, a **clove hitch,** a popular knot that is always on anyone's list of the first seven knots to learn.

The clove hitch, you will learn, isn't quite as useful as it is advertised to be, for the very good reason that it is so easy to adjust, it can even overadjust itself (loosen) when you don't want it to. If there is a changing strain on the clove hitch, it slips so much you might say it tends to untie itself. But if the clove hitch is in the middle of a line, as it might be when using one long dock line to reach two cleats and both ends are under strain, it works fine.

A point worth noticing: The clove hitch is good if your dock line is under strain as you tie it. The first part of it will usually hold the boat while you complete the hitch.

There is a solution to the slipping clove hitch: Make a security half hitch around the line itself after you make the clove hitch.

But there are better ways to tie up a boat than with a clove hitch.

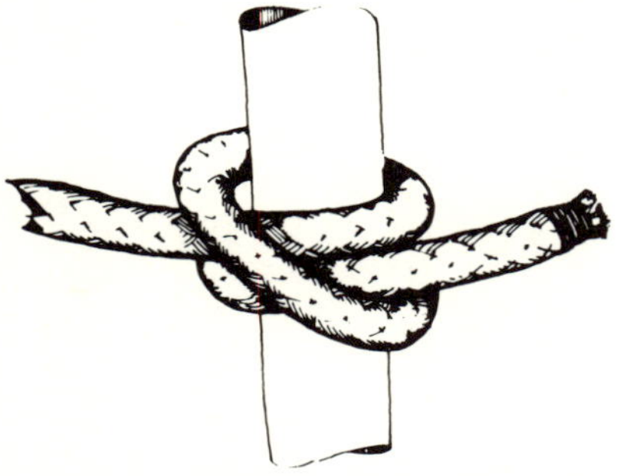

The clove hitch is so adjustable it can even work itself loose. Use it with care.

The cleat hitch is one of the better ways, and as we noted, a variation of the half hitch. Most people don't even give it a name. *Cleating down* and *belaying* are other terms that are often heard. In any case, there is a right way, which is easy, but there are also a

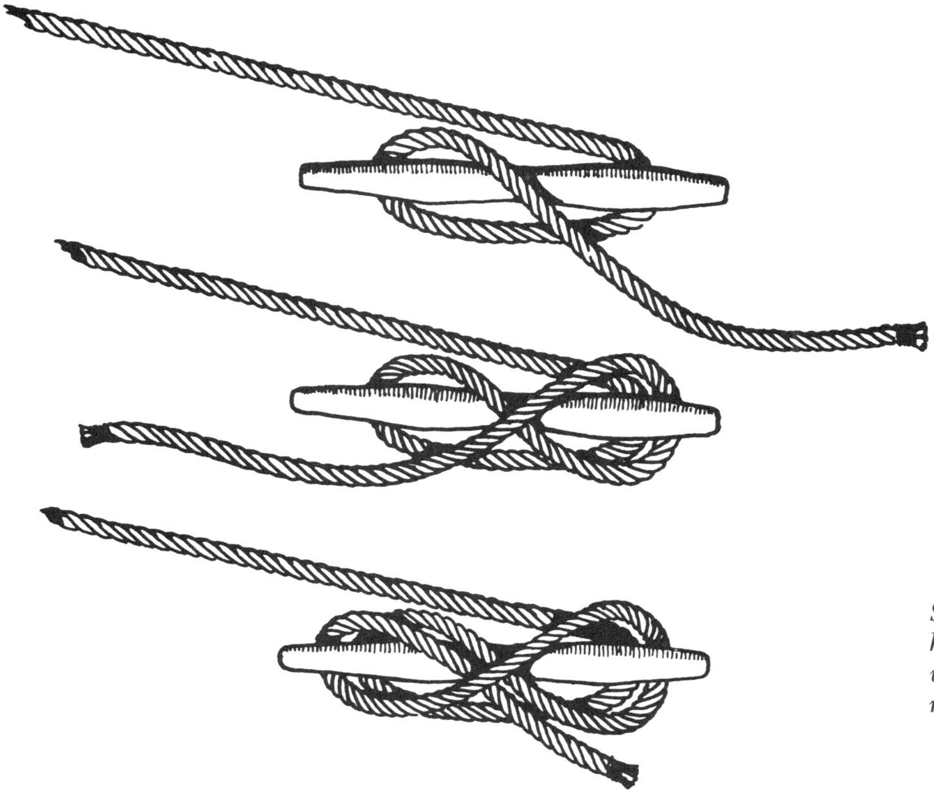

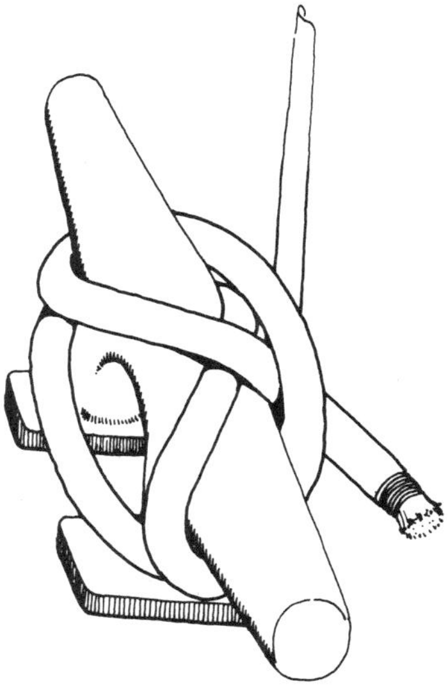

Small mistakes in making the cleat hitch may make it awkward to undo. Most beginners make too many turns.

The bowline is the king of knots, the strong knot, the knot that can always be untied, the knot with a thousand uses.

The square or reef knot can be tied rapidly. It holds when used to secure something—a sail or a package—but it is not good for tying two lines together.

number of small mistakes you can make. They're not fatal; they're just unhandy.

As you learn to make fast to a cleat, start with the line leading to the cleat. Take it under the farthest horn and around it, *then* angle it across. That's the best start, because now the line has enough friction so it is easy to hold while you complete the job. (This is called snubbing, naturally.) Now go around the horn, making a couple of figure eights.

Here are three common mistakes made in cleating down a line:

- ▲ Leading the line to the nearest horn of the cleat or clear around the base of the cleat on the first turn so that the line tends to jamb later on when you want to release it.
- ▲ Putting too many criss-crossed figure eights. A couple will hold; more will only take time to undo later on.
- ▲ Making a final locking turn in cases where a quick release may be necessary, or making it with the wrong twist, which looks sloppy.

The same turns are used in making a line fast to a pair of bitts or to a belaying pin.

We have been observing that there are often several ways of doing things. In some cases there is a *best* way.

THE KING OF KNOTS

The bowline is one of the best ways of all to solve the problem of dropping a loop (strictly, an **eye**) over a piling. One of the other ways is with a previously made **eye splice,** which of course is a closed loop. But if you don't have an eye splice already in the line, you can make a strong eye, of whatever size you need, in a hurry by tying that bowline. Of all the useful knots, safe knots, dependable knots, and easy-to-untie knots—the bowline is number one.

The bowline is neither hard to remember nor difficult to tie, but it is used so often and in so many ways that you may want to consider giving yourself some special training, to look expert and feel expert. If you could have only one knot, you would surely choose the bowline.

Some bowline pointers:

- ▲ Be sure you learn it "upside down and backward." It has to be right or it isn't a bowline, and an approximation is not much good. As with other knots, make sure you know what it looks like no matter which side is up.

▲ Practice tying this, and other knots, in various positions and situations. You may first learn it sitting in a living room chair and tying the bowline in front of you. But now try putting a loop of the line around a table leg and *then* making the bowline. Try making the small loop first, with either hand.

▲ You might even try the bowline in the dark, just to get to the point that you can always do it. Surgeons have been known to practice tying surgical knots with one hand, and that hand hidden in a coat pocket. The American Indians were also good at tying knots in the dark.

▲ You will notice two ways of using the bowline: to fasten a line to something and to make a loop . . . which has a number of uses.

There are some important bowline variations, including one with a double loop for special uses. The other bowlines will be found in Chapter 3.

All the knots we have been looking at up to now have been tied in the end of a line, for one reason or another. All except the bowline are more or less variations on the half hitch.

Reef knot or **square knot** may be about to leap into your mind. "For tying two rope ends together," obviously. Yes, and no. The reef knot is a prime example of the knot that's good for one purpose and inadequate for others.

It's excellent for tying up a package or for tying a sailstop around a sail, although many persons improve it by tying half a bowknot, a **slipped reef knot,** for a bit of security and for quick undoing. The reef knot is also the knot of obvious choice for tying in an old-fashioned reef, and with a double bow it's the excellent shoelace knot that does its job while looking good.

But the reef knot is less than mediocre for tying two ropes together. Here's why: When the reef knot is holding something, under a constant strain, it holds itself. However, if it is subject to changing stresses, to alternately going loose and being jerked, as might happen in a towline, it tends to twist itself out of shape. It can slip. Its normal virtue, that it is fairly easy to untie, does not always hold when it is used for the wrong purpose. If the reef knot is used in an attempt to fasten a large rope to a smaller line, it is even less dependable.

Lobstermen often use a variation of the double becket hitch (plus the farmer's tuck into the strand for added security).

The plain becket hitch is more quickly undone, because there is only one half hitch through the loop . . .

. . . while with the end seized to the standing part the same knot would require a knife to get it undone.

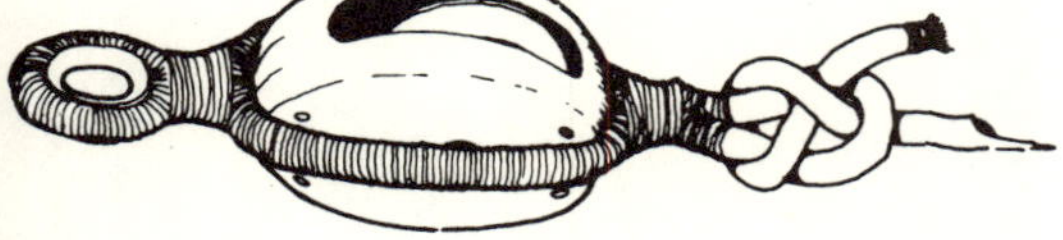

A half hitch, in and around a loop, makes a secure becket bend—a form of knot that is centuries old.

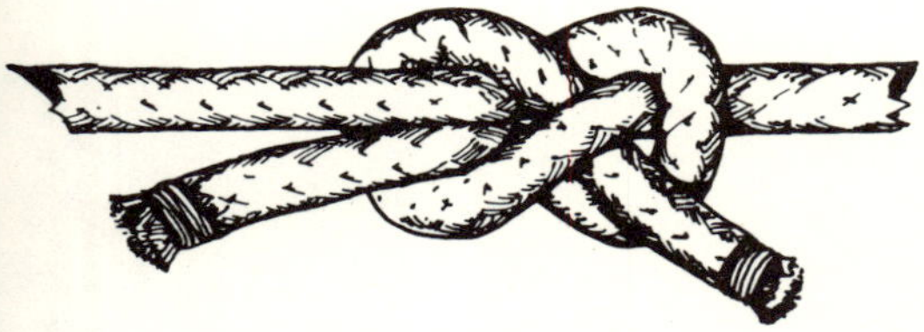

The sheet bend, for tying two lines together, is one of the older "sailor's knots." It is really like the becket bend.

The anchor bend is a special purpose knot—easy to remember, easy to make. An extra touch is a seizing, to make it semipermanent.

TWO LINES TOGETHER

The sheet bend is a better way to fasten two lines together. Compared to the reef knot, it takes only a slight, slight variation—in the way the turns of line cross each other—to make the sheet bend. But the sheet bend holds, is easy to unfasten, and has several useful variations and even one surprising revelation about itself.

Suppose you want to fasten a line to an existing loop, such as an eye in a rope. The best bend for this purpose is called the **becket bend,** because that loop is called a becket. Upon close examination, the result turns out to be really like the sheet bend. As you are already guessing, many knots are variations of each other. In fact, take a very close look and you will see a startling lookalike between the sheet bend, the becket bend, and that wonder knot the bowline.

There is also another excellent way to fasten two lines together. Herb Hild, sailor and sailmaker, says that two bowlines are his choice. The lines can be of different sizes, different kinds or textures of rope, and the bowlines will always hold and can always be undone. The only disadvantage is that the two parts that bear on each other are under great stress; if you were towing a barge across Lake Erie, you might worry that the rope would chafe and break. The solution: Take more time, and do a reeving line pair of bowlines. Now you have two parts of the line taking the strain.

The anchor bend, with sometimes other uses than this name implies, is the last of the basic knots to look at. Once again, it's a variation of two things you already know: a round turn (around the ring on the anchor) and what is really two half hitches. Since this is usually a semi-permanent knot and often is doing its work where it can't be seen and inspected (under water), it's a good idea to reinforce it by seizing the end to the standing part. Another name for this good knot is the **fisherman's bend.**

Either the anchor bend or the bowline is an excellent knot for attaching anchor lines to anchor rings or painters to the bows of dinghies.

Dan Fales, an excellent boatman and one of the top editors at *Motor Boating & Sailing,* says you need only know seven basic knots. The bold face names in this chapter may look like they add up to more than a dozen, because some are instructional and some are just variations, but here are the knots that will take care of most situations:

The **figure eight,** as a stopper, although it's a minor knot.
The **reef knot,** as a fastener, when using both ends of the same line, but not for attaching two lines to each other.
The **bowline,** for almost everything.
Two **half hitches,** for fastening a line to an object.
The **clove hitch.**
The **sheet bend.**
The **anchor bend.**
The **cleat hitch** variation you'll use hundreds of times a year.

There is also the fender hitch, but that is really the clove hitch with a slippery hitch added to make it quick to unfasten.

It is true that there are other knots and ways of using them, to be covered in the next chapter, but until you get to giving magic shows or otherwise demonstrating your dexterity with amusements like making macrame, you'll seldom need them.

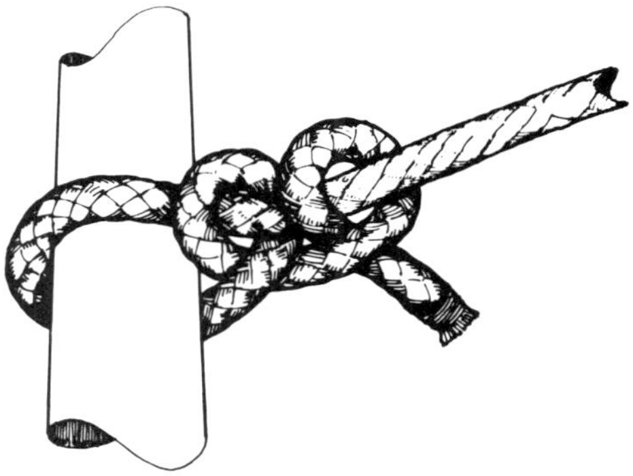

Two half hitches (here shown with modern braided rope) are good for securing a line to an object.

WRINKLES

As you handle different kinds of rope, note the different textures, the varying degrees of softness and stiffness. The choice of a knot, even a simple knot, may vary with the kind of rope. Notice the knots used by Coast Guardsmen and other professionals aboard their small boats. Often you will see an eye made with a bowline for one end of a dockline, rather than an eye splice. Another Coast Guard way to make a loop is to use two half hitches, then seize the end to the standing part. This keeps the loop the size you want it.

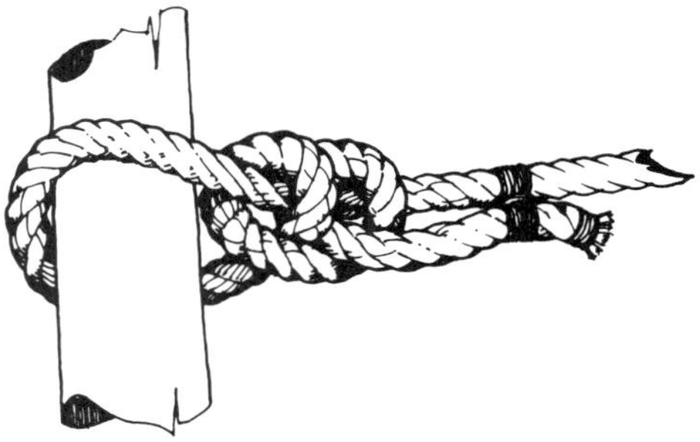

Two half hitches, with the end seized (wound with a light line) to the standing part, are secure. The loop won't change size.

Water does not have much effect on synthetic fiber ropes, although wet nylon is weaker than dry and does swell a little, but if you occasionally use the older types—manila or cotton—beware the wet knot that cannot be untied.

A quick way to measure a length of line: Your outstretched arms will reach about six feet, or one fathom. A person of small stature might have to stretch a bit.

To estimate the length of coiled line without measuring: A typical small line, coiled, has three feet per coil. A heavier line, such as an anchor line, will measure about four feet per coil because the coils are larger.

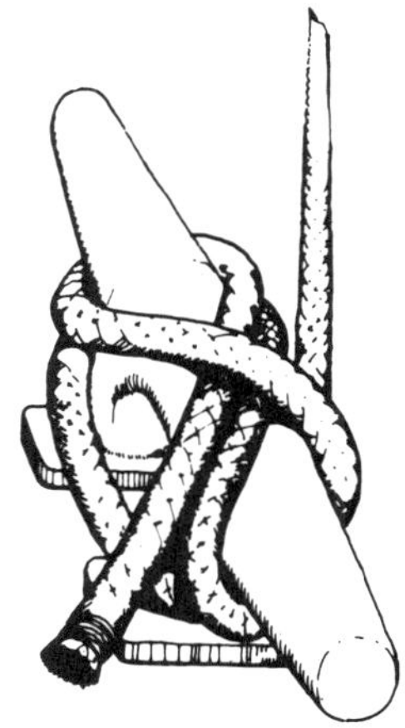

Chapter 3

Special-Purpose Knots

After looking at seven basic knots in the previous chapter, you may be thinking about the hundreds of other knots and all the technical lore about rope still ahead of you.

No! That's not the way it is. You may learn another seven or eight knots, with variations, but that's about all that anyone operating a modern pleasure boat will use.

The double carrick bend is a pretty knot—but people on pleasure boats today don't really tie carrick bends, single or double, let alone sheepshanks or some of the other knots that you've heard about.

In the days of the clipper ships, rigging was an elaborate technique using hand-made methods. Sailors whiled away the time devising macrame and fancy work. These are interesting hobbies—but today's high-tech sailing is actually simple and precise.

If you won't be sitting in the lee of the longboat aboard the clipper ship *Dreadnaught*, watching the bosun demonstrate knots, bends, and hitches plus a few other useful bits of rope lore, try improvising your own snug corner. The idea of practice is still a good one.

Three or four short lengths of line and perhaps a spool of waxed sail twine (or even nylon dental floss) and a knife (preferably one with an extra spike blade) are all you need. One piece of line might be a smooth three-strand "medium lay" nylon—exactly what you think of as "rope." Another might be a thinner, smaller braided rope, the kind that's used for the running rigging of a small sailing dinghy or the flag halyard of a large yacht. And a

◄
An old knot revived for high-tech sailing, the buntline hitch is strong and compact. It's good for halyard shackles, traveler control lines, trailer hitches.

third piece might be double-braid Dacron, the type with a fuzzy texture.

KNOTS, BENDS, AND HITCHES

A knot, speaking very broadly, is a configuration of rope or other flexible material (leather shoelaces, tape, straps) to *hold*—to another rope, to a ring or post, or even to itself. A historian of the sea or someone discussing the niceties of nautical language would even include splices as knots.

A bend is a kind of knot that fastens to another rope.

A hitch fastens a rope to a solid object: a spar, cleat, ring, shackle, becket.

There are exceptions to these statements, but that's a start.

In the choice of which knot, bend, or hitch to use, one of the questions to ask is about ease of tying, even in the dark.

In other situations, a small size of the finished knot can be important, as we shall see.

Some knots are fine for fastening one rope to another—provided both ropes are the same size and texture. If there is a difference in the two pieces of cordage, there are alternate knots that work better.

Among the common mistakes: the wrong choice of a knot for a given purpose (even though it is a perfectly good knot for other purposes), or overtying, or the opposite, not making the one extra turn that will keep the knot safe, secure, and easy to untie.

Certainly you will get a feeling that a good knot holds for as long as it is supposed to and can be undone when it is time. Indeed, after you learn the next seven or eight knots, you will begin to feel that you also know the easy way to untie each of them.

We will look briefly at seizings and splices. One or two, like the farmer's hitch, might be called semisplices. In most other cases a splice is more of a workbench project than something you make in a hurry as you approach the club float.

A useful knot around the water is called the farmer's hitch. It's easy to make with three-strand line, but not with braids.

A FEW MORE USEFUL KNOTS

The farmer's hitch is a quick way to add a little security to a plain knot in plain three-strand rope. Put a loop of rope around an object and tie two half hitches. Now, use your fingers to untwist the rope and tuck the end under. That's a knot used by Rhode Island lobstermen when they fasten a potwarp to the float. You'll find it useful when tying a dinghy to some odd rail on a float or if you create a rope belt to hold up your blue jeans. You can even use the tuck-between-the-strands with just one half hitch or with a clove hitch.

Making this tuck will also give you the feeling of the twist in the rope. If the piece of three-strand that you use is the typical rope used aboard most boats, it is "medium lay." If it's very loose and almost silky, it's "soft lay," and you'll soon realize why it seems easier to work with—but really isn't. If the rope in your hands is very stiff and difficult to open up, it's "hard lay," and again, not the best thing to use.

Now, back to the two half hitches. One advantage of this knot is that as soon as you have made the first "half hitch" you find the knot is holding, which may be a help in the work you are doing at the moment. Actually, the second half hitch doesn't always hold as well as you'd like unless it's pulled up very tight or you add the farmer's hitch or seize the end to the standing part by wrapping it with twine.

It just happens that there's a variation, only a little more difficult to tie.

The buntline hitch sounds like clipper-ship days, but it's actually a simple and useful knot that has been revived in modern times.

The buntline hitch doesn't hold until the second turn is taken, but it is snug, secure, and strong. This old hitch is a modern rigging trick of experts.

As you can see, the first hitch is *outside*, and it won't hold at all unless you use your fingers and make the second hitch on the *inside*. Now, when you tighten it, against a ring or shackle, you find it is very secure, very small and neat. One modern use of this hitch is to fasten a halyard to its shackle. When the sail is fully hoisted, the knot is tight against the swallow of the block, but it can't jam. An eye splice, being longer and thicker, can jam and won't allow the sail to be hoisted quite as high.

Another use for this new/old hitch is on the pull-up line of a boat trailer. Once again, you can pull the boat tight onto the trailer bed and snug against the winch.

An interesting point, discovered by the man most responsible for the rebirth of the buntline hitch, Rod Stephens, is that this knot is stronger than a bowline or two half hitches and almost as strong as a good splice.

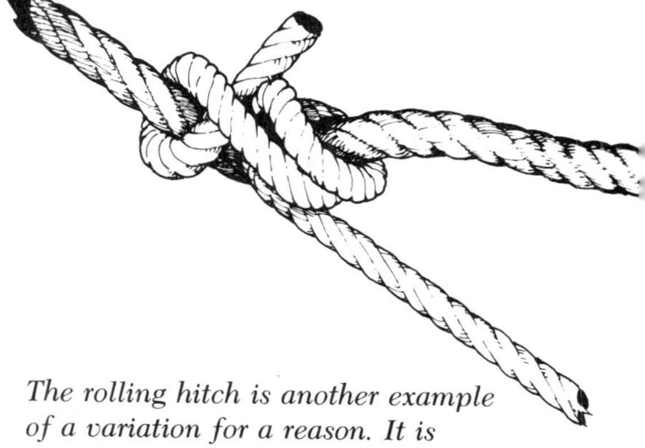

The rolling hitch is another example of a variation for a reason. It is based on the clove hitch, but used to make one line fast to another.

The rolling hitch is a variation of the clove hitch. It is used to fasten a line to the standing part of another line. If you want to

The double sheet bend takes a moment longer to make, but it is always secure.

The bowline on a bight, made with a doubled line, is a knot for lifting persons or objects.

haul on the line or be able to adjust the line—let's say, on one corner of a cockpit awning—the rolling hitch is the one to use. There could come a time when you would want to use another line to haul on an anchor line from the stern, to turn your boat; the rolling hitch will work. If you ever have to hoist a spar, use a rolling hitch. As you can guess, or easily demonstrate to yourself, it doesn't slide easily along the line or spar unless you want it to.

The flag halyard hitch is still another variation of the clove hitch. It works like a rolling hitch. You take three hitches around the burgee staff, then move a foot or so along the staff and make another triple hitch. When the halyard is used to hoist the staff and then tightened, the tension at each end keeps the staff vertical so the flag will fly in the breeze.

The double becket hitch, or **double sheet bend,** is particularly useful if there is a big difference in size between the two lines, as there is when a heaving line is attached to the eye of a dock line or hawser. The double becket hitch is the one to use on a bosun's chair if you want to feel absolutely secure. This is also an example of the language of knots: The same knot is called either a hitch or a bend, depending on whether it is made onto a free end (looped) or an eye or becket.

A becket, you'll note, is a grommet or loop of rope, as for a handle or a small and handy place to attach a line.

VARIATIONS IN THE BOWLINE

The bowline, the king of knots, also has some useful variations. **The bowline on a bight** is made with a doubled line. It then has

The running bowline and the Portuguese bowline are other useful knots to know.

two secure loops, which make an improvised bosun's chair to hoist a crew member aloft in a sitting position. Or if someone who has fallen overboard is being hoisted back onto the vessel, the bowline on a bight provides one loop for each leg and a line to hold on to. The bowline on a bight can be made when neither end of a line is free.

The running bowline forms a noose when a normal bowline is made around the starting part. This is sometimes useful when fastening a boat to a large diameter piling.

The Portuguese bowline is made by taking two loops and then tying a regular bowline. Sometimes called the French bowline, it is another way to improvise a bosun's chair. Some sailors use this as an anchor bend.

Ashley's stopper knot is a hefty one to use on the end of a line. It is harder to tie than to untie, because it has to be drawn up (tightened) with your fingers.

The miller's knot or **bag knot** is a knot to use when you are fastening the end of a sail bag or any other bag. There are several interesting variations of bag knots. The choice is not critical.

The constrictor knot is based on other bag knots. It has a peculiarity: Even though it is simple, it is difficult to loosen. This makes it a good knot for a quick, if temporary, whipping on the end of a rope.

The reverse surgeon's knot or **batten pocket knot** is a good one for tying the ends of batten pockets because it doesn't shake loose in a breeze as a reef knot can. The regular surgeon's knot is good for tying parcels when you have no one handy to put a finger over the first part of the knot. That extra turn holds it fairly well.

The carrick bend has such a symmetrical look that it is always showing up in nautical books. The diagram of it is pretty, even in some of the incorrect and dangerous variations shown in some books on seamanship. In the single version, this knot can easily jam so tight, as it "capsizes," that it cannot be undone.

To be sure, the double carrick bend is a fine one for joining stiff hawsers, such as a tugboat might use. If you don't seize each end, the knot will draw up and jam. No matter how pretty the pictures are, they do not justify using the carrick bend on a pleasure boat. It can be tied in four or five incorrect variations, some of which might be okay for ornamental sennet or to make an old-time rattan carpet beater. One author even presented a picture labeled "carrick bend" that was in fact a granny knot.

Tied in the end of a line, a stopper knot keeps the line from "getting away" through a block or fairlead. This is Ashley's stopper, better than a figure eight because it's bulkier.

Bag knots are elaborations on the clove hitch. The miller's knot and the constrictor knot are two to practice on.

Two knots that hold well while being tied are the so-called surgeon's or "suture" knot, and its reverse, useful for awnings and batten pockets.

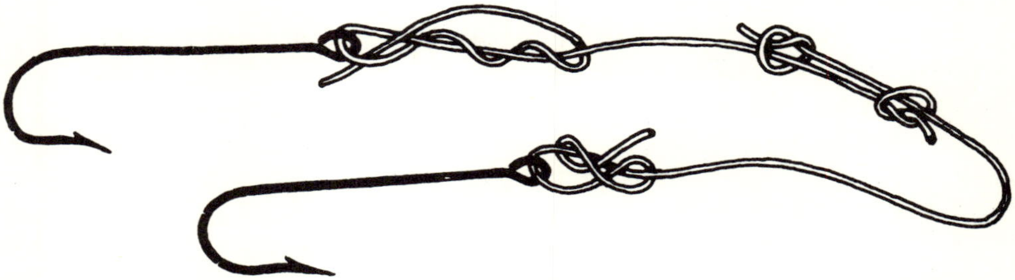

Knots for monofilament line, used by fishermen, are a special situation because of their stiffness. The buntline hitch works well in some sizes, because as it tightens it binds. Another standard fishing knot for joining two lines is made by tying an overhand knot around the standing part of the other line, then duplicating the knot with the other piece of line.

Two bowlines, to fasten two lines together, are always secure, even if the lines are of different types of rope or different sizes.

To fasten two lines together, as you might when using short dock lines to make a towing line, use a sheet bend or two bowlines. These knots are stronger, can be untied, and are the choice of innumerable professionals. The strongest way known to fasten two lines together with knots is the special variation of two bowlines shown in the illustration.

The lark's head or **cow hitch** is often used on small sailboats to fasten a jib sheet to the clew of a sail, since it is smaller and smoother than two bowlines would be and thus less likely to get hung up or add to wind resistance. It is better to add a seizing. An ocean racing sailboat will use either bowlines or snap shackles for strength, despite the danger to personnel of a flailing metal shackle.

OTHER FIBERS, OTHER STRUCTURES

The carrick bend is among the most beautiful of knots—when drawn and when first tied. In use, as it tightens it loses its lovely form.

As you practice tying knots and as you use them in real situations—which means under strain, in the rain, when the wind is whipping the line out of your hands, or perhaps in the dark—you discover the braided Dacron line with a fuzzy surface, used on modern sailboats, has a different feel, a way of holding that is unlike soft, slippery nylon.

The older rope fibers are seldom seen aboard today's recreational boats, but at various times, a great variety of natural materials have been used for rope: grass, sisal, coir, hemp, jute, cotton, linen, and even silk.

Manila fibers come from the leaf stem of the abaca plant, a wild banana found in the Philippines and some areas of Central America. The fibers are separated and combined into ribbons, then repeatedly combed before spinning into yarn. The finest "yacht manila" was a beautiful light yellow rope. One advantage over the older hemp was resistance to rot without the necessity of tarring.

Sisal is about three-fourths as strong as manila and is a widely used substitute. It is made from the Agave plant. Sisal is used for rope boat fenders and for smaller tying twines.

Hemp is made from the Cannabis Sativa plant, the source of hashish and marijuana. Hemp rope, when not tarred, was called "white rope." Hemp was usually tarred to prevent rot. It is still occasionally used for ratlines, marlines, and other tarred cordage.

Jute has less strength than manila, sisal, or hemp. It is used in making lower grades of cordage, for tying twines, and for bags.

Cotton is used for smaller ropes, for products like clotheslines and sashcord.

The synthetic fibers, although all are based on continuous filaments of long molecular-chain polymers, vary considerably in their characteristics and properties. Among the properties that the Cordage Institute recognizes are:

- Strength
- Stretch with load
- Permanent stretch
- Recovery from stretch
- Floatability
- Stiffness
- Twist direction/torque
- Chemical resistance
- Flex life in bending
- Slipperiness
- Limpness in handling
- Texture
- Water repellency
- Hygroscopicity (water absorption)
- Toughness against wear
- Ruggedness in shape
- Temperature resistance
- Friction melting
- Combustibility
- Rot resistance
- Marine growth resistance
- Color
- Aging
- Contaminating
- Uniformity
- Service costs

The newer fibers used for cordage are developments of the chemical industry. Often, research for fabrics and for automotive tires leads to new kinds of rope and of course new materials for sailcloth. A significant fact about the synthetic fibers is that there are many ways to control their characteristics and this in turn allows development of the geometry of rope.

Nylon (polyamide) has high tensile strength, high elasticity, good energy absorption, and high impact resistance. It has a high melting point (480°) and good dry abrasion resistance. It is approximately three times as strong as good manila. Nylon not only absorbs water, but it stiffens and shrinks when wet and can lose as much as 15 to 20 percent of its strength. Nylon is not harmed by the chemicals it normally comes in contact with in boating.

Polyester is the generic name for a family of fibers manufactured under various trade names. A.C.E. (Allied), Dacron (DuPont), Fortrel (Celanese), Kodel (Eastman), Terylene (British), Tergal (French), Terital (Italian), Terlenka (Dutch), and Tetoron (Japanese) are among the manufacturers' names. Some rope manufacturers use modified fibers and their own names, as Duron (Samson) and Esterlon (Wall). Other trade names are used for composite ropes and for special constructions. Polyester is low-stretch compared to nylon; the strength is similar. It too resists ultraviolet degradation.

Polypropylene is an olefin, made in monofilament, multifilament, and film form. Some of the trade names are Herculon, Polypro, Meraklen, Nestron, Novolen, Ulstron, and Vestalen. One brand, Manilex, is colored to simulate manila—not to defraud customers, but because the beauty of manila is still admired. Polypropylene has about half the strength of nylon or polyester, a low melting point, low abrasion resistance, and high positive buoyancy. It does not absorb water, nor do oil and gasoline affect it. Sunlight degrades it, especially white and light-colored polypropylene.

Polyethylene, also an olefin, has a little less strength and is a little heavier than polypropylene. It is sometimes used in noncritical applications because of its low cost. But it, like polypropylene, is useful for water-ski ropes, dinghy painters, and some fishing applications. It gains strength when wet.

Allied's Spectra-900 is from the same olefin family and has the same advantage of low weight. However, this newest of the rope fibers is stronger than other fibers and has the least stretch. It is self-lubricating.

Kevlar, a DuPont aramid fiber, is used for the high-tech rope of the racing sailor because of its minimum stretch and high strength. It deteriorates with flexing and is therefore frequently combined with other fibers, particularly polyester.

Iceline, a new product of Tubbs Cordage, is a floating line that is stronger than nylon.

Other materials, including fiberglass, other aramids, shredded Mylar, and many composites, are used in making rope. Most of them have special applications and are not generally useful in recreational boating.

Rope construction or geometry is as important as the fiber material. Qualities like spliceability, torque or twist, and ease of handling depend on the construction of the rope. Even the strength and the durability of the rope are affected by the method of construction.

Laid or stranded rope is the oldest construction known, no matter whether the material is coconut husk fiber, leather, or silk. The thousands of knots used by weavers, tentmakers, horsemen, farmers, lumbermen, campers, magicians, and sailors were all invented with laid rope.

The fibers are twisted together to make yarns. Yarns are twisted to make strands. Strands are twisted, in most cases three strands, with a right-hand or Z-twist. In some cases four strands have been used, for shrouds of sailing vessels. Some hawsers for large ships are made with six strands. For special purposes, a left-hand twist has been used. But for thousands of years three-strand laid rope was the standard. It not only makes excellent knots, it is easy to splice. By interweaving the strands it is relatively easy to make an eye splice, a back splice on the end of a rope, or a splice to join two ropes together.

Laid rope has built-in problems, caused by the very nature of the construction. A rotating spinner, towed behind a vessel to measure speed and distance, would obviously have problems. Any laid line, used constantly on a winch, will take a set. Laid line can kink and hockle, actually for the same reason: the built-in twist. Laid line has a torque or twist in its very design.

Braided or plaited line not only avoids many of these problems but has extra advantages. Rope engineering has advanced to the point that braid-inside-braid, using one or more synthetic fibers, can be designed for any of various special characteristics: low stretch, high resistance to abrasion, flexibility, or floatability.

The typical solutions to marine applications include: (a) using

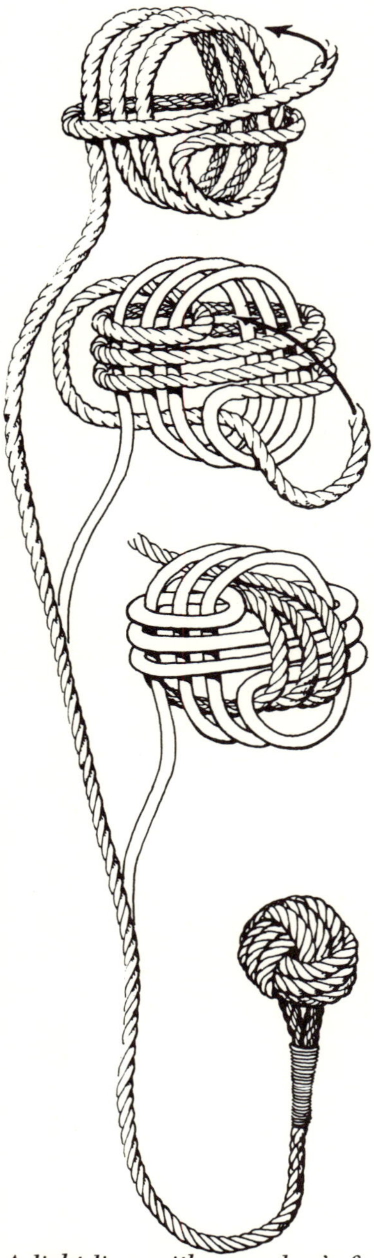

A light line, with a monkey's fist (with or without an extra weight) can be made up to serve as a heaving line, to get a heavy line from boat to dock.

the elasticity of double braid nylon for anchor lines that are superior in strength to the same size laid line; (b) using the high-strength and low-stretch capabilities of double braid polyester and Kevlar lines for large sailboat running rigging; and (c) using strong lightweight polyester braids for light air spinnaker sheets. Many small sailboats use other combinations of both the fibers and the constructions.

Texture is one of the controllable characteristics. The outer cover of double braid to be used on sheet winches can be given a "wooly" texture, for a better grip on the winches and with the hands. Or where abrasion resistance is very important, as on a halyard, triple-strand construction can be used.

The double-braid type of construction will not unlay, kink, or hockle under load or with the sudden release of load.

Composite construction, such as using a polyester cover over a Kevlar core, can be made stronger than wire and near zero stretch.

Splicing techniques for most, but not all, types of braided constructions have been developed. Essentially, these involve substituting the core and cover for each other, in the manner of the child's version of "Chinese handcuffs," so that one part of the cover is threaded inside the opposing core to make an eye.

Additional information on the use of special types of rope constructions is given in the chapters on sailboat rigging. Chapter 13 shows how to make typical splices of three-strand and double braid.

RIGHT WAY AND WRONG WAY

The wrong way to do things is not just a matter of amusement for those in the inner circle. Nor is a sailor's concern with doing things "shipshape and Bristol fashion" mainly concerned with neat appearance. Someone can tie a dinghy to a float by making a quick loop around a bollard; someone else, without thinking, can kick the loop and cast the dinghy loose to drift across the harbor. A helpful hand can put eighteen turns of a dockline around a piling, thinking to get it out of the way—three hours later the next boat on the pier catches fire and the crew loses precious seconds trying to get the lines free.

One reason for always putting a line on a cleat the same way, the standard way, is so that it can be automatically undone when the time comes. One reason for not taking a jamming turn on a

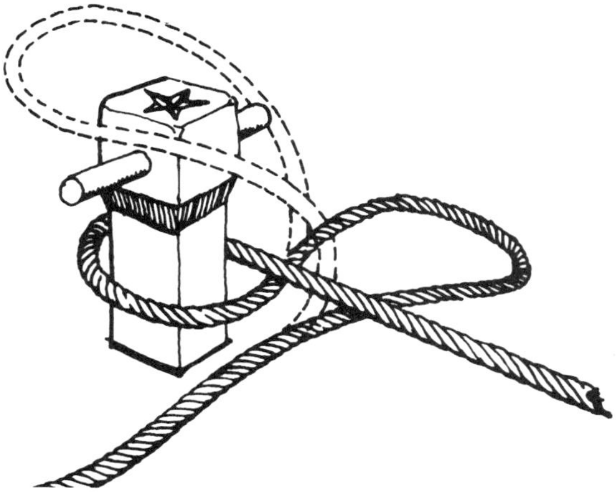

cleat with the sheet of a small boat is that a gust of wind might knock the boat down and that might well be the instant to release the sheet and ease the pressure.

The towboat hitch is quickly cast off in an emergency.

WRINKLES

The towboat hitch is useful because it can be cast off under strain, even if it isn't one of the hitches every beginning boatman has to know. This hitch can be used at either end of the towline, preferably on bitts or a bollard, but a workable approximation can be made on either a stern or a bow cleat.

Cutting rope with a knife is not done as often as it was in the Age of Sail (an electric "hot knife" is far better when you're working on running rigging). If you need to cut nylon or Dacron rope with a knife, tape it first—it keeps the strands from snapping open. Even tape from the medicine chest is better than nothing. Or make two whippings, using dental floss if you have no whipping twine, then cut between them.

Mousing a hook can save your life—if it's the pelican hook on the gate of the lifeline and you run into rough weather. In port, or least at the dock, the sliding ring on the hook may seem secure enough. At sea a serving of light twine, called mousing, will keep the sliding ring in place and prevent the pelican from opening.

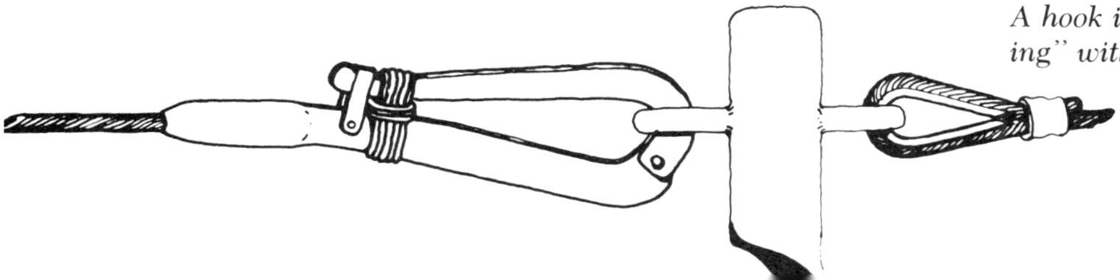

A hook is made secure by "mousing" with light twine.

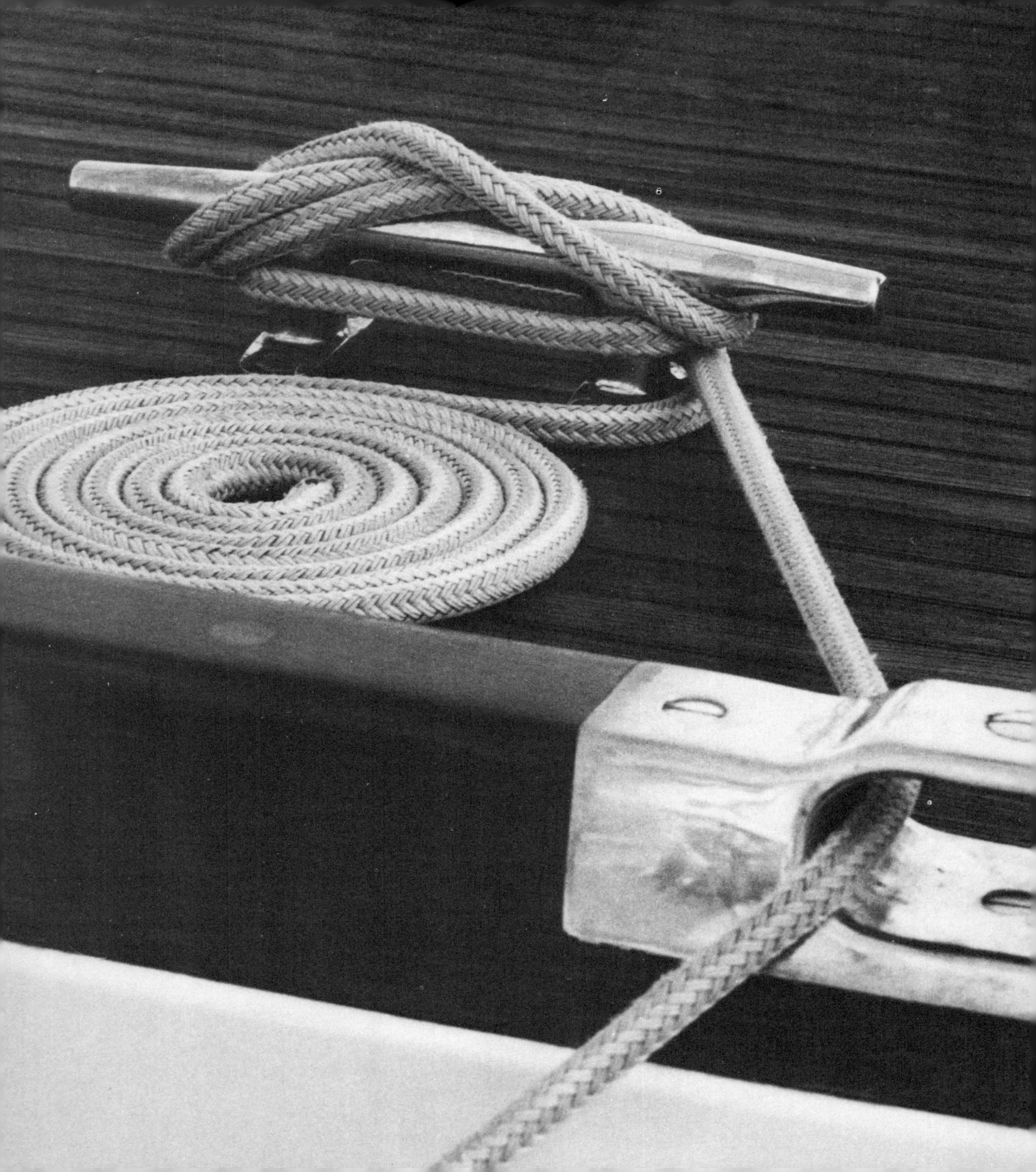

Chapter 4

Decks and Deck Hardware

You can't push on a rope . . . but you can use it to apply power in sophisticated ways. Rope is such a remarkable transmitter of power that one of the latest devices, found aboard high-tech racing sailboats, is called the magic box. Inside the mysterious-looking black box is a new mechanical device that also spans the centuries. It used to be called a block-and-tackle, but with ball bearings and space-age materials, it might just as well be called a power amplifier.

Basic deck hardware, like most other marine equipment, has gone through changes and improvements over the decades. Basic mechanical principles, utilized with new alloys, low-friction bearings, and the superplastics, are capable of improving even the simplest sailboats and powerboats. But even though there is a high-tech look to it, deck hardware does not always get the attention from boat builders that should be required.

Only the very best of today's boats are well laid out on deck, and the quality of the installations on new boats is often inferior to the design and manufacture of the hardware.There are other cases of stock boats whose builders economize by using cheap or too small hardware. Finding out what the standards should be is not difficult.

In this chapter we will look at the hardware and fittings related to all line handling, at deck hardware and deck layouts in some detail, and then take a first look at the ways in which they are used aboard both powerboats and sailboats. The way rope works and the various types of rope are also involved in how the hardware works, so we will be looking more closely at cordage itself.

◀
Ideal set-up: a nylon double braid line, led through a good chock, fastened to a well-designed cleat, and Flemished down on deck

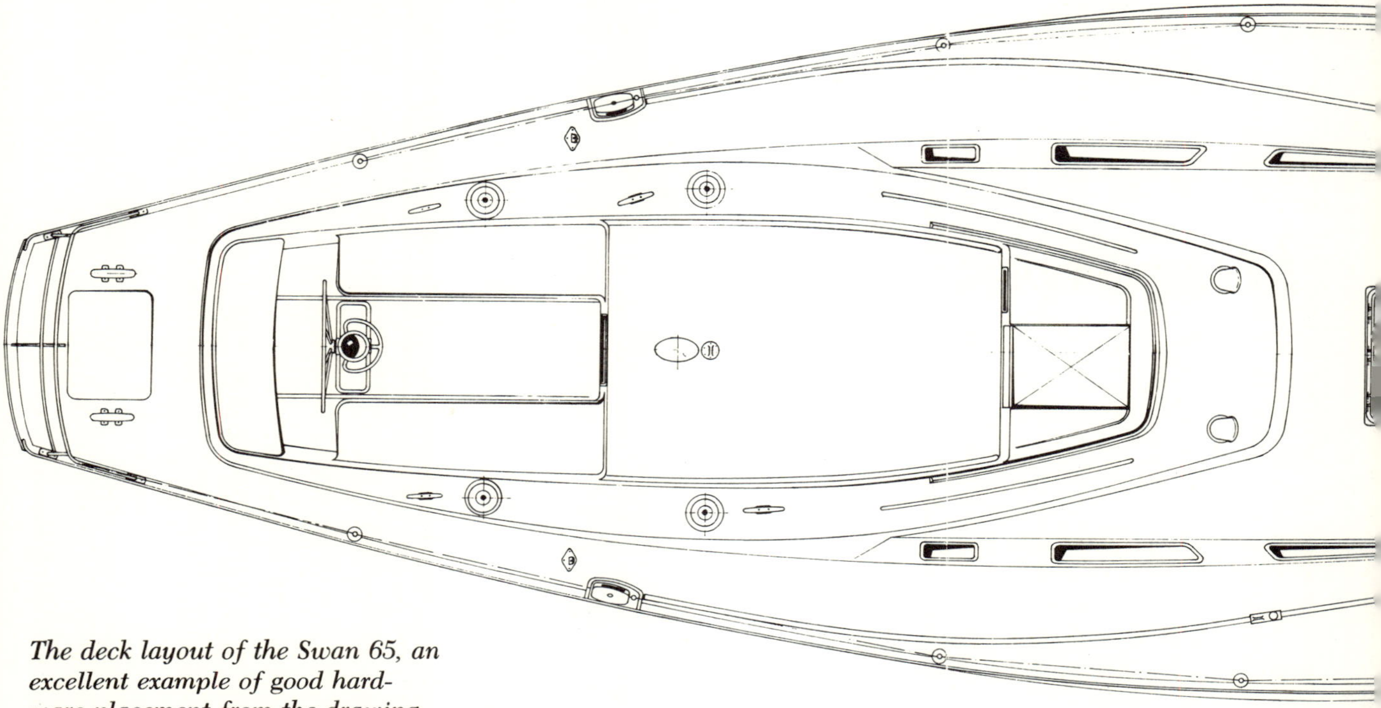

The deck layout of the Swan 65, an excellent example of good hardware placement from the drawing board of Sparkman and Stephens, shows one detail that Rod Stephens says could be improved: "I would put the hinges of the hatches forward, to keep out water."

CHECKING DECK HARDWARE

If you are buying a boat, power or sail, go over the deck plan and the actual deck installations as though you were doing it with a naval architect. Or if your present boat can stand some functional improvements, get professional help to see what an ideal deck layout might be. New boat or old, there is only one way better than having a professional surveyor do the job for you: that is getting him to survey the boat in your presence. If he talks and explains, while you make notes, you can end up with a better decision or a list of improvements to make. Here are some points to check:

Cleats and chocks for size and quality. A large proportion of production boats have basic deck hardware that is too small for the lines that will be used. Consider that it is often necessary to put two dock lines on the same cleat: Will the biggest cleats on the bow and at the stern take two hefty lines?

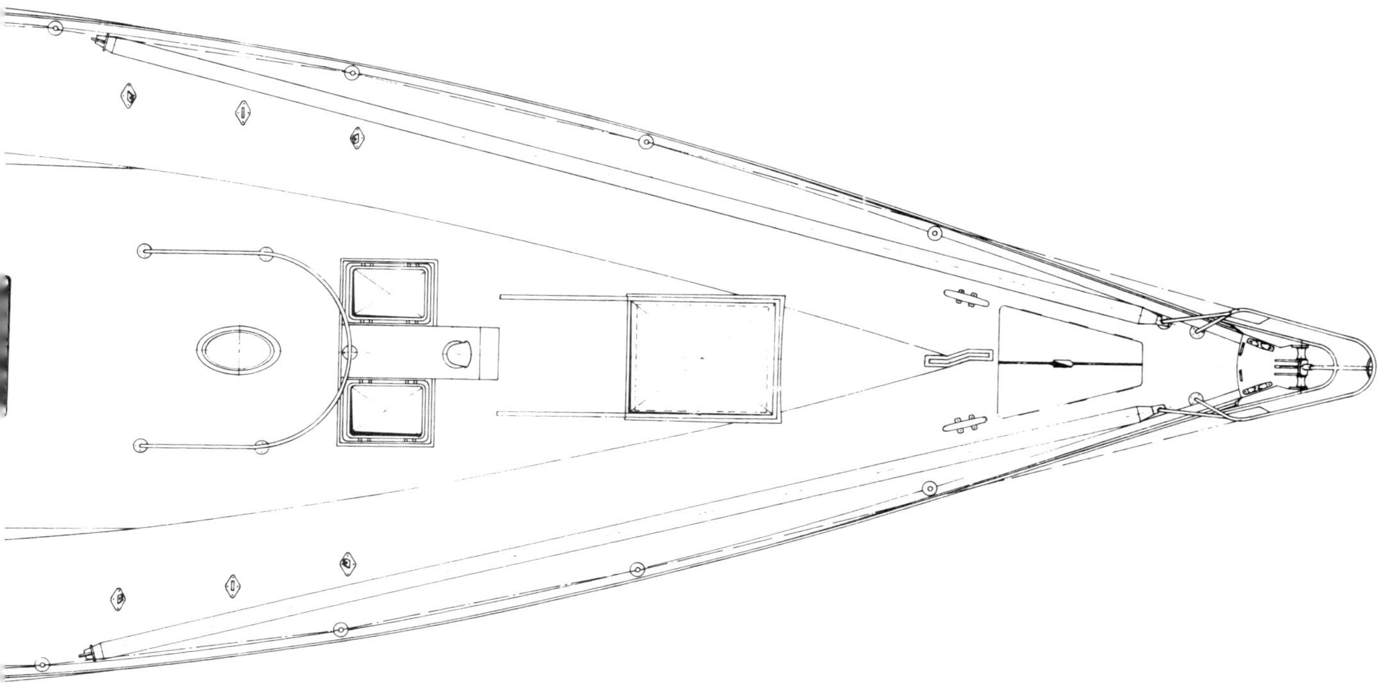

Even good-sized boats are seen all the time with cleats made of cheap metal under polished chromium, with hollow cleats that won't take the strain of a boat surging at her mooring in a storm, and with hardware that is styled to look pretty without regard to the sharp angles in its design. It is hardware like this that leads to extra chafe on dock lines and anchor lines.

Correct installation. This means that deck hardware should not only be through-bolted, but that there should be adequate backup plates under cleats, bitts, and deck winches particularly. Many times, chocks are installed backward or cleats are improperly positioned for efficient use. In any place where the position of the line is known—next to a chock for a stern line, for example, or in place for a sheet winch—a cleat should be positioned at an angle of from ten to fifteen degrees to the line that leads to it. This makes it easier and faster to cleat down and reduces potential strain on the cleat. The perfect boat will have cleats set so that cleating down is clockwise, which makes for a standard operation every time.

Another version of a closed chock, this one a special latching model designed by Cape Dory for its own boats

Among the typical problems in deck hardware: a chock installed incorrectly, so the line can slip out. Remedy: Switch sides.

No chock at all here, so dock lines can chafe on track. The cleat is barely large enough for even one line.

LOOKING AT DECK HARDWARE

Elementary though it may seem, let's look at the functions of deck hardware. You can make a checklist from these points.

Chocks in one sense are guides for lines and in another sense keep the lines from abrading the toe rail or bulwarks. A dock line led through an open chock will give no problems when the boat is tied up at a float or at a pier that is at all times lower than the deck. But if it's not a float, a very low tide can lift the line right out of the chock. Closed chocks solve that problem but are not as convenient to use. Some excellent latching chocks are available. One is called the Locking Chock.

The **skene chock,** with angled horns, is a practical solution preferred by many naval architects, builders, and boat owners. However, perhaps one in five is installed incorrectly, leaving the opening angled so that the dock line can lift out inadvertently. Happily, the solution is almost always easy: Switch the port and starboard chocks.

New chocks should cause no chafe problems, but periodic inspections should be made to find and correct rough spots. If chain is used for the anchor rode, it is particularly necessary to inspect the anchor chocks for nicks and abrasions.

This foredeck has no chocks for dock lines, although there is a roller chock for hoisting the anchor. Open base cleat is good.

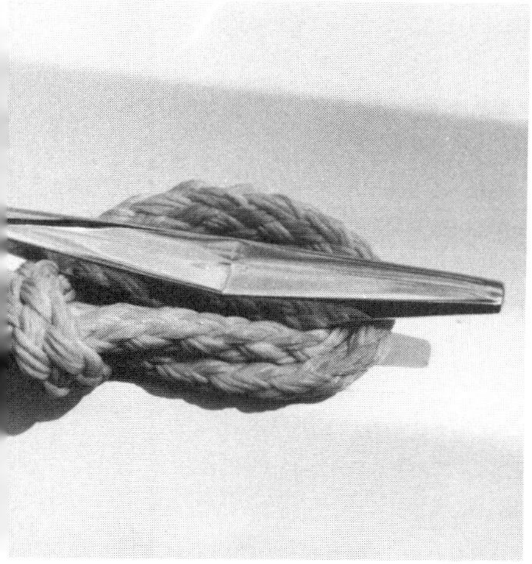

Some sharp cleats may gleam with a "designer" shape, but they tend to abrade lines. Avoid bare feet on deck.

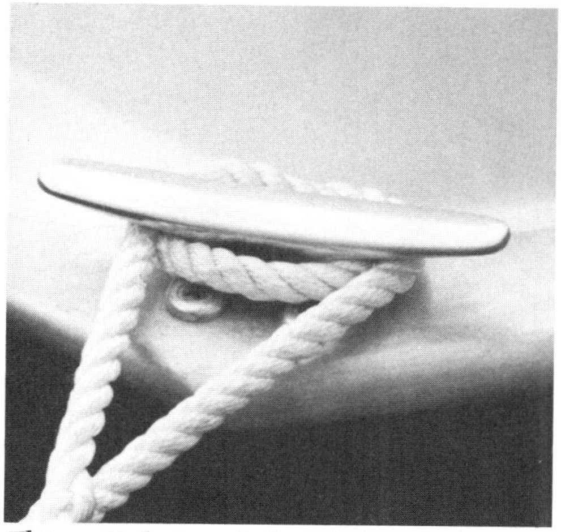

This well-designed cleat is installed at the transom without a chock.

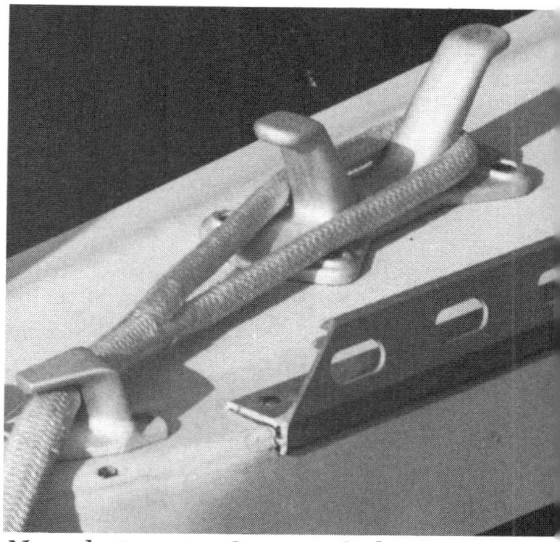

New designs in cleats and chocks keep showing up. A strong method of through-bolting with a back-up plate is always required.

WINCHES: APPLYING POWER

Anchor winches, windlasses, and capstans, of course, must be installed with similar care.

An anchor **winch** is a general term. A **windlass** normally has a horizontal drum. When several turns of the anchor line are taken on it and tension is applied, turning the drum with a hand lever or by power lifts the anchor. A **capstan** usually has a vertical drum. A **gypsy** is a horizontal drum to take the line, in the U.S. In the UK a gipsy, or gypsy, is a similar wheel or drum with notches to take chain links, or it can be the rope type drum. **Wildcat** is an American word for the wheel to take chain.

The typical hand-operated windlass for cruising boats has a warping drum, for rope, on one side and a chain wheel on the other. Newer designs, especially of power winches, have improved upon this. Some models put both types of "wheel" on the same side so that the usual setup of rope plus six to eight feet of leader chain can be quickly handled. Similar drums are available for the vertical axis type.

A windlass, or a winch, of course, multiplies the strength of one person. The hand-operated lever alone can have a power ratio of ten to one, or a lot more. Most power winches have a lever.

A large cleat, with an open base, next to a large chock in the bulwark, is a good example of proper deck layout.

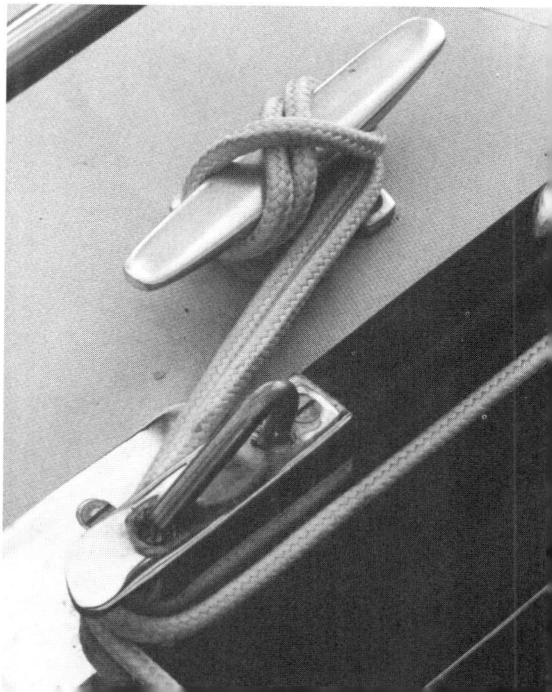

Ankoralina is a new "flat rope" from Sweden, which can be coiled on a reel to save space aboard smaller boats.

One special type of windlass, the angler's, is used by fishermen who change anchorages frequently. Some use a wire cable. Recently, a Swedish company started making flat rope, called Ankarolina, to coil on a reel, for such special uses.

For larger cruising boats as well, the improvement in power winches, and the use of even the simplest hand winches, has been made possible by the improvements in rope. In the days of manila line, you wouldn't store a wet anchor rode belowdecks, but today's nylon line is not a problem. Instead of having a crew member forward on deck to bring the anchor up, operating the winch controls with a foot switch or lever and the anchor rode by hand, the new automatic electric anchor windlasses, operated from the bridge, put the anchor line directly into the rope locker. Note: One company, Powerwinch, recommends using medium or hard laid line, because the winch has to "grab" the line. Some double-braids are too soft.

SPECIAL DECK HARDWARE

Deck pipes, or navels, are used on most larger cruising boats. If properly fitted, they don't let rain belowdecks and very little "green water," even in rough going. One of the best of the recent improvements in cruising-boat design has been the addition of an anchor well on the foredeck—a place where anchor and rode can be stowed under a hinged deck lid.

Anchor davits were once used only on large yachts or merchant ships, but today, as already mentioned, excellent small davits, a form of anchor bowsprit with two roller chocks, are available.

Deck chocks for anchors and spinnaker poles have to be carefully located on deck for ease of access. Some of the ingenuity of cruising sailor-inventors shows up in the ways that have been devised to carry lightweight anchors on the bow pulpit and lashed upright at the shrouds.

For small powerboats, one company makes a good combination bow handle, for lifting, with a centered anchor or dock-line chock.

Larger power cruisers and sailing auxiliaries frequently have chocks installed on the rail amidships in addition to the standard bow and stern chocks. These handle spring lines, sometimes more than one, and at times such items as shore power lines. They need to be large or they are of little use.

The roller chock, a special type, is a great convenience in handling the anchor. If these chocks were limited to their original conception, installed on the side of a sailboat's bowsprit, they might be rare indeed on new boats. But fortunately for cruising boat owners, many excellent installations of roller anchor chocks are made nowadays on the bow or on a special anchor sprit. You can buy an anchor davit for a powerboat that gives you the advantages of a bowsprit with roller chocks. There are also worthwhile other variations of roller chocks.

Deck cleats come in more shapes and sizes than almost any other item of marine hardware. Many are too small and a few look as though they had been designed on the off day of an automotive stylist whose highest achievement was working up a "streamlined" door handle for a 1965 sports brougham.

The open base type of cleat allows you to pass the eye of a dock line through before looping it over the cleat. This adds security if the eye is either too large or too small. If you splice your own eyes and make them the right size for your mooring cleats, you don't need to face the situation.

Some excellent cleats are made using teak rods in stainless steel bases.

A cruising boat that will frequently be tied up with bow line, stern line, and two or more spring lines needs cleats large enough to hold two dock lines at once. Any boat that may need to have dock lines doubled up for a severe storm needs full-size deck cleats.

Mooring bitts and **samson posts,** in the days of wooden construction, were solid oak extending from the keel through the deck—reinforced by adequate timbering. Today, excellent metal bitts are available. They must be installed properly, which means with large stainless steel or bronze bolts and a heavy backing plate. On large power craft you will occasionally see twin bitts, or towing bitts, at the stern.

Thimbles are metal or plastic devices, used with rope, around which you can make an eye splice. Improved versions such as the combination shackle and thimble and the envelope thimble continue to be invented. The shackle and thimble, distributing the strain and preventing abrasion, enable you to quickly and securely attach a line to an anchor ring, for example. Delrin thimbles are stronger than those made of hard nylon, although the two may look alike.

Shackles, as used for anchor lines, are essentially harp-shaped or D-shaped fittings with a removable pin across the end. Proper siz-

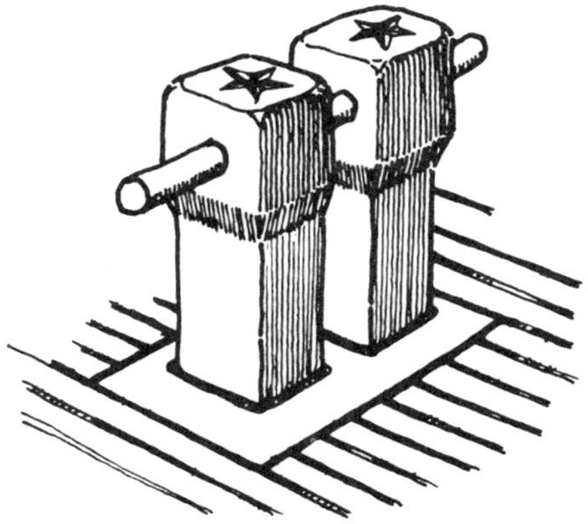

A pair of bitts, with a norman bar for cleating tow lines and anchor lines, is one of many types used on the foredeck.

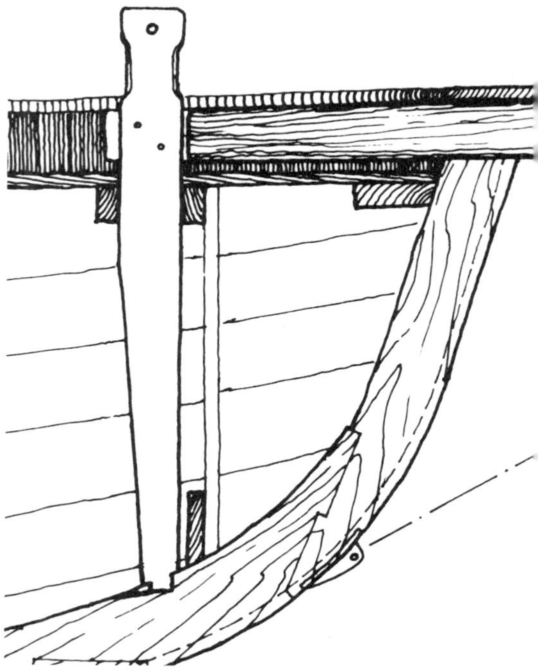

A good chock, large enough for a pair of dock lines, is well installed in the toe rail here.

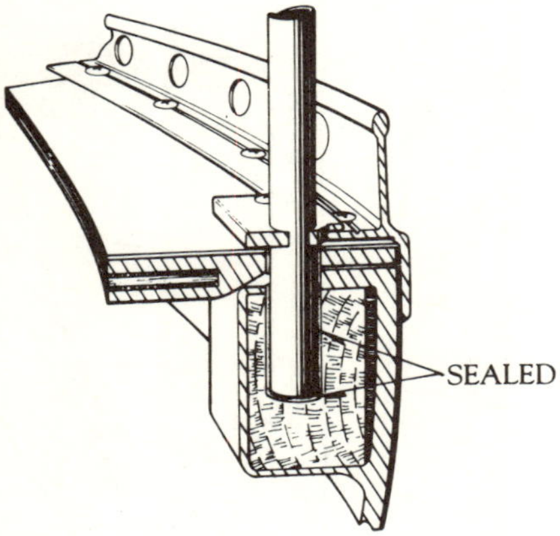

Stanchions are not a real safety factor unless the bases are well secured, as in this Irwin yacht installation.

ing is important because you need strength yet must fit a shackle on a given thimble.

Because many marine hardware items were originally designed and manufactured when manila rope was the standard, it is a good idea to check on the strength of actual hardware if the application is critical. Synthetic ropes are so strong that the fittings can give before the rope does.

Pulpits, stanchions, and lifelines need proper installation too. If the lifelines are so low that they become tripping hazards, beware and refit. Both the ocean racing organizations and the American Boat and Yacht Council (ABYC) specify 24 inches from the deck as a minimum. Many yachtsmen prefer 27 to 30 inches. Especially when the opening between toe rail and upper line is greater than 22 inches, intermediate lines are recommended.

The normal standard for lifelines is 7 x 7 wire rope (the cable size depending on the size of the boat) covered with PVC plastic. The ABYC says: "The maximum longitudinal spacing of stanchions should be seven feet. . . . stanchions should be designed and located to permit attachment to structural members of the hull . . . bolt fastenings and back-up plates should be used. . . . All stanchions, pulpits, and liferails or similar members shall be mounted . . . to have a minimum strength to withstand a 400 pound static load at any point in any direction."

Any surveyor can tell you about lightweight stanchions that bent, hull attachments that were flimsy, and other inadequate arrangements.

A wise precaution: A standard way of providing a gate in the lifeline, for access at a dock or float, is with a pelican hook. This is fine for the situation at the dock, but at sea it may pose a hazard. Even if the lifeline is well tightened, the locking ring can accidentally work loose. Once the boat is under way a sensible precaution, advocated by Rod Stephens, Jr., is to mouse the pelican hook, wrapping it with light twine.

Family cruising boats and many racing sailboats sometimes share another safety device: a netting under the lifelines, to keep small children, pets, or racing sails temporarily retained on deck from going overboard. It is not necessary to make your own netting, macrame-style, however. Nylon netting, easily made fast, is available through larger chandleries.

Ladders, such as to flying bridges, are best installed at an angle, with suitable strong handholds. The rise between steps or rungs should never be more than 12 inches. A tread is desirable.

DECK STOWAGE

A thoughtful surveyor, a wise naval architect, or any experienced cruising man would point out the need for adequate deck stowage. This ranges from small boxes, located in Dorade-type ventilator boxes, to lazarettes, spaces under cockpit seats, or powerboat deck boxes. Ready dock lines can be hung on bow pulpits as you enter a harbor, but they need a proper stowage place. Winch handles need their own sockets, next to the winches they fit.

Even when space is already available, it takes some ingenuity to get the most from it. A cruising boat may have a socket at the toe rail, to hold a boat hook—with a simple ring or grommet on a shroud to hold the upper part. Another boat may have space on the cabin top or belowdecks, but within reach.

A row of dowels or pegs, set in a piece of board, often makes a good place to hang spare lines. Others use rust-proof hooks, Velcro holders, and canvas slings on the bottom side of the cockpit seats. Still others use such places for flashlights and ready-access tools.

INSTALLATION OF DAVITS

Davits for dinghies, tenders, and inflatables can be installed on the stern of either an auxiliary or a power cruiser. The tender can have up to a 64-inch beam and a total weight as high as 600 pounds if the proper davits are used. Factors to consider in the installation include the freeboard and the transom shape. A boat with low freeboard should have higher davits. A boat with a curved transom should have davits with a longer projection.

Back-up plates of steel, aluminum, or wood must be used.

The space between davits is determined by the distance between the inside edges of the forward and aft seats of the dinghy. The lifting rings ideally should be within a foot or so of the bow and stern of the dinghy. Gunnel bosses must be securely installed so that the dinghy is "locked" in the stowed position.

Other deck attachments that require careful installation include hardware for boarding and swimming ladders, fender hooks, special hooks that are now used for electrical shore power lines, and the brackets for horseshoe buoys.

Family cruising, with netting as well as adequate lifelines, has a bonus: easier sailhandling on the foredeck in a blow.

STEEL, BRONZE, ALUMINUM

The best materials for deck hardware are excellent. The worst are close to execrable.

Strength under stress is an obvious requirement. Resistance to surface corrosion is another factor.

Stainless steel comes in a number of formulas, depending upon ductility and other factors. These variations are of more significance in the specification and construction of running rigging for sailboats and are discussed in Chapter 9. Stainless 316 is one of the most used steels. Like any, it is not completely "stainless"—a small amount of surface corrosion can take place. Keeping the surface clean prevents this.

Manganese bronze is widely used and has excellent qualities such as high strength, a low friction coefficient, a good resistance to seawater corrosion. If bronze is chromium-plated, it keeps a good surface shine. If not, a small amount of oxidation discolors it, but of course does not weaken the fitting. Everdur bronze and Alloy #90 have an ultimate strength of 90,000 pounds per square inch and a yield of 40,000 psi. Alloy #70 has an ultimate strength of 70,000 psi and a yield strength of 24,000. Naval or Navy bronze has much greater ductility. Its ultimate tensile strength is 40,000 psi and its yield strength is 18,000 psi. Another high-strength, corrosion-resistant alloy is nickel aluminum bronze, with a tensile strength of 115,000 psi and a yield strength of 75,000 psi.

Marinium, an alloy of aluminum and bronze, has great strength and a fine finish, either highly polished or satin.

Other alloys of aluminum are used for parts of winches, and for spars, including reaching struts, spinnaker poles, booms, and masts. Alloy 356 and Tenzaloy are used for castings such as aluminum deck plates and some rigging parts. One of the points that must be watched with aluminum is the type of fastenings used. Stainless steel or brass screws and bolts can lead to corrosion and severe deterioration caused by galvanic action. Aluminum is best protected from surface corrosion by a process called anodizing, which forms a surface oxidation harder than the aluminum itself. Anodized aluminum may be either black or the natural color.

Galvanized steel cleats and bollards are often used on piers, floats, and similar structures. The steel is strong enough, but the only pleasure boats likely to use hardware of this material are the ones trying to look like work boats.

Zinc alloys and even the wrong plastics are sometimes used for objects such as cleats, which should be made of stronger materials. Chromium plating on pot metal or "metalizing" on plastics does not make them any stronger or reduce the chances that they will break under stress.

However, some plastics are excellent for certain deck plates or inspection port covers, and many special plastics are used for the operating parts of blocks and other rigging equipment, where their low friction and freedom from corrosion make them good choices. Delrin, Cycolac, Celcon, hard nylon, PVC and ABS plastics, as well as others, have important marine uses.

ROPE AS A POWER TRANSMITTER

"Rope is a power-transmitting connection between two points," it says in *Gleistein Yachting*, of George Gleistein & Sohn, GMBH. Most boatmen already have a partial knowledge of the basic but fascinating mechanical devices that make rope such a useful tool The special characteristics of rope itself are also worth a closer look.

When rope goes "around a corner," as inside a block, some of the fibers are stretched and, if the line is under strain, some are compressed against the sheave. One result is that some of the strongest rope materials, with the least stretch, actually wear out faster. In any case, line going through a block will work better and last longer if the sheave is of a large enough diameter so that the rope does not make too sharp a bend. Similarly, a line attached to a shackle or other fitting (with a splice or a knot) will be stronger if the fitting is large enough to give a proper bearing surface.

A **block** is a seemingly simple device. It consists of a grooved wheel, called a sheave, turning on an axle inside a case. But when a line goes through a block, which of course may have two or three sheaves, all the marvels of the wheel become evident. You can reverse the direction of the force and in so doing get the continuous lever action of the wheel. If the axle has a roller or ball bearing, there is very little friction, especially compared to making a similar directional change with even the smoothest fairlead.

If you attach even a single block by its becket to something you want to move, you can almost double your power. Pull the rope two feet with a force of 50 pounds and the block and its becket

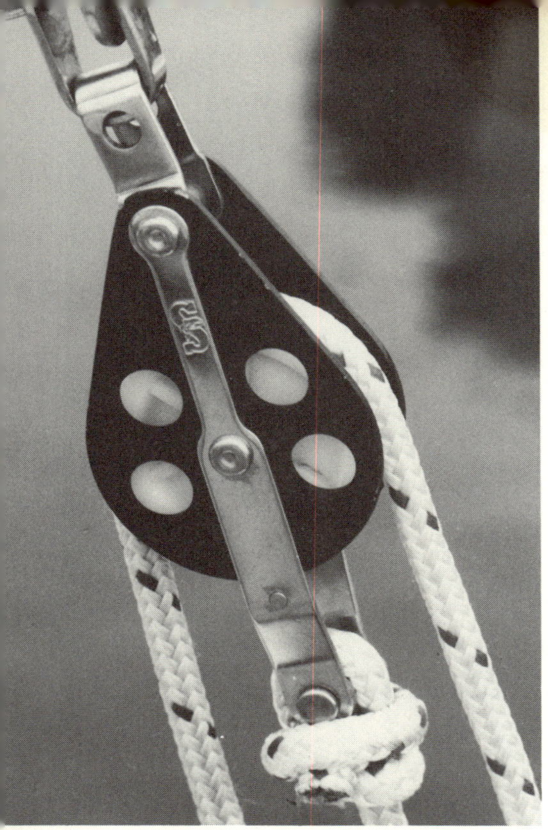

A simple block is a wheel on an axle, inside a shell.

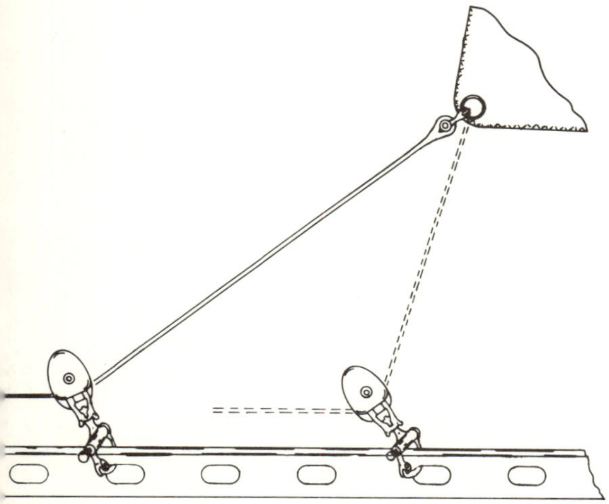

Blocks redirect power, but they must be able to absorb tremendous loads.

pull upon your object with a force of 100 pounds. The tradeoff, of course, is that the object is moved only one foot.

Because we will look at many variations and uses of blocks in this and other chapters, here is a short look at how a block is made.

Anatomy of a block. The sheaves run on an axle, which may be a plain pin, or a roller bearing, ball bearing, or self-lubricating type of axle. Teflon-impregnated bearings, for example, are widely used in sailboat rigging.

In an old-style wooden block, an inner strap and an outer strap held the pin and the shell that enclosed the whole. A modern block may have one fabricated steel piece that is shell and strap in one. Sheaves are made of bronze or a superplastic, acetal. One trade name is Delrin.

The larger opening, through which the line is rove, is called the swallow. The smaller opening at the bottom of the block is the breech. The place on the bottom, for attaching a line, is called a becket. It may have a thimble through it. The similar place at the top is called the hook.

A **tackle** is the combination of **falls** (ropes), blocks, and hooks used for applying power (losing speed but gaining in force, as we have seen). The name **block-and-tackle** is also generally used. Lifting power is applied to the **fall, the hauling part.** The **fall block** or **running block** is the block attached to the object to be moved. It is also called the movable block. The **standing block** is fixed to a permanent support. The end of the rope that is attached to a block at the becket is the **standing part.** A brief study of a block and the way a tackle is assembled will clarify the terms.

How blocks work: Consider the strain put on a block when a jib sheet merely goes through the block and makes a 180° turn. If someone is hauling on the sheet with a force of 50 pounds, you could measure the force applied to the corner of the sail: also 50 pounds. But the forces acting on the block, if measured, will prove to be 100 pounds. The explanation is plain: There are two forces of 50 pounds each on the block.

Now look at another everyday block-and-tackle, the downhaul on the boom of a simple sailboat. There are two single blocks in this setup, and when a crew member pulls up on the line with a force of 50 pounds, the boom is pulled downward, again with a force of 100 pounds. Why isn't it more? The second block acts only to change the direction of the pull in this case. You count the number of lines coming *from the movable block* to find the ratio of the purchase. A simple block-and-tackle, which might be used to lift an object, is sometimes called a single whip. It is convenient but does not change the power.

Most block-and-tackle arrangements add both convenience and a change in the power.

Another typical arrangement to be found on the falls of a davit for a dinghy or on the main sheet of a small sailboat is one with one double block and one single block. Count the lines *from the movable block* (in this case, three) and you know that this purchase has a ratio of 1:3. Apply 50 pounds pull and you get 150 pounds of lifting force, minus a small amount for friction.

Besides the change in force, you note that there is another change: speed and distance. You have to pull in three feet on the line to move the boom one foot, and while you are doing it, you can see that the line in your hand moves three times as fast as the output force. If it weren't for the design and construction of modern blocks, friction would make all this a difficult thing.

More elaborate arrangements of blocks produce still greater ratios. Although you may not have a need to know the old-time names for these, you can tuck them in your memory in case you are reading a book about nineteenth century seafaring or watching a lobsterman haul up his traps.

A single whip changes the direction of force but gives no mechanical advantage. The same arrangement does give an advantage if it is rigged so that the block moves.

A gun tackle purchase gives a ratio of 1:2 if the block with two lines is the one that moves. If it were rigged with the other end up so that the block to which the end of the line is made fast, at the becket, was the movable one, the ratio would be 1:3.

A luff tackle or **watch tackle** has a single block with a becket and a double block. The advantage is 1:3 if the single block is the movable one and 1:4 if the double block is movable.

A two-fold (double) tackle has two double blocks and may be rigged so the advantage is either 1:4 or 1:5.

A Spanish burton is another commonly used tackle on shipboard, particularly fishing boats and work boats. It has two single blocks, each with a becket.

As we have seen, the same combination of blocks may be rigged in more than one way. To get the greatest mechanical efficiency, the hauling part should lead from the block with the most sheaves. If both blocks have the same number of sheaves, it is best to have the hauling part lead from the movable block.

Several other ways of rigging blocks are shown in Chapter 9.

Single whip

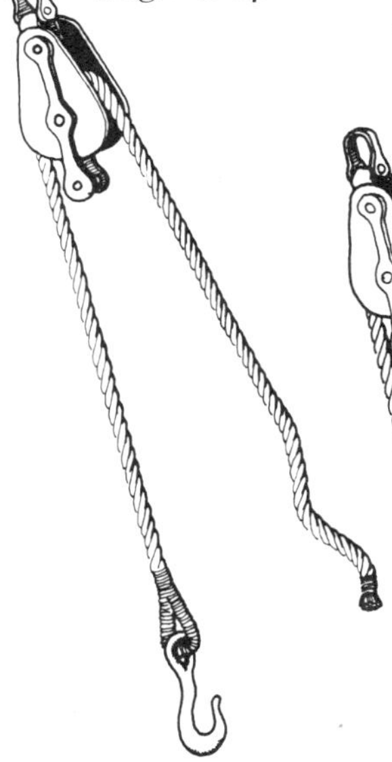

Gun tackle or watch tackle

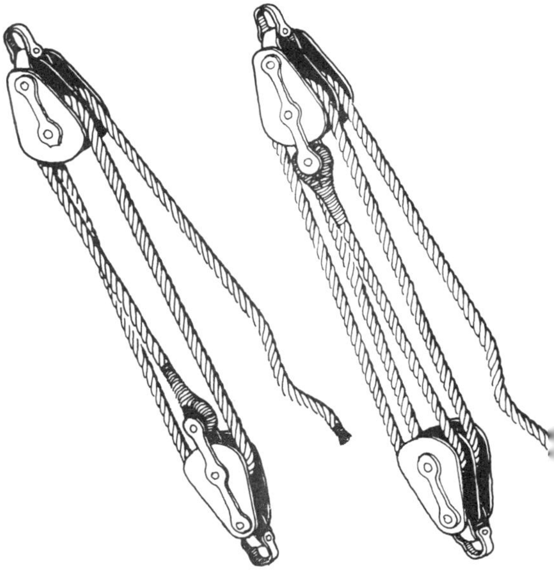

A tackle may be rigged so either end moves.

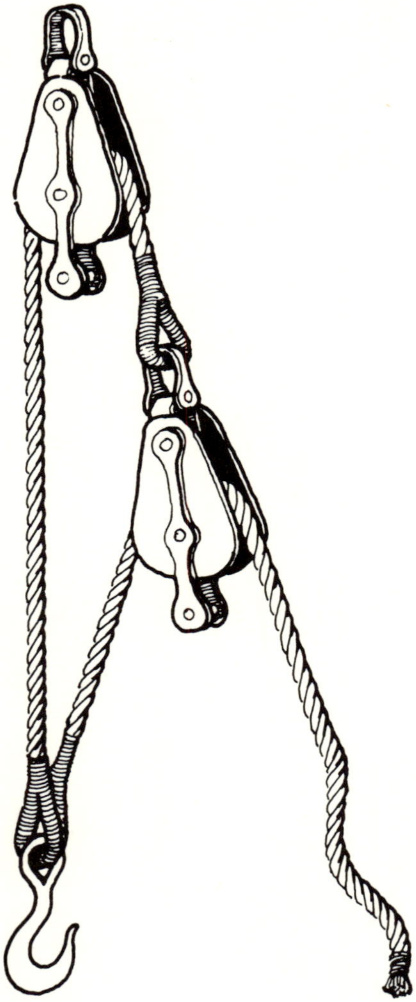

A Spanish burton

The mechanical principles are the same, but it is possible to apply the force from either end of a line or to have a choice of fast or slow from the same setup of blocks and lines.

Aside from sailboat rigging, there are various other situations where a knowledge of rigging blocks and tackles comes into play. Some of them involve rarely encountered situations, like lifting weights in an emergency. Tremendous force can be applied.

THE STRENGTH OF ROPE

The rope in a block-and-tackle is just as important as the blocks. If you use three-strand rope and it is under a heavy strain going around the sheaves, the natural twist to the rope takes a set that gives an awkward twist to the whole block-and-tackle. Double braid, on the other hand, does not take a set, and the difference is obvious when you look at a modern rig for a main sheet. When possible, end-for-end any rope periodically. Using a laid rope on a winch, always the same way under severe strain, will also give it a set that can lead to hockles.

Standard advice to those using rope is to find the tensile strength—the breaking strength—and then use rope with a working load not more than 11 percent of the breaking strength in the case of laid rope and not more than 20 percent of the breaking strength for braided rope.

However, there is a great difference between a steady load and a shock load. "Sudden drops, snubs, and pickups" as well as excessive temperatures end up weakening rope. Nylon rope is a little weaker when wet. So setting a safe "working load" depends on circumstances. A line used for towing is not only subject to risk because of the extra strains on it—but the hazards of its breaking are more significant. On a sailboat, jibes and knockdowns obviously can cause excessive loads to be applied to lines that otherwise are many times strong enough.

A simple lever is one means of getting mechanical advantage with a hand-operated anchor winch. A sheet winch on a sailboat may have both a lever, the handle, and an internal gearing system. Some outhauls on booms are as simple as a single movable block with one line to apply the force. Others make use of worm gears inside the boom. Chapter 9 goes into more detail on the mechanisms used.

A hand-operated anchor windlass uses a lever, of course.

Once you have a feeling for the various ways of applying force, you may decide that in a way, you *can* push on a rope. You certainly can get just about the same effect.

WRINKLES

A handy billy can be rigged ahead of time and carried in the bosun's locker on a long cruise, ready to be clapped on for emergency lifting. Rig a double block so that a lizard, a short length of line, is attached to the becket. Rig a single block the same way. Now make up the tackle with a fair length of line and you have a **handy billy,** ready for heavy work.

Lengths of spare line should be ready aboard almost any boat—for an emergency tow, to tie down loose gear if a tropical storm warning is raised, or to teach your nephew a few new things about knot tying.

Size of a block: An old rule of thumb stated that the size of a block should be about three times the circumference of the rope being used, and the diameter of the sheave should be at least twice the circumference of the rope. With the low-stretch ropes, particularly Kevlar, another way of putting it is: The sheave should have ten to twelve times the diameter of the rope.

To finish off the ends of spare lines, learn to make at least one kind of whipping. A West country whipping, not to do with American cowboys, but with the West Country of England, is described in Chapter 13. A quick temporary whipping that's easy to learn is Ashley's constrictor knot. One way to tie it, using perhaps a foot of whipping twine, is to make a clove hitch, then to rearrange the two ends so that they come up between the two bights. This little gem is a tight knot, also useful for the end of a bag, but when it is once pulled tight, it is so secure it may need to be cut open. This can be avoided by making a third bight that is a slip knot, good for a bag knot but not needed for the quick whip on the end of a line.

If you wear deck shoes with laces that tie, here's the knot that looks neat and doesn't keep coming undone: the **slippery reef knot,** not to be confused with the granny bow knot, which has neither grace nor security.

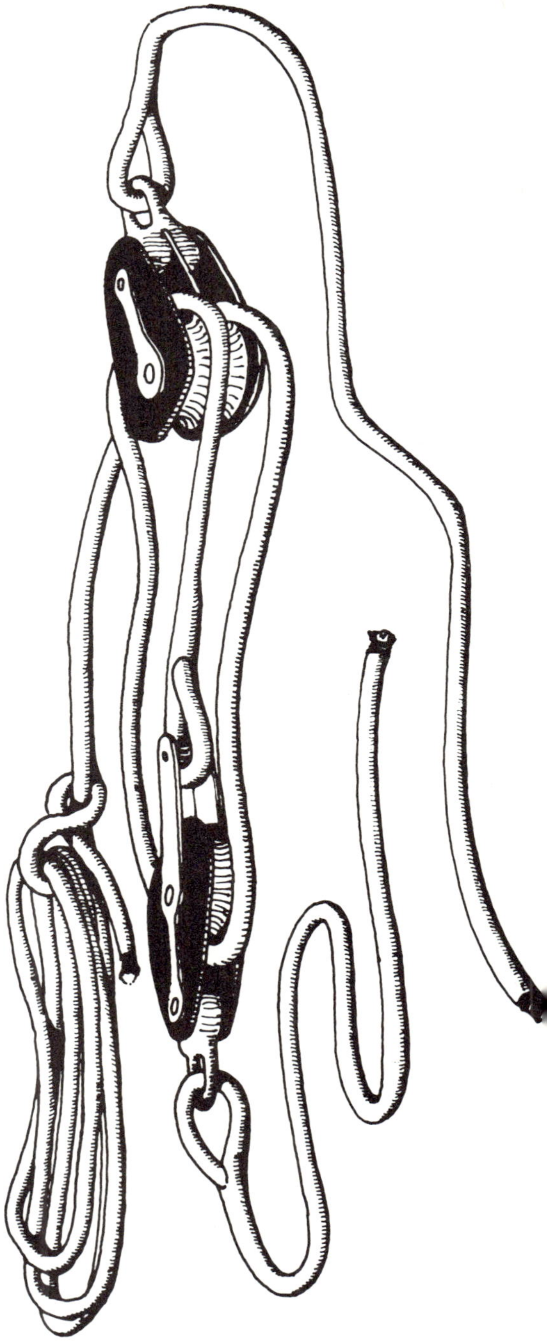

A handy billy

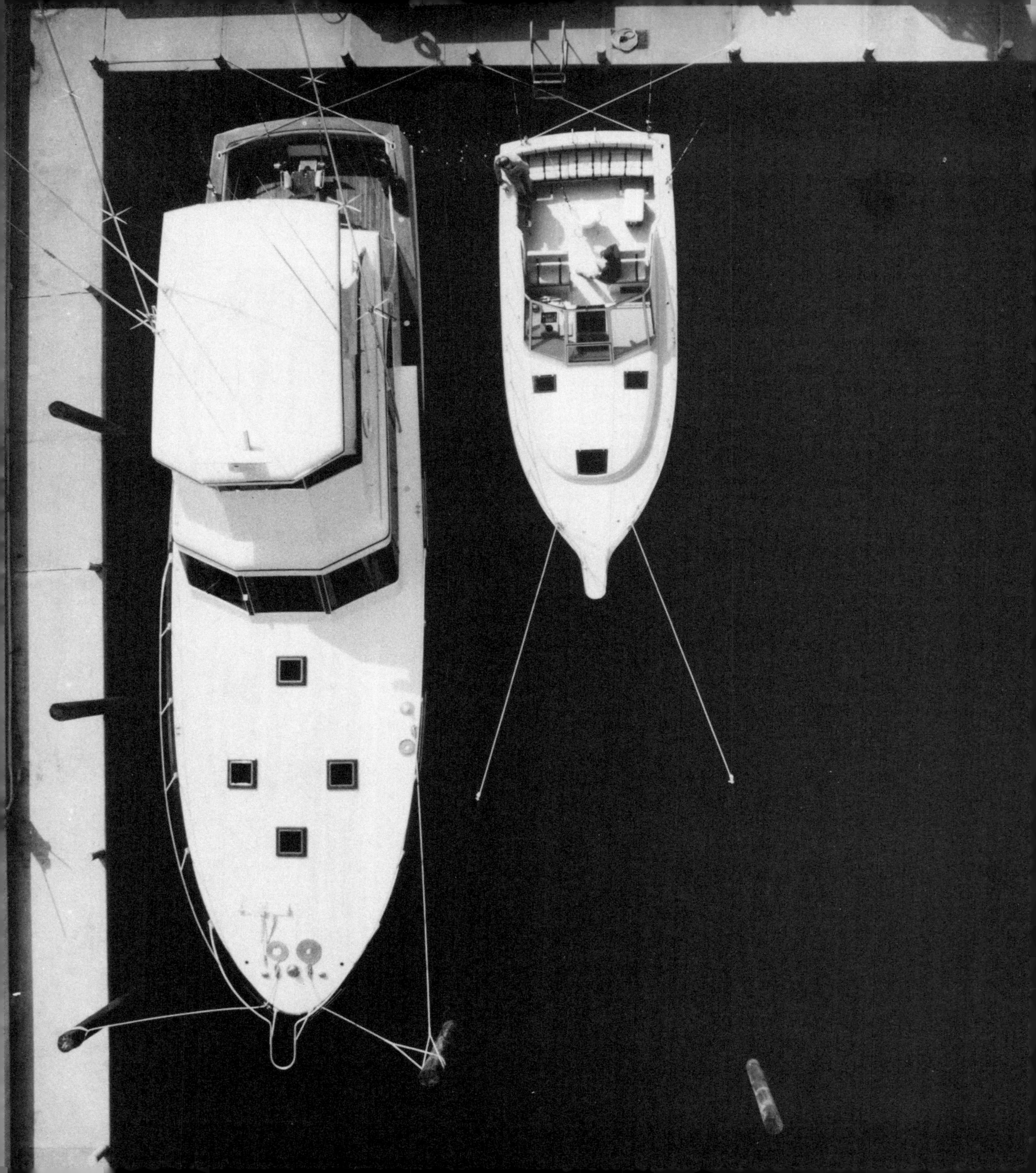

Chapter 5

Deckmanship

The beautiful yawl *Finisterre*, some years "retired" after winning the Bermuda race three times in a row, was coming into a float at the end of dock five at Yacht Haven, in Stamford. A young man wearing Docksiders, and in other ways looking like the willing type he was, ran down to help with the lines. He took the bow line that was tossed to him and immediately began to pull on it, while another person took the stern line. In a couple of minutes they had made *Finisterre* fast, neatly and properly cleating down the lines.

There was a look on the young man's face that said: "What can I learn from Carleton Mitchell?" He was hanging on every word.

Mitch, the owner of *Finisterre*, recognized the eagerness, as well as the degrees of experience and inexperience, and a little later gave a couple of pointers.

"You don't usually need to *pull* on a dock line. Just take a turn around a cleat or bollard, and hold it. If you start pulling on the line, the way most people do, with a keel sailboat you're going to pivot the boat. That just makes the stern swing out from the dock.

"Other times, of course, it's part of the job, to carefully haul a boat along a dock to the space where she'll be tied up. Then it's easy, even with a boat larger than *Finisterre*, to move her, especially if two persons are at the lines, one forward and one aft."

One way or another, helpful hands on boat, pier, or float can do it smoothly or make small errors in bringing a boat in and helping tie her up. A fresh look at the basics, applicable to power or sail, as well as at some of the many useful little tricks, is a good idea even for those who have been around boats a good deal.

◀ *A full set of dock lines holds the boat, even if wind or current change completely. Springs are to control fore and aft movement; they also are used in maneuvering.*

Standard dock lines, when the job is all done, are as follows: Bow line, stern line, forward spring, and after spring. As all boating persons know, the bow line and stern line hold the boat to the dock. The spring lines keep her from moving forward or aft and, in the case of a boat docked at a pier where there is a large rise and fall of tide, are an effective way to keep the boat in place as the tides change.

There will be times, even with a fairly small boat, when there will be more lines in use because of a special situation. There is more than one "right" way to arrange these lines, depending on the available cleats, pilings, or bollards on the dock, as well as on the boat's own deck hardware and the proximity of other vessels. At times, variations of the methods used on big ships may be useful; at other times the boat owner gets an idea from the way local fishing boats tie up in a particular harbor. In any case, the size and type of boat, the length of stay, and the condition in regard to the wind as well as the tides and currents have a lot to do with the way a boat is made fast, the way she leaves a pier or slip, and how a boat is towed.

Expert line-handling and deck work includes a number of skills and specialized bits of knowledge: estimating distance, coiling lines, throwing a line, preventing chafe, and avoiding both small and large accidents.

The length of dock lines for any vessel depends somewhat on the type of service. For a typical pleasure boat here are suggested lengths:

Bow line—twice the beam.

Spring lines—one and a half times the length overall.

Stern line—twice the beam.

The type of rope for dock lines, for years, was twisted manila. This was replaced by twisted nylon, preferably medium lay. The new technologies of synthetic fibers and of rope construction have made a still better choice possible. Double braided nylon lines are 30 percent stronger than three-strand rope. They are non-torquing and non-hockling. Their elongation or stretch characteristics smooth out surges caused by waves and wind and thus reduce the strain on fittings. The braided lines stay flexible, and loss of strength caused by abrasion is less. However, as with anchor lines, age, dirt, and wear take their toll. Inspection is a necessary part of the maintenance of dock lines.

The size of rope depends on the vessel's size, of course. Based on absolute strength, rope that is 9 mm or 3/8″ in diameter is adequate for boats up to 35 feet in length, but the mere bulk of a rope reduces the effect of abrasion, so many persons would choose 12 mm or 1/2″. The following table gives the comparative strengths of double braid and three-strand twisted nylon rope in a few sizes, showing how an increase in the diameter of rope results in an increase in both the minimum tensile strength and the recommended working loads. In many situations, such as towing or lying in a dock area exposed to violent storms, where shock loads might occur, even these "working loads" are not necessarily applicable.

Comparative Strengths: Nylon Double Braid and Nylon 3-Strand

DIAM. INCHES	METRIC MM	DOUBLE BRAID TENSILE (LBS.)	WORKING LOAD (LBS.)	3-STRAND TENSILE (LBS.)	WORKING LOAD (LBS.)
⅜″	9	3,700	336	3,340	278
½″	12	6,550	655	5,750	525
⅝″	16	10,200	1,130	9,350	935
1″	24	26,000	3,250	22,600	1,030
Working load rating		20%		11%	

Source: The Cordage Institute.

Making up a dock line. Each line should have at one end an eye splice or a loop made by tying a bowline, large enough for any bollards or pilings likely to be encountered. Marine dealers sell nylon dock lines already made up, including the eye splice and a finish, such as a whipping, on the other end. This is a convenience, except when these prepackaged ready-mades are soft-lay three-strand nylon. Although it is shiny and pleasant to touch, this kind of rope in time will kink and get hockles (permanent distortions that weaken rope).

If you can find double-braid nylon, properly spliced and of the right size, you're better off. The Canadian Navy, the U.S. Navy, and the U.S. Coast Guard use this type of dock line for small boats. In Chapter 13 you will find instructions for making an eye splice in double-braid rope.

Three-strand laid rope, to be sure, is easier to splice if you are going to make up your own. Use medium-lay, not the soft kind (the ease of working with it is an illusion), and certainly not the hard

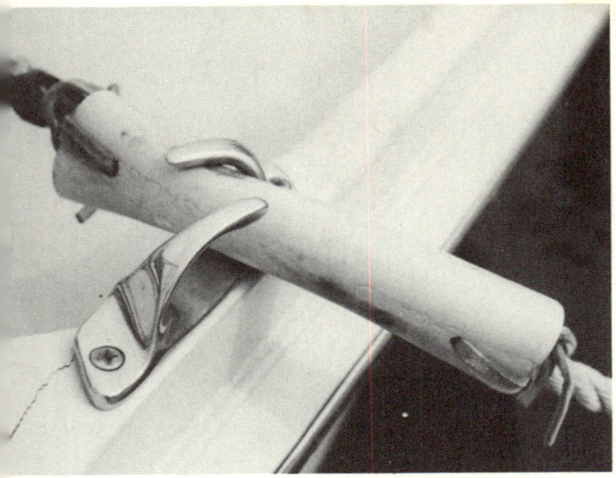

Chafe guards protect lines and sometimes help keep them snug in their chocks.

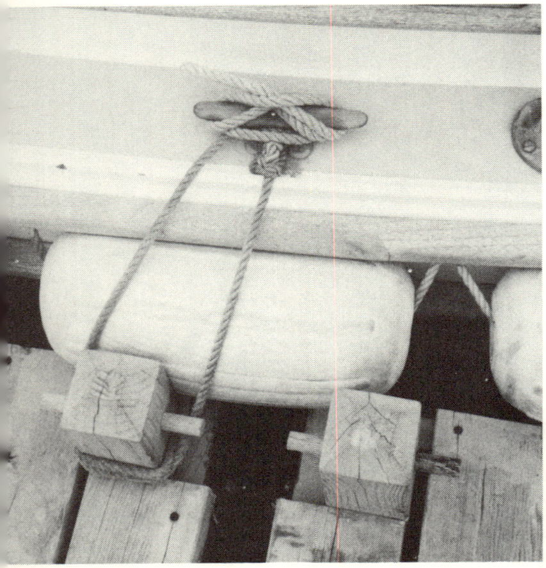

Careful use of fenders keeps the dock from scarring the hull of the boat.

lay, which requires tools and professional skills. However, making up your own dock lines of double-braid rope is not unduly difficult.

The ends of a cruising boat's dock line or a spare line that might be used for towing or lifting should be handled as follows: Although one end can be an eye splice or a loop made with a bowline, it is usually best to keep the other end plain so it can be put through a block or fairlead if necessary. Whip the end to protect it. Putting a backsplice on it limits what can be done with the rope. If it is necessary to keep the end of a line from going through a block, tie a stopper (figure eight or Ashley's stopper knot).

Of course a dock line fitted exactly for a permanent berth may have eye splices and antichafe protection as part of the setup.

Chafe guards at the chocks are often desirable, particularly at a permanent berth, where rocking from the wakes of passing boats or from storms may increase the chances of wear. The best chafe guard material is leather, but plastic and rubber antichafe material are more readily available.

Fenders and fender boards are an important adjunct in docking, except in a situation like a fuel dock, which may have built in fenders. Protecting the hull from the rough edges of pier, float, or pilings takes some careful adjusting at times. At a permanent home berth, it is often possible to put corner rollers or other protection on the float or dock.

Fenders, plus a fender board, are an even better method of protecting the topsides.

DOCKS, PIERS, AND WHARVES

Dock is a word with a number of meanings. Strictly speaking, a dock is the water area between two piers; loosely, it is a place, such as a wharf or pier, for loading and unloading. A general meaning is all the port installations. There are dry docks, also called graving docks, which can be emptied of water, to allow working on a vessel.

A wharf is a structure, parallel to the shore, where boats can tie up or moor.

A pier is a similar structure, but projecting from the shore (although a pier can also be a breakwater or a promenade). A finger pier is a narrow pier projecting from a wharf or pier.

A float is a pierlike structure that rises and falls with the water level. A camel is a long, narrow float between a large vessel and a pier or wharf used as a work platform.

A slip is a mooring area, sometimes between two finger piers or between pilings so that the boat's bow or stern is against a pier or wharf.

A mooring is a place where vessels are made fast, as at a pier, or secured to a permanent type of anchor, such as a mushroom. Moorings are the general area where boats or ships are docked, moored, or anchored.

A berth is an assigned anchorage or docking (mooring) space.

A bollard is a wood or iron post on a dock, pier, wharf, or float to which vessels can attach their dock lines. If it has a horizontal cross piece, that is called a norman. On shipboard, a bollard is more likely to be called a samson post or a bitt (or there may be a pair of bitts.)

Piles are long slender columns, usually wood, driven into the ground, used to support wharves and piers and to hold floats in place. The part of a pile or piling that projects above the surface of a pier is often used in place of a bollard to attach a mooring line.

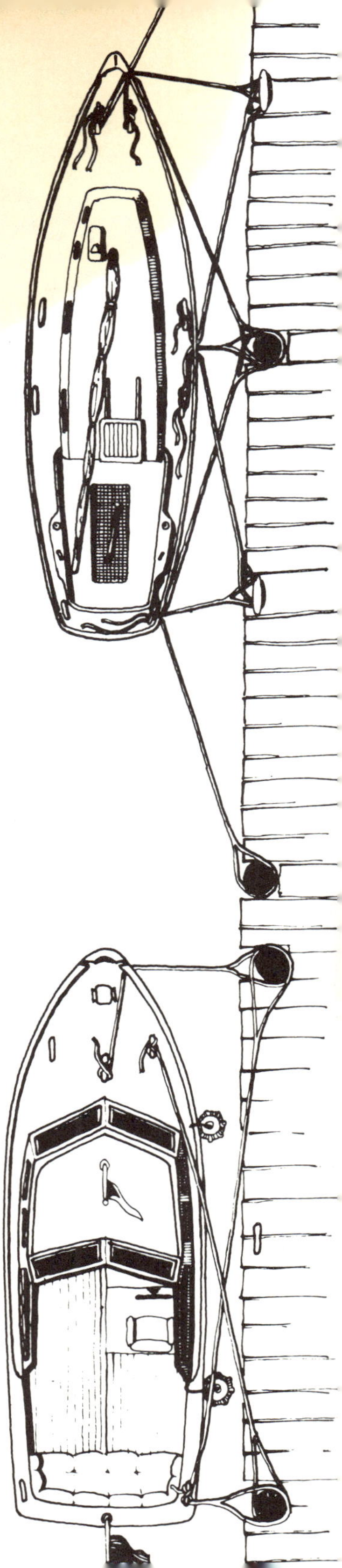

A boat under power can use reverse to bring the hull into the dock, once a bow line is made fast. Reversing is often a good way to leave the dock.

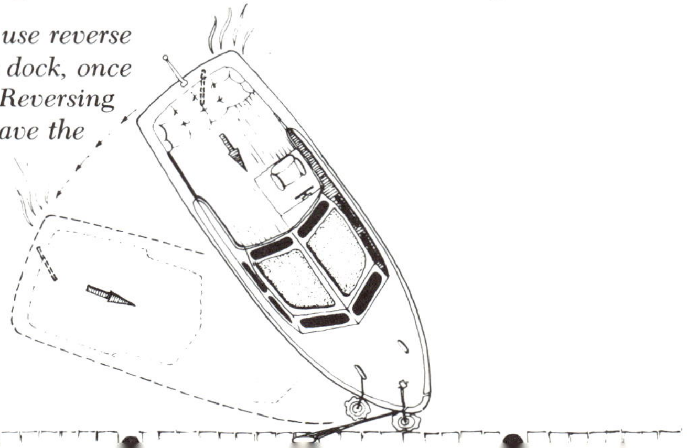

DOCKING PROCEDURES

While approaching a pier or float, the skipper and crew make preparations.

There are two parts to this. First, the skipper notes the wind and tide so that he can decide which direction will make the best approach. The way other boats are tied may help him determine this. Second, the necessary lines and fenders are readied.

A short stop, to get fuel or pick up guests for an afternoon's outing, may require only two lines (one at the bow, one at the stern) and perhaps a couple of fenders. The lines should have been coiled and hung neatly when last used. It is a simple matter to check that they are not fouled. At times it may be desirable to overhaul the lines, especially if it may be necessary to throw a line to the pier.

Loose gear on deck or in the cockpit, which might be a hazard to working crew members, should be secured. If the sails have been dropped, they should be well furled and the sheets and halyards coiled so that they won't interfere with the work of docking.

A bow line and a stern line are normally taken through their respective chocks, then up and back to the lifelines, so they will already be in position when taken to the pier.

With fenders and dock lines rigged, a power cruiser enters a marina and backs smoothly into her slip.

PAP

PAPILLON

The wrong ways to fasten lines include bypassing chocks, tangling up on cleats, tying to lifeline stanchions, and overwrapping.

Because boats under power maneuver more easily with the port side to the pier or float, the usual choice is to approach in this way, but there are many exceptions because of wind, other boats, or the direction to be taken when leaving.

Sometimes in berthing a boat in a slip, it is desirable to back in, especially if getting on and off the boat onto a float or dock would otherwise be a problem. Backing in to a slip is a lot easier with a twin-screw powerboat than with a single screw auxiliary sailboat. The sailboat crew may have to use lines and muscle and have fenders ready for temporary fending.

If the wind is blowing against the incoming boat, one way to get the boat in is to approach bow on, make a bowline fast, and then use reverse power to bring the port side of the boat close enough to the dock to use a stern line effectively. An alternate way is to make a stern line fast first and then go forward. The boat will move herself in, more or less parallel to the pier or float, especially if the rudder is used to help.

Normally, with little set of wind or current, a pier is approached at an angle—about 10° with a single screw vessel. The power is cut early enough so that she comes to a stop at just about her right position. If it is necessary to use reverse, the normal action of the propellor will swing the stern in.

Edging slowly into a short space at a pier, with other boats close by, may involve throwing a line to a helping hand on the pier. The technique of throwing a fairly light dock line is to divide the coil in half, then throw one half of the line with the right hand, letting the weight of the line pull out the second half of the coil from the left hand.

A LINE AS A MESSENGER

It can be another matter to toss a heavy coil of line, such as might be used on a large yacht or work boat, or to throw a line against the wind. The solution is to use a heaving line, a light line sometimes called a messenger, with a weighted knot called a monkey's fist. Because adverse winds or difficult situations do arise, many boatmen keep a light line available for this purpose, even though it may never be needed.

If it is necessary to lie against a pier or float with the wind bringing the boat against it, rigging fenders and fender boards may be the most important preparation.

Making fast each dock line is a procedure that may need to be repeated if adjustments are required. If a dock line already has an

The right methods to fasten lines allow for security, a quick release if needed, and protection of boat and gear.

A dozen extra turns on a piling can get in the way of other people, too.

eye on the end, it is usually convenient to put this over a bollard or a piling and to adjust the length from the boat. If there are cleats on the pier, the eye can be put over a cleat or through an open base cleat or doubled for security.

A knot is sometimes needed. A line can be made fast to a bollard with:

- ▲ A clove hitch. This is seen often, partly because it is so easy to adjust and readjust the line. Expert sailors are not the ones who use a clove hitch, however, unless an extra half hitch is taken. The clove hitch can work loose if it is not under steady, constant tension.
- ▲ Two half hitches. This is a more secure knot, tied rapidly.
- ▲ A bowline. Even if a line has been passed around a piling, making a bowline is not difficult. It is the most secure knot of all.

Avoid multiturns around a pile or bollard. This is an error frequently made, no doubt because boatmen want to get the excess line out of the way.

A Flemish coil, on the dock or on board the boat, is a better way to keep excess line out of the way. In the days of manila rope, a flat coil tended to collect moisture and promote rot. With synthetic lines this is no problem.

In most cases the boat is secured fore and aft, then spring lines are rigged. There are a variety of ways to use these, depending on the available space. Sometimes a line is taken from the quarter furthest from the pier or wharf so that something like a thwartship spring line results. For large ships and small yachts, a customary way of handling the lines to the pier is with a Mediterranean moor. The bow is held by one or two anchors, the stern is at the dock. In this and other situations, using the chocks to help control the lines is important.

If a boat is to be left unattended for several changes of the tide, special precautions may be necessary, such as rigging an extra snubbing line to keep a spring line from getting caught on a projecting part of the dock structure. Another protective measure that is sometimes taken is to rig an extra line to a nearby piling, assuming it won't be in the way of other boats, so that your boat will be held off the pier or float when the wind changes.

After the boat is secured with all necessary lines, adjusted for anticipated changes of tide, wind, or current, it is often necessary to rig shore power electric lines. Here's one good way to prevent a "disconnect" caused by the boat's motion: Add a knot. An overhand knot, tied as you plug one wire into the female end of another, is one way to avoid pulling out. Or if the receptacle is on a post, either make the overhand knot around the post or add a short piece of line as a tyer.

Water hose is another shore connection, usually for a short period. A common mistake is to forget that coils of tangled water hose left on a dock can trip passersby. One excellent kind of water hose, if you carry your own, is the kind that stows flat on a reel. It takes less space.

Changing berths or adjusting the boat's position is sometimes more easily done by using dock lines. The technical name is **warping**. If the vessel is turned end for end, using only her lines, that is called **winding ship.** If proper lines are rigged and the crew works to a plan, it is relatively easy to turn even a good-sized boat end for end without starting the motor. This might be desirable to catch a cooling breeze in the cockpit or to avoid a driving rain.

Avoid gear carelessly left on a pier, frayed rope ends, and mooring too close to another boat's topsides.

An overhand knot is useful for keeping electrical power lines in place.

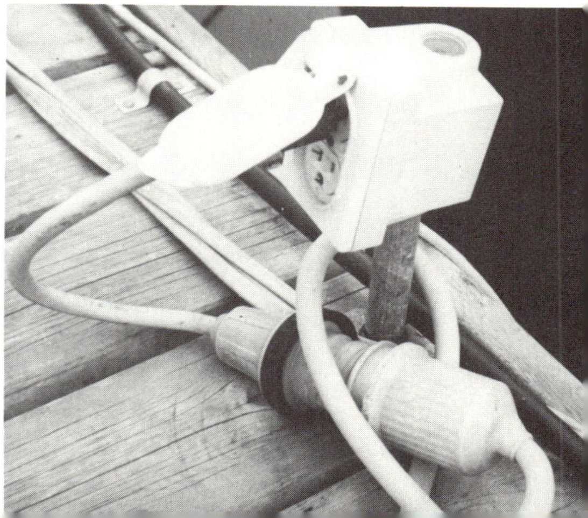

BACKING OUT

Departing the dock is a procedure that sometimes requires advance planning, especially if other boats are in the way. In many cases the easiest way to get away from a float or pier is to back out. Captains of small naval ships that may have to maneuver without tugboats know how to do this.

In other cases, the spring lines are needed to get away from a dock. If the wind is holding the boat to the dock, backing while the bow spring is still fast, or using the after spring while going ahead, will usually do the trick. Sometimes it is necessary to rig a special spring line, to use a short line, or to move a dock line to another piling, in order to maneuver.

► *With a young crew member handling the lines, an auxiliary comes up to a Maine dock to pick up a passenger.*

Timing everything correctly, the crew use fenders, two lines—and a few muscles.

▼ *Leaving a dock is easy when wind and current aren't fighting the boat. Many times a spring line is needed to help control the boat while it backs away from the pier.*

Taking a dock line properly: Hold the boat with a half turn or full turn around piling or cleat; don't let the boat pull you into the water.

A BOAT STEERS BY THE STERN

There are a number of ways that spring lines are used to move a boat around a piling, against the wind or current, in and out of a slip. One important point: Three times out of four it is easier to back away from a dock than to try to run out like a car leaving a parking space. A car steers by its front wheels. A boat steers by its rudder, at the stern.

The control of the boat, when using her power, is sometimes dependent on the propeller, of course. But the effect of the propeller is often determined by the rudder's position. At times, without the boat moving, a short burst of power, with the rudder at a fairly sharp angle, will move the boat sideways. In other situations, as you know, the normal action of the rudder is effective only when the boat has way on.

Put the boat into reverse, apply power for a short burst, and the stern will swing sharply to port. The turning effect of the rudder is more pronounced when the boat is going astern. Use brief spurts of power.

Use the wind and the current, as well as the dock lines and power, in close maneuvering in a dock area.

A balance between caution and sureness is needed. It doesn't pay to run at speed to a dock and then stop by applying full reverse; sooner or later the worst will happen. But if you are edging up to a dock, against a strong wind, you can get within a foot without fear of hitting the dock. Similarly, it is often better to let the wind ease the boat away from the dock, using a little power in short bursts, than to try to speed the process.

After departing a dock, make sure that all lines are promptly coiled and stowed, along with fenders and fender boards.

COILING LINES

There are several ways to coil lines, depending on the purpose.

If you are packing up large lengths of rope for transportation, a good way to keep the coils secure is to tie them at four evenly spaced places.

If you are stowing the coil and it won't be used soon, there is a standard stowage coil, shipshape and secure. A coil for hanging a halyard on a cleat, ready to be cast off in a hurry, is made by leaving a section of the standing part from the cleat to the coil (less than a foot, usually) and using this to make a bight with a twist, to hang the coil on the same cleat.

A gasket coil, used to hang up a dock line or spare rope that won't be needed as quickly as a halyard, is made by taking four or five turns around both sides of the coil and then putting either a bight or the single end through the small opening between the round turns and the end of the coil. This is used to hang up the coil. One use for a gasket coil is to hang up a main sheet when the boat is moored.

Overhaul a coiled line if it has become fouled. If awkward kinks keep it from coiling properly, start over. If you pull a line back through a coil, while getting the snarls out you may be adding a knot without knowing it. If you are coiling braided line, you may have to settle for figure eights; don't use the coiling method that works for laid line and put a twist into braided line that started out without torque. Braided rope can also acquire a twist or set from constant use on a winch, always in the same direction.

One exception to an obvious rule about letting line pile up is a rope locker for an anchor line. Braided line can be dropped into the stowage area and will come out just as smoothly. Even laid rope will fake down evenly enough so it does not need to be coiled or stowed. The concern about storing wet rope—that it will mildew and rot—is no longer valid with synthetic fibers.

To fasten two lines together, to make a longer line in a special situation, use either of the following methods:

Tie a bowline, and then make a bowline through the loop, with the other rope.

Use a sheet bend or double sheet bend. For extra security, seize the free end to the standing part. When you're through, cut the seizing.

Having everything ready, with lines properly coiled, makes boat handling easier. These lines are in "gasket coils."

TOWING AND BEING TOWED

The situations requiring towing vary a great deal.

If you are merely helping move a fairly small boat a short distance in smooth water, you can take a line from the bow cleat of the boat to be moved. You may not think you need to make it fast at the stern of your boat, but do so. It is dangerous to have someone try to hold the line.

If you are moving a boat from one place to another in smooth water, one way is to lash it alongside in much the same way as rafting, which is described in Chapter 6. Your speed will be curtailed, but you will usually have good maneuverability.

Almost any towing situation may require someone to stay aboard the towed boat to steer it out and in and when difficult situations develop. Set up a system of signals so that the towed boat and the towing boat can communicate with each other. The hand signals suggested for anchoring situations elsewhere in this book should be adequate, unless towing at night, when additional flashlight signals or radio telephone may be needed.

Towing at night calls for special supplements to the running lights: two white lights on the masthead, one above the other. In international waters, tows are supposed to fly day signals, one at the masthead of each vessel.

Emergencies, including bad wind and waves, may put such a strain on both boats that special measures must be used. These sometimes include putting the towline around the mast of the boat being towed, if the bow cleat or bitts are not adequate, and using a towing bridle at the stern of the tow boat. The bridle makes it easier to steer the towboat as well as distributing the strain of the towline over more than one fitting. It is not always feasible to rig a towing bridle, however.

As a general rule, towing in rough water requires a much longer towline, to absorb the shock of the waves.

Usually, it works best for the towboat to pass the line to the vessel to be towed. If emergency weather conditions make it difficult, try floating a line to the vessel in distress. You can use a floating water-ski rope or a light line tied to a float and then let the other boat haul the heavy towline aboard. Methods of tying two dock lines together have already been discussed.

Towing under sail: It isn't always necessary to use power for towing. It is quite feasible to tow a fairly large boat behind a sailboat or a whole line of small racing sailboats.

Double-braided nylon line is the best for towing, because it has some stretch but not as much "snap-back" as three-strand laid line.

Safety in towing requires that all persons know about the danger involved. A towline, under heavy strain, becomes a potential weapon, loaded with stored energy. A broken line, snapping across a deck, is a fearsome thing. Inspect a towline carefully before using it. Keep from overloading the line and keep people from being in the way if the line should break.

Backing an auxiliary sailboat (with only one screw) takes skill at the helm and on deck.

If it is necessary to tow a vessel that is on fire, approach from the windward side so the flames are blowing away from you.

Be ready to cast off, or even to cut the line, if an emergency should require it.

When towing a long distance, adjust the line as much as possible so that the two vessels are both on the crests or both in the troughs of waves at the same time. Alternate surges on the line, caused by waves, strain the line and the fittings. A long line lessens the strain.

As you approach a harbor, shorten the towline to aid in maneuvering. When going around a buoy or the end of a dock, and in passing moored vessels, take a wide swing.

A large boat should not try towing a small one at too high a speed. The smaller vessel may be difficult to steer and will often have difficulty in following or "tracking."

A home berth can have special stern lines rigged to keep the boat (power or sail) in place. A convenient boarding ladder can be a swim ladder at an anchorage. Some docks have antichafe protection built on.

WRINKLES

The rule of three. The meticulous skipper who knows how many minutes are required to get the dock lines, fenders, and fender boards ready can match this information against estimated distances as he enters a harbor and approaches a dock or marina. The trick is to use the rule of three, which states that in three minutes, a vessel proceeds a distance in hundreds of yards equal to her speed in knots. Here are three examples: At a speed of 15 knots, your boat is moving 500 yards each minute. As you slow down to 6 knots, you move 200 yards a minute. And at 1 knot, you are moving 33 yards a minute.

Remember, the propeller gives lateral thrust in going forward or reversing: The thrust is in the direction that would result if the blades were aground as they turn. Think of them as wheels.

Make dock lines to size, for a permanent mooring in your home slip, with the correct size eye splice at each end. The ratio of the length of an eye splice to the diameter of the piling should be a minimum of 3:1 and preferably 5:1. That is, a one-foot bollard or piling should have a three- to five-foot eye, to avoid straining the throat of the eye. It is always possible to make a large loop by using a small eye and bringing the loop through it.

Many persons put plastic antichafe sleeves on the eye splices for these dock lines and leave the lines in place when going out for a morning's fishing or an afternoon of sailing.

A heaving line, ready to carry a heavier dock line from boat to pier, is best made of light, floating line, such as polypropylene, which isn't propeller prone.

Padlock plus chain, encased in old fire hose, keeps an aging runabout secure at a small dock.

RI 2052 J

Chapter 6

Anchoring

It's a stormy night. The only thing that's keeping your boat from going on the rocky beach at the other side of the harbor is an anchor, a short piece of chain, and a length of line hardly thicker than your thumb . . . plus a couple of shackles, a well-made eye splice, and the expert technique with which you anchored the afternoon before.

Anchoring is a seaman's skill that involves: (a) the selection and preparation of ground tackle; (b) the choice of the anchorage, including the kind of bottom and protection from wind and seas; and (c) proper procedures.

Ground tackle is the inclusive term applied to the anchor line or anchor rode, the shackles and lengths of chain, and the anchor itself.

When you are noting the variety of anchors on the foredecks of various boats as you walk through a marina, there seem to be dozens of types. Some are better than others: What are the choices?

As everyone knows, the function of an anchor is to hold a vessel in place. It isn't weight alone; a good anchor does its job by digging into the bottom. The harder the wind blows, the deeper the anchor digs in. Yet it will be necessary, after the blow, to get the anchor up—so an anchor is designed so that a horizontal pull digs it in and a vertical pull gets it out. This makes designing an anchor a neat problem in geometry. Since it is also necessary to manufacture the anchor, make it strong enough, and find the proper weight to make it dig in yet be easy to handle, you can see why

◄ *On the beach with plenty of scope—but a fouled anchor wrapped in its own chain*

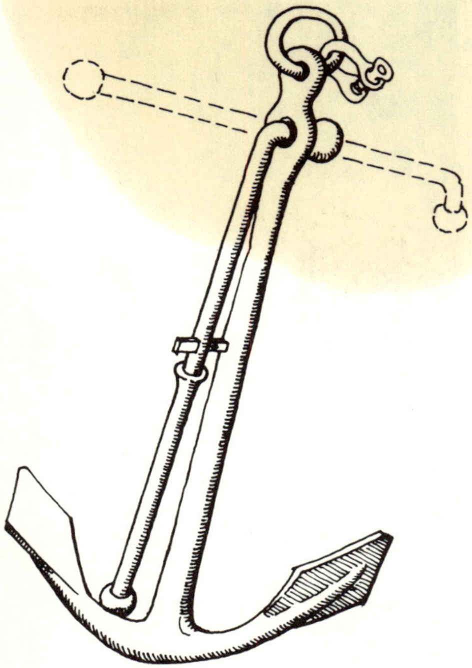

some popular anchors have evolved over centuries and other excellent models have been invented by engineers.

The kedge was originally a small anchor that could be handled by boat crews, but as this shape has evolved and been refined by knowledgeable craftsmen, the word *kedge* has become generic.

One variation is called the Herreshoff model, since the great Nathaniel Herreshoff improved it. Another is called the Fisherman or the Yachtsman. One excellent variation had a few touches of angle and convenience added by another famous boat builder, Henry B. Nevins; you may not be able to find one, because those who own them keep them. The British like the Admiralty model.

In one form or another, these old/new anchors are still in use despite certain disadvantages.

The old-fashioned kedge can be carried flat on deck, in chocks. Before it can be used, it has to be "made up" by extending the cross-arm and inserting a key to hold it in place. A kedge, unless it is already made up and hanging from a bowsprit, is not ready for instant use in an emergency. Yet one of these anchors, with its time-tested shape, will dig in on most kinds of bottoms, holding well with a comparatively short anchor line.

In some boating areas there are special variations of the kedge to dig into the sand or to hold in grass or weeds.

An anchor has centuries-old names for all its parts; even the latest designs use about the same nomenclature. Before looking at some twentieth-century anchors, we will look at these special words, the names of the parts.

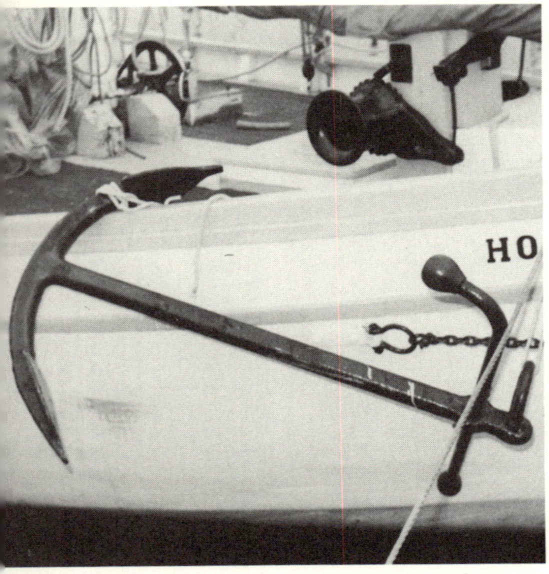

Anchor anatomy, ancient and yet always subject to experiment and development

THE PARTS OF AN ANCHOR

The anatomy of an anchor, a classic anchor, includes the central shank, with a ring to fasten the line to at one end, called the head. The digging-in parts are at the other end, the crown. From the crown extend two arms and two flukes. The bill is the face of the broad part of the fluke. Sometimes the fluke is called the palm. At the head of the anchor, set crossways to the flukes, is the stock.

The stock is intended to lie flat on the bottom while one fluke digs in. If the anchor comes to rest "properly," that's what will happen. If it gets "upset," the pull on the anchor line will usually dig in the stock just enough to make the anchor turn over or "capsize" and cause the fluke to start burying itself. If it's digging into hard shale, the anchor may skid along the bottom for a while before digging in.

If a loop of anchor line accidentally gets twisted around a part of the anchor, stock or fluke, the boat can be in trouble as the anchor drags. This tendency is a particular weakness of the kedge anchor. Attempts at "anti-fouling" anchors were patented as early as 1838.

IMPROVEMENTS IN ANCHORS

Inventors have often set out to improve the anchor, with several kinds of new technical problems to spur them on. Landing craft in World War II needed an anchor that would hold as the boats were beached to land troops and equipment. Power winches were used to haul the landing craft off the beaches.

The Danforth anchor was one that resulted from this military requirement. The Danforth, invented by R. S. Danforth and Robert D. Ogg, has become popular in most sections of the United States and elsewhere in the world. The Danforth anchor, for pleasure boats and work boats, is manufactured in many sizes and with some variations, such as high-tensile steel in one model to keep the weight down still further. It is an anchor that holds in sand, mud, clay, and other kinds of bottom—but not very well where the bottom is grassy.

The Danforth anchor has a moving part: twin pivoting flukes that are sharp yet wide. These large flukes, and their exact angle, are what give this anchor its great holding power. The Danforth has a stock, but on the crown end, and this is intended to prevent the anchor from rolling or rotating. Occasionally, clam shells or oyster shells get stuck in the space between the movable flukes and the shank, and this may interfere with the anchor's proper functioning.

Because of its great popularity, "add-on" inventors have figured out new ways to chock the Danforth on deck, upright at the rail, or in special anchor wells. The Danforth is always made up ready to use—no assembly.

Although it will usually come up with a strong vertical pull, the Danforth often tends to bring part of a mud or clay bottom with it. Particular boatmen who don't like mud on their decks figure out ways to slosh the anchor up and down in the water before hauling

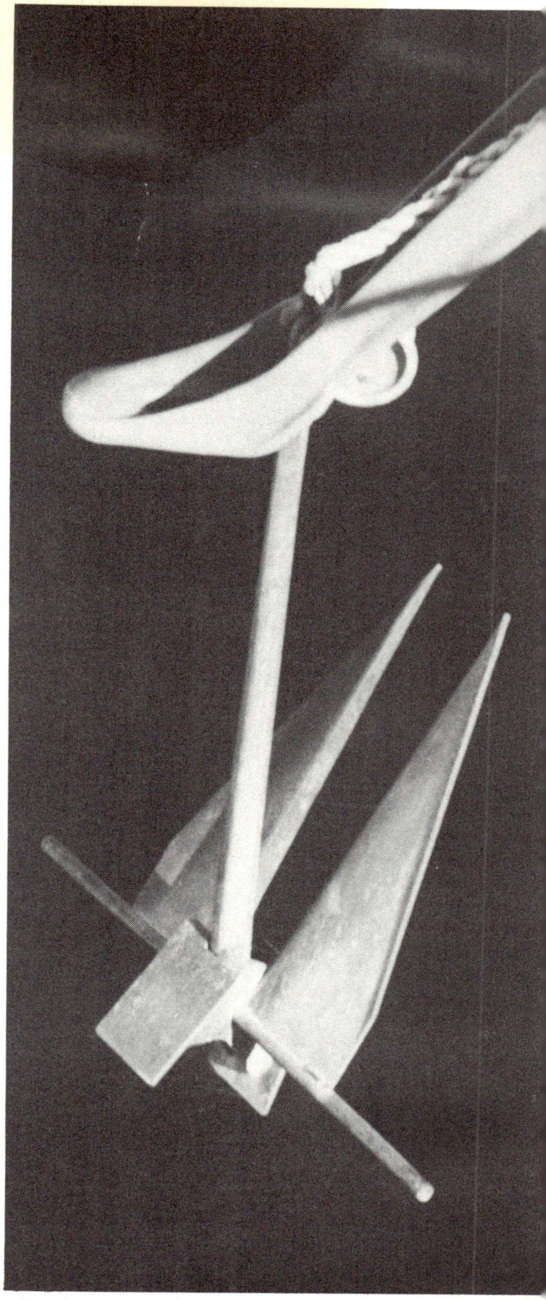

The Danforth design was carefully tested. Exact angles, engineers found, were critical.

aboard. Some throw buckets of water on the anchor, and those with larger boats use a hose.

The Northill is an anchor originally developed for use by waterborne aircraft. It comes in several models and sizes for small boats, including a folding version of stainless steel and a heavier galvanized version. With its stock across the head, it is somewhat like the small boat anchors used for centuries by the Chinese. The Northill has not attained the popularity of the Danforth, except in certain regions of the U.S., notably on the Gulf Coast.

The Danforth and the Northill are generally called lightweight anchors because they work well in weights as low as eight, fourteen, or twenty pounds—digging their geometry into the bottom instead of depending on sheer weight to hold the boat. There are also aluminum anchors, for boats as well as for aircraft.

The CQR Plow is a third type of lightweight anchor, invented by G. I. Taylor of Cambridge University in Great Britain. Indeed, it looks like an agricultural implement, but works like a major nautical invention. Its enthusiastic users claim it holds better in more kinds of bottom than any other anchor; it comes up clean; it is easy to set, always starts digging in, and is less likely to foul.

The Plow also has a moving part, a pivot or swivel. Because the CQR is somewhat awkward to handle and is not easy to stow on deck, cruising sailors often carry one under a bowsprit. Some use a special anchor pulpit.

So still other variations have been designed: the Wishbone type, with one big fluke in the center and the Bruce anchor, which might be described as looking like a cross between a plow anchor and a bent teaspoon. No matter what comparative anatomy words are used, the Bruce anchor, also from the United Kingdom, works well, although it is not noted for great holding power.

The Bruce anchor was originally developed to secure floating oil and gas rigs. It comes in sizes from 2.2 to 110 pounds (1 to 50 kg.). Its design is self-righting, and it breaks out easily with a vertical pull.

Choosing an anchor—that is, buying one for a particular boat—should involve some knowledge of the conditions that will be encountered. A boat owner new to boating or to the waterways and harbors of a particular area can inquire of others and note which types are popular.

Of course, a cruising boat may venture into other areas and meet with new conditions. It is not unusual for a boat that is doing extensive cruising to carry three anchors, of different sizes and types, for special situations or conditions that may be met.

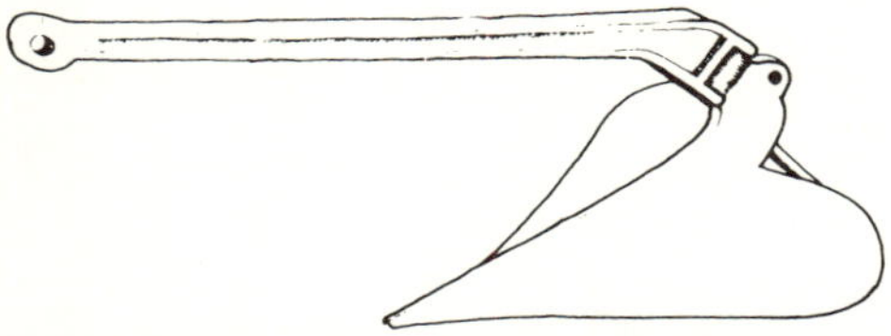

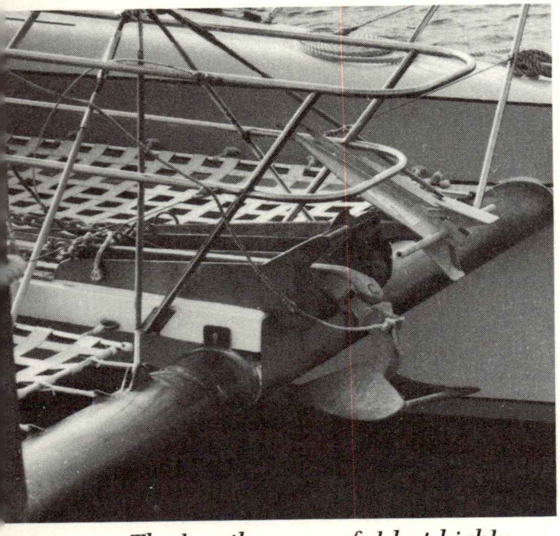

The less than graceful but highly praised CQR plow is a favorite with cruising sailors in most areas.

As you spend time on the waterfront, you see still more variations. A store may still have on hand a supply of small, squat "stockless" anchors called "Navy type." They're not for small boats. This general type of anchor was originally developed for large ships with steam winches. The head of the anchor can be drawn up into the hawse pipe. This, and variations such as the more recently developed British A.C. 14 (vaguely like the Danforth), require chain and tremendous winches. The anchor for an aircraft carrier weighs 20 tons and has a shackle almost as tall as a man. There are few small boat uses for any of the navy types of anchor.

The mushroom anchor is excellent for a permanent mooring. If it's heavy enough and has had weeks to dig into the mud and clay, it holds in a blow. Some small boat fishermen use mushrooms for short stops. A folding anchor, easily carried in a dinghy, or a five-pronged grapnel, for retrieving something lost on the bottom, or sometimes for a grassy or weedy bottom, can be very useful—but knowledgeable boating people know these are not suitable for a cruising boat's main anchor—or in the colorful old language of the sea, "its best bower."

OTHER PARTS OF THE SYSTEM

The anchor rode fastens to the ring at the anchor's head by means of a shackle. On well-found boats there is the first shackle, a short length of chain, and then another shackle. The chain serves two purposes: Its weight helps keep the pull of the anchor horizontal and the chain links are easier than rope to clean on occasions when the anchor has been in mud. The shackle on a permanent mooring will be a swivel shackle, but this is not needed on a working anchor.

Anchor shackles are generally galvanized steel or stainless steel. The shackle should be many times stronger than the strains that will ever come on it and large enough to take a thimble with an eye splice. The pin that closes the shackle should be pregreased, tightened firmly, using a tool such as a shackle wrench, Vise-Grip pliers, or a spike through the eye. It should always be fastened, against the gremlins that unscrew shackle pins, by mousing, preferably with stainless steel wire.

An anchor system ready to use on a cruising boat is normally set up in the manner illustrated. The anchor rope has a small, tight

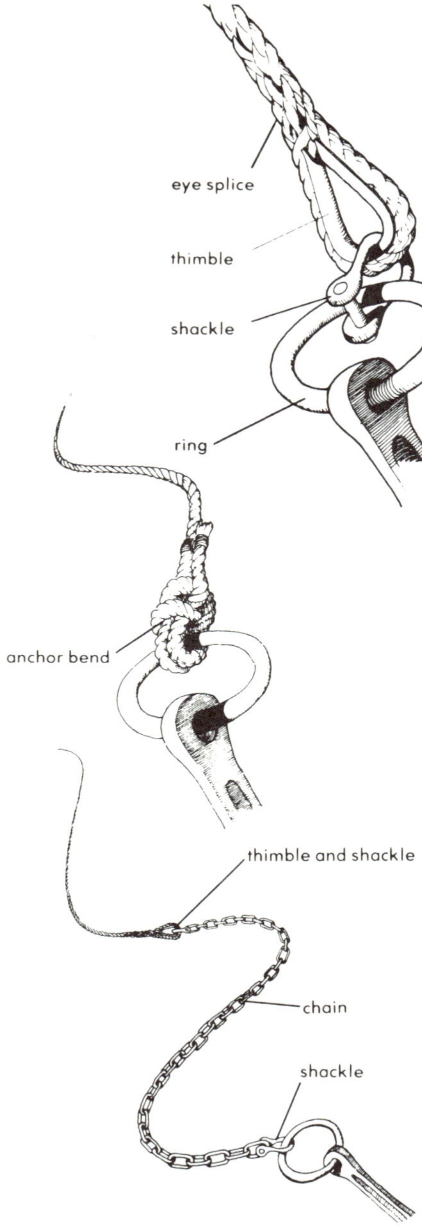

Three ways to attach an anchor rode to the anchor's ring: (1) With shackle and eye splice over a thimble (2) with an anchor bend, plus a serving for extra security (3) with shackles and short length of chain.

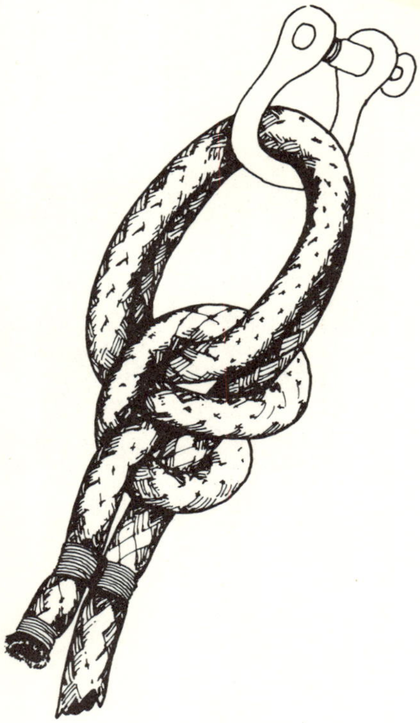

An anchor bend is one of several ways to make up the line. A bowline, with an extra turn, is stronger.

eye splice made over a thimble (and often reinforced by a seizing and perhaps a few stitches of sail twine) and this thimble in turn is either left shackled to the chain or can be quickly readied for use. New types of thimbles with "ears," well suited to this use, have been coming on the market. A useful trick is to boil the eye splice after it is tightly made. Boiling in water shrinks nylon rope.

At other times, when a boat does not need to have an anchor ready for every night's stop, the anchor line may be stowed apart from the anchor or there may be more than one anchor ready (a light lunch hook with a light anchor line, for example). There may be situations calling for two anchors to be used at once, as we shall see. In these cases, you need a quick way to fasten a line to either the anchor ring itself or to the shackle at the end of the short chain. One standard way is a secure knot.

The anchor bend is the knot most generally used. Those with experience add a little extra security by seizing the end to the line so it's out of the way and can't possibly come undone. Perhaps the best choice, quick and sure, is the bowline. A good variation is the **anchor bowline,** with an extra turn around the ring. Why are there choices of eye splice, anchor bowline, anchor bend, or short chain? Why doesn't someone settle on "the right way"? The answers to questions like these involve the use to which the boat is put and such matters as available stowage space for anchor lines. If an anchor is kept ready for use—and for most kinds of operating conditions this is a desirable safety practice—the line must be available through a deck pipe or coiled on deck when entering harbor. It should be secured at the bitter end.

If a boat is used mainly for afternoon sailing, the anchor may not be needed as often, so the anchor line can be kept neatly coiled, perhaps in the lazarette or in an anchor well or other locker space. If a boat is going on a three-month voyage, with many harbors and many conditions foreseen, it would be well to carry a storm anchor, a regular working anchor, and a "lunch hook" for short stops plus as many anchor lines. One line might be merely spare line with other potential uses. It is easier to turn an anchor line end for end if an anchor bend, or some other knot, instead of eye splices and shackles, is used.

The short length of chain suggested as part of the made-up ground tackle has a tendency to scratch the deck or the wooden toe rail. Many boat owners use chain coated with soft plastic to prevent this small abrasive damage.

HOW DEEP IS THE WATER?

How long should an anchor line be? What diameter? What kind of rope is best? Who uses chain?

As we will see when we look at anchoring procedures, it is often desirable to have line out as much as seven or eight times the depth of the water in the anchorage. This suggests that one of the anchor lines aboard a boat should be eight to ten times as long as the depth of the deepest harbor that will be visited. One hundred and fifty feet is a minimum length for most pleasure boats. Gale P. Foster, who has personal knowledge of island cruising, says those who cruise extensively should carry one anchor line that is three hundred feet long. Captain Horatio Hornblower would have called that "half a cable's length."

The line should be strong enough to carry any load it could possibly be subjected to and large enough in diameter to take a lot of wear and chafe and yet remain strong. But there is another test: An anchor line should be large enough in diameter to be easily handled. A small line cuts one's hands, so even if it is strong enough to do the job, it might still be too thin for easy use. On the other hand, as Bob Ogg points out, the other function of an anchor line is as a "shock absorber," and too thick a line will have no stretch when used on a small boat.

For centuries, manila rope made a good anchor line. It is still seen occasionally. But since anchor lines are often stored wet, any rope that mildews and rots is on the minus side. Nylon is the best choice even though it is not the strongest of the new fibers. Nylon has excellent stretch characteristics to reduce the strain both on the anchor and on deck fittings in storm conditions. Nylon doesn't rot, nor is it affected much by sunlight. It does lose some strength when wet, but if you use the proper size, this does not matter. Nylon is easy on the hands.

Braided nylon anchor line is the ultimate choice even though laid rope is more easily spliced by amateurs. Double braid, more supple, is easier to handle. It is more likely to flake down in a figure eight pattern compared to laid rope. Chafe weakens braided rope less significantly than it does laid rope because of the way only a few small strands are exposed. Most important of all, braided nylon stretches smoothly when a boat is riding to anchor while laid rope has more of a "yo-yo" effect.

Chain is preferred for a working anchor rode by some boatmen, especially those who cruise where there are rocks or coral. Ralph Naranjo, after sailing from California to New Zealand in *Wind Shadow*, had had enough troubles with coral in French Polynesia and various storms. In his book *Wind Shadow West*, he tells how he finally coped:

"At that point I vowed to upgrade the ground tackle and install an adequate handling system. Both were accomplished in New Zealand. I purchased 250 feet of 10 mm chain and added a stainless steel roller fairlead as well as a powerful Nilsson manual windlass. The anchor could be dropped, retrieved, and housed in the fairlead without my ever touching it. The heavy chain minimized yawing at anchor. It was nice to be in our bunks and have confidence in the ground tackle holding *Wind Shadow* no matter what."

The skipper of a small boat, seldom going far, would find there are reasons for not using chain. Here is an abbreviated table:

	APPROXIMATE WEIGHT IN AIR		BREAKING STRENGTH	
DIAMETER	NYLON ROPE	BBB CHAIN	NYLON	CHAIN
⅜″	3.8 lbs.	170 lbs.	4,000	5,500
½″	7.1 lbs.	295 lbs.	7,100	9,500

The weight of the chain in the bow of a small sailboat, obviously, would affect her trim.

Other ground tackle items include a trip line. This is a fairly light piece of line that can be fastened to the crown of the anchor, usually to a ring or bolt hole put there by the manufacturer for the purpose. The trip line is needed on occasion to pull a fouled anchor up (backward, so to speak) and out of rocks, so those who cruise in areas where the holding ground is rocky should know when to rig one. It's easier than sending down a diver to recover the anchor or cutting the line and ordering a new anchor. One brand of lightweight anchor is made with a double shank so the line can be fastened to a ring that slides up and down—a built-in trip line.

On deck there are a few other related items of equipment. If there is a bowsprit or bow platform, anchor rollers are a convenience. Some boatmen fit rollers to the bow chocks at the rail. Proper anchor chocks, including tie-down lines, and whatever else may be needed to lash the anchor in place in rough going, are commercially available. Some boat builders and some boatmen make their own, to fit, using teak or locust. Many new boats come equipped with an anchor well, covered by a hinged section of deck. Anchor and line can be kept in one. A look at similar boats' methods of handling anchor chocks is a good idea.

Later in this chapter we will look at how the anchor rode is made fast. There must be adequate hardware, properly installed. The newer boats usually have a good-sized cleat. Many older cruising boats have a samson post. Large, strong chocks or roller chocks are not part of the basic ground tackle, but they make using it easier.

CHOOSING AN ANCHORAGE

Choice of anchorage is not always entirely up to the boatman. A storm may force him to take to the nearest sheltered harbor, or he may come into harbor so late that the best places have all been taken by other boats.

Have one or more harbors in mind, just as the pilot of a small private aircraft keeps his eye on the chart and on the ground, with an emergency airport or landing strip always "there."

Keep an up-to-date harbor chart at hand as you look for your spot, and take a good look around for (a) recent changes, such as a line of anchored barges, that might modify your plans and for (b) clues in the way other boats, already anchored, are lying. For many cruising areas you can find a book with aerial photographs of popular harbors. These make interesting and useful supplements to harbor charts.

As a general rule, if you are aboard a keel sailboat you can get an idea of what the currents and wind will do by observing similar boats in the harbor. Or if your boat is a power cruiser, you'll tend to lie to wind and tide like the other power cruisers already anchored in the harbor. You'll want to consider how other boats might swing, or even drag in a blow, during the night, so that you can anchor "out of harm's way."

ANCHORING, STEP BY STEP

The anchoring procedure starts ahead of time. Well before you actually drop the anchor, there are two preliminary steps: (1) freeing the anchor from its chocks and getting it and the anchor line ready; and (2) making a careful inspection for loose shackle pins, severe chafe, or other potential problems.

At flood tide, in a typical harbor on the coast of Maine, the current can be seen catching moored boats so they swing, putting a strain on anchors.

The favored corner of the harbor may already be crowded. Consider the direction of the wind (at anchoring time and as forecast for the night) and anchor pretty much on the windward side of the harbor. The water will be smoother, the strain on your ground tackle will be less if it should blow hard, and there will be fewer boats that might drag into you during the night.

Of course you must allow for a change of wind. Think ahead so there will be sufficient depth no matter which way you eventually ride to your anchor.

The other factors that might affect a choice is the depth or the kind of bottom, the holding ground, in one corner or another. Certainly you don't want to anchor in eight feet of water at high tide if the rise and fall of tide is six or seven feet.

As even most beginning boatmen know, when you have picked

your spot (and looked astern), you head into the wind and do your best to bring the boat to a stop with the bow just over the spot where you want the anchor to be.

Just as you put the motor into reverse and start to slowly back down, the crew member on the bow gets the anchor over the bow and pays out the line as the boat moves astern. Take care not to drop loops of line over the anchor. When the boat is backing down and sufficient scope is out, he snubs the line, taking a turn around the bitts or the deck cleat. If the anchor digs in at once, everything is fine. If it's skidding along a hard bottom, you may end up too far from where you want to be—and you'll have to start over.

Assuming the anchor digs in, your crew on the foredeck pays out the line handsomely (slowly and carefully) as you back the boat until enough scope is out—even a little more. If the depth of

At slack tide (which could be either high water, as here, or low water), the boats drift idly. But this is when a line or chain can foul the anchor.

At ebb tide, the boats (except for the trawler again entering the harbor) now ride the other way. A good practice is to set the anchor again if current changes.

water is 12 feet, this may mean four times twelve, or perhaps 48 feet. The amount of scope required may vary. An old-fashioned anchor will usually work with a scope of three or four times the depth. Most of the lightweight anchors, even with a short length of chain added, require a scope of four or even five in good weather and a good seven times the water's depth to hold well in a blow. Mud and clay, which usually make good holding ground, may require less scope. A gale on its way might mean letting out your anchor line to eight or ten times the depth.

When you're sure the boat is in the right spot and the anchor is holding, the hand on the foredeck makes the line fast, usually with a cleat hitch. Check that the bitter end has been secured.

If there is little or no tide, then this may not be a factor. If you're in an area where the rise and fall of the tide is ten feet, of course, your scope should be figured on the depth at high tide.

If the wind or the current changes completely during your harbor stay, you may end up on a local shallow spot.

Although you seldom hear them talk about it, there are those who forgot to allow for the tide, anchored at low tide with a short anchor line, and found themselves drifting across the harbor when the anchor was lifted out.

Finally, take a bearing so you can check if you are dragging.

Anchoring under sail takes a little more sense of time and distance. The procedure described above is essentially for a powerboat or a sailboat under power.

If you sail into the harbor, you have two choices: (a) start the motor, head into the wind, get the sails down and furled, and then proceed with your anchoring; (b) do the whole anchoring maneuver under sail. If you have room, the wind isn't too strong, and your crew executes every step smoothly, you may get some admiring glances from others in the harbor. If the current fools you, the wind dies, and you find yourself drifting into another boat, that's another story.

Anchoring under sail, especially, calls for having all the gear ready, with lines that run free and sailstops or other furling gear at hand. The jib is dropped first and bagged or put down the forward hatch so the foredeck is clear. It takes coordination with a practiced crew and quite admirable skill in timing to round up, drop the mainsail, let go the anchor, and drift back while the sails are being furled. You surely don't want to be tacking around the mooring area as you drift backward. For that matter, many a powerboat has sailed about on her mooring, refusing to settle down.

Either way, under power or under sail, some sternward movement of the boat is necessary to dig the anchor in. There are those who anchor under sail, for the sake of their pride, and then use power, backing down to get the anchor safely set. At times a steady wind or current may do the job.

Hand signals are a useful means of communication in anchoring and in picking up a mooring. If there is one crew member on the bow to indicate "go to port" or "more to starboard" or "okay, start reversing" without needing to shout, the whole procedure runs more smoothly.

Wind and current changes are among the circumstances that may alter your original plan. If the wind changes, make sure your

CT 5243 X

anchor is dug in as your boat is swinging in a new direction. If necessary, reanchor entirely. If the changing wind results in another boat dragging or drifting into you, there are limited choices. It is customary for the boat that anchored earliest to claim "seniority." If you are able to talk the other skipper into reanchoring, fine. If it is your place to change anchorages, do it. If the other skipper argues, and some do, the way to protect your boat is by reanchoring in a safe place.

Special problems can arise. With a change in the wind you may find your boat is directly over the anchor of another boat—and the other boat has decided to leave. Sometimes some pushing and a few fenders over the side will solve the problem—or you may need to shorten up to give the other boat room. Or worse, two anchor lines can get crossed. It takes patience and a little thinking to get straightened out—plus a resolution to avoid *that* problem in the future.

Anchoring in a place where you know the current will reverse during your stay sometimes calls for setting two anchors—one upstream and the other downstream. Storm situations sometimes make it advisable to get two anchors down for extra holding power.

The anchor light, required by law for some places, such as high traffic areas, and for boats longer than 7 meters (23.4 ft) in length in all except "designated anchorage areas," may be something that goes on with a flick of a switch. Powerboats are generally equipped with an anchor light; it should be visible all around. Sailboats generally have a masthead light that is satisfactory for an anchor light. A common practice is to carry a separate anchor light, powered by dry cells, to hang on the forestay. The rolling hitch is the appropriate knot. If the light swings when the boat pitches, a tie-down line is often rigged.

Weighing anchor, of course, is the nautical term for the procedure of getting the anchor up and departing. It is usually easy, especially for those who know some of the tricks. At other times it is a job to try the patience of a St. Elmo.

Standing on the bow and trying to pull an anchor up can take muscle. Here are some easier tricks:

▲ Half an hour before departure time, shorten up on the anchor line. The small motions of the boat and the nearly vertical line will tend to start the anchor breaking out of the mud or clay.

◀
One boat had a long anchor line out, the other was on short scope; when the wind shifted the boats drifted.

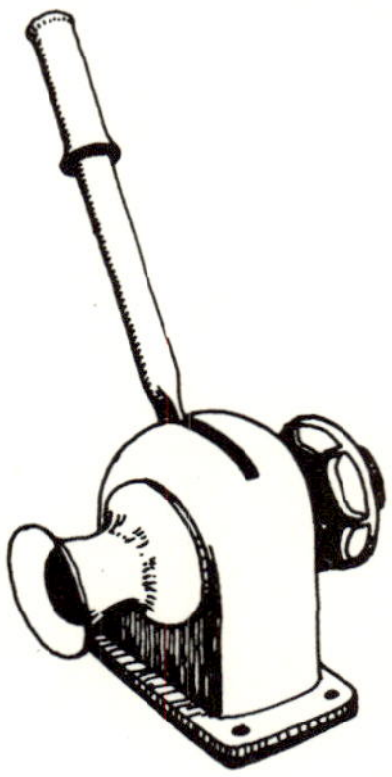

A windlass, for rope or chain, is an old method of applying power to a line that is efficient . . . whether by muscle or by electric motor.

▲ If the tide is coming in, the task is even easier. As the tide rises, the boat on a shortened line will lift and the anchor that seemed well dug in the night before will work itself out of the clay. Be careful to watch, lest the boat drift across the harbor carrying her anchor.

▲ Assuming there is room, supplement the muscles of the foredeck crew with the boat's motor by going slow ahead. Or do it the old-fashioned way—sail the anchor out.

▲ Use a winch, as many a cruising sailor has done. No anchor winch? Use a sheet winch. After an all night's blow, the anchor may be four feet into the clay.

An anchor windlass on a cruising boat more than ten meters (31 ft) in length is practical.

Here's a pointer from Powerwinch: "After the anchor is raised, using a winch, secure the chain or anchor rope to a chain stop or cleat. The windlass is not designed to serve as a cleat or mooring bitt for a sustained period of time."

SPECIAL ANCHORING SITUATIONS

Special situations, like rafting, kedging off, turning the boat on the anchor line, using two anchors, and the Mediterranean moor are usually a matter of applying common sense, using previous experience (including that of others), and having the right gear on hand.

Kedging off, as any reader of Captain Hornblower knows, is a masterful feat of seamanship that saves the vessel in distress.

Often, the distress is being lightly aground. You may be in shallow water with a sandy bottom and fearful that prolonged running of the motor, with the propeller churning the sand, will foul the water cooling system. The kedging off procedure is simple: taking an anchor out in the dinghy and then hauling in on the anchor line to move the boat.

The details are easy to work out, provided you plan each step in advance.

Step One: Organize a very long anchor line, perhaps by fastening two lines together, carefully coiling it on the deck of your boat so that a crew member can pay it out easily.

Step Two: Instead of trying to carry the anchor *inside* the dinghy, hang it over the dinghy's stern. The kedge type of anchor is the easiest to use because the stock can be hung on the dinghy's transom. Other types of anchors may require a short lashing.

Step Three: Row to deeper water while the crew member on the deck pays out the line. Using an outboard, with an anchor over the stern, is more difficult than rowing unless your yacht tender is a fairly large boat. When you reach the place to drop the anchor, usually at the end of the available line that has been paid out, ease the anchor over the transom. At this point you realize how hard it would have been to stand up and get an anchor out of the bottom of the dinghy and into the water without capsizing.

Step Four: At the mother vessel, start hauling in. It may take two strong hands or the use of the windlass or even a block-and-tackle to get the boat free. If you're helped by a rising tide, so much the better.

To turn a boat while at anchor is a neat trick. You won't need to do it so your guns will bear on some fort ashore, as might have been the case two centuries ago, but you might want to catch the light breeze if you're riding to a current. Just take a line from the stern to the anchor line at a place a few feet below the chocks. Haul in the line at the stern until the boat is turned to your requirements.

When to reanchor: If you stay anchored for several changes of tide or several wind shifts, you may find you have circled your anchor—chain and line included. If you reanchor, you are safe; if you don't reanchor, you run the risk that you have fouled the anchor. If a blow comes, you have a perilous situation.

Rafting, putting two or more boats on the same anchor, is a common practice with recreational boats. Fenders, a bow line, a couple of spring lines, and a stern line are necessary. Naturally, even in a snug harbor, an approaching storm should be a signal to anchor the boats separately. In many harbors, overnight rafting is not permitted.

Do not use two anchors when rafting. If the current swings the whole raft around, you may find you have tangled your lines. Getting out of a large raft is awkward enough. As long ago as 1802, the U.S. Navy regulations included this sentence: "It is the duty of the sailing master to keep the hauser clear and see that she is not girt with her cables."

A riding sail is not often seen in anchorages except where experienced cruising skippers find a snug hole. A mizzen sail on a yawl or ketch or a small triangular sail set on the backstay of a sloop will hold an anchored boat steady in a light to moderate breeze. Many trawler-type powerboats use the riding sail at anchor and in

In good weather a raft is pleasant and sociable, but if the wind changes direction, moor separately.

some cases as a steadying sail while under way. Now and then you see an improvised riding sail: a dinghy sail hoisted on the backstay.

A Mediterranean moor, used in some crowded harbors in Europe, is useful in a very small harbor where there isn't good swinging room, and sometimes for a short stay off a beach.

Here's how: At an appropriate distance from the pier, perhaps a hundred feet, *while heading away from the pier,* drop the anchor and make sure it is set by backing down, and then pay out line as you reverse until your stern is almost touching the pier. Rig two dock lines, one at each quarter, but rig them as though they were springs, add a couple of fenders, and then a way to get from the stern to the pier.

The small harbor variation is to end up bow in to a suitable part

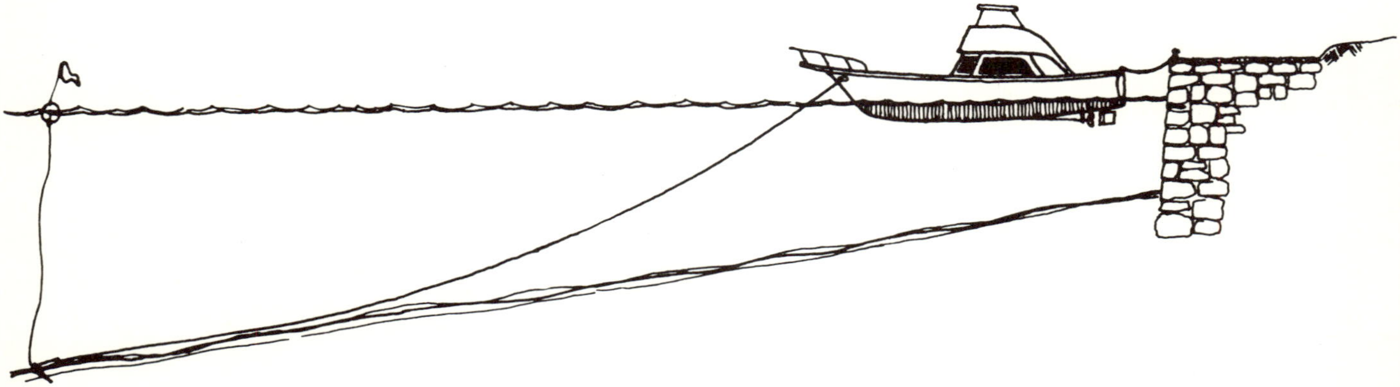

of the shoreline, perhaps a steep beach, being careful not to go aground, with your stern anchored out.

Drop the anchor some distance from the beach, back down and set it, then move the anchor line to the stern of the boat and let one crew member tend it, playing it out as you head the boat toward the shore. At this point, let one person take a light anchor with its anchor line ashore and set it securely. Sometimes this requires a dinghy, sometimes the crew member can wade ashore.

Sometimes you can take the bow anchor, or a sand-spike, ashore first, then back off and anchor from the stern.

STORM SITUATIONS

Adding a weight, partway down the anchor line, is a workable way to increase the security during a blow. The use of a sentinel (sometimes called a kellet) adds two improvements to the system:

First, the catenary, the curve of the anchor line, is increased, and this means that the actual force pulling on the anchor will be more nearly horizontal. Second, the weight acts as a spring, easing the force of sudden surges caused by wave motion.

A float to which the anchor line is attached, plus a second line from the float to the vessel, is an alternative storm system suggested in Chapman's *Piloting, Seamanship & Small Boat Handling.* In this case, the boat rides more freely, without the anchor line dragging her bows down, and the extra spring in the line acts to absorb the surges caused by heavy seas.

The Ogg system of carefree anchoring, without using heavy anchors, is described by Robert Ogg, co-inventor of the Danforth, in his small book *Anchors & Anchoring*:

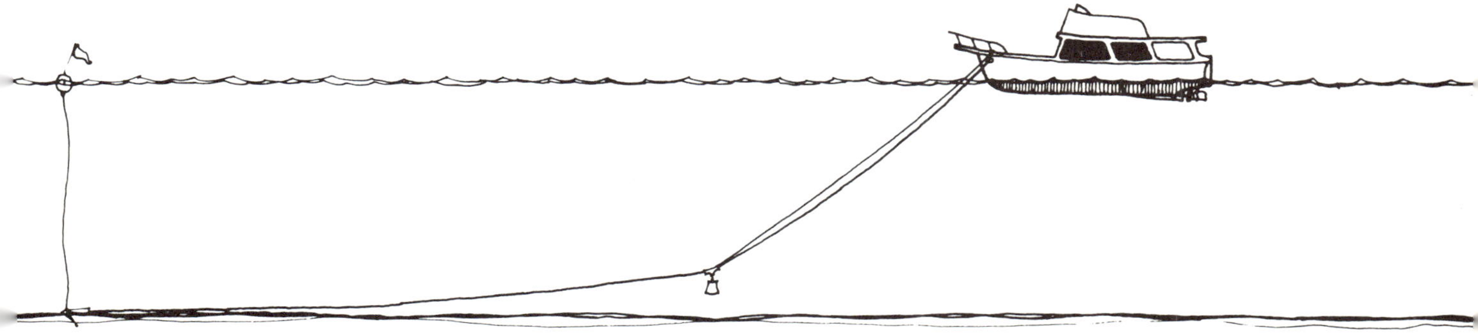

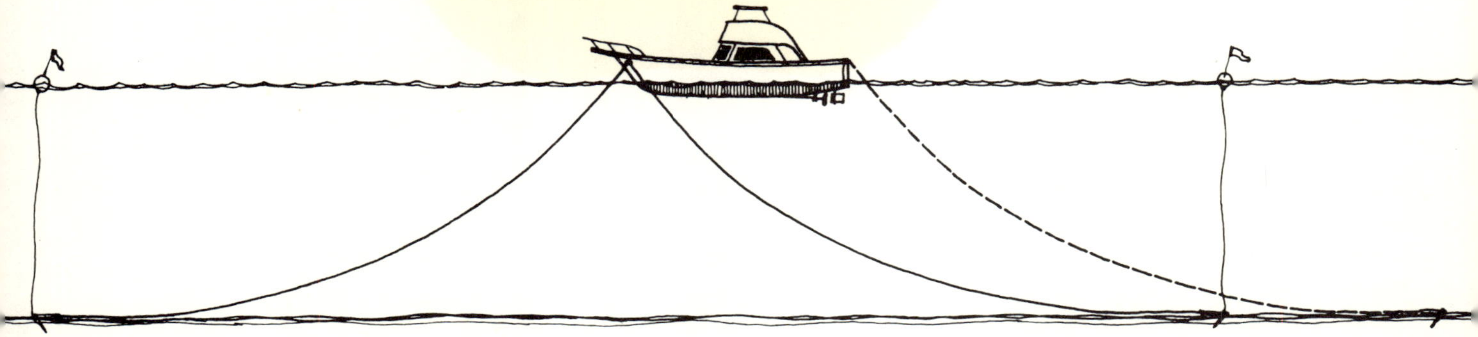

"Whether the harbor is crowded or not, you have to estimate where you want your boat to end up when she finally lays to her hook. Let's call this spot 'X.' Now figure how much scope you will need, allowing for depth of water and tide. Say it's 150′. When you are about 150′ upwind of X, kill your headway, lower and set the forward anchor. After dropping back to Point X you can either drop back an additional 150′ to drop the second, or after, anchor, or you can use a dinghy to drop the second hook.

"Set the after anchor and take the rode forward, allowing 20 to 30 feet of slack to prevent a direct strain on the line, and lead it through the same chock as the bow rode. Make both lines fast forward, on separate bitts if available.

"In a crowded anchorage this system allows virtually full scope on each rode and yet cuts the swinging room to less than one quarter of what it would be with one hook down. The double rig provides more security than one large anchor and eliminates the possibility of fouling the anchor, a problem that can develop with a change of wind and/or current when you are swinging on a single hook. If the boat swings with the twin anchor lines, they possibly will be twisted once or twice but this is easy enough to untangle.

"I call this the carefree system because once the anchors are set you can forget about them for the night. If the breeze stays in the same quarter you swing to the bow anchor. If the wind should come abeam, you will lay to both anchors. They will pivot slightly

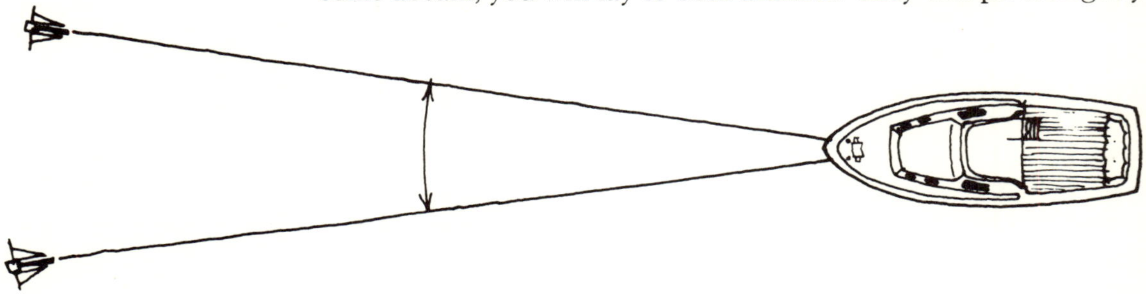

and hold the strain. Naturally, if the wind shifts 180° you fetch up on what was set out as the after anchor."

Two anchors in a storm is a time-tested way of adding security. There is a recommended procedure. Set one anchor first, settle back to proper scope to make sure the anchor is dug in, then go ahead with rudder hard over until the first anchor line is taut abeam. Then drop the second anchor, drop back, and equalize scope.

WRINKLES

When rafting so that two sailboats are together, take care that the boats are not lined up mast-to-mast so that the spreaders are in danger of touching. Drop the add-on boat back a few feet to avoid damaging the rigging if a passing boat should set up a rocking motion.

The hand lead, in these days of electronic depth sounders, is sometimes forgotten. You may not need one that's twenty fathoms long with all the traditional markers, but an easy-to-use small lead line for anchoring situations is handy. Get a small sounding lead and attach a light line with a bowline. Ten meters or thirty feet will do. Make a loop in the other end (an eye splice or a bowline) so you'll have a becket to hold the line. Put a figure-eight knot six feet (one fathom) from the lead, two figure eights at the next six feet, three knots at the next six feet, and so on. As you poke your way around a new harbor searching for the right corner to drop the hook, you have a better idea of the bottom. You can even tell where it's six feet on one side of the boat and nine feet on the other, or at the stern, which is more than an echo sounder can tell you. Or if you put waterproof grease in the hollow of the lead, you can bring up a sample of the bottom.

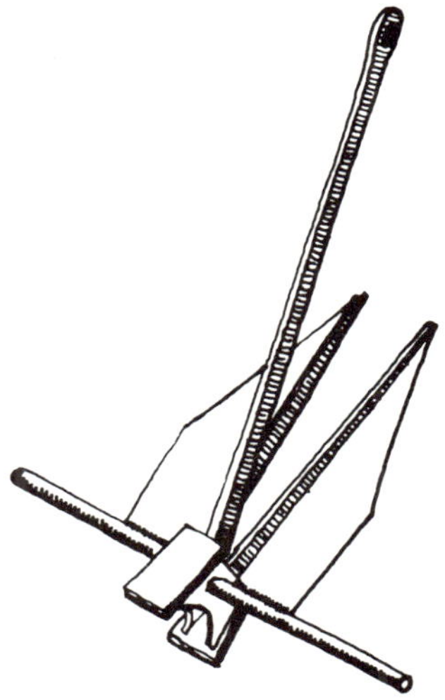

Servings on the anchor line, every thirty feet or so, make good chafe guards, especially if you cruise the same general area, going to harbors with familiar depths of water. You can then let out scope to a predetermined amount and have the chafe protection in the anchor chocks or over the anchor rollers as soon as your hook is down. Regular anchor markers are available in the marine stores, but you may still need the antichafe guards.

Turn your anchor lines end for end every season or two. They'll last longer.

US 15

Chapter 7

The Dinghy

The ideal dinghy is easily put in the back of a station wagon, will row well and tow well, can be operated with an outboard motor, boasts a usable sailing rig that stows inside the sturdy little hull for easy transporting, is unsinkable and large enough to serve as a lifeboat for the small yacht she accompanies. She fits the definition of a boat: "A small craft that can be hoisted aboard a larger vessel."

If such a dinghy existed, she might be named *Reasonable Facsimile,* but she always seems to be in some other harbor. However, there probably is one named *Compromise.* Yachtsmen keep looking for her; now and then one claims he has found her.

The most beautiful are made of wood, none more so than when built of varnished cedar planking with copper rivets for fastenings. The most practical, and certainly the most often seen, are made of plastic reinforced fiberglass. There is such a choice of designs, and of course so many conditions under which small boats are used as tenders, that there is no one way to answer the question "Which kind is best for me?"

A person new to boating looking for a dinghy would do well to ask what are the most popular models or makes of small dinghies in the area. The consensus way of making a choice works well, because it is essentially the "survival of the fittest," especially if the ways in which the boat will be used are considered. Here are questions to ask:

Design and construction: Was the boat designed by a recognized naval architect? Most of the better dinghies are. Is it carefully built? Is the hardware right? If it is to be used with an outboard motor, is the transom (stern) strong enough?

◄
Like gulls around their nests, dinghies cluster together at the dock.

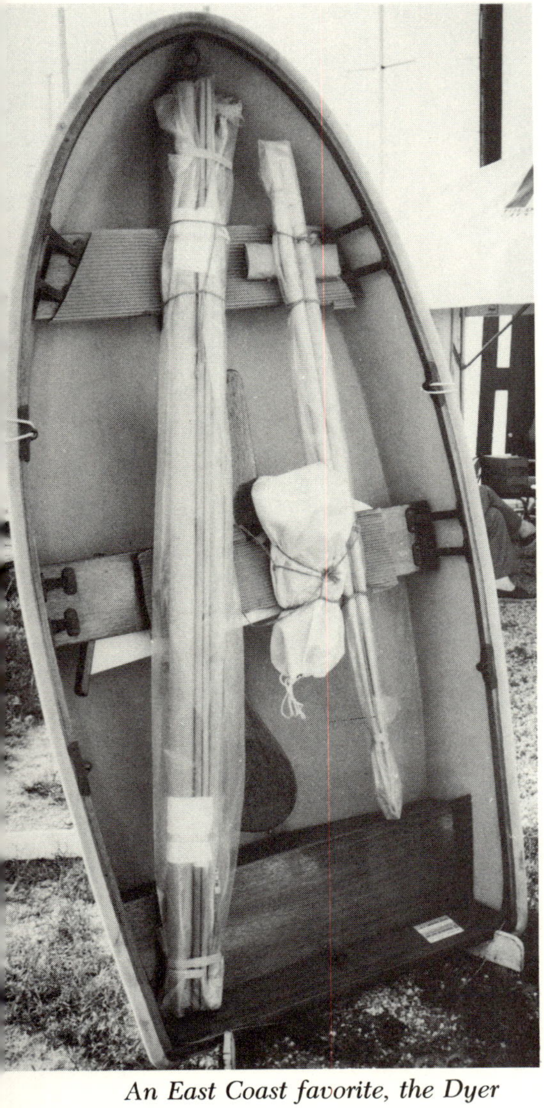

An East Coast favorite, the Dyer Dhow, carries oars, spars for sailing, and all gear required for sport.

The dinghy under oars: Does the small boat row reasonably well?

Towing characteristics: If it is to be towed—and most dinghies are towed part of the time—how well does it tow? Is the bow ring strong and properly installed on a through-bolted eye?

Sailing: If it is also a sailing dinghy, does it sail reasonably well? Does the sailing gear (mast, boom, rudder, tiller, and sail) fit inside the dinghy for transportation?

Can it be taken aboard your boat? This means, does it have a proper place to attach a sling or bridle at either end? Can you use a halyard or davits to get it aboard, and can proper chocks and other equipment be installed?

Equipment for the small yacht's dinghy varies somewhat, depending on the use. Later we will look more closely at equipment.

A plastic dinghy should not leak, but it can ship water under tow or in use. A bailer, preferably made fast with a lanyard, should be standard equipment. A sponge is also useful. Some few dinghies are made with duck boards, to keep one's feet dry. Others have a sort of bilge drain built in when they are molded, letting the bilge water run down to a small well, where it can be sponged or dipped out.

Other built-in qualities to look for include:

▲ The location of the through-bolted towing eye: A screwed-on eye will come adrift, not later but sooner. A towing eye that is too high in the bow will have a tendency to make the dinghy drag under tow.

▲ Proper lifting eyes, also through-bolted: One at the bow and one at each quarter usually provide a balanced support. You can rig a bridle across the stern, or in some cases the wire traveler of a sailing dinghy makes an adequate stern lifting bridle. If the dinghy is to be in davits, the falls (block-and-tackle for lifting) can be attached directly at the bow eye and the stern bridle. If a halyard or topping lift is to be used, a fore-and-aft bridle will be necessary. Naturally, any bridle must attach above the dinghy's center of gravity.

▲ If the oars are carried in the dinghy, they should be lashed in when the dinghy is to be towed, of course, except for a short run across a placid harbor. One workable method is to fasten the oars to the thwarts with a couple of shock cord ties, with an eye in one end and a toggle in the other.

- ▲ The rowlocks may be removable or the kind that can't be lost because they can't be removed. This has two small disadvantages: (1) some expert sailors will profess to look down at the "patent oarlocks," and (2) since the rowlocks can't be removed and taken along for your walk in the town, you lose one method of "semi-theftproofing" your dinghy. Removable rowlocks should have a short length of brass or bronze chain with a toggle so that they can be taken out of the sockets and stowed elsewhere when desired.
- ▲ A dinghy on a cruising boat is occasionally used after dark. One easy installation is a flashlight bracket, under a thwart. You don't have running lights, but Coast Guard regulations say you should be able to show a flashlight when operating after dark.

The painter, after the oars, is the most important piece of a dinghy's equipment. Decades ago, a yachtsman would use a manila painter and put cork floats on it to prevent it getting in the way of the propeller. Today there is an alternative that most boatmen prefer. They use a dinghy painter made of floating rope. Polypropylene rope, as strong as old-fashioned manila but considerably lighter, makes a good dinghy painter. However, the ultraviolet component in sunlight tends to weaken it. Rope experts say the darker colors or black polypropylene line resist the degrading effects of ultraviolet light. In any case, use a heavier line than you might otherwise think of; renew it at least every season.

The size of rope (diameter) for a painter should be not less than 3/8 inches. Half an inch is better. A dinghy painter should be considerably longer than three times the length of the dinghy itself if it is to be towed. Even an auxiliary sailboat has enough speed to require letting the dinghy tow well astern, so the painter should be longer than the boat that is towing it. Usually, it is best to fasten the painter to the towing eye with an eye splice over a thimble to prevent chafe. The other end of the painter can have a plain whipping or be made up into a small eye splice to fit over the towing cleat on the mother boat. Or use a bowline.

In addition to the painter, a small boat should have at least one extra line aboard. This may come in useful when leaving the dinghy at a float, to tie it off so that the wake of passing boats or a shifting wind will not lead to damage. Under many circumstances a small anchor is useful—for fishing, for occasionally mooring the

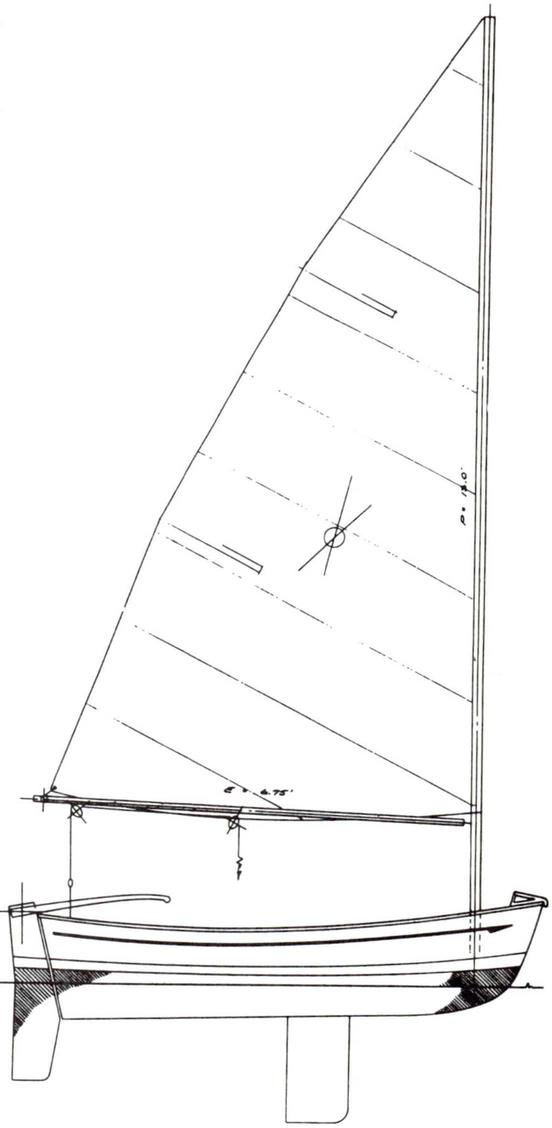

Perrywinkle is one of many beautiful dinghies designed by good naval architects. Robert H. Perry drew her and supervised her excellent construction.

Chocked on deck . . .

boat at a float so it won't chafe against other boats, and even as a safety device. Sponge, bailer, and life preserver cushions complete the equipment list of a plain vanilla rowing dinghy. One equipped with an outboard motor may require a spare fuel tank.

Some people give a formal boat name to their dinghies (and who is to say that *Tender Behind* or *Trailing Arbutus* isn't definitive?). There is one other old-time custom so practical that it needs to be reintroduced where it has been forgotten: painting the name of the mother vessel inside the transom of the dinghy. This serves to identify the small boat in case of loss-and-find, of course—but it also makes it easy for you to pick out your own dinghy at a float crowded with six almost identical Dyer Dhows or Optimist prams.

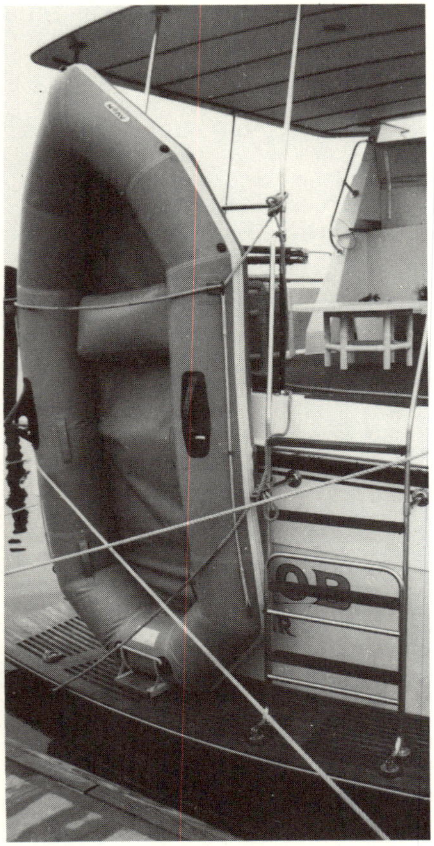

. . . lashed on the stern . . .

HOISTING A BOAT ABOARD

Pleasure craft under thirty feet, whether power or sail, usually tow the dinghy. Indeed, many larger boats tow their dinghies part of the time because of the convenience. However, there are two excellent ways of carrying a small boat aboard a larger vessel.

The first is with davits. Boats less than fifty or sixty feet in length are more likely to have the davits at the stern and of course larger yachts often carry their small boats amidship in the same fashion as large ships. A typical dinghy carried on deck, upright in chocks, is aboard the motor sailor *William Hand* at Block Island. It's a seagoing method that keeps the small boat out of the way but not necessarily ready for quick use.

Henry Keene of Edson International, makers of a popular line of aluminum davits, passes on this advice for boat owners using davits:

1) When maneuvering your boat, be aware of the davits! With the dinghy stowed in davits, the overall length of your boat increases four to six feet. Be careful when docking or backing into a slip. Hitting a piling, dock, or an-

other boat can damage the davits and the dinghy. Do not moor your boat with the davits extending over a fixed dock on an ebbing tide.

2) The dinghy or inflatable that is carried in the davits should not extend beyond the sides of the boat so as to catch waves during a roll (or, in the case of a sailboat, when heeled). A boat with a narrow stern or low freeboard needs to carry a shorter dinghy or use davits with greater height than a boat with a wide transom or high freeboard.

3) At no time should water be allowed to collect in the dinghy or inflatable while on the davits. Tenders *must* be equipped with a suitable drain plug to allow water to escape and/or be covered to prevent water from getting into the dinghy.

4) Oars, gas tanks, or anchors carried in the dinghy must be properly secured and distributed evenly throughout the dinghy. Unsecured items will move in a seaway, causing the dinghy to swing and put excessive side loads on the davits.

. . . tied at the quarter . . .

5) The dinghy should not become a "catchall" for loose items such as barbecues, hoses, fenders, and dock lines. Davits have specific load ratings which must not be exceeded.

6) Edson has found that the practical lifting capacity of a davit rigged with a 3:1 block and tackle is between 75 lbs. (34.1 k) and 175 lbs. (79.5 k). A greater weight is not easily lifted and cleated.

. . . the dinghy is on hand.

7) The lifting rings in the dinghy must be located above the center of gravity so that the dinghy will not tip when hoisting or launching. Gunnel locks must be securely installed so that the dinghy is locked to the davits in the stowed position.

8) The dinghy must be well secured in the davits at all times. When operating in a seaway, additional cross straps that go under the dinghy and secure it are required. These further prevent the dinghy from swinging and putting undue side loading on the davits.

Putting a small boat into the water is relatively easy if the davits have been properly rigged.

Step one: Check that all necessary gear is aboard the dinghy, including an accessible painter to tie the boat up when it is in the water. *Step two:* If the small boat has a drain plug, make sure it has

Well-installed davits add to the convenience of having your own water taxi aboard.

been replaced. *Step three:* With one person at the falls (the hauling parts of the lines that make up the tackles) at each end of the dinghy, lower away, keeping an eye on the boat so that it is kept horizontal as it is lowered and does not catch on any gear on the way down. *Step four:* Make sure the painter is fastened to the large vessel before casting off the falls.

It is just possible, but not easy, for one person, using care, to lower a small boat using the two lines of the davits. The easiest way is one fall at a time, letting out only a foot or so alternately at the bow and stern. Holding both falls at once, something like a nineteenth-century coachman driving a team of horses, is more difficult, even though a small dinghy may weigh no more than sixty pounds.

Some trawler yachts and motor sailors have a mast and boom that is suitable if not ideal for getting the dinghy aboard and launching it. Usually, this requires two persons or at least a great deal of step by step planning. By using the main halyard, most auxiliaries thirty feet or perhaps a little longer can also take the dinghy aboard. The boat is brought up alongside, a bridle is rigged from bow to stern, and the halyard attached to the lifting point or eye of the bridle. A halyard winch is a great convenience, but on boats without winches the job can be done. One person hoists the dinghy. A second crew member keeps the dinghy straight as it is hoisted out of the water and helps swing it to the correct location on deck. After the halyard is detached, two persons turn the dinghy over and get it into the chocks. Fasten the gripes diagonally across the dinghy's bottom, secure the halyard and the bridle, and you're done. Of course on a larger boat the dinghy might be carried upright, perhaps with a boat cover.

The place to stow the dinghy depends on the deck layout, particularly the vertical space between the cabin top and the boom. Built-on or movable supports, usually for the dinghy's transom, sometimes also at the dinghy's bow, hold the small boat in place. Good strong tie-downs or gripes are required. A standard arrangement is to criss-cross them over the hull of the dinghy.

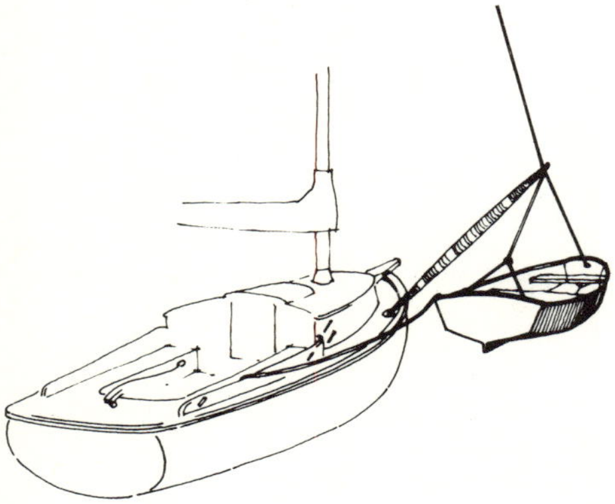

If this arrangement can't be worked out because of space limitations, some boat owners find a way to carry the dinghy in the deck area on one side of the cabin top (or the coach-roof in British terminology). This means special lashing must be used and the crew must always remember to walk on the opposite deck when going forward or aft (muttering, meanwhile, about the benefits of towing the dinghy, such as ready access to the foredeck).

INFLATABLE BOATS

Stowable, towable, and handy, inflatables are getting a bigger market share every year. Continuing product improvements, spurred by standards such as those of the ocean racing clubs, make them an acceptable alternative to more conventional boats.

But inflatables do have some drawbacks. Let's look at the negative points first:

Because of their low freeboard, they don't give you a dry ride across the harbor on a choppy day. The seat positions are low, so if spray comes aboard, it hits you in the face. These boats don't row well. They're so light that they become a problem in a strong wind. If you want a sailing dinghy as an extra, the pumped-up boats won't do.

But here's the good news: Inflatables operate fairly well with outboard motors. They carry a big load; the Coast Guardsmen sometimes see them overloaded. They have been improved, so that the strong construction and the repairability are impressive. Maintenance is minimal. A typical life expectancy is ten years.

The inflatable dinghy can be stored in a small space. Pumping one up by hand or foot is a small chore, but electric pumps and CO_2 bottles are workable.

The quality variations are large. An inflatable for light use is one thing. A top-quality inflatable, made by one of the companies that also make survival rafts, is as expensive as any custom cedar dinghy.

Although these boats are probably at least as good as conventional small boats when it comes to lifeboat capabilities, they are not to be confused with genuine life rafts, such as the ones carried by ocean racers.

Inflatable dinghies, like this one nestling between the hulls of a catamaran, are the local transport in harbor. Bicycles, especially folding ones, are a good form of local land transport.

THE DINGHY UNDER TOW

Dinghy towing seems easy for those who get the hang of it and a problem for those who haven't learned the basics.

- ▲ Under way, tow far enough astern so that the dinghy is riding *down* the wave caused by the wake of your boat, usually the second or third wave astern, not fighting gravity by trying to climb up. By letting out the painter an arm's length at a time, you can adjust the towing length for the least resistance.
- ▲ There will be times, with a cross sea, changing winds, or what seems like just plain crankiness, when adjustments have to be made frequently (and a few bad weather times when it is well nigh impossible to tow a small boat).
- ▲ Coming into harbor, or in special slowed down conditions such as sailing in a fading breeze, gradually shorten up on the tow line.
- ▲ In crowded traffic conditions, around docks and floats, tow with a very short line and keep an eye astern to make sure the dinghy isn't fouling a mooring line as you pass.
- ▲ When moored in a slip or at a pier, keep the dinghy painter at a proper length and fastened to a cleat on whichever quarter comes nearest to keeping the boat out of the way. As tidal current or wind changes, it may be necessary to take a fresh nip on the painter, or to use the dinghy's second line to tie the boat at a convenient angle, free from possible problems like chafe or making a keep-awake noise all night.
- ▲ Many powerboats get the dinghy on the swimming platform, at least in harbor and in quiet waters.

RIGGING A BOAT BOOM

To keep the dinghy from banging against the hull while in a harbor, there are time-tested ways used by large ships and yachts that can be adapted to even the small cruising boat. One of these is tying the dinghy to the mooring float if the mother ship is large enough. Use an endless line to retrieve the dinghy. The other method is the boat boom. There are two working arrangements: (a) the standard big ship method, with lines (including a man-rope line) to retrieve the dinghy, an accommodation ladder, and even a place to pipe the officers aboard, and (b) a smaller improvised set-up for a weekend racer-cruiser using the spinnaker pole, a topping life to hold it up, guys forward and aft, and one endless line to take the dinghy out to its quiet berth.

Getting aboard. Working out ways to get from the dinghy to the deck of the mother vessel is a matter of trial and error. The small cruising boats are so low in the water that people with average agility can clamber from dinghy to deck. If the distance calls for a ladder, the swimming ladder, a special accommodation ladder, a stern ladder, or a bosun's chair well fastened to the lifeline or the fittings at the deck may be the best solution.

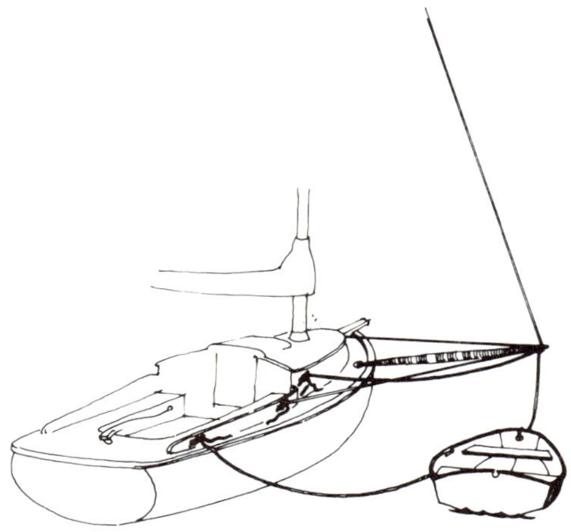

A boat boom, on a quiet night, keeps the dinghy from growling and nudging the mother vessel.

THE ART OF ROWING

Anyone watching an expert, from an Olympic oarsman on down, gets a sense of the graceful skill, the ability to use the smooth flow of muscles to build up speed, and the charm of the art of rowing.

Handling an eight-foot dinghy is somewhat less of a way to look heroic. Instead of rowing with long, even strokes and feathering your oars expertly, you use a fairly short stroke. Instead of letting the boat glide between strokes, you have to keep it moving, especially in choppy water.

Short quick strokes don't always mean you can't feather the oars to keep from "catching a crab."

It's a matter of practice and of changing your rowing style to suit the boat and the condition of the water at the time. Those who row frequently and who handle a variety of small boats—including seemingly awkward prams and the somewhat better looking dhows—learn to get the weight balanced, to handle turns with aplomb, and to have just the right amount of forward motion as they stop rowing and fetch up at their destination. They learn to take the painter in one hand, their duffle bag in the other, and step aboard, or ashore onto a float, with a firm and graceful step.

As you know, most rowing is done while you're facing aft. To see if you're on course, there's a better way than constantly turning your head. Learn to (a) get on the correct course and (b) line up a course astern of you by taking a quick visual bearing, such as the stern of one boat and a point on the harbor shore. Just follow the course with fewer turns of the head.

Rowing is one of the special delights of boat-owning. The usual custom is to paint the boat's name on the inside of the dinghy's transom.

Here's a little dinghy rowing trick Dr. Henry Wharton of Huntington, New York, found somewhere. When rowing ashore from *Many Moons*, one member of the family, seated in the stern of the dinghy, always watched the course, quietly keeping one finger pointed at the destination. If the person rowing got off course, he would see the finger pointed to one side or the other and correct by pulling harder on the appropriate oar. No need to interrupt the conversation.

Oars should be stowed on the dinghy's thwarts when leaving the boat—never left in the rowlocks. Similarly, when bringing a dinghy alongside a larger vessel or a float or pier, always ship the oars (take them out of the rowlocks) as you come alongside.

When a dinghy is to be tied up or towed, of course, always ship the rowlocks. This preserves the topsides of the mother vessel when the dinghy is later brought up to the side of the boat. When a dinghy is to be towed, the oars should be either secured to the thwarts (shock cord ties are excellent) or taken aboard the mother vessel.

OAR LENGTH FORMULA:

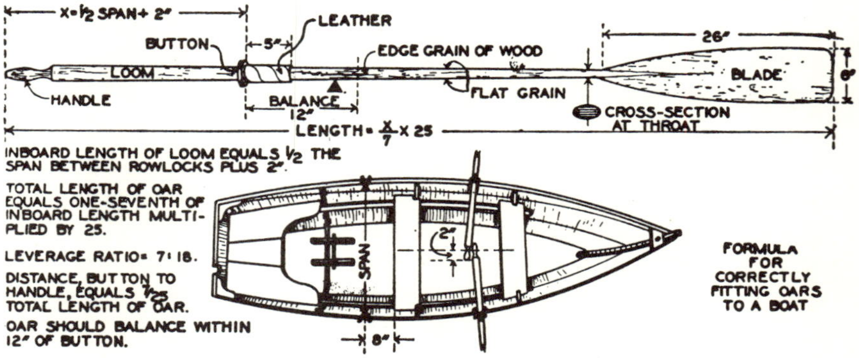

To choose the right length of a pair of oars for a dinghy (or other rowboat) use the old formula of Shaw & Tenney, makers of oars and paddles in Orono, Maine.

A ONE-HOUR SAILING COURSE

If the reason you venture forth upon the waters is to find quiet relaxation, it just may be that the time has come for you to discover the simplest kind of sailing there is—dinghy sailing or boardboat sailing.

It's inexpensive. It's safe. It is simpler—to do and to learn—than most non-sailors realize. You can rig the single sail, centerboard and rudder (and that's all there is) of a Dyer Dhow, a Sunfish, or a Phantom in seven or eight minutes.

If you have been around boats, you already know half of it. If you want to get someone to teach you to sail, find someone who will leave out the blarney, the extras, and the special language. You can find those things in various good books. All you need to know about learning to sail a small sailboat in a harbor, in a light breeze, you can learn after supper on one summer evening, by yourself. Here's the one-hour course in plain sailing.

First twelve minutes: Rig the boat. Follow the directions. You put the centerboard in. You attach the rudder at the stern, taking care that the tiller is underneath the wire traveler across the stern. You step the short mast. On some boats you attach the boom first, because the mast goes through a ring on the boom. On others you attach the boom, near the base of the mast, and the sail, which is usually attached to a sprit or gaff. Check that the halyard, holding the sail up, is securely fastened. Make sure the sheet, which will control the boom and thus the angle of the sail to the wind, is properly rigged and not tangled. (It's very simple. Island fishermen who can't read or write can do it.)

Next three minutes: While the dinghy is still made fast, get comfortably seated, low down in the boat, where the boom will not hit you in the head. Get one hand on the tiller and one hand on the sheet, the control line. Check everything again. Never mind any sailing words—just be sure you have the feeling that when you push the tiller to port, the boat will turn to starboard and vice versa. If you pull on the sheet, the boom will come toward the center of the boat; if you ease it, the boom will be able to swing out a bit. By this time the sail, being up, may be slatting in the light breeze. You may even feel the boat trying to move ahead. Not to worry—let your helper on the larger boat fend off. One last point: Make sure you have a feeling of the direction of the wind. As a boating person, you already know about that.

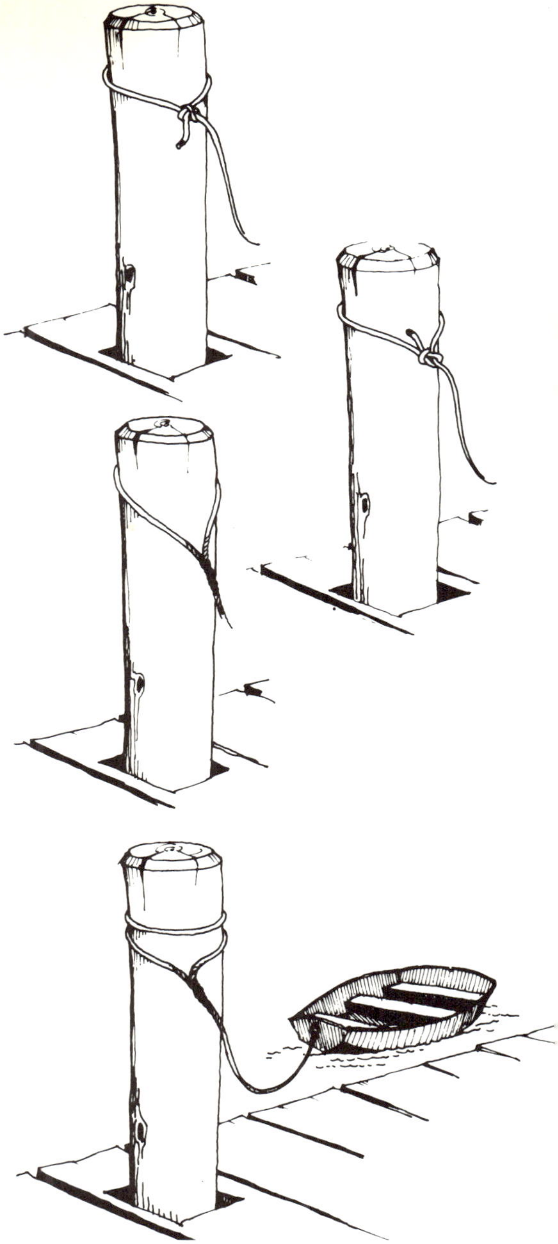

The adept sailor has at hand at least four ways to fasten a dinghy painter to a piling. Half hitches are quick. A bowline can make a loop ahead of time. If the piling is too large for the eye, make a loop. Not shown: a clove hitch, which all too easily works itself loose.

THIRSTY LADY III
47

Next ten minutes: Cast off and start sailing. You'll find the dinghy (or boardboat) tends to start moving forward on its own. Once you have some motion, you can steer (another thing you already knew). Keep all your motions slow and gradual. If you steer a bit directly toward the wind, the sail begins to slat again and the boat slows up. So turn away! Let the sail fill and find out how to get some speed . . . let the sheet out a little, adjust the rudder. Sail across the wind, and you'll be going the fastest. Just keep an eye out that you don't run into other boats or get too close to the shore and run aground (you already knew that, too).

Next twenty minutes: Make some bigger turns. Here's how: when you have the boat sailing fast, gradually haul in on the sheet until the boom is fairly close (nearer the center of the dinghy) and at the same time steer the boat more nearly toward the direction the wind is coming from. Make sure you're still moving well through the water so you have good steerageway. *Now*, make a slow and steady turn into the wind and past . . . so that you are heading almost at right angles to your previous course. First the sail will slat for a moment, but as you continue turning on your momentum, the boom will settle down on the opposite side and the sail will fill *from the opposite side* and you'll be sailing on a new tack. Try it several times, until you get the hang of tacking (which is all you have been doing—changing tacks is going from sailing with the wind on one side of the sail to sailing with the wind on the opposite side). By now *you can sail*, and if you wanted to, you could get back to the mother ship or the float.

The rest of the hour: Practice a few more changes of course. If you let the boom pretty far out and turn, always using your rudder slowly so that the wind is approximately behind you, you're sailing downwind. You have to steer more carefully, you don't feel you're going as fast (because you're with the wind, of course), but you have mastered the third way of sailing. (The other two are broadside to, which is called reaching, and close-hauled, when you were most nearly heading into the wind.) Changing tacks is easier when you're close-hauled, generally possible when you're on a close reach, and as far as sailing downwind is concerned, the one thing to leave for a later lesson. (You can do a lot of weekend dinghy sailing without ever learning to jibe.)

After one hour in a light wind, if you are someone already used to small rowboats and the normal details like the direction of the wind and keeping your eye out for other boats, you actually can be sailing a small dinghy. Another time you can practice your skills

◀

A quiet harbor on a weekend afternoon makes an ideal place for sailing dinghy practice.

and learn to jibe properly. You will learn that as with any boat, you must be moving to steer. If the boat is momentarily going backward, which can happen, the action of the tiller/rudder is reversed.

WRINKLES

Dinghy at the bow. A power cruiser, especially, has such a wide transom that there is often little room for the dinghy to be tied up next to it when in a marina berth. One solution is to tie the dinghy at the bow, usually with two lines so it will not drift about and make annoying bangs against your own or other people's hulls.

A shore anchor can be improvised from a railroad spike or an improvised tent stake, for a dinghy's short stay on a beach.

Splash! When a sailing dinghy with a centerboard is operated as a rowboat or with an outboard motor, a common annoyance is seawater sloshing through the centerboard well and into the boat. A thin piece of foam rubber or foam plastic insulation can be fitted to the inside of the centerboard trunk cover or kept aboard to be wedged into the slot in such cases.

Upright! With one person aboard, operating a dinghy with a small outboard has its minor perils and problems, such as trimming the boat under way. You certainly can't sit too far aft. An ingenious way of holding on to the dinghy while keeping one hand on the outboard steering control is to grasp the dinghy painter, perhaps three feet from where it is fastened to the bow. Sit amidships and use the grab line as a steadying line.

Solution. If your rowlocks are stolen or lost overboard, there is a way you can still row—provided you have some light line aboard. Put a piece of line, a lanyard, through the rowlock socket on each side, and then make loops large enough to hold each oar. If you had a pin to make a hole pin in the socket, you'd be even better off and able to row in one of the old standard U.S. Navy ways. But the lanyard improvisation works.

Mayday! If the dinghy has to be used as a lifeboat, fasten extra buoyant cushions, fenders, and Personal Flotation Devices under the thwarts to increase flotation in case of swamping. Take a flashlight, drinking water, food, signaling apparatus, and warm clothing for the crew.

"Boat your oars!" You may never want to use the old-time commands to a boat crew—but you may hear them used informally. "Give way" means to start rowing. "Hold water" means to slow or stop the boat with the blades of the oars. "Oars" means stop rowing, holding the blades horizontally, out of the water. "Stern all" means to row the boat backward. "Toss" means to lift the oars out of the water and lay them down inside the boat, blades forward. "Way enough" means to cease rowing, lift the oars out of the water, and be ready to boat them at the word *toss*.

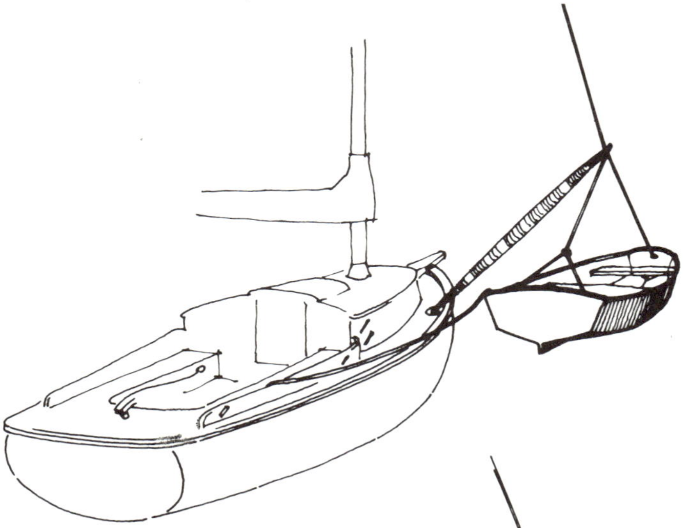

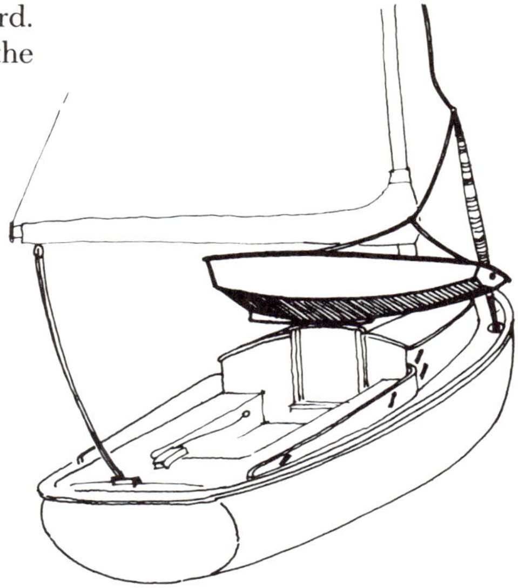

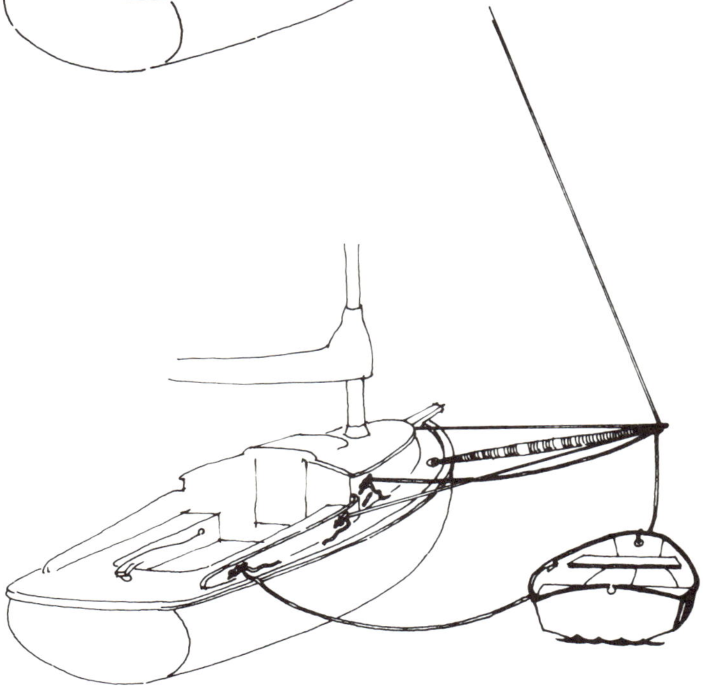

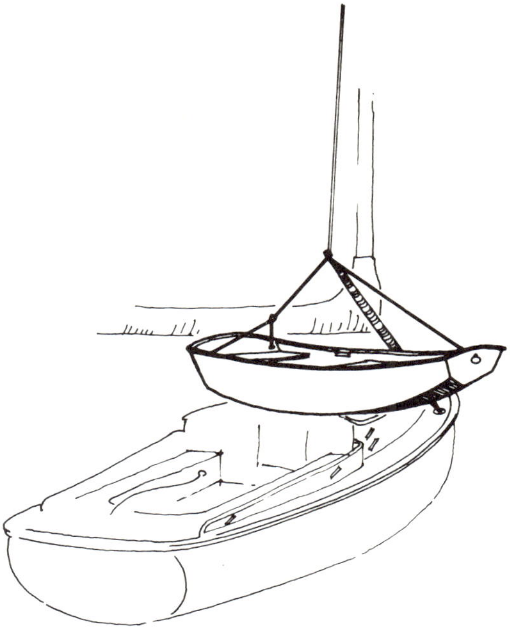

SERENITY

Chapter 8

Flags and Signals

Before "wireless" and radio-telephones were invented, boats and ships communicated with each other, and with the shore, by using flags, lights, and other kinds of visible signals. A surprising amount of marine communication is still handled in this way. It is fast because it is direct.

Consider a harbor such as the anchorage called the Salt Pond at Block Island, off the eastern tip of Long Island. A cruising sailboat, *Thirty Mule Team*, is anchored out and wants the launch to come and take the people to shore. The skipper can call the launch on his radio, and usually that will work . . . except that he has to take time to describe *Thirty Mule Team* and where the boat is anchored. Instead, the skipper blows the horn three times, or waits until the launch, circling the harbor, is fairly close, and hoists the tricolored "Transportation" flag—an outsized T, in the International Signal Code—at the starboard spreader. The launchman then knows *exactly* who is looking for a ride to shore. *Thirty Mule Team* doesn't have to have all the international signal flags aboard, just the big red-, white-, and blue-striped T.

Watch a really expert water skiing team and note how they use hand signals for turns, to slow up, to stop.

Or watch a cruising boat coming into a small harbor. One person is forward, to handle the anchor and anchor line, and the other crew member is at the wheel and throttle, controlling the boat. Better than shouting, they use hand signals.

First, a look at the basics of using flags. With most persons, the best-known flags are the national ensign, perhaps a yacht club

◀ *At anchor on a holiday, a sailboat shows all her signal flags, while her neighbor has added a dozen extra.*

burgee, and the ensign of a national organization such as the U.S. Power Squadrons or the Coast Guard Auxiliary. These are recognition flags. Even if you are not a member of the Power Squadrons or the Auxiliary, you may notice that boats flying these ensigns are the likeliest to lend a helping hand—and generally, the most capable—if another boat needs a tow or other help.

CORRECT USE OF FLAGS

In the U.S., the use of flags and ensigns is a matter of custom, not law. A few of the accepted customs have been changing and a few other variations, which may not be as acceptable to all persons, have been noticeable.

The U.S. Ensign, by custom for many decades was flown from sunrise to sunset, afloat or ashore, except at the White House, where it was flown twenty-four hours a day. In recent years it has been more usual to see the flag flown at night, lit up by a spotlight, particularly at official or formal places such as government buildings. Careful persons avoid merely leaving the flag up all night.

A useful standard for flying the American flag, the U.S. Ensign, and the Yacht Ensign aboard boats and ships is this: It should be flown from the stern staff of a powerboat or sailboat, in port or under way on inland waters. The old custom said that it should not be flown at the stern staff by a sailboat while under sail. This was a practical idea when long booms of gaff-rigged sloops and cutters swept the entire stern of a sailboat every time the boat came about or jibed. A yacht on the high seas should fly the ensign at times when recognition is desirable.

An old ketch under way, flying a private signal, a voyaging pennant, and a yacht club burgee, with the U.S. Ensign on the leech of the mizzen sail.

Many sailboats quite properly fly the ensign from the leech of the aftermost sail, approximately two-thirds of the distance from the clew to the head of a Marconi sail. On a gaff-rigged sailboat, the flag traditionally is flown from the peak of the gaff.

A foreign yacht visiting the U.S. should fly a small U.S. Ensign at the starboard spreader, just as an American boat in foreign waters should fly the ensign of the country being visited in the same way.

The Yacht Ensign, with the circle of thirteen stars surrounding an anchor, once reserved for documented vessels, may be flown in place of the fifty-star American flag, but this should be done only in U.S. waters, not abroad.

Instead of the U.S. Ensign, it is proper for a boat owned or chartered by a member of the U.S. Power Squadrons to fly the authorized ensign of that organization at the stern. However the U.S. Coast Guard Auxiliary flag is not flown in place of the U.S. Ensign.

Making colors, the ceremonial raising and lowering of the U.S. Ensign, is a practice with certain customs of its own both at yacht clubs and aboard boats in a harbor. The usual signal, at 0800 each morning, is the firing of a gun, at which time the yacht club's national ensign is hoisted, followed by those of the club boats in harbor. On a yacht club cruise or at a regatta, the senior club officer present hoists his ensign at the 8 o'clock signal and other boats in the club, and usually others in the harbor, follow suit. The U.S. Power Squadron ensign, the club burgee, and any private signals would be hoisted in that order, after the U.S. Ensign.

At sunset colors, except those flown on a day and night basis, are lowered in reverse order, the U.S. Ensign last.

An old custom aboard large yachts is seldom seen today: flying the Union Jack, a blue flag with white stars, on the bow staff.

Other national flags may be recognized or honored in U.S. waters in various ways, and of course anyone operating a boat in the waters of another country should learn the appropriate customs and practices.

State flags are often flown. On a vessel with more than one mast, a state flag is flown at the main masthead in place of the private signal or other flags. A state flag should not be flown from the stern.

A yacht club burgee may be flown on the bow staff of a powerboat or on a small staff at the masthead of a sailboat. Rules about day and night or on which mast or about flying the burgee while racing are set by individual clubs.

Private signals of owners are generally flown from the masthead of powerboats and sailboats, and sometimes at the bow staff of a larger powerboat or from the starboard spreader of a sailboat.

Officers' flags and pennants of various clubs and organizations are flown in accordance with the rules of those organizations. Those who like to observe who is visiting the harbor can look up these rules, and many of the flags, in books such as Chapman's *Piloting, Seamanship & Small Boat Handling.*

Flag dimensions: The hoist of a flag is its vertical dimension and also its inner side, by which it is attached. The fly is the horizontal length. The union is the blue part of an American flag, with the stars. A burgee is rectangular, triangular, or swallow-tailed (as is a private signal). A pennant is a flag, usually triangular, used for signaling or decoration.

A small craft anchored, flying the U.S. Ensign and a club pennant at the bow

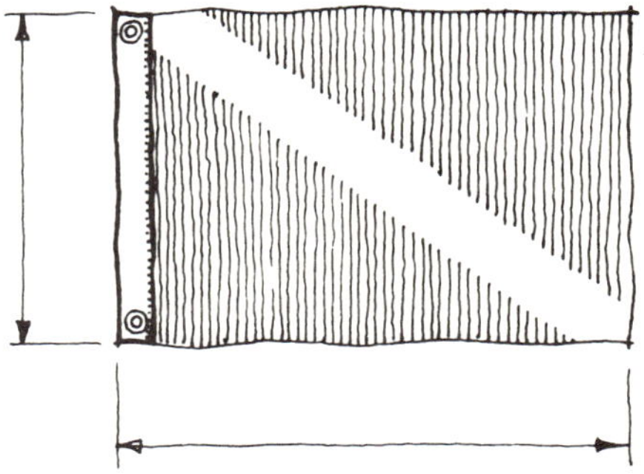

The U.S.P.S. ensign is on the starboard spreader, the private ensign on the main, the club burgee on the mizzen, and the U.S. Ensign is on the stern staff.

A member of the Power Squadrons under way, flying the U.S.P.S. ensign, his officer's flag, his squadron pennant, and the yachting ensign at the stern

FLAGSTAFFS AND FLAG HALYARDS

Flags that are flown from a staff, such as the Union Jack, the U.S. Ensign, and the burgees of most organizations and yacht clubs, are more or less permanently attached to the staffs, in some cases with a short halyard. Many boat owners like to keep ensigns on a staff, when not in use, in a small cloth bag made for the purpose.

A yacht club burgee, attached with clips to a staff, may be hoisted to the masthead on a flag halyard. Flags flown on halyards attached to the spreaders, another customary way used for signal flags and others, may be attached to the halyards in one of several ways.

Small spring clips tied to the ends of the halyard can be quickly attached to the corners of the flag. At times when no flag is flown, the spring clips can be attached to each other. However, this system has the disadvantage that if one end gets loose in a breeze, it may be hard to recover or the whole halyard may unreeve and come down.

An alternative, particularly at the masthead, is to use an "endless" flag halyard, made by tying or splicing the two ends together. This can't unreeve, but it is necessary to attach a staff to it by using halyard hitches—essentially a pair of rolling hitches, one above the other, so arranged that the flag will project above the masthead when hoisted.

Braided line, usually low-stretch polyester, is most used for flag halyards. Usually, a small block is fastened at the proper place near the masthead. For a spreader halyard a good alternative is a screw eye, fastened to the bottom side of the spreader, or a ring seized to the spreader.

Folding a flag properly reduces wrinkling during storage, saves storage space, and makes for easy retrieval and use. A signal flag or an ensign, folded correctly, is easier to hoist and break out.

A yacht club flag pole is usually a nautical affair; it may even be a salvaged mast from a wrecked or outmoded boat. The gaff, although not always the highest point, is customarily used for the U.S. Ensign. The club burgee flies from the masthead. Usually, there are a number of signal halyards attached to spreaders or to a crossed yard. These halyards are used for flying officers' flags, for honoring foreign visitors, for National Weather Service signals (storm warnings), and for "dressing ship" days.

SIGNAL FLAGS

A number of special flags are in general use for various purposes, ranging from functional and fully communicative to amusing. Saving for last the description of the International Signal Code flags, let us take a brief look at flags commonly seen.

Diver Down, in the international code, is Alpha, a blue and white swallow-tail. In practice this is used chiefly by commercial salvage ships with deep sea divers at work. Obviously, and the rules of the road specify this, other vessels in the area should take care. The other version of a diver down flag is the red rectangular flag with a diagonal white stripe, used on even very small boats and floats when a diver using **a** **S**elf **C**ontained **U**nderwater **B**reathing **A**pparatus (SCUBA) is working in the vicinity. Until 1984, the U.S. Coast Guard took the position that the Alpha flag was the only correct flag to fly, but the popular red flag is now officially noticed by the Coast Guard, and boatmen are encouraged to use it to mark the operational area of free-swimming divers.

Just don't try to pick up a small black floating object with your boathook—it may be a diver looking for seashells or a lost anchor. Slow down, watch carefully, and if possible, avoid the area entirely.

Transportation or **T** flags (also called **T**ender flags) are such useful and generally recognized flags that everyone on the water should be familiar with them. Yacht club tenders and public transportation water taxis are the boats generally hailed by a **T** flag, usually with three or some other number of blasts of a horn to call attention.

The size of flags should be appropriate to the size of the vessel. A good practice is to use an ensign that is one inch on the fly for each foot of overall length. Burgees, private signals, and officers' flags should be about one half inch on the fly for each foot that the tallest mast is above the water. For powerboats, a little more than half an inch for each foot of overall length works out to be good.

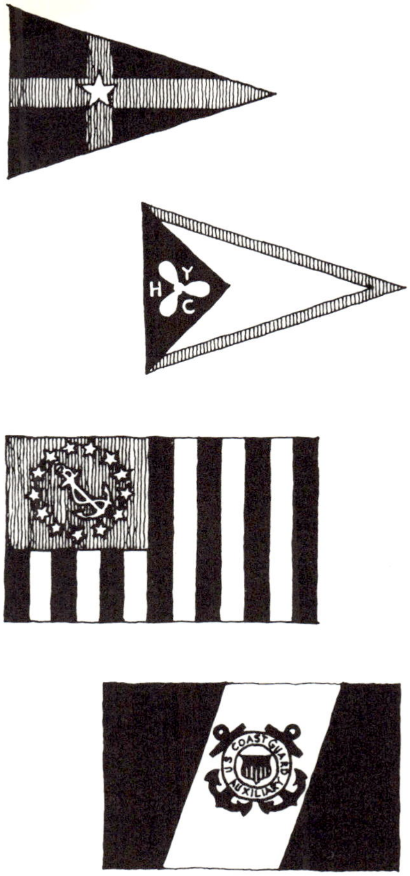

The burgees of the New York Yacht Club and the Houston Yacht Club, top, and the flags of the U.S. Power Squadrons and the Coast Guard Auxiliary

THE INTERNATIONAL SIGNAL CODE

Everyone has seen some of the alphabet flags of the International Signal Code. A few of the flags, such as the yellow Q (Quarantine) are easily recognized by anyone. Although the flags stand for letters of the alphabet, they are rarely used to spell out

International code flags. All are blue and white except for vertical red bars. JX: Leak is gaining rapidly. JW: I have sprung a leak. NC: I am in distress. See text for other signal meanings.

words, let alone messages. There are a number of one-flag signals and some two-flag signals that are easily remembered.

The International Signal Code has the advantage that its meaning is the same in all languages. There are a total of forty flags. First there is the code flag itself, also used as the answering pennant. It has three vertical red stripes, alternating with two vertical white stripes. Then there are twenty-six square flags for each letter of the alphabet, ten pennants for the numerals 0 to 9, and three special burgee-shaped flags called first repeater (or substitute), second repeater, and third repeater.

Even on a boat that does not have a complete set of flags, some of the signals, such as **T** for Transportation, can be used (and often are), and of course a boat operator can memorize or have available a list of the most used signals. An understanding of how these signals are used is desirable.

A **group** means a set of letters and/or numerals flown together to make a signal. A **hoist** is one or more groups displayed from a single halyard. Except in commercial or naval situations, it is rare for more than one hoist to be used at a time. **Complements** are numerals added to the basic signal to answer a question or to supplement the same basic signal.

To send a signal, hoist the name or number of the boat you are calling. If you don't hoist a call sign, it is understood that the signal is addressed to every boat in sight. It is customary to fly a yacht club burgee above the first flag if members of the club are being signaled, a common situation when a club fleet is on a cruise or holding a regatta. A vessel to which signals are addressed should hoist the code flag (answering pennant) at the dip to show that the signal is being observed, and full up or two-blocked when the signal is understood.

If you do not understand a signal, fly ZQ: "Your signal appears incorrectly coded; check and repeat," or ZL: "Your signal has been received but not understood."

Repeaters or substitutes are used to duplicate an alphabetical or numeral flag in the same group. To fly "Oscar Oscar," hoist "Oscar and First Repeater." Presumably, this would mean that two men are overboard.

To spell out names or words, clear text should be preceded by the code YZ.

The system is basically divided as follows:

Single letters are important signals; two letters are next in importance.

A single letter with a complement (numeral) is used for azimuth, time, speed, distance, or other information.

Two-letter groups with complements are used to answer questions or explain details.

Three-letter groups in the code are used for medical signals.

Some yacht clubs have their own signals for place names and cruise or race information. The U.S. Yacht Racing Union has signals, shown later in this chapter, used by race committees. Further information on signal flags and other visual communications is contained in *H.O. 102*, which has approximately 1300 signals. This is a U.S. government publication, obtainable from chart agents.

Following are some of the most used signals used in emergency situations, listing first one-letter messages, then two-letter, with two using numerical complements:

From the anchor light, ready on the forestay, the anchor ball above it, and the radio call sign on the halyard, one can guess: This cruising boat would like messages and perhaps visitors.

A—I have a diver down

C—Yes (Affirmative)

D—Keep clear; I am maneuvering with difficulty

F—I am disabled; communicate with me

G—I require a pilot

K—I wish to communicate with you

L—You should stop your vessel immediately

N—No (negative)

O—Man Overboard

Q—I am healthy; request free pratique

U—You are running into danger

V—I require assistance

W—I require medical assistance

AL—I have a doctor on board

CJ—Do you require assistance?

CK—Assistance is no longer required

CS—What is the name/identity signal of your vessel?

CV—I am unable to give assistance

ED—Your distress signals are understood

FA—Will you give me my position?

GN1—Take some persons off; skeleton crew will remain

GV—You should endeavor to send me a line

IL—I can only proceed at slow speed

IM—I request to be escorted until further notice

IT—I am on fire

IW—Fire is under control

JG—I am aground, in dangerous situation

JW—I have sprung a leak

JX—Leak is gaining rapidly

KM—I can take you in tow

KN2—I cannot take you in tow but can take off persons

MC—Uncharted obstruction in channel; caution

NC—I am in distress; require immediate assistance

NF—You are running into danger

PM—You should follow in my wake

QX—I request permission to anchor

UH—Can you lead me into port?

US3—Nothing can be done until visibility improves

UW—I wish you a pleasant voyage

VL—Tropical storm approaching

XT—Weather expected is bad

YZ—The words that follow are in plain language

The same signals, with the same international meanings, may be given by signal light using Morse code or other means, including radio. The glossary gives the meanings of all one-letter signals in their alphabetical place.

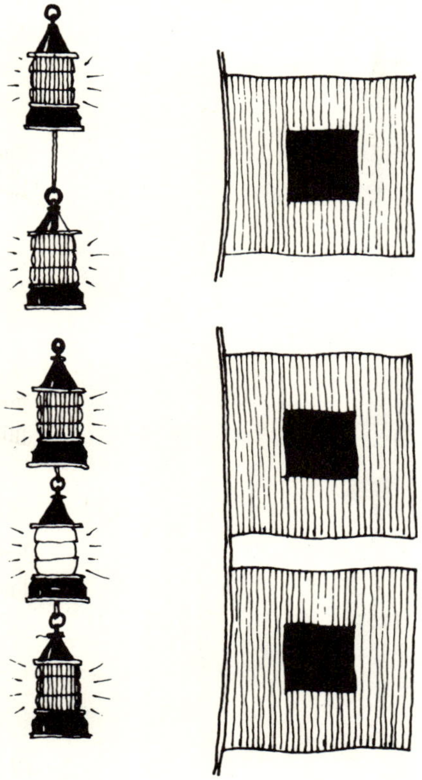

Weather flags (and lights at night) are flown at yacht clubs, Coast Guard stations, and at some commercial marinas.

DRESSING SHIP

One of the visual delights on the water is the holiday scene when one or more sailboats dress ship. There is a standard way to do this. First, fly the national ensign in its proper place. Then arrange the flags, using the toggles, tacklines, and loops that most flags have, interspacing swallow-tails, rectangular flags, and pennants. Between every two alphabet groups use a numeral or a repeater. If the size of your flags and the size of your boat match up, you will be able to start at the waterline at the bow and go to the top of the mast, using the jib halyard, with half the flags. Using the main halyard as a hoist, set the other line of flags from the top of the mast to the waterline at the stern.

Dress ship only at anchor or at the dock, except when a waterway parade has been arranged.

WEATHER FLAGS AND LIGHTS

One of the clearest systems of visual signals are the flags by day and lights by night shown at Coast Guard stations, many yacht clubs and marinas, and by the National Weather Service, which provides the basic information. Many boatmen make it a practice to glance at the weather flag whenever they pass it to see if it has changed, although if no bad weather is predicted, no flag will be flying. Usually, a weather flag will be easy to find in a new port because those who fly them use a high mast, unobstructed by trees, advertising signs, or other confusions. The National Weather Service provides maps that show many of the locations for weather flags, and in some cases fuel companies show them on their cruising charts.

These signals are advisory flags for small boats, not complete weather forecasts.

Look for red! The small-craft warning is a red triangular flag and may signify a lot for a small boat. For a larger boat, it can be considered advice to tie everything down. Two red triangular flags, one above the other, are a gale warning. A square red flag with a black square is a storm warning and two of these flags, one above the other, is a hurricane warning. At night the warnings are conveyed by arrangements of red and white lights.

There are other visual indications of the weather that experienced sailors watch for—ranging from noting that chimney smoke

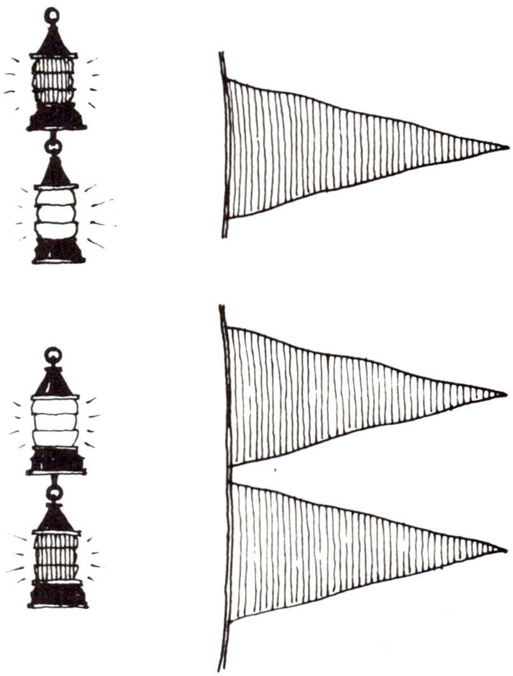

The flags and lights to watch for when bad weather is coming: small craft warning (red pennant), gale (two red pennants), storm (red and black), and hurricane (two red and black flags). Lamps are red and white.

The easy way to keep flags ready for use is to fold them in a standard manner.

and flags in general are showing how strong the wind is to noting that large boats are sailing with a reef in the main, or small boats are coming into harbor with the crew wearing yellow foul weather gear on a bright sunny day—telltale signs of heavy winds, waves, and spray outside.

DISTRESS SIGNALS

Almost any signal will attract attention in an emergency, of course, and when none other is available it may save a life. Some of the first ones you think of have disadvantages.

- ▲ Flying the American ensign upside down. This may not be noticed, unless some other signal is used to attract attention.
- ▲ Slowly and repeatedly raising and lowering both arms, outstretched at sides.
- ▲ A gun fired at one-minute intervals. (If you have a gun, which may be illegal.)
- ▲ Continuous sounding of fog signal apparatus. If the horn is powered by a small pressure tank, it will soon run out of pressure.
- ▲ Rockets, flares, and even a controlled fire, as in a metal bucket, to make smoke and attract attention.

NEW VISUAL DISTRESS SIGNALS

U.S. Coast Guard regulations: All boats used on coastal and territorial waters, including waters directly connected to the Great Lakes, and U.S.-owned boats on the high seas are required by law to be equipped with visual distress signals. There are certain exceptions, for some boats operated only in daylight hours, but even these boats should carry a minimum. The signals approved by the Coast Guard include:

Pyrotechnic red flares, hand-held or aerial.
Pyrotechnic orange smoke, hand-held or floating.
Launchers for aerial red meteors or parachute flares.

A wide variety of signaling devices, both pyrotechnic and nonpyrotechnic, can be carried to meet the requirements. There is a complication: In some states the pistol launcher for meteors and parachute flares may be considered a firearm and therefore illegal unless you have a firearms permit.

- ▲ Recommended visual distress signals: an orange flag with black square-and-disk; special electric signaling flashlight to signal S-O-S; three orange smoke signals, hand-held or floating; or three red flares of hand-held, meteor, or parachute type. Boats under 26 feet in length are not required by law to carry these signals unless operating at night or carrying passengers for hire. However, any well-equipped boat should have necessary equipment aboard, safely stowed, accessible—and known to the crew.
- ▲ To signal S-O-S, as everyone should know, does not require a complete knowledge of the Morse code . . . just the memorizing of dot-dot-dot, dash-dash-dash, dot-dot-dot, for S-O-S.
- ▲ Conveying additional information or requests, such as asking for a doctor, warning a rescue boat about a nearby rock, or making plans for a tow requires more elaborate communications. The flag code and Morse code were discussed earlier.

Under some circumstances it is necessary to communicate with a search aircraft. Orange dye marker on the water is one of the standard methods. Another recognized signal is an improvised or enlarged version of the distress flag, preferably made by using orange-colored canvas with a black square-and-disk.

Commercial fishermen towing nets, navy teams practicing with torpedoes, and towboats with very long tow lines pulling a string of barges are among the other possible dangers marked by visual warning signals. These are real situations that at times have involved serious accidents. One way to keep out of harm's way is to become familiar with the parts of the rules of the road that seemingly have nothing to do with the required lights for your own boat. Knowing the nighttime appearance of the lights of a string of barges or a submarine on the surface or a harbor channel dredge isn't that difficult. See Chapman's *Piloting, Seamanship & Small Boat Handling* or other books that cover regulations.

A standard arrangement for a flagpole at a yacht club shows the U.S. flag on a halyard at the gaff, while the club burgee is at the top of the mast. Other halyards are for signals or to show officers' flags.

Watch the Committee Boat (which normally flies a very large blue R-C flag) to see what the action is all about. Stay out of the way of the competing boats.

WATCHING A SAILBOAT RACE

Among the pleasures of boating is being able to tell what's going on by using one's eyes. Many of the activities of regatta and race committees can be followed through the flag signals to the racing boats. Knowing the "code" can give you a ringside seat at the action as well as enabling you to keep your own boat out of the way.

The R-C flag, a large rectangular blue flag with the white letters R-C will be flown on the committee boat. Look closely and you will see two variations of signal systems. One is a signal hoist on which a few of the regular alphabet flags are flown, to signify a postponement, a shortening of the course, a warning to wear life jackets, or other standard messages of the United States Yacht Racing Union, although many clubs add some of their own.

As the time comes to start the race, the second system comes into play. A white or yellow cylinder is hoisted at the firing of a gun to mean "10 minutes to start." This "warning" is hauled down, and exactly as the five-minute gun is fired, a blue cylinder ("Preparatory") is hoisted. At the starting moment the blue cylinder has been hauled down and a red one goes up smartly with the starting gun: "Go!"

Watching the sailboats maneuvering around the starting line, which as you know is between the anchored committee boat and a designated buoy or another anchored boat, you can see how their skippers are using the time warnings to try to get into a favorable position, sailing fast with a clear wind. Some boats get a good start, some lag behind—yet every now and then you will see one boat pull a sneaky start at the other end of the starting line and go on to win.

If a boat crosses the line before the gun, the chances are she will be recalled and have to cross the line again. All in all, watching a sailboat race is not necessarily what the newspaper sportswriter Red Smith wrote: "like watching grass grow."

Here are some of the signals to watch for:

A boat flying the red "Protest" flag at her starboard spreader is planning to claim a foul. If you watch exciting action at a turning buoy and then one or two of the boats hoist the Protest flag, you are seeing typical action.

Two guns and/or the code flag or Answering Pennant means all races are postponed until later in the day.

The first substitute is a General Recall.

N means all races are abandoned. If it's a windless day, start your motor; if it's blowing hard, batten down.

S means "shorten course."

Y means "You must wear life jackets."

USING HAND SIGNALS

Except on the smallest boats, it isn't always easy to shout from the steering position to the bow. And even two boats close together on the water cannot always communicate by voice. So systems of hand signals have been created, with some variations, depending on the purpose.

Water-ski signals are easy to remember. A hand across the chest, thumb up, is the way the skier signals the towing boat to go faster. Turn the thumb down—go slower. Hold the right arm outstretched—turn to the right. Left arm—turn to the left. Hand up—skier wants to stop. Finger across the throat—stop the motor. Hand on top of head—skier wants to return to the dock or the shore. Two hands clasped together above the head—skier is OK after a fall. Ski sticking up out of the water—skier is signaling his presence to other boats.

That last is a good point. Just as the American Water Ski Association (AWSA) has been getting skiers to observe safety and courtesy standards, other boating persons should give the skiers room and safety.

Water skiers who are observing the good practices recommended by AWSA, you will probably observe, try to work out courses that are away from swimming areas, low speed mooring areas, and marina channels. A corridor, about 200 feet wide and 2,000 to 3,000 feet long, is established. When a traffic pattern is established, it is generally in a counterclockwise direction, similar to the flying patterns of flight instruction and of private planes at small airports.

In California and some other states, if you see a blaze orange flag in a water ski area, it means "water skier down," or "traffic control." Skiers who had fallen were injured and killed before this safety flag was adopted.

Towing and mooring hand signals are more likely than any others to be useful—as well as observable—to a wide variety of boat operators. The ones described below are adapted—partly from U.S. Navy signals to use in directing a tug boat, and partly from those excellent signals of the Water Ski Association.

A crew member on the bow of a boat coming into a dock, approaching a mooring pickup float, or standing ready with the anchor can use these simple signals:

Point to the right—turn to starboard.

Point to the left—turn to port.

Open hand, palm down, moved slowly up and down—dead slow.

Palm high and steady—stop.

Signaling a boat that is to tow you or a helicopter attempting to rescue a person or crew is more complex. The signals to a rescue helicopter are given, with other information, in Chapter 15.

WRINKLES

To keep a small flag, such as a club pennant, clean while the boat is not in use, put a plastic sleeve over the rolled up burgee.

Mark your mooring. Put a very small colored pennant, perhaps even using Day-Glo or reflecting tape with your initials or buoy number, on the top of your mooring buoy or its pickup rod to make it easier to find and identify when returning to your home anchorage at night.

Your own flag. You can design and make—or get made by a good flag maker—your own private signal. Most are triangular, rectangular, or have a swallow tail. Two colors are "distin-

Philip G. Wright, the sailor artist

Walter Cronkite, the sailor newsman

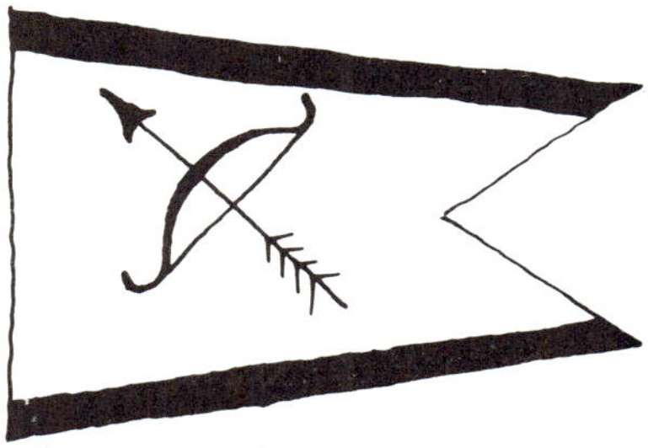

Charles F. Chapman

the schooner yacht America

John Whiting

Rod and Olin Stephens

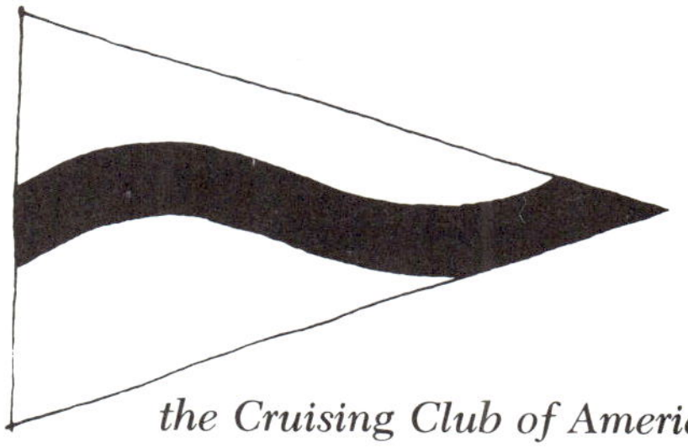

the Cruising Club of America

guished"; it takes more artistry to use extra colors and still avoid gaudiness. Simple designs look best. Two ideas: Try for a visual pun, like a cross if your name is Cross, and use nautical flag motifs, such as stars, seagulls, or flying fish. Rod and Olin Stephens use a white seahorse on a plain blue rectangle. Trademarks are not the authentic touch.

Identify. An idea from the days of packet ships and large private yachts is relatively easy to adapt: Paint a small decorative stripe, using your private signal colors (or any other family colors you choose) on the blades of your dinghy oars, your fender board, and your mooring buoy. You can paint a miniature of your private signal on such items or use decals of code flags. Varnish over to protect the identification.

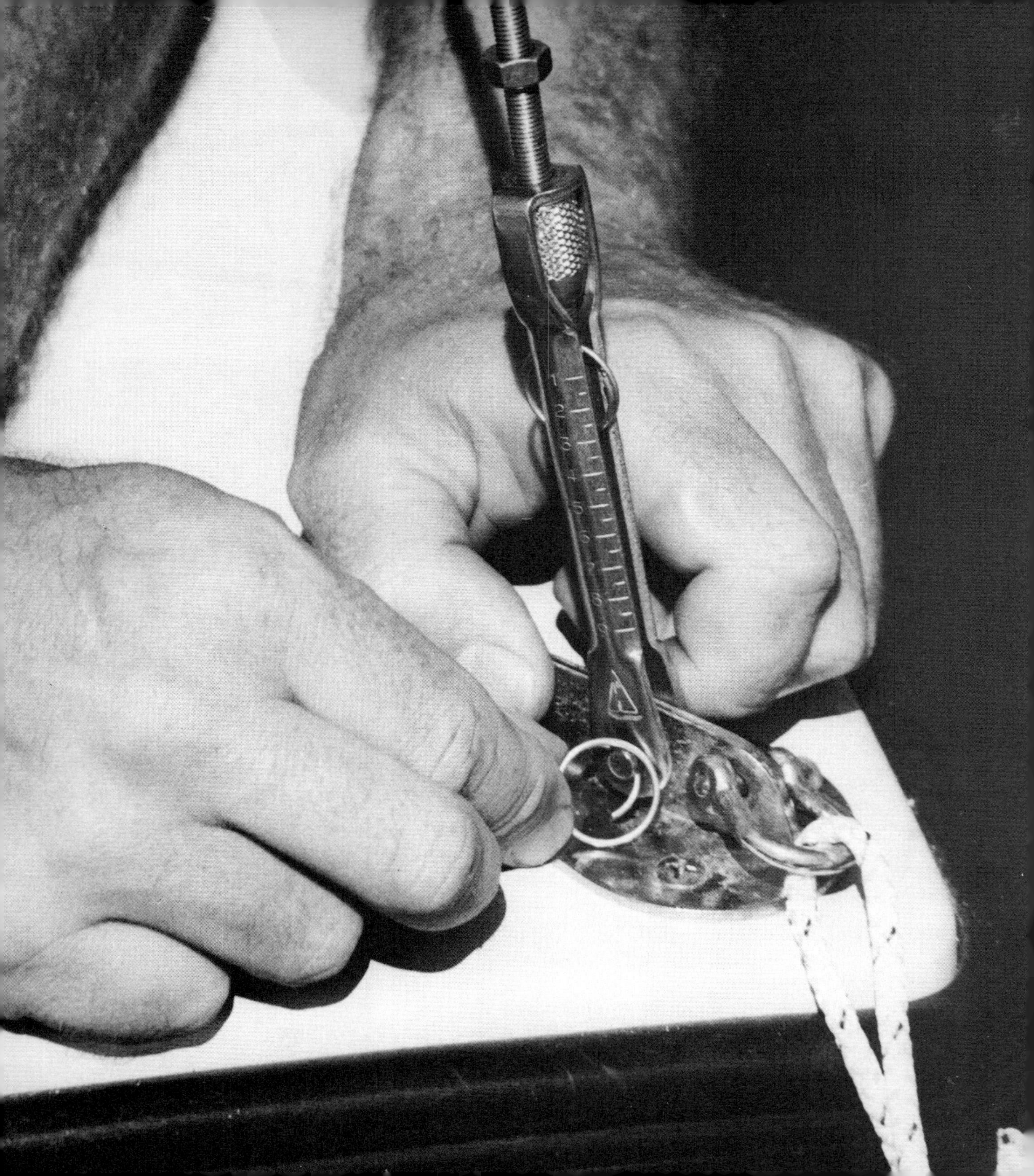

Chapter 9

Sailboat Rigging/ Hardware

In two hours on the Atlantic Inland Waterway, at a place like St. Simon's Island, Georgia, one can count, as they go past, a trimaran; a catamaran; seven stock new-tech boats built of fiberglass; a wooden sloop with high bulwarks, topmast, and a long bowsprit; a giant cruising cat boat; and a new-tech motor-sailer with what looks like a sawed-off transom, all heading down the waterway. You can't talk about sailboat rigging without being aware that there are hundreds of types and thousands of sizes.

So, to take an anatomical look at sailboat rigging, let's start somewhere near the middle. We'll look at a thirty-foot production boat made of modern materials but without high-tech gear. Since abbreviations like *Qk F1 R* are now acceptable for boat names, let's call this one *Any-Aux*.

Even without new-tech, a cruising sailboat is a fairly complex set of spars and wire rope, sophisticated hardware, and double braid running rigging. There are perhaps a hundred and fifty items in the rigging—not counting the deck hardware for anchoring and docking. Between stainless steel, superplastics, super lubricants, and new inventions based on ancient principles, even *Any-Aux* is quite a boat.

If you know the basics, save the next few pages for your neophyte nephew and just skip lightly. As we look at how all this rigging works, the experienced sailor will be reviewing familiar facts, of course, while your nephew will be absorbing some new terms. In addition, we will do a little inspecting to see what might be improved, altered, or adjusted aboard *Any-Aux*.

◀
Turnbuckles, using the power of the screw (an inclined plane), are the standard adjuster

This isn't a complete buying guide, of course—but for someone who may be checking out a boat there are a number of useful pointers. Last year's racing machine, to some extent, is this year's cruising boat. The small day sailer and the mighty twelve-meter or the maxi-boat seemingly do not have much in common—yet both keep changing. Some of the changes have been ways to use aviation shock cord, some are improved roller furling, or a few rigging hardware items that have a touch of space age technology.

STANDING RIGGING

The standing rigging, piece by piece, is easy to figure out. Start with the stays forward and aft that (to put it a little too simply) hold the mast up. More precisely, they hold the mast in the exact right place for efficient sailing and the headstay itself has another function: The jib is fastened to it.

On our hypothetical thirty-footer, the headstay or forestay runs from the stem to the masthead. A boat rigged this way is said to have a "masthead rig." Without the help of a naval architect, though, the boat owner is not likely to make a successful conversion from an old boat with the forestay three-quarters of the way up the mast to a full "masthead rig." Which rig is better? That depends on what you want to do, because in sailing there are few absolutes but many strong opinions. In any case, there are some improvements you can make yourself. Some additions will require the tools and expertise of a good rigging shop. Some are best planned and supervised by a competent naval architect.

The backstay extends from the stern to the masthead and in practice is linked to the forestay. Each affects the other.

Both the headstay, or forestay, and the backstay are adjusted for tautness by means of turnbuckles, or "rigging screws" as the British say, made of bronze or stainless steel. In a properly rigged boat there are toggles, so that the slight working at the stemhead and at the fitting aft is not a cause of strain. In the case of the headstay, a toggle at the masthead is also desirable, because the strain of the headsail in a stiff breeze, making the stay sag off, can put a strain on the tang, which will eventually break it.

We'll come back to those turnbuckle adjustments more than once, because that is where some of the sophistication in today's rigging comes in.

The name for the stays on each side of the mast, the lateral sup-

A sloop's standing rigging is basic: backstay and forestay plus shrouds on each side. All are precisely tuned.

ports, is shrouds. There are different arrangements of the shrouds, depending largely on the size of the boat. In our idealized example there are two lower shrouds on each side, a typical arrangement. These are fastened to tangs about two-thirds of the way up the mast at the spreaders. The third, the upper shroud, on each side goes over the end of the spreader to the masthead. On larger boats, of course, there are often more elaborate arrangements of struts, special stays, and other hardware to keep the whole structure properly tuned.

The naval architect designs the combination of stays, shrouds, and spreaders, and the builder's rigger installs them so that the right degree of tautness in the rig will keep the mast straight and transmit the various strains imposed by the sails. Because wire rope stretches a little in time, occasional adjustments have to be made. Because those adjustments become critical in a racing boat, a lot of technology is now available.

Check that the mast is absolutely straight, fore and aft and port and starboard.

WIRE ROPE

Wire rigging is actually wire rope. Not too long ago, galvanized plow steel was widely used, and for some applications, such as in fresh water areas, it still is. Today, however, most shrouds and stays are made of preformed stainless steel strands.

Stainless steel may be one of several alloys. Type 316 was pioneered in Europe and has improved corrosion resistance, achieved at the expense of strength. The most commonly used in the U.S. may be 302/304 alloy, which is exceedingly strong. The MacWhyte Wire Rope Company's Jack Bush says it has good resistance to corrosion and staining, except that the combination of salt water and the tropics does cause problems. There are nitrogen-based alloys with high strength and improved resistance to corrosion. The newest MacWhyte alloy is called Sailbryte and has the same strength as its 302/304 but twice the resistance to corrosion and staining.

The cable for standing rigging is designated 1 x 19. This has the least stretch of any configuration. It is laid up in one strand composed of 19 wires, which is the highest strength to diameter ratio possible. The smaller the diameter, the less the wind resistance. This type of wire works well with terminal fittings installed by either rotary or roll swaging machines and also with swageless terminals, which use compression to lock the terminal onto the end of the "wire." The other common configurations of wire rope, such as 7 x 7 and 7 x 19, are described in Chapter 10. Flexibility is their special virtue.

Wire terminals are of various types, with some variations in the way the wire rope is attached to the terminals. Lifelines have a stud on the end, which is a threaded pin for insertion into a turnbuckle. Some terminals incorporate insulators so that the backstay can be used as a radio antenna.

The swaged terminal is made with a stainless steel alloy that can be worked cold. About three inches of "cable"—that's the correct term—is inserted into the terminal sleeve or barrel. The sleeve is then put through a swaging machine, which rolls and compresses the barrel (in the words of the MacWhyte Wire Rope Company, which ought to know) "a bit like squeezing a tube of toothpaste" until it forms a tight bond with the rope. A simple type is the roll swager, found in smaller rigging shops. The rotary swager is far better; there is also a hydraulic press type.

In rotary swaging, the terminal is placed between two dies, which rotate around the axis of the terminal. The terminal is "hammered" for a few seconds, with many light blows. The finished terminal is straight and smooth.

In roll swaging, the terminal is also placed between two dies and is squeezed with a couple of passes. This can create unequal stresses within the metal structure, which can make it more vulnerable to shock loadings and "stress corrosion." Terminals done with a roll swager often have a shorter life, particularly in tropical conditions. The terminals sometimes bend during the swaging (look for a banana shape). Yet if done right, this makes a good terminal.

One point about swaged terminals: Don't walk into a rigging shop and ask them to shorten a stay "just an inch." Because of the barrel, the minimum reduction is usually three inches, as the old terminal must be cut away and discarded. A full three inches of cable must be inserted into the new barrel.

Swageless terminals are a comparatively recent development. They offer these advantages:

1) A terminal can be attached at sea, on an emergency basis, if you're an ocean racer or a trans-ocean cruiser.

2) These terminals are more or less reusable and can be used to make a more precise fit, as in shortening a cable component by as little as half an inch.

3) Only hand tools are required.
4) The connection can be opened for inspection—at the time of installation or at regular maintenance intervals.

An even simpler emergency connection, at least for sizes of 1/8″ and smaller, is the compression sleeve, which uses a double-barreled sleeve of malleable metal, a thimble, and a special crimping tool. Its appearance is not graceful, but it's a little better than a bulldog grip.

SIMPLE RIGGING ADJUSTMENTS

The turnbuckles are the primary means of making rigging adjustments, both when the boat is commissioned and during the season. The threads should be sprayed with silicone or Teflon lubricant or greased with anhydrous lanolin (which resists washing off in rain or salt water) about four times a season, so that it is a simple matter to take up or ease off on the turnbuckles.

How taut? If your boat has been correctly rigged and is performing well, get a feeling of the shrouds and the headstay and backstay . . . try to remember the tension. In a general way, lower shrouds are a little looser than upper shrouds and the fore and aft stays are as taut as they can reasonably be made without putting a corkscrew shape into the mast. Try it to see how much is too much!

Or for the price of a dinner, you can buy a simple tension gauge. In that case you should set the stays up, by the gauge, to match winning boats of the same class or to the specs of a knowledgeable rigger. Not technical enough for you? You can buy hydraulic backstay adjusters with built-in gauges—for the price of a lot of dinners.

At the deck, the shroud turnbuckles fasten—not directly, but with toggles—to metal strips called chainplates. These in turn are bonded or bolted to the sides of the hull—sometimes with strapping clear around the boat and under the mast step. When a boat is sailing hard, all the pressure on the sails is transmitted by the standing rigging to the mast and the chainplates. That's where the strength has to be.

The headstay fastens in a similar way to the stemhead fitting. The point of the forestay or headstay tension is to give a good set to the jib—so as near to "straight" as can be is the right way on our "plain vanilla" auxiliary. Not straight enough to suit you? Now

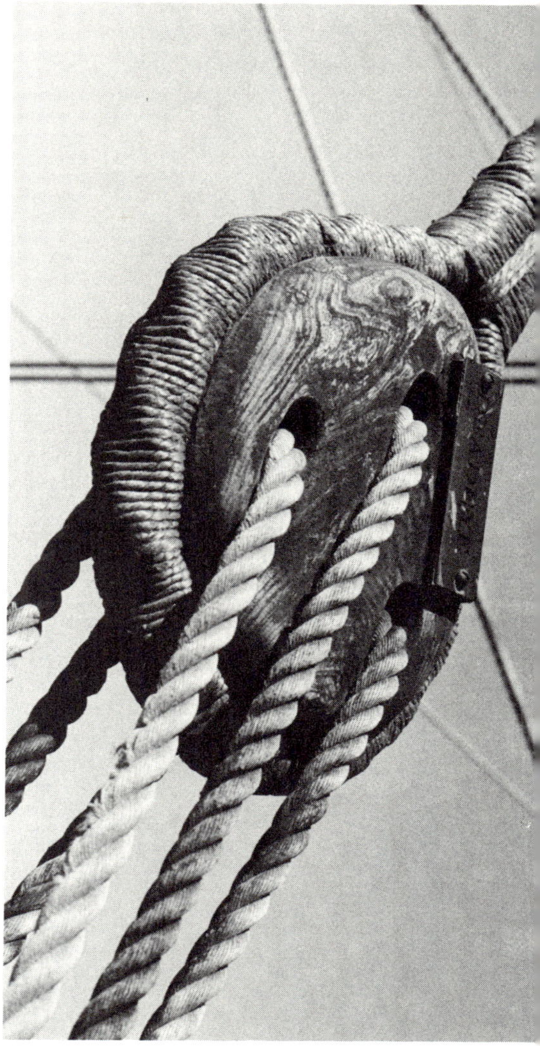

Deadeyes, using rope lanyards for power, had the beauty of wood and the curse of inefficiency.

▶
A range of adjustments, at fitting-out time and now and then during the sailing season, must be made.

you know why some racing boats have rod rigging. For that matter, some boats need a little sag in the headstay, at times, to give the maximum shape to the sail. But this is a cruising boat, not one for infinite variations in the tuning.

SETTING UP THE RIGGING

Observe and take notes. If you have never watched an expert rigger set up your boat's rigging, arrange to do so. Learn how to sight up the mast along the track to make sure it is exactly straight. Of course you should make sure the track is perfectly straight when the mast is out of the boat. You can't bend straightness into a crooked track.

Your rigger may show you how hard to pull on the fore and aft stays to get them to deflect two inches; on a typical boat this will take a good strong effort, putting your weight into it. This is an informal tension gauge, but it is worth getting the feel.

The basic deck hardware must be placed right. Here a MacLear winching platform is a feature.

Watch how the rigger adjusts the stays to get the mast straight. He'll start with the lower shrouds—usually the forward lowers first. When the bottom part of the mast is straight and the lowers have equal tension, he'll shift to the upper shrouds. The whole drill is designed to get tension and a straight mast, and this takes some back-and-forth adjustment.

The spreaders may need adjusting too. They should bisect the angle of the shroud, which means a slight upward cock to each spreader. Even though the spreaders may be taped to the shrouds, every time you approach your boat, take a look at the angle. Spreaders do slip down. Look at a dozen sailboats and, unless you are in a crack racing fleet, you'll see one or two with saggy spreaders.

Adjusting the rigging at the dock is the primary thing. But while the boat is sailing, and again after it has been sailed close-hauled in a moderate (fifteen-knot) wind, fine tuning is necessary. Sail first on one tack, then on the other. Again, start adjustment with the lowers. At this point you will notice that the leeside lower shrouds are almost slack when under sail. If the boat is right, this slackness will be the same on each tack.

When the rig is tuned, put cotter pins in the turnbuckles, to keep them from backing off. Don't bend the pins all the way back—that can lead to failure. A 10° spread will hold. A file and a touch of silicone sealer smooth out rough ends—although boots or tape are usually added. Or use circular pins. Your boat's turnbuckles don't use cotter pins? They have locking nuts instead? The toggles look different? That just goes to show the ingenuity of naval architects and rigging manufacturers.

All terminal fittings should be "inspectable." There are closed-barrel turnbuckles available, but you can't tell if there is an inch and a half of thread left or only a quarter-inch.

As you can readily determine, turnbuckles have right-hand threads in one end and left-hand in the other. If they are properly installed, of course, they are the same way up at all points, so that a person making rigging adjustments won't inadvertently loosen when he thinks he is tightening. If yours are wrong, fix them.

Your rigger should know how to adjust diamond stays, baby stays, running backstays, twin backstays, jumper struts, and the other variations that abound on yawls, ketches, schooners, and other rigs.

The skipper, or a designated crew member, should know how to check each of the parts of the rigging—and the whole, which is a tightly assembled structure.

KEEP A RIGGING NOTEBOOK

There's more than one name for a rigging notebook. One sailor in the United Kingdom calls his the Defect Book, because notes are always being made of parts to buy and adjustments to make.

A good rigging notebook will contain a list of all the stays, with their cable sizes and the specs of any special terminals, plus sizes, part numbers, and other necessary notes on all the fittings, turnbuckles, and other parts that might need emergency replacing. It will also contain similar specs on the running rigging and the sails, of course, including details on blocks, special shackles, winches, and winch handles.

Here is a typical, though partial, list:

Standing rigging:

Upper shrouds 3/16″ dia. 1 x 19, preformed

Lower shrouds 3/16″ dia. 1 x 19, preformed

Headstay 7/32″ dia. 1 x 19, preformed

Backstay 7/32″ dia. 1 x 19, preformed

Upper and lower shrouds to have eyes at both ends

Headstay and backstay to have one end eye, one end jaw

All swagings carefully inspected for hairline cracks

All rigging assemblies to be tested to 1/3 breaking load after swaging.

The specs for cable, you'll note, are given in thirty-seconds of an inch or in millimeters. The complete specs for turnbuckles give the wire size and the body "size" of the turnbuckle. They include the length extended, the length closed, the diameter of the clevis pin, the tensile strength, and the weight. The specs also include the information on the swage fittings, the toggles and jaws, and such details as the availability of link plates, to add still more adjustability. Merriman Yacht Specialties, an old-time maker of rigging fittings, says: "Working load should not exceed 40% of tensile strength."

There might be notes, such as: "Chainplates need better aligning with the shrouds." Or this one, on Lake Michigan: "Change bronze turnbuckle on backstay. Rigger says it will cause corrosion in the galvanized wire backstay."

In the good old days all this was done with deadeyes and lanyards, just as the running rigging included mast hoops, the gaffs had jaws, and it took two halyards to hoist the main. There was a time when standing rigging was considered the fixed type and the running rigging was the adjustable type. Nowadays, with movable and bendable masts, sails that furl inside the mast, and aviation devices added to the gear, Joshua Slocum might decide it would be easier to go around the world in a balloon.

WRINKLES

Small collisions, like the bow hitting the pier, call for a careful examination. Look to see if a turnbuckle was bent. Sailing mishaps, like a jibe all-standing, also call for a second look to find the bent shackle or the twisted thimble in the wire topping lift that could give trouble later.

Rigging spares, including toggles, clevis pins, swageless terminals, D-shackles, snapshackles, and cable, should be checked for size against the standing rigging. If a cable steering system is under the deck, be sure that the spares on hand, and temporary fixes like bulldog clamps, will take care of any breakdown.

Sail measurements and rigging measurements start with these standardized conventions:

I is the distance from the deck to the top of the mast.

P is the distance from the boom (lower black band) to the upper black band (highest point) on the mast (the luff of the mainsail).

J is the distance between the forestay attachment and the forward edge of the mast.

E is the length of the foot of the mainsail.

Chapter 10

Adjustable Rigging

Hold a beautiful black and stainless steel block in your hand and spin the sheave with a finger touch. Smooth!

Put the same block on a genoa track, under the heavy strain of sailing in a strong breeze, and you have friction, real friction loss. The moral is: Use the right size and type of block, with appropriate low-friction bearings, for the job at hand.

Hold a piece of braided rope in your hand. Feel it—it's smooth; flex it; try the weight; see if it stretches. The truth is, you cannot tell if this particular piece of double braid is nylon or polyester. Oddly, few professionals could tell, although they might identify the colored markings of the rope. But your specification of the right type of rope for halyards, sheets, guys, vangs, downhauls, and topping lifts is important.

Let's look at the running rigging, the adjustable rigging, of a boat only a little more complex than *Any-Aux*, whose standing rigging we looked at in the preceding chapter. Let's call her *New-Tech.*

We'll be looking at the main systems in her rigging, the gear that works them, some smaller systems and their components, and at details about rope for adjustable rigging.

Internal halyards are used aboard *New-Tech* to reduce wind resistance and some of the risk of getting fouled with spreaders or another line. On *New-Tech*, the halyards leave the foot of the mast at "exit-blocks," then pass through fairleads and sheet stoppers to the winch on the cabin top. This is almost fiendishly clever: Get a halyard taut with the winch, snap a lever, and you can use the same winch for the next halyard.

◄

XLS-900, going around a sheave, resists strains on inner fibers. The new core material, Spectra-900, is strongest rope material.

On a simpler boat, like *Any-Aux*, only a cleat is needed. Boats with what might be called "later-tech" have line tensioners; these actually get the last bit of tautness in the halyards.

The usual arrangement is for the main halyard to be on the starboard side and the jib halyard on the port. There are many such conventions, good to know about because they enable any experienced person to lend a helping hand on another person's boat with a minimum of questions.

The sheets, too, on *New-Tech* are rigged with more sophistication than those on *Any-Aux*, even though the boats are about the same size. This is not just a racing matter; *New-Tech* is a more strongly rigged boat and easier to sail.

Let's compare. *Any-Aux*'s genoa sheets lead to snatch blocks on tracks along the toe-rail, port and starboard, then all the way aft to the end of the track and another snatch block, on each side, before returning to the sheet winches. That's a cheap way, commonly seen, and it works in pleasant weather sailing, but it isn't right. Those aft snatch blocks would not hold up under hard sailing.

New-Tech has blocks of about the same size on each track, but they are wide sheave genoa blocks, to take each sheet and lead it aft. At the after ends of the tracks, there are turning blocks, also called foot blocks. These are bolted on, are a great deal stronger than the snatch block arrangement and, with the genoa blocks, actually provide better leads to the winches. Unlike the snatch blocks aft, foot blocks cannot get twisted and bend under a heavy strain. Moreover, since both the genoa blocks and the turning blocks have ball bearings and are a trifle large, rather than a trifle small, they turn freely, even with the heaviest loads.

Any-Aux's sheet winches are large enough for light cruising work and are fairly well positioned. But the jib sheet cleats are just bolted straight on. They work, but there's a small difference: *New Tech*'s cleats for the jib sheets are at a proper angle. This makes cleating down faster and easier.

The main sheet on *Any-Aux* is like hundreds of thousands of others. A block on the boom, a block at the center of the deck, and a slightly modern innovation: a cam cleat. Haul on the sheet and the boom comes in. Lift the sheet out of the cam cleat, ease it, and the boom is eased. Simple.

What could be better? The boom can be hauled toward the center of the boat, can't it? Yes, but the sailing would be better if the sheet led to a traveler on a track, so that the boom would be hauled *down*, on either side . . . and the setting could be predetermined, depending on the strength of the wind and the point of sailing—close-hauled, on a reach, or downwind. Later, we'll look more closely at big boat travelers.

Sailing, like baseball, is a game of inches.

MAIN SHEET VARIATIONS

Any of a few score other variations in the main sheet rigging might have been chosen. Both *Any-Aux* and *New-Tech* sheet to the end of the boom. Other boats have rigs that lead the sheet forward to the mast and back along the cabin top. Still others sheet to the center of the boom. Both these systems require extra blocks; extra blocks mean more potential for friction—and you have one more reason why careful planning is needed to get good rigging setups. The more blocks in the sheeting system, the more important it is to use low-friction blocks. The sheet has to be pulled in three feet (or let out three feet) for every foot that the boom is moved. Because of the angle, it might be correct to say five feet on the sheet for one foot of boom adjustment.

Main-sheet arrangements are designed for boom control and convenience—but extra friction can be the price.

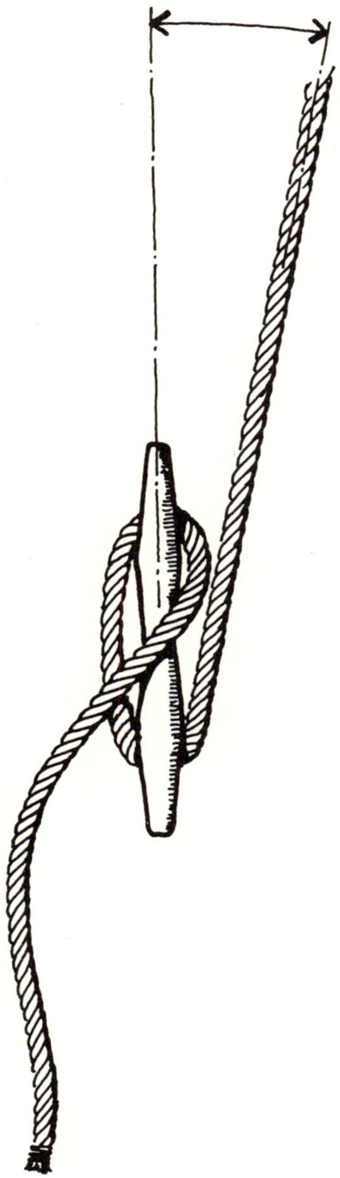

The angle of the cleat to the winch should be between ten and fifteen degrees as the sheet leads to it.

POWER FOR THE JIB SHEETS

There is the same requirement for extra power to adjust the jib sheets, but the power requirement is met in a different way. Each jib sheet goes through a block, but in this case only to adjust its direction. The power is applied by winches, which can be defined as fast-moving hand-operated continuous levers. There is one sheet winch on each side of the boat, at least on these two boats. More about winches will come later.

There are also a variety of ways in which the angle of the jib sheet can be adjusted. A working jib, on the simplest rigs, may have the sheet led through a fairlead or a block that has only one or two positions, perhaps on a pad-eye. The genoa jib poses a more complex problem, so the block may be on a car or slider moving on a track (essentially on the gunwales, again with exceptions such as certain hot racing boats) and can be fastened in any of a score of places, forward or aft, by just setting a spring-loaded pin.

THE ANGLE OF THE CLEATS

Normally, each time a jib sheet is adjusted, it is refastened to a cleat. If the boat has been well designed and built, the cleat will be at an angle somewhere between 10° and 15° to the normal position of the sheet as it comes off the winch. The cleat will be set counterclockwise to the line that leads to it (this means a different set to port and starboard cleats, of course), and a minimum of 12 to 18 inches from the winch. Many good naval architects say "two feet, if there's space."

On a boat you are considering buying, this business of the positioning of the cleats is a quality point to look for. On a boat you already own, some of the sheet-handling problems, such as overrides and other foul-ups that you may be experiencing, can be eliminated by making the necessary changes in the position and angle of the cleats.

The vertical angle of the winch, relative to the oncoming sheet, is also important. Naval architect Gary Mull, in the Nicro-Fico *Rigging and Fitting Guide*, says: "In order to avoid overrides, lines leading to winches should strike the winch drum at least 5° below a line perpendicular to the winch axis. NEVER lead a line to a winch from above perpendicular to the winch axis! The further away from a winch the lead is, the more the winch will have to be tilted back away from the load to avoid overrides."

Because of the constant readjustment of jib sheets and the necessity to do it smoothly and rapidly whenever the boat comes onto a new tack, a new variation has been developed: the self-tailing winch. Hauling on the sheet and cleating it down are no longer part of the drill—although many boats are built with the spare cleat in place, just in case.

The running rigging and related hardware just described are the essentials. A boat can sail with only halyards and sheets to hoist and control the sails. Thousands do.

ROTARY JIB FURLING

Now for a closer look at some of the subsystems of the running rigging, with now and then a stop for a detail. Let's start from the bow of the boat and move aft.

On that simpler boat, *Any-Aux*, a shackle is used to attach the tack, the forward corner of the jib, to the stemhead fitting. Cruising boats, where sail changing speed is not so critical, can use good screw-pin shackles. The racing boats need the rapid type. If it is desirable to have the jib a little higher on the stay, which might be the case with a small jib in a head sea or one of the cruising reacher-chutes that is set to the stemhead, a short pendant, made of wire or synthetic rope, will be used.

There are various ways to attach the sheets to the clew of the jib; a standard way is with a snap shackle—but again, some shackles are more suitable than others. Knots, especially the bowline, have the advantage that they inflict less pain than steel shackles when they hit the crew on the side of the face. A cruising boat, customarily, uses the same set of sheets, so they can be left attached to the clew. A lark's head, served, makes a good attachment for a day sailer. The excellent bowline is seen most often. Racing boats, often switching between lighter and heavier sheets, not to say headsails, require the operational speed of well-designed shackles. The best lock, so that they won't flog themselves into the open position.

Jib furling gear is the most important innovation. The principle seems simple: To shorten sail, rotate the headstay and wrap the headsail up on it. Just put a wind-up drum at the bottom, with a

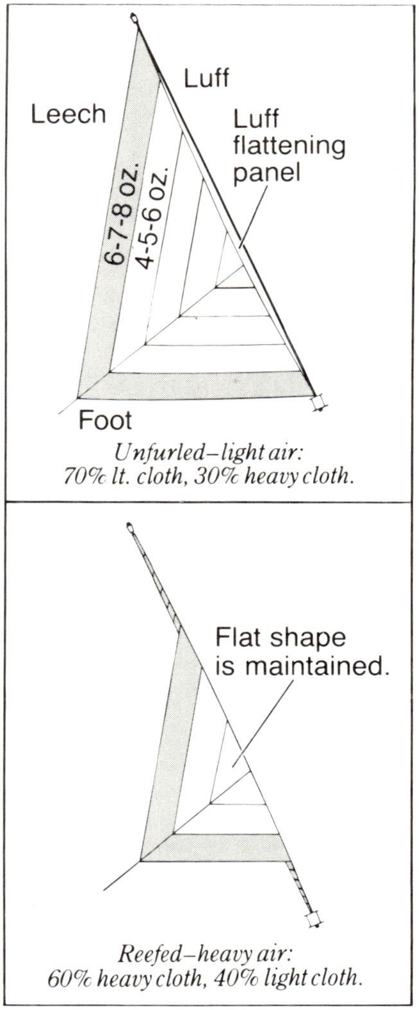

Unfurled–light air: 70% lt. cloth, 30% heavy cloth.

Reefed–heavy air: 60% heavy cloth, 40% light cloth.

Jib-furling gear allows the skipper to vary the size of the sail in use, yet keep a good shape in the sail.

line coiled. Pull on the line, wind it up. Release the line and pull on the sheet, and the sail area increases.

The sailmakers, rigging manufacturers, and designers who have been improving on this idea have analyzed their problems and found all sorts of solutions:

- ▲ Rods instead of wire, for the headstay.
- ▲ Grooved luff extrusions, to take the headsail luff.
- ▲ Ball bearings, to reduce friction.

Some of the solutions involve using the newest materials. Here are examples:

- ▲ Stainless steel bearings, bathed in lubricant.
- ▲ An open ball-bearing system, using Duratron ball bearings in Teflon-impregnated races, flushable with a hose or by the rain.

One drum—to look at the materials—is made of spun stainless steel. The opening is cut with a laser. The parts inside and outside are made of nickel-plated silicon bronze, and Hardkote Teflon anodized aluminum.

The simpler versions, for nonracing day sailers, may not even require new jibs. In the top-rank sailboats, however, special sails, carefully engineered plans for the exact fitting of the complete roller furling gear, adjustability, and precise use have resulted in exceedingly workable systems. There are differences between systems for cruising boats, small racing boats, and larger performance boats. Some use a padded luff to maintain the correct sail shape. Another uses a swivel system to keep the tack and head of the sail on independent swivels. In this, the center of the sail begins to furl before the tack and head, gathering up excess cloth, for better shape when partially furled.

For the most competitive racing boats, a way has been designed to remove the furling gear but leave the twin luff foil for headsails. In another system, an internal halyard for the jib is included.

The advantages of combining reefing and furling the jib in one system include easier spinnaker handling—no jib on the foredeck—and for smaller boats, ease in getting the jib out of the way so you can right the boat after a capsize.

Double luff headstays are another development that reaches both the cruising sailer and the racer. Twin headsails, for easy downwind sailing while making long passages, have been used for decades. The solid rod headstay, with a more or less airfoil shape and twin grooves, has made it possible to set one sail while the other is still working. But if the sails are wet, it has been found, the time that might have been saved is lost fidgeting the wet sails up and down. There are alternate ways of setting a jib, while the first is still up, even on a single headstay.

A POLE FOR THE JIB

The whisker pole, improved by a number of clever sailors, is one of the most generally useful of the "modern" improvements. It is used to "wing out" the regular jib or genoa on the side opposite the mainsail. Out of the main's wind shadow, the jib provides increased speed and a better balance on downwind sailing. On a reach the whisker pole opens a larger slot, helping the boat go faster.

Some whisker poles are telescoping. The spike end is designed to fit into the clew of the jib, if the clew grommet is large enough, or into a properly tied bowline. The other end of the pole snaps into an eye on the mast. The eye is mounted on the mast, unless a track is used, at the right height to match the clew of the average headsail used.

The adjustable poles are normally set at 100 percent of the foot length of the sail being used. If a number of sails are used, the crew marks the various lengths on the pole, using a felt tip marking pen. Another way to determine pole size is to multiply 1.4 times **J**, the distance from headstay to the mast.

All there is to trimming the whisker pole is keeping it at 90° to the wind, using the masthead wind vane or telltales on the shrouds as a visual guide. In practice, this means that on a reach or a run the pole is set as though it were an extension of the main boom, on the opposite side of the mast.

Whisker poles are used for boats from mini-size to 50 and 55 feet long, at least in light airs.

A variation, the downwind pole, is a good deal more like a conventional spinnaker pole, since it uses a topping lift. For long-range cruising, twin downwind poles, storing vertically at the mast, have been developed.

Reaching struts, used with spinnakers, are outwardly similar to whisker poles. They allow a better control of the after guy on a

The whisker pole (once improvised) is now a fine auxiliary spar for cruising and racing boats.

reach and save the wear and tear on the guy by keeping it off the shrouds.

Barber hauls are normally sophisticated additions to racing gear—but in fact any cruising boat can improvise a Barber haul to improve the set of the jib. It is simply a lateral adjustment, to control the clew of the sail by means of a line with a snatch block riding on the jib sheet.

The boom downhaul is one of the means used to get the luff of the mainsail as taut as possible. In certain cases, downhauls are used on headsails, to increase the luff tension.

Boom vangs, in either of two modes, might be said to extend the boom downhaul's control still further, usually by means of a tackle. The first development of the vang was a rough-water idea, to keep the boom from slatting or being caught in an accidental jibe. A claw around the boom, or a way of attaching the vang to a heavy bail under the boom, is used at the upper end. The tackle then leads to the rail. Whenever the boat is tacked or jibed, of course, the vang must be cast off and then reset on the other side. The center boom vang is a similar tackle, extending from a midpoint on the boom to the base of the mast. It supplements both the main sheet and the downhaul, allowing tacking and jibing, but keeping the boom down. It thus helps control the shape of the mainsail's leech and the "twist" in the sail. Used in conjunction with the main sheet traveler, the vang gives greater efficiency to the sail.

The Cunningham is a sail control device, using a small but powerful S hook, with a special shape, grommets set into the sail, and a control line. The Cunningham, by pulling down on the loose corner of the mainsail, at the tack, under certain wind conditions, changes the draft of the sail.

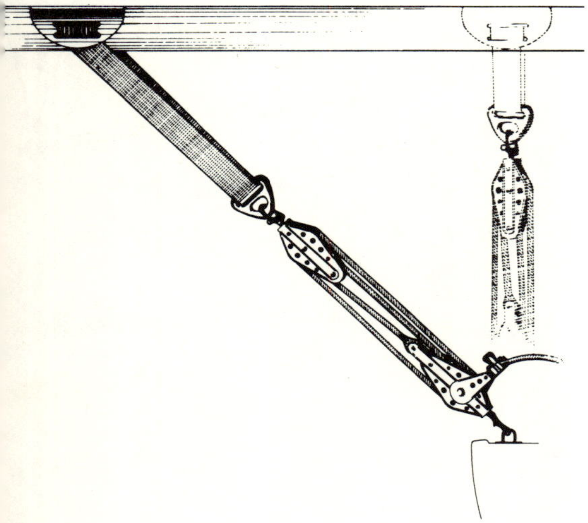

A boom vang attachment, from Nicro-Fico, has proper webbing, fittings, and blocks.

MAINSAIL REEFING AND FURLING

Anyone who ever read *Two Years Before the Mast* knows how hard it was to get out on a yardarm, standing on a footrope, and get a wet canvas sail under control. By contrast, furling a mainsail on a small sloop on a rainy, windy day is easy, but only by contrast.

There are five ways to shorten sail:

1) Reduce the number of sails.
2) Use smaller sails.

3) Reef, using reef points, thus reducing the area of a sail along the foot.
4) Reef, with roller reefing boom.
5) Roller furling.

Modern technology has improved on the standard ways the ancient Phoenicians used to cope with too-strong winds and added a couple of better ways.

When it blows too hard, you can always do what the ancients did—reduce the number of sails. A modern sloop will handle fairly well under mainsail alone. A good one will do well in a blow with just the jib. She'll sail downwind and reach, and fairly comfortably.

Changing sails, using a smaller headsail, for example, is just as good seamanship as it ever was. It's just easier.

As the wind pipes up, taking in a reef gets harder and harder, especially in one of the older systems using reef points.

About halfway through the twentieth century, the designers added roller reefing to the high-tech sailboat. It still required a couple of persons working together. One, at the halyard, lowered the sail a foot or two at a time. The other cranked the boom-turning mechanism while trying to keep the sail from bulging unevenly. It was, perhaps, good to have in case of necessity, but not always good to use.

Then came technical improvements. One is just a better way to rig the old reefing system. The others are variations of the window-blind method.

Slab reefing, sometimes called jiffy reefing, is possible because of stronger polyester sails and better rigging on the boom. The sail sets better because the line through the reef points, rather than separate ties, allows for a balanced strain on the sail. The preset lines, through properly spaced cringles and using correctly spaced cheek blocks on the boom, are faster to operate. It is difficult to get all these details correct on the drawing board—some try-and-fit work is usually necessary.

A flattening reef, like the Cunningham, is a way of making a small change in the shape of the sail. It is similar to a slab reef in operation but does not substantially change the area of the sail.

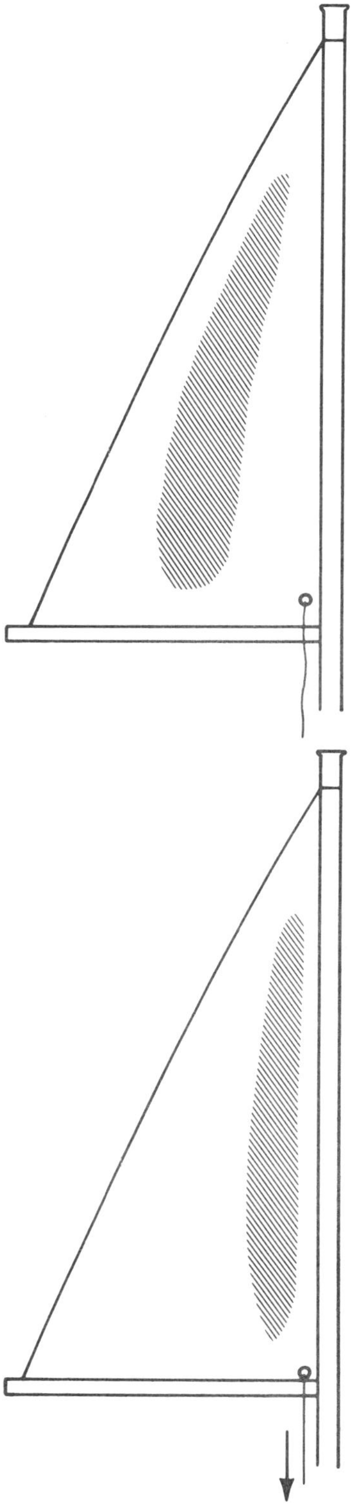

The Cunningham alters the shape of the sail, moving the full curve part forward for windward sailing.

A ninety-three-foot schooner, from Frank MacLear, has dozens of electric motors for sail handling.

MAINSAIL ROLLER FURLING

Like many other inventions, mainsail roller furling was built on other developments. The most popular versions, such as that of sailmaker Ted Hood, roll the sail up inside the hollow aluminum mast. Instead of horizontal roller-boom reefing, vertical furling is working out satisfactorily for cruising boats, successfully shortening sail and stowing it.

Frank MacLear, the naval architect who specializes in larger cruising boats, feels that small cruising crews are better off with the roller independent of the mast. A few inches of space between the roller and the mast cuts down on the sail's efficiency, but it does away with the problems that can be caused by a high wind making the sail bind against the slot in the mast.

MacLear has simplified both the rig and the handling of his larger cruising boats in many ways. Electrically operated furling systems and boomless mainsails are two of the ways he has moved sailing into the age of automation.

MacLear boats range in size up to *Centurion*, a ninety-four-foot brigantine. Since the three squaresails on *Centurion*'s foremast, as well as the six fore-and-aft sails the boat carries, are electrically controlled, a few extra methods of generating electricity were included on the vessel. She has solar panels, and her three-bladed, controllable pitch propeller is also rigged to generate electricity under sail, through two 3.8 kilowatt alternators. Of course, when *Centurion* is under power, her main diesels run generators, each producing 22 kilowatts.

Falcon II, a smaller MacLear design, is a sloop. She has the mainsail trimmed to her beefed-up backstay. As a boomless cutter she is a pretty boat, as well as one easy to handle for a small crew. Other MacLear boats without booms range from forty-two feet to the beautiful eighty-seven-foot cutter *Aria*.

On a smaller and more experimental scale, devices to pull a zippered bag down the length of a sail are being developed by various innovators. Some of these, for spinnakers, have sailmakers' strong endorsements.

CHOOSING BLOCKS

Unless your naval architect specified the complete list of blocks for your boat and they have proven to be exactly right under all sorts of sailing, with none lost or damaged and a couple of spares in the bosun's locker, you want to look more closely at these beautifully made mini-machines.

The three choices you have are: 1) the correct type of block; 2) the right size; and 3) the rated strength.

Some types of blocks, such as **exit blocks** at the foot of the mast and **masthead sheaves,** are built in. If the block is for a rope halyard, the sheave will probably be plastic. Wire halyards require a metal sheave, usually anodized aluminum or bronze.

Cheek blocks, mounted on a spar, usually require a curved plate. A flat plate is used on deck, deckhouse, or coaming mounts. As in all cases, the sheave should fit the line used, as to size and type.

Turning blocks, also called foot blocks, are used for turning jib sheets and spinnaker sheets. Heavy through bolting is usually necessary, because of the tremendous loads. For the same reason, low friction bearings, under load, are required.

Fairlead blocks, for genoa sheets when used on the rail and for leading external halyards at the base of the mast in some cases, come in a wide variety of designs. At one end of the scale are suitably sized snatch blocks. At the other end are wide-sheave blocks,

A turning block, heavily bolted, is needed for handling jib and spinnaker sheets.

A well-suited snatch block has to match the expected strain—which can run to many tons.

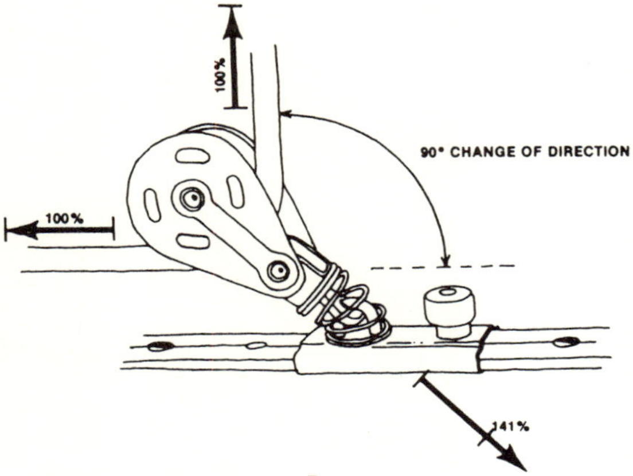

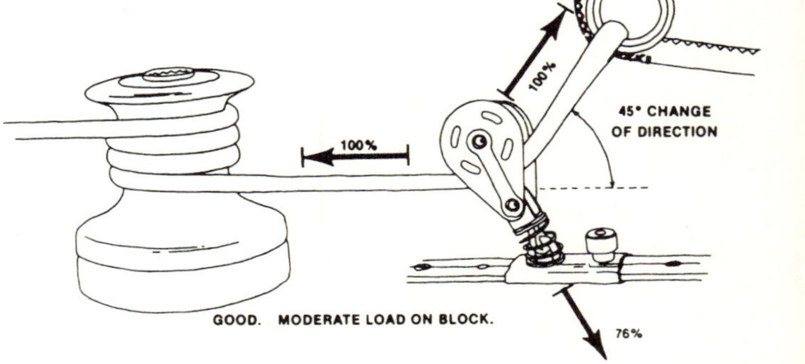

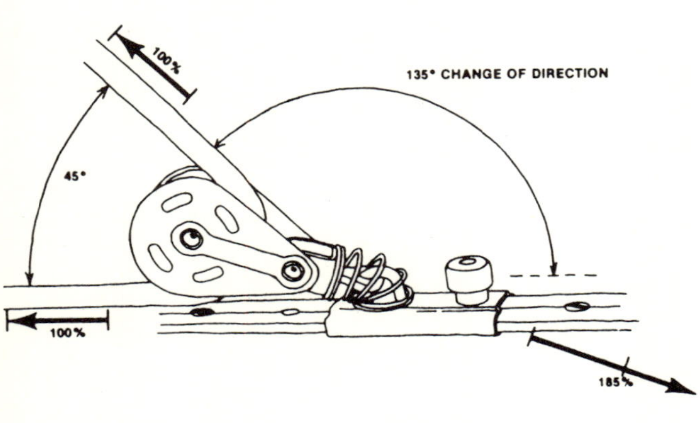

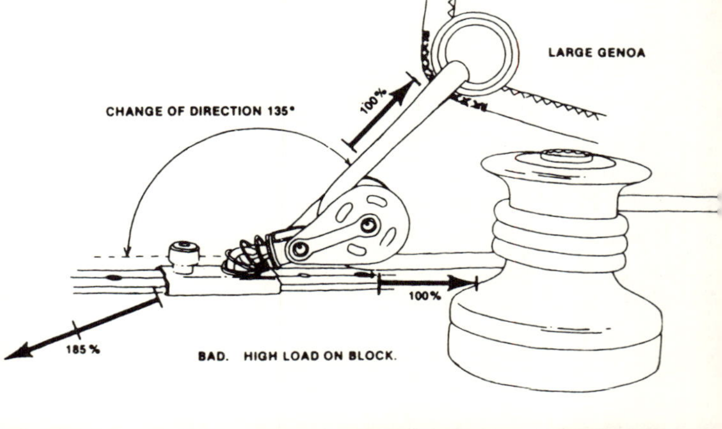

to take two sheets at once, for rapid headsail changes and ease in sheet handling. One kind will even pass special shackles. Offshore racing boats require lead blocks that can be adjusted under extreme loads; Harken blocks, for example, have Duratron (plastic) ball bearings and are adjustable on the track by either single part lines led aft to winches or multiple purchase tackles led to the cockpit.

Special reaching sails, with much less elaborate rigging than the spinnaker, have been developed recently. Radial cuts and improved sailcloth, combined with such new-tech ideas as using computers to lay out the sails, have made these sails very useful. Some are super-genoas, some are mini-spinnakers, one is called a radial drifter, and all have colorful names, coined by sailmakers, to match their colorful panels of cloth.

Spreacher blocks have been developed for fast, efficient sheeting of spinnakers and reaching sails (hence the name) and bloopers. The smaller sheave inside the larger one simplifies inside-out spinnaker changes. A racing block, the spreacher must have virtually no friction during light air drifting conditions and yet withstand heavy loads in a blow.

Snatch blocks, as improved by rigging manufacturers, are one of

Modern rigging hardware, if chosen properly for the job, is strong, cleanable, and corrosion resistant.

the modern-day contributions to seamanship. These blocks can be opened quickly to accept a line, without having to reeve it through the entire block. So they are used for Barber hauls, genoa fairleads, spinnaker sheet and guy fairleads, and many improvisations. They are made with screw pin shackles, swiveling snap shackles, and with a trunnion snap shackle. Snatch blocks, on a small car on the track, should not be used as turning blocks for genoa sheets even though some builders furnish boats rigged in this inadequate way.

Fiddle blocks are similar to spreacher blocks. They are used for main sheet multipart systems, boom vangs and for special setups like a riding monkey to keep a topping lift out of the leech of a sail.

Blocks come with snap shackles, cam cleats, beckets, swivels, upset shackles, reversible shackles, and with spring mounts or on slides. Depending on the use to which they will be put, they have various kinds of bearings. They include roller bearings, stainless steel ball bearings, plastic ball bearings, Teflon-impregnated bearings, and needle bearings. Many small blocks will withstand loads of two tons and more. Multiton blocks are an impressive example of what can be done with stainless steel.

Choosing a block is more complicated than it used to be. The sheave for Kevlar rope, for example, must be exactly right, to avoid flattening the rope under strain. The widths of sheaves, of course, should match the sizes of the lines that go through them, but the shape of the sheave groove must also suit the type of rope. Kevlar and polyester rope, being low-stretch, last longer if the core section is not overstressed. The diameter of a sheave to be used with Kevlar, it is generally recommended, should be at least twelve times the diameter of the rope.

WINCHES

The modern winch is the device that makes rope such an amazing transmitter of power. While a simple, small cruising boat might have only a couple of plain geared winches, with power ratios like 7 to 1, some of the two-speed and three-speed winches generate power ratios of 43 to 1 and 58.6 to 1. Others, primarily for the short-handed cruisers, are electrically operated.

Frank MacLear's *Aria* has six out of ten of the winches on her winching platform operated by electric motors.

SPINNAKER GEAR

The basic gear for flying a spinnaker is a sheet, a guy, a spinnaker pole with a topping lift, and an extra halyard. Double sheets, double guys, trip lines, a strut for reaching, and various items like track on the mast are added to the list—yet Roger Marshall, N.A., one of the clearest writers on the subject as well as an expert sailor, says a spinnaker can be a boat's best friend.

You don't need all three kinds of spinnaker until you get into serious racing, as Marshall points out. A running spinnaker is cut full at the shoulders. A triradial is the general purpose spinnaker, with each of the corners cut in a radial pattern. The star-cut spinnaker is flatter; it is used for reaching, but in racing may be used in strong winds when a larger, fuller chute would be too much for the boat.

The easiest way to understand the basic gear is to study the drawing and observe other boats when they are flying their chutes.

The latest change in the how-to of spinnakers has been the American development of dip-pole jibing, as compared with the older standard method, in which the pole is taken off its mast attachment and turned end for end. Dip-pole jibing involves dipping the pole under the forestay, through the foretriangle. This may sound simpler . . . but it requires more crew (a total of three or four) and a second sheet plus an extra guy. In the standard jibing method, "the sheet becomes the guy, the guy becomes the sheet."

MAGIC BOXES AND THEIR COUSINS

When it comes to the old-fashioned block-and-tackle principle, nothing aboard a modern sailboat is more fascinating than the magic box and its cousins.

Main sheet traveler systems, complete with tracks, ball-bearing races, and built-in blocks, are elegant devices for precise control of the way the main sheet is adjusted. Main-sheet rigs are elaborate enough, with their many ways of combining blocks, fiddle blocks, ratchet blocks, and cam cleats. One of the most ingenious is the Easymatic system, which combines two purchase ratios in one block system. As Tod Sackett at Merriman Yacht Specialties says: "Pull one line for power or pull both for fast sheeting." The two lines of the sheet run through a double cleat. The sheaves may be double ratchet or not.

But the marvelous ingenuity of the rigging designers is not always seen in something brand new. Decades ago, riggers figured out a way to put one end of the main sheet on one side of the cockpit and the other opposite . . . for ease of handling, in a "double-ended" tackle setup. Other rigging innovators have worked out a way to put the block-and-tackle of a boom vang inside a tube, to keep all lines free.

The magic box, although it has limited applications, is the Harkens method of putting blocks, line, tracks, ball-bearing races, and a few high-tech materials into a control system that turns manual power into tremendous short-haul leverage. Outhauls, downhauls, vangs, Cunninghams, jib halyards, shroud tensioners, baby stays, and backstay adjusters are all used with magic boxes.

Marty Rieck, of Harken Yacht Fittings, writes: "There really is no mystery or magic to a magic box. It is simply a powerful multi-purchase system housed in a compact aluminum extrusion. If you took two triple blocks, one with a becket, and ran a line through them you would have the same thing as a six-part purchase magic box, except that the blocks take up more room and the exposed lines would need to be kept free and clear. In the magic box the lines are contained and perfectly organized. The disadvantage of the magic box is that it has a limited length of travel, which is no longer than the box itself."

The magic box

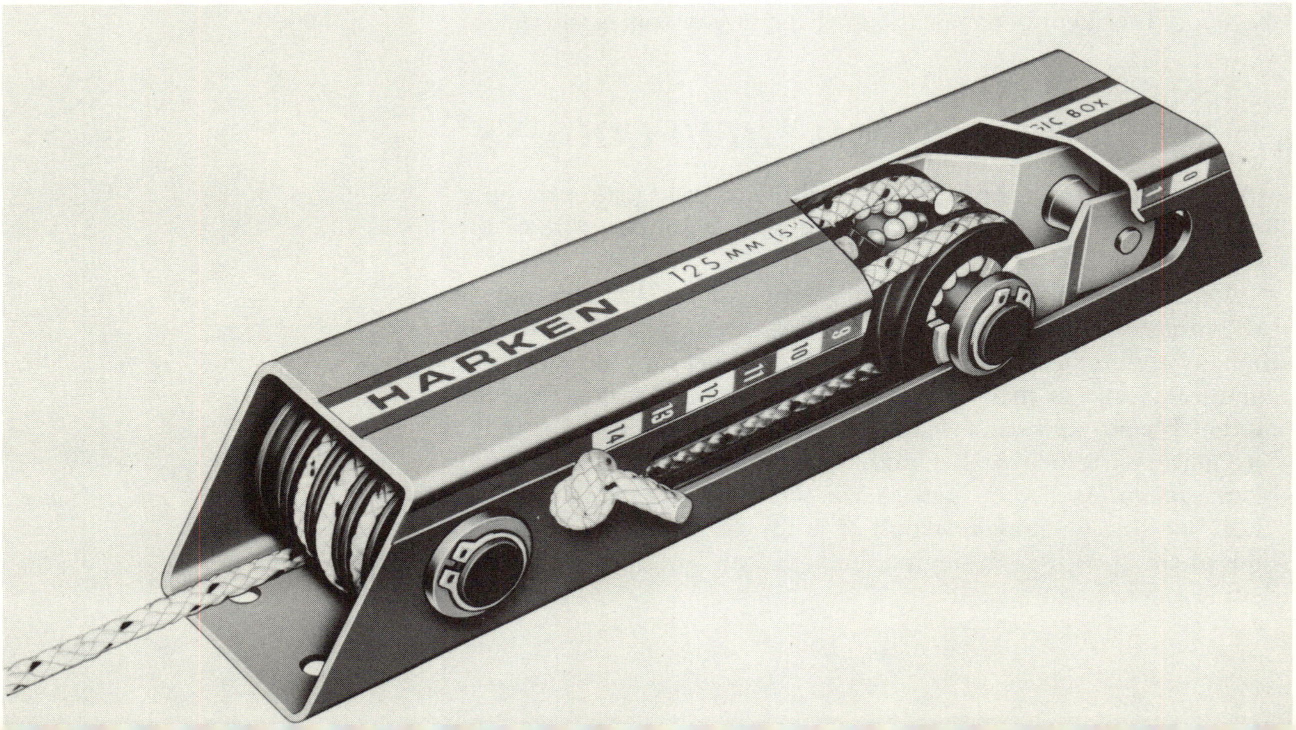

A six-part magic box is 32 millimeters square (narrower than 35 mm camera film, only 1 1/4 inches). The whole thing is less than nine inches long. Fastened to the deck, the mast, or the boom, it provides a 300-pound working load with steel ball bearings and twice that with Duratron bearings.

A larger box, which might be used for vangs on a small keel boat, is 15 inches long. It has a 1,200-pound working load, and, with an exterior double purchase, gives a 16:1 advantage.

One set of sheaves is fixed at the end of the box (three or four sheaves). The other set rides in slots in the box, with a common axle that has a becket. A hook or a line can be fastened to the becket. You just pull on the light line at the back of the box and marvel at a low-friction system.

HYDRAULIC RIGGING

For both racing and cruising boats, the positive control of hydraulic systems is now being used to good effect. Where the control is for a high load but to be applied over a short distance, hydraulics are effective. A winch is more effective when working with long lengths of line.

Racing hydraulics first began to be used for control of sail shape; backstay adjusters and vang adjusters are increasingly accepted on racing boats, especially since the higher speed pumps were introduced.

The Navtech hydraulic vang not only allows you to flatten a sail, but it can add draft by lifting the boom in light airs. A topping lift, with its windage, is no longer needed; the hydraulic vang holds up the boom and the furled mainsail.

Flattening reefs, hydraulically controlled, are not only powerful but sensitive to fine tuning.

Main-sheet fine tuning, main and jib Cunningham adjustments, and other applications are also being made.

The cruising sailers are adding centerboard control with hydraulics, as well as some of the racing applications. A backstay adjuster makes roller jib reefing easier, by keeping the headstay straight.

Hydraulic controls have the advantage that you are dealing with an easily measured force: pressure. Gauges can be noted and the rigging set to a previous marking to duplicate sail control, for example.

ROPE FOR HALYARDS

Wire rope, when used for halyards, is formatted in a 7 x 19 configuration, or sometimes in 6 x 37, for maximum flexibility. Reel winches, racers complain, are a slow way to get a sail up. With rope tails, making the wire-to-rope splices can be a problem, although not for the best rigging shops. Eventually, the improvements in low-stretch and prestretched rope satisfied the racing sailors. Some of them know that a difference of .05 percent stretch is significant.

Double-braid rope, with a Kevlar core and a polyester prestretched cover, is one super-tech answer, requiring only money. Even newer is Samson's XLS-900, with a polyester cover and a core of Spectra-900.

For most sailing, including plenty of successful racing and cruising, double-braid halyards are the most popular. The all-rope halyards have to withstand small flexing, under great stress, at the masthead. The ideal ratio of the sheave diameter to the rope diameter for polyester is probably 8:1. For combinations containing the stronger but less flexible Kevlar, 10:1 and 12:1 are recommended.

The width of the grooves in the sheave should be 10 percent greater than the rope diameter. Using sheaves intended for wire rope will pinch the fibers and result in more rapid abrasion. However, a rigging shop can "dress down" an old wire rope sheave.

"The load on a halyard," say the Samson Cordage people, "does not normally come near to reaching the breaking strength of the rope. The possible exceptions are spinnaker and reacher halyards, which are sometimes subject to shock loading." However, higher strengths result in a longer working life and less stretch.

Note: "Shock loadings can cause any synthetic fiber rope to become brittle and lose strength."

The permanent elongation in a halyard can be removed when it is first put in service, by heavy loading. There will always be some elastic elongation, and this is another reason for using the stronger line.

Two configurations of wire rope used on boats: 7 × 19 is flexible, makes good halyards. Stays are made of 1 × 19.

Halyard Size Guidelines

WIRE SIZE SS – 7 × 19 DIA.	TENSILE STRENGTH LBS.	ROPE SIZE DIA.	TENSILE STRENGTH LBS.	USE (TYPE OF BOAT)
⅛″	1,760	¼″	2,200	Small One-Design
5⁄32″	2,400	5⁄16″	3,300	Medium One-Design
3⁄16″	3,600	⅜″	4,400	Cruising to 32′
7⁄32″	5,000	7⁄16″	5,800	Cruising to 40′
¼″	6,400	½″	8,300	Larger, to 55′
5⁄16″	9,000	9⁄16″	11,000	Offshore, over 55′
⅜″	12,000	⅝″	13,600	Spin. halyards & guys
¾″	19,000	⅞″	28,200	Large offshore boats: halyards, sheets, guys

The buntline hitch doesn't hold until the second turn is taken, but it is snug, secure, and strong. This old hitch is a modern rigging trick of experts.

TERMINATIONS

The strongest way to secure a halyard to a headboard or a snap shackle is with an eye splice, secured and whipped at the throat. The strain on the splice is considerable.

There are several advantages to using a knot, especially for spinnaker and reacher halyards. The knot will act as a stopper, preventing an eye from getting wedged in the throat of the block. The halyard can be turned end for end with a minimum of trouble.

The ideal knot is an old one, the buntline hitch, revived for American sailors by the noted sailor and naval architect Rod Stephens, Jr.

This knot takes up on itself, in a manner of speaking, so the halyard can be drawn so tight that the sail gets its maximum height. Because the knot acts as a stopper it won't get jammed in the throat of the block. The story of its rediscovery for modern yachting is told by Stephens in the introduction to the Glossary.

One other rope terminal is favored by some: a British Gibb fitting that compresses the end of the line, like a swageless fitting on wire rope. You cannot inspect it; when someone develops a transparent, strong plastic for the compression ring, he may have the ultimate terminal.

As headsails get bigger, reaching spinnakers grow in size, and sailors get so "courageous" that they carry sail until the boats are in danger of being overpowered, even jib sheets can break, al-

Snugged up, it is good for a shackle on a jib sheet (to get the clew close to the track) or on a halyard: It won't jam in the throat of a block.

though for most sailors the comfortable-to-the-hand approach to choosing rope size is more than adequate.

Up to 20 percent of the breaking strength of the line is considered to be the normal working load for double-braided synthetic rope. It is only 11 percent for three-strand rope. When the size of a sheet is increased, there is an advantage in relation to reduced stretch.

One rule of thumb says the load on the jib sheet will be four pounds for each square foot of sail area.

Here is an example, provided by Samson Cordage:

Head Sail Area = 300 sq. ft.
Jib sheet load = 1,200 lbs. (estimate)
Line size = 3/8″ Yacht Braid
Breaking strength: 4,950 lbs.
1,200 lbs. load is 24% of breaking strength
Elastic stretch at 24% = 2.5%

If the line size for the sheet is increased to 7/16″, the breaking strength will be 6,600 lbs. The jib load, at 1,200 lbs., is now 18 percent of the breaking strength, giving a larger margin of safety. The elastic stretch is reduced to 2.1 percent.

Textures of the rope are one of the other important considerations. Woolly rope grips the drums of winches more readily. It is easy on the hands. The woolly textures of some polyester ropes used for sheets are built in by using a "spun" fiber to begin with,

A variety of types of rope, eye splices, special end splices, and terminal fittings is shown here. The tool shown is the Fid-O McGrew splicing fid.

even though this kind of fiber is neither as strong nor as free from stretch. The smooth ropes will fuzz in time. The fuzziness does not weaken the rope; it protects it.

WRINKLES

Whip the ends of all lines.

After heavy winching (as in tacking), counterrotate the line to remove any spiral set.

To clean lines, use conventional laundry detergents in a home washing machine. Put the rope inside a mesh bag or a pillow case to prevent tangling.

The technical basics of rigging sailboats can be acquired by taking a course in naval architecture. You may not want to become a competitor of the established firms, of course, but to gain familiarity with the working loads, the standards, and the available mechanical solutions. More than one top racing and cruising sailor has added to his expertise by correspondence. Write to the Westlawn School of Yacht Design, Department D, 733 Summer Street, Stamford, CT 06904.

Color coding for the running rigging is desirable on a boat with a multitude of lines. A suggested standard from Gale Foster is:
Main sheet, main halyard: white.
Jib and genoa, sheets and halyard—blue.
Spinnaker—sheets and halyard: red.
Topping lifts: green.
Vangs and travelers: orange.

Jib hanks are another detail of ingenious improvement. One kind allows you to hoist a jib under another jib—with the old hanks releasing as the new ones go up through them.

The old way to get the halyard taut on boats with extremely simple rigging and no halyard winches may be almost forgotten in these days of electricity and hydraulics. The crew person raising the sail gets the halyard tight by putting his/her weight on it, then snubbing it around the cleat on the mast. Holding the line tight with one hand, the crew person "sweats" the long halyard by pulling it away from the mast . . . gaining a few inches. Then a quick pull on the snubbed end captures the gain. Repeat. Repeat. Cleat down. Captain Slocum used a block-and-tackle.

Use a stopper knot to keep from losing a halyard.

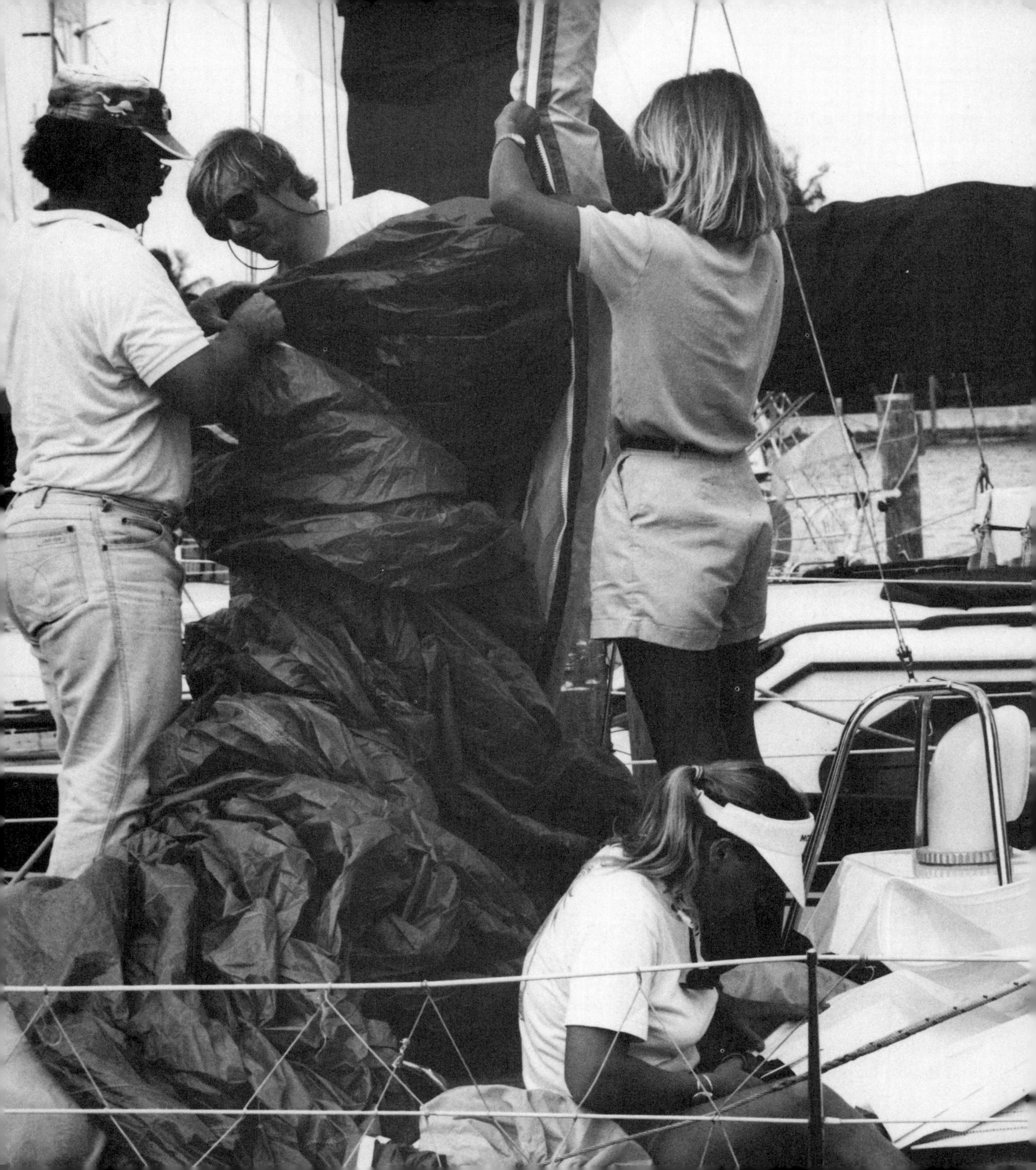

Chapter 11

Sail Handling/ Sheet Handling

The race started in light airs. Half an hour later, the breeze died. Along with forty other boats, we were like a scene from *The Rime of the Ancient Mariner:* "as idle as a painted ship upon a painted ocean."

Two crew members sat quietly, watching the water for the telltale streaks that indicate a rising wisp of wind, watching the other boats, and listening to the occasional slatting of gear. One of the crew was smoking a cigarette; the smoke spiraled straight up. It was turning into a sleepy afternoon.

Suddenly, my two crew members looked at each other, but said nothing. The cigarette smoke was slanting toward the east.

No words were spoken. One moved quietly below to get the spinnaker. He got it out of the bag and under the forward hatch. The other crew member was laying out the sheets and guys on deck, outside the shrouds. He moved the pole out of its chocks and into position.

So quietly did they work that no one aboard the yawls and sloops around us, some as close as a hundred yards, even opened his sleepy eyes. So quickly did they work that the entire spinnaker rigging was ready in a couple of minutes.

Then the blue streak on the water darkened. The cool feeling on the back of the neck confirmed it. In thirty seconds, our spinnaker was up and drawing as the breeze freshened, and *Merrywend III* was off and running before any other boat crews had finished yawning. It was as rewarding as winning a race—to see how a couple of borrowed 210 sailors handled the lines and the sail on a

◀ *Getting a spinnaker ready before a race . . .*

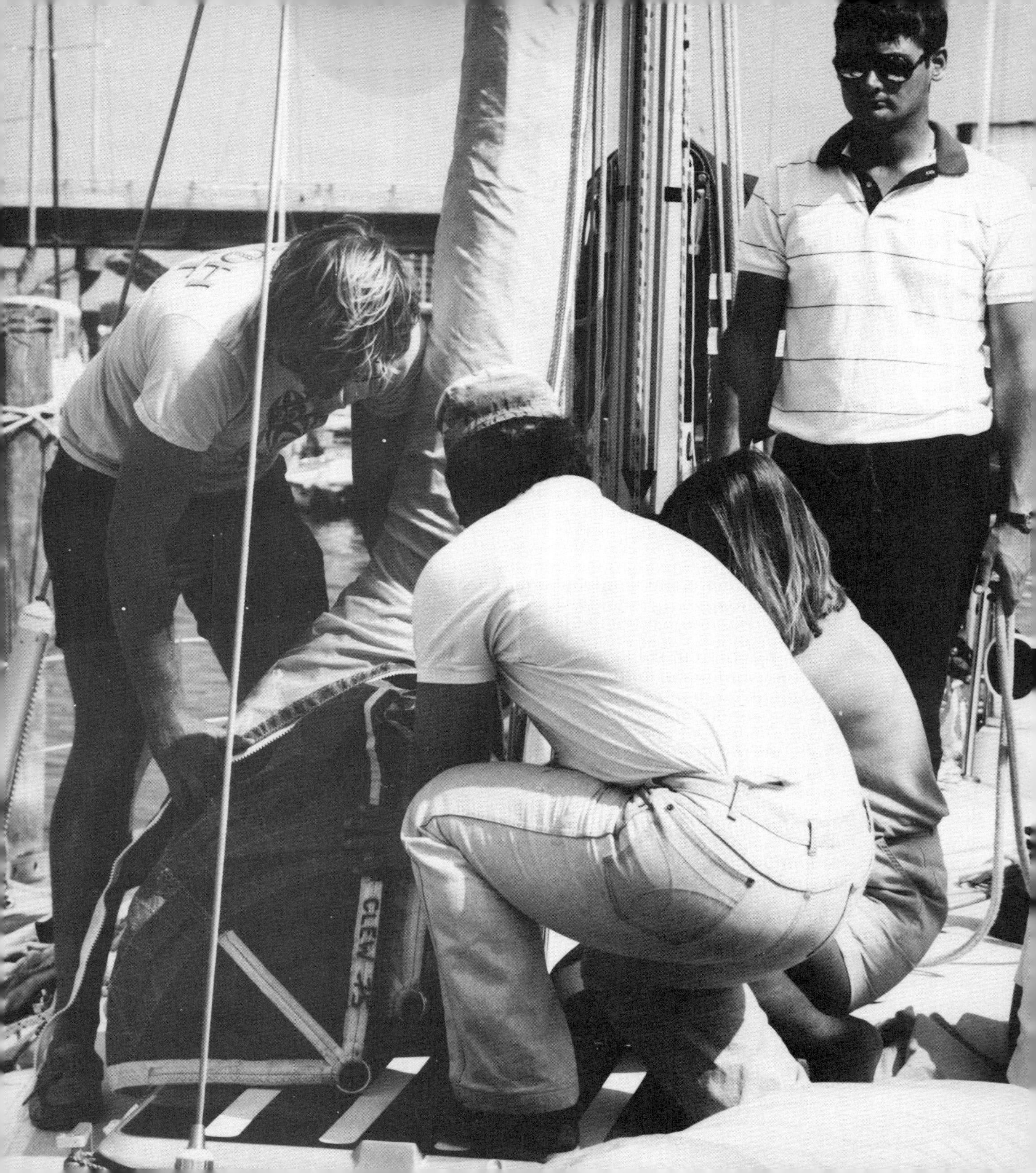
CLEW

thirty-three-foot cruiser/racer and got us moving ahead of the pack.

That's the essence of all sail handling and line handling for any boating situation, not just racing:

- ▲ Know where all the gear is and that it is all in perfect order.
- ▲ Set running rigging so it is exactly right, so there will be no hitches. Bend sails properly.
- ▲ Handle halyards, sheets and guys with smoothly practiced skills and the right timing.

Naturally, there is a lot of variation in the required sail-handling gear. A small day-sailer, a racing-cruising auxiliary, or a boat for long ocean passages with many spares will each have specialized equipment. The checklist that follows is a broad one, so not all items will apply to every situation. Some of these checkpoints are for once a year, some are for every day.

A CHECKLIST FOR SAILORS

- ▲ Is your propeller shaft properly marked—two daubs of white paint are needed, one on each side of the shaft—so that you will know when your propeller blades are perpendicular for minimum resistance while sailing?
- ▲ Are the genoa track holes numbered (perhaps every fifth number) so that blocks can be positioned at the same place every time? Some people use waterproof felt-tip marking pens, some apply sticky tape numbers from the store.
- ▲ Do all jib snap-hanks work freely? Usually, Teflon spray lubricant at the end and the beginning of the sailing season does it. But check.
- ▲ Are all sail slides smooth, so they don't stick?
- ▲ Are all shackles on halyards and sheets the correct size, and do they work smoothly?
- ▲ Are any rigging parts that require lubrication working smoothly? Reel halyard winches should not be lubricated—they depend on friction. Geared outhauls and roller reefing systems on the main boom, which may not be used all the time, should be checked for smooth operation at least once a month. Turnbuckles should be lubri-

◄

. . . is easy with a zipper and six willing hands.

cated lightly so they can be easily adjusted. Rod Stephens recommends anhydrous lanolin; others feel silicone spray is good.

- ▲ Do the sliders on genoa tracks and main-sheet travelers work smoothly all the time? Sometimes spray lubricant is needed, sometimes a small dent needs filing.
- ▲ Is there a stopper knot—a figure eight or Ashley stopper knot—in the end of every halyard?
- ▲ Is the mast straight? In most cases this means is the track straight, are all the track joints smooth? If you have problems getting the sails hoisted quickly, note whether it is a particular slide or a particular place on the track where most slides hang up. Resolve the problem!
- ▲ Do the sheaves of all blocks run freely? Spray lubricant should be used on masthead sheaves before stepping the mast, and all sheet blocks should be kept lubricated so the sheaves are easy spinners.
- ▲ Have you checked all wire rigging terminals for hairline cracks, for bending or distortion, and for alignment? If a terminal or a toggle is taking a twisting strain, you are heading for a rigging failure. At every point where a tang and a swage fitting come together, check for a fairlead, otherwise you are putting a bending load on the end of the fitting or the tang.
- ▲ Do you find any unusual stains or corrosion spots in your wire rigging—or any fittings? Inspect these carefully; they are the first warning of trouble.
- ▲ Are cotter pins bent just enough to keep them in (not bent clear over) and cut short (unless you use circular pins)? Are all pins new?
- ▲ Do you have your spares on board? Depending on the type of boat and the service, a spares list would include turnbuckles, toggles, shackles, cotter pins, sail stops, tape, whipping twine, lubricant, small lengths of line in various sizes, and probably an extra winch handle.
- ▲ Are all sail battens aboard?
- ▲ Are all halyards free of twists, not caught on spreaders, and running smoothly in their sheaves (including exit sheaves for internal halyards)?
- ▲ Are lifelines, pulpits, and stanchions secure and in proper working order? If there is a gate, the lifeline must be very taut when the pelican hook is fastened. Better yet, when at

sea, the pelican hook should be moused so it cannot open accidentally.

- ▲ Does the rigging look and feel right? You get used to the proper tension on headstay and backstay, the slightly looser feeling of shrouds, and should know immediately if something has changed. Every time you use a halyard, check it for chafe and inspect the eye splice or the knot that attaches it to its shackle.
- ▲ Especially if you use line tensioners, cam cleats, or jam cleats, are the sheets and halyards free of chafe?
- ▲ If you have a roller furling jib, is the take-up line free of chafe, kinks, or binding? Does the roller mechanism turn smoothly?

Checklists, perhaps, apply mostly to skippers and those crew members of racing boats assigned to pre-race inspections. Yet the expert sailors always keep a watchful eye. They notice a rigging part that may give trouble, they make a note of something that needs renewing before the season is out—even if they are not in competitive situations.

THE SAILING CREW'S DUTIES

Many sailboats, even forty-footers, are sailed single-handed. Two or three people can easily handle most auxiliaries. Racing crews are larger—yet the various tasks that must be accomplished are essentially the same.

Here, for starters and for smiles, is the crew of a twelve-meter:

The bowman's or foredeckman's primary job, of course, is to hank on the jibs, take them down, hook up the spinnakers, handle the lines and the pole in jibes, and to help coordinate the folding of sails when he isn't otherwise busy.

The man in the foxhole (forehatch) hands sails up and down, mans hydraulics like outhauls, and helps in the winch grinding when needed.

The mastman hoists the sails, helps get the sails on deck, and helps on winch grinding.

The grinders crank the winches.

The tailers pull—they tail on the jib sheets, spinnaker sheets, and the guys. They trim the sheets.

The main trimmer handles the main sheet.

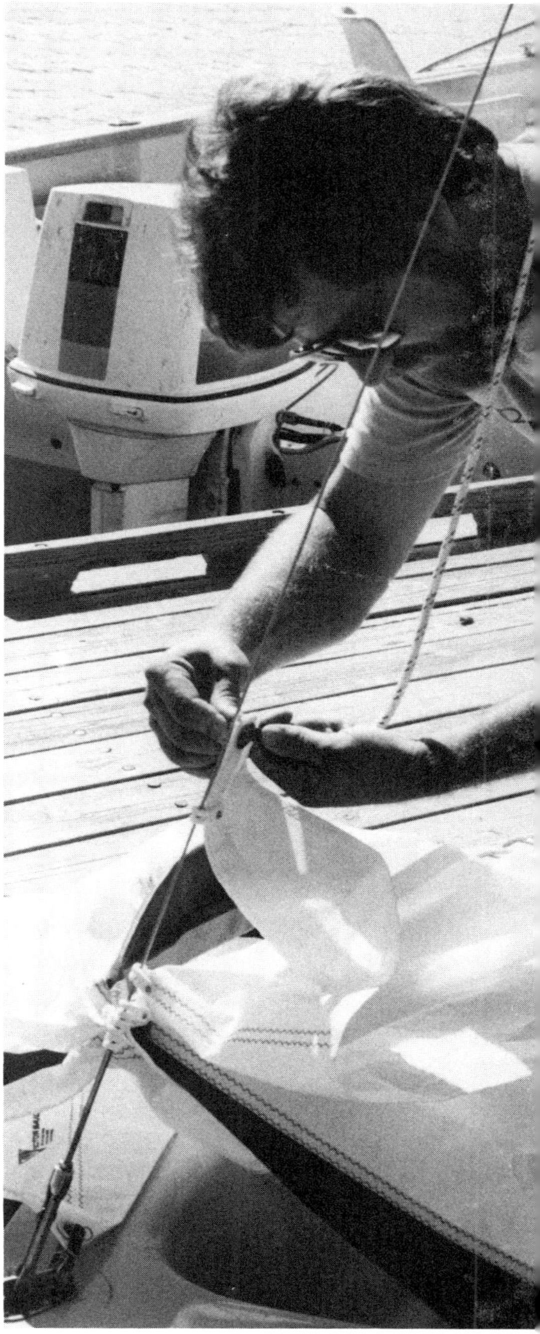

Hanking on the jib is awkward for a beginner, smooth for an old-timer.

The tactician watches the wind, the other boats, and the boat speed. He thinks ahead. The navigator tells the skipper where the boat is, how close it is to making a buoy on a given tack, and how it is doing in relation to wind speed. The skipper steers.

Except for the tactician, who generally is furthest aft, the crew in the list above are described in their positions from bow to stern. Your crew, no matter how large or small, does about the same chores, plus many boatkeeping tasks.

On even the smallest boat there are a few hundred details of sailing that have nothing to do with the theory or principles, the strategy or tactics of racing, or decisions about what kind of rigging or gear is needed. Here are some reminders of the highlights of a sailboat's crew duties (some of which may be handled by the skipper), presented approximately or in a general way from the bow aft and from the start of an afternoon's sail to the end.

On a small boat, the sails may not even be bent—they'll be in the bag. A typical small cruising sailboat will have the main already on the boom, except on the first day of the season. So we'll start with the first day of the season, with the sails in their bags.

If the sails were put into the bag properly, the right corners are at hand. In any case, a typical mainsail is put on the boom by starting with the clew, at the mast, and sliding each slide into the track and toward the end of the boom. When they're all on (and none has been inadvertently put on with a twist) and the sail is stretched along the boom, two attachments remain to be done.

First, the tack (the bottom, forward corner, of course). The fitting is opened by removing the pin, the cringle slides into place, the pin is replaced and locked, usually with a twist. Then the same procedure is repeated at the clew, the outboard end. Usually, the outhaul needs to be slacked to make it easy, so it has to be taken up again. On a small boat the outhaul may be only a line through a fairlead or a small cheek block. On larger boats it may be a worm gear and a crank or an internal wire outhaul on a block.

The next job is similar: getting the luff of the sail onto its track. There may be slides on a track, slides in a groove, or a luff rope in a groove. There may be a loader. Again, you start with the head of the sail, naturally. When all the slides are in place, you tighten whatever gizmo is in use to hold them in place: a thumb screw and a special slide at the bottom, a latch on the track (or, on a plain vanilla boat, a piece of line around the mast).

The halyard shackle is attached to the headboard *after* you check that the halyard is free all the way aloft.

Now come the battens. In general practice, there are four, and they are usually arranged so that two short ones go top and bottom, fitting into their pockets precisely. The two long battens get the middle pockets. On virtually any modern sail you have a piece of internal elastic to keep the batten tight and a special slanting pocket to keep it in when the sail slats, as it will sometimes. On some old-timers, you may find a batten pocket with twine ties at the end of the batten pockets; these are also found on some headsails. Here's where you need a correct knot. A square knot, sooner or later, will whip itself undone and you'll see the batten fly into the water. But a "batten knot," a reverse surgeon's knot, which is just as easy to tie, stays in place.

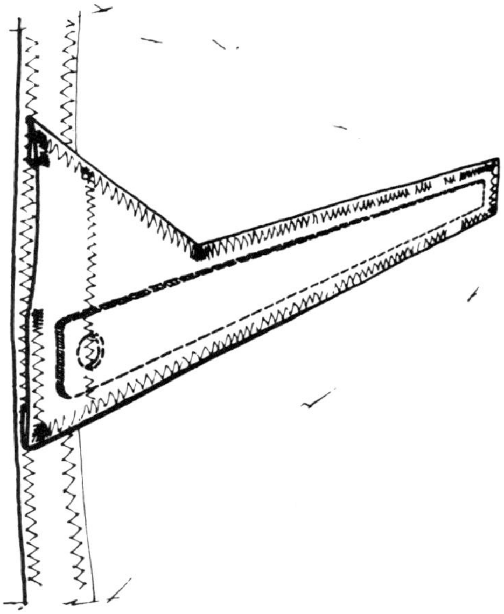

A batten pocket is usually cleverly made to position the batten and prevent its loss.

When attaching a jib to the headstay, especially if the wind is really blowing, keep the jib in its bag until it is attached; this prevents the wind taking charge. Start with the tack, the lowest corner, and make sure the shackle isn't twisted or binding. Then put on each hank, starting from the bottom with the kind that snaps on the stay, and from the top with the type that slides into a groove.

Take special care that no jib hank is twisted and upside down on the stay. If it is, it will give so much trouble when the jib is hoisted that you will remember it all your life and never make that mistake again.

Before attaching the halyard shackle to the headboard, look aloft and make sure the halyard is free—not caught on a spreader and running freely on the sheave.

You may not be planning to hoist the jib immediately. If you unbag it and it's ready to hoist, fasten it with a sailstop or two, a piece of light line tied around it, or perhaps a shock cord holddown that is already in place across the foredeck.

Often the jib sheets are already attached to the clew. There are several ways to do this. On an ocean racer that will be sailed under maximum stress conditions, stainless steel shackles will likely be used. On most boats these clatter against the mast and rigging every time you come about. They sometimes hit people's ears. Some people splice the sheets to the clew. This works smoothly, but makes it more difficult to change or replace a sheet. There are bowlines, lark's heads, and lark's heads reinforced with servings as other ways to attach the sheets.

Make sure the sheets are properly attached, then, and in place through their fairleads or blocks on each side. A working jib sheets inside the shrouds. A genoa jib sheets outside. The genoa snatch blocks should already have been put on their proper place on the

Gary Jobson (world class sailor) starts hoisting the jib on a small sloop.

track—according to the number that works for the kind of sailing you'll be doing.

When the jib is to be hoisted (and it is an old-fashioned idea that the jib is *never* hoisted until after the mainsail is up; do it the skipper's way, he should know), check that the other half of the halyard—the part from the block or sheave down—is free. As with any sail, hoist smartly, keeping one eye on the jib hanks as the sail goes up the forestay, lest there be a glitsch. Keep the other eye on the clew and the sheets, as the crew member in the cockpit gets the sheet in, to make sure nothing is caught on a ventilator or the projecting end of a carelessly chocked boathood. We'll come to belaying the halyard in a moment.

Getting the mainsail up, which usually does come first, requires one or two other eyes to be peeled. If the boat is heading directly into the wind, the main sheet may require no attention other than slacking it a trifle from its "in port" tautness. But there are variations. If the boat is under power and in a harbor with no seas running, it will be easy to keep her headed into the wind, so it will be just as easy to get the main hoisted in a hurry. But sometimes you find you are hoisting the main and starting to sail at the same time. The pressure on the sail keeps it from going up. What next? The helmsman lets her fall off a bit and get moving, then heads up again as you finish getting the halyard tight. Or you are at a mooring and although you try to hoist the main while the boat is headed into the wind, something interferes—a current keeps the boat at a small angle, for example. No problem. Just wait a minute, and as she sails at her mooring, she will luff up on her own and once again you get the mainsail all the way up.

It is often situations like the one described—the boat at her mooring riding to the current and a light breeze blowing—that make it desirable to get the jib up first. Then your skipper says, "Drop the mooring," and the boat sails off on an easy reach until there is room and headway enough to luff up head to wind and hoist the mainsail.

There you are standing at the mast, with the sail up, the halyard in your hands, and it's time to get it tight.

Here is where the next step depends on the type and size of boat. If the boat has a reel halyard for the main, and some still do, you have already gotten the halyard tight by cranking hard on the winch handle. A standard winch works with rope on it—the whole halyard may be rope, or it may be a wire halyard with a rope tail, made by a rope-to-wire splice.

Once the halyard has been hauled up hand over hand, the quickest way, you put a couple of turns of the line on the winch, put in the handle, and take a few turns with one hand while taking a strain on the tail with the other. When all is tight, you belay the tail to the correct cleat, which should be just below the winch, coil up the line and hang it, and take the winch handle out to drop into its nearby pocket or stowage place in a handy deck box.

A smaller and simpler rig may require less use of winches, but it won't get the halyard quite as tight. You get your weight on the halyard.

Proper stowage of halyards keeps them ready for use.

HANDLING THE MAIN SHEET

Because the main sheet on any size boat above a sailing dinghy is a tackle to give you extra power, you will soon find that letting out twelve inches of line may let the boom move only four inches, which may be the exact amount the skipper wants it eased. Even so, bringing in the main sheet or easing it should be done smoothly. In light air, jerking on a sheet whips the sails and slows the boat. In strong winds, you have to keep complete control and not let the sheet get away from you.

Some main sheets are rigged so that they have two ends for control—one on either side of the cockpit. Others have two lines coming together in the middle—control one, and you get "slow speed." Use both at once, and you can get five or six feet in much more quickly. Still, do it smoothly.

Besides controlling the sheet, and thus the boom and the sail, if you are the one in charge of it at any given time, you should keep the excess line neat. Usually, it is best to coil it loosely, ready to run out a bit. If you have been sailing hard on the wind for hours and it is time to turn and make a run, you had best overhaul the sheet to make sure it hasn't acquired a small tangle or two and will run smoothly when you let the boom out.

JIB SHEET WORK

The person on the jib sheets should have several senses, skills, and knacks and use them all simultaneously.

The boat is sailing closehauled. You round a buoy and are able to safely turn 30 degrees to starboard. The skipper starts to turn and says, "Ease the sheet a bit."

You get one hand on the sheet between the winch and the cleat, and the other starts taking turns off the cleat. If the wind is light, you can take all turns off and ease the sheet a few inches at a time with no trouble. If it's really blowing, you probably keep one turn around the cleat, even though there are two or three turns around the winch. If you know the boat is on its new course, you can make the decision, easing the sheet until the sail is drawing better. You feel the boat speed increase, and a quick glance tells you there's no flutter in the leach, no flutter in the luff—but almost. If the skipper wants to direct you, inches at a time, as he steers the boat with a similar sensitivity in the way he holds the tiller, that's his choice. If he wants the main eased too, as he probably will, the boat speed may pick up—but you may have to take the jib sheet in a few more inches—trimming is that sensitive.

The boat continues on the same course. You feel the wind changing, coming more on the quarter. Now you become the diplomat. "Shall I ease the sheets a bit more?" you ask.

READY ABOUT!

An hour later, it's time to tack. Timing skills, this time. The helmsman says, "Ready about!" You make sure the new sheet is in place, ready to hand. You get one hand on the sheet that's still in use, taking it almost off the cleat. You look to make sure the long coil isn't tangled—it will have to run free.

"Ready about!" The helmsman puts the tiller over, the boat starts to turn into the wind. Not yet! Wait until the jib has stopped drawing and is flapping as it reaches the centerline. Now cast off the sheet . . . and go to the opposite sheet.

Get it in fast, hand over hand. Take two turns around the winch, three if it's blowing, and start hauling while you get the winch handle into action. By the time the bow has swung over another 40 degrees, you should have the sheet just about right—knowing from experience how tight to get it. As the sail starts to draw, you check and adjust . . . probably using the winch handle, and a steady pull on the tail, to get it in a few more inches. You watch the sail and the course of the boat. When you're on course exactly, you trim . . . a little in, a little out, inches at a time, either relying on your knowledge of what the jib should look like when it's working at its best, or letting the skipper give a hint or two.

Can something go wrong? Well, you could have been sloppy

with the loose sheet and gotten an overriding turn on the winch. It's easy to do. You won't be the first. In light airs, it's easy to fix. In a breeze, you have a problem. The helmsman can probably luff up and take the strain off to help you get it straight, but it's as hard to get a riding turn out as anything you are likely to do on a sailboat. You can also get a riding turn because the winch is not installed at the proper angle, but even so, an ounce of prevention is worth forty pounds of hard hauling.

Wrong way! If you get too many turns on a winch, you can get an override that might take ten minutes to undo.

AN OLD TRICK THAT WORKS

What if it's really jammed? The best thing to do is to use a square-rigger trick: Put a stopper, a jigger, on the standing part, the part of the jib that's doing the work. Another rope is attached to the errant sheet, using a rolling hitch. A jigger is a small block-and-tackle, kept handy for emergencies. Often, a more direct way is this: Lead the stopper line through a block or two, to get the direction right, and then to a free winch to do the work. Haul it in until the strain is off the problem winch, unwind the lazy end, breathe a sigh of relief, and make a resolution about not getting overrides on the winch.

All in all, handling the jib sheet during the few seconds it takes to come about is one of the delicate arts of sailing. In a racing situation it's most likely a two-person job . . . one to throw off the old sheet, one to take in the new sheet, and then tail onto it while the first crew member switches sides and gets on the winch handle. Self-tailing winches speed things up, but they can get overrides too.

All it takes for perfect jib sheet handling is practice, analysis of all the motions, practice again, and perhaps watching experts do it (Don't ask them. Who can put into words the directions for playing a Stradivarius or hitting a slider out of the ballpark?).

Properly done (on a properly positioned winch) the jib sheet will never override.

DROPPING THE SAILS

Coming back to the home mooring, it's time to take the sails down. Assuming you have been sailing with a main and a jib, either one might be taken down first. Sometimes it is possible to get the main down and furled and come easing up to the mooring under the jib. More usually, the jib is dropped first, partly to get

A quick way to furl a mainsail, using shock cord instead of sail stops. Hooks on boom hold furling gear in place.

▶
The conventional way to secure the main sheet when the day's sail is over, coiled and hanging ready at the end of the boom

▶
The main halyard of a small and simple sloop is coiled and hung neatly (well, fairly neatly) under the cleat on the mast.

An older form of easy furling on a gaff-rigged boat, using a marling hitch to hold sail and spars in place

the foredeck clear, and either tied in a bundle and put in its bag while still on its stay or taken off, folded, and bagged.

Here's the drill: Get the coiled halyard off the cleat, make sure the bitter end is secured and that the coil will run free, check aloft and that you know how the sail will be gathered in. In a light breeze, the crew person at the halyard can smother the jib alone. If there's plenty of searoom and the helmsman is good, a smart way to get a headsail down is to run off before the wind and let it come down smooth and easy in the lee of the mainsail.

Preparation for dropping the mainsail, unless you have roller furling right on the mast and don't need to drop it at all, is simple. Get the sailstops ready, or if a shock cord system is used, get it in place, get the main sheet in, wait until the helmsman heads up and gives you a luff, and bring the sail down. A little practice teaches the whole team how to time it. If the teamwork is clicking, the helmsman can be sailing on the jib in a minute or two, while those

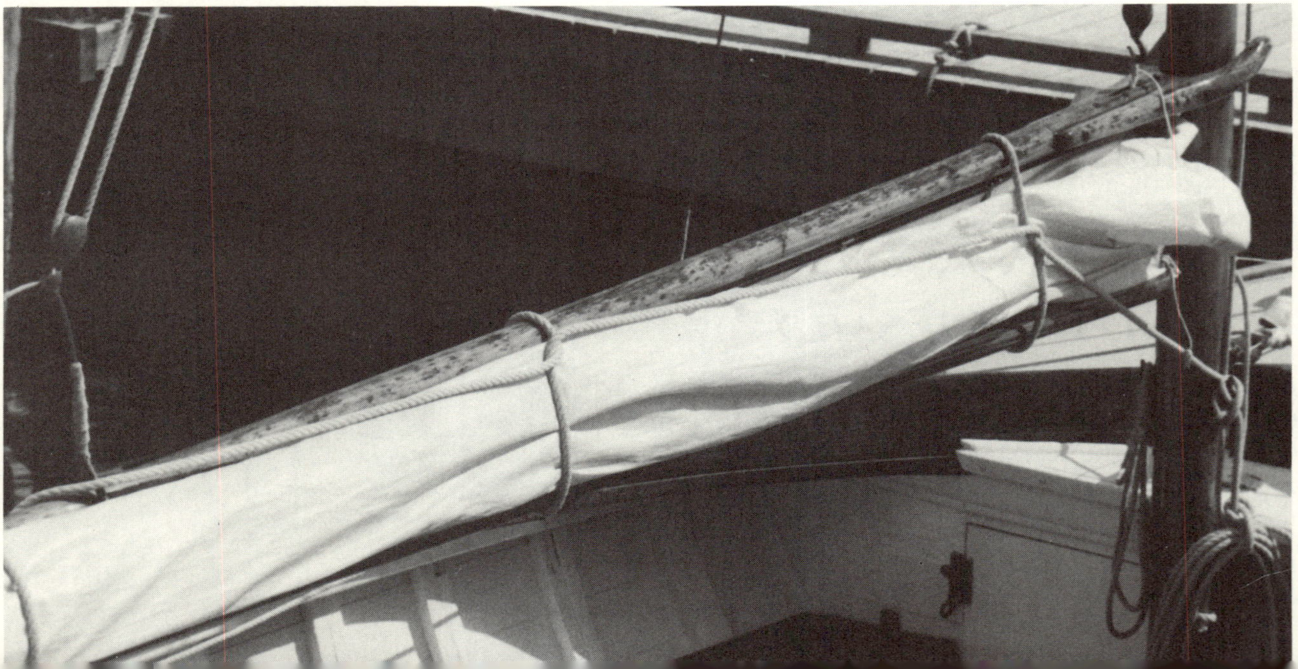

at the boom are still furling the sail and getting it snug in the stops. Or if the trip is ending under power, into the dock, the helmsman watches to make sure the mainsail furling is under control before turning, lest the wind catch the sail and upend the sail handlers.

Headsails are usually bagged. If they are folded first, they take up a third as much room. If room below is a problem, bagging a jib while it is still hanked to the headstay and leaving it secured on the foredeck is a standard cruising boat device.

SEND IN THE CLOWNS . . .

The following step-by-step procedure is not recommended, but it is sometimes seen. The crew drops the jib on the foredeck, then drops the mainsail on the cabin top. The dock lines are brought out; someone drops a coiled line on the deck near the bow cleat, but that can't be seen because the jib is on top of it. As the helmsman brings the boat into the dock, turning so the wind is abeam, the mainsail flaps, obscuring his vision. Meanwhile the foredeck person, ready to toss a dock line to the float, steps in the coiled dock line, while his helper is tripping over the loose boathook. The boat is docked without the wind taking the jib halfway up the forestay (as can happen), but since the wind is setting the boat onto the dock, a special scramble is necessary to find the fenders and the fender board.

SPINNAKER HANDLING CHECKLIST

More seriously: There is more than one way to rig a spinnaker, depending partly on the size of the boat. A racing boat that will jibe the spinnaker with the dip-pole method needs more lines and more crew. Here is an excellent checklist for spinnaker work, adapted from *The Nicro-Fico Spinnaker Booklet,* written by Roger Marshall, naval architect and author of the books *Designed to Win* and *Race to Win.*

HOISTING

▲ Do you have the correct spinnaker?
▲ Are sheets and guys led correctly?
▲ Are halyards clear? Check aloft.

- ▲ Foreguy cleated?
- ▲ Pole set at approximately the right height?

Procedure:

- ▲ Preset the pole.
- ▲ Raise the stopped spinnaker.
- ▲ Break out the sail by pulling on the sheet.
- ▲ Drop the jib.
- ▲ Trim the spinnaker.

JIBING

Basic checklist:

- ▲ Mainsail vang/preventer removed?
- ▲ Is the new guy/sheet led correctly?

End-for-end jibe checklist:

- ▲ Is the foreguy/topping lift ready to be eased away?

Procedure:

- ▲ Trim the mainsail in to the center line.
- ▲ Trip the pole off the sail, then off the mast.
- ▲ Pass the pole through the foretriangle.
- ▲ Hook end of pole onto the sail and then onto the mast.
- ▲ Jibe and ease the mainsail out.

Dip-pole jibe checklist:

- ▲ Is the inboard end of the pole at the right height?
- ▲ Is the inner forestay removed?
- ▲ Is a man ready on the topping lift?
- ▲ Is the new guy led forward?

Procedure:

- ▲ Bring mainsail in to the center line.
- ▲ Trip the pole off the sail.
- ▲ Lower the outboard end of the pole.
- ▲ Swing the end of the pole through the foretriangle as the bowman pulls in the foreguy.
- ▲ Connect the new guy.
- ▲ Top up the pole.
- ▲ Pull the new guy aft.
- ▲ Trim the sheet.
- ▲ Jibe and ease out the mainsail.

TAKING THE SPINNAKER DOWN

Checklist:

- ▲ Are the spinnaker halyard and the guy free to run?
- ▲ Is the jib ready to hoist?
- ▲ Are the jib halyard and sheet ready?

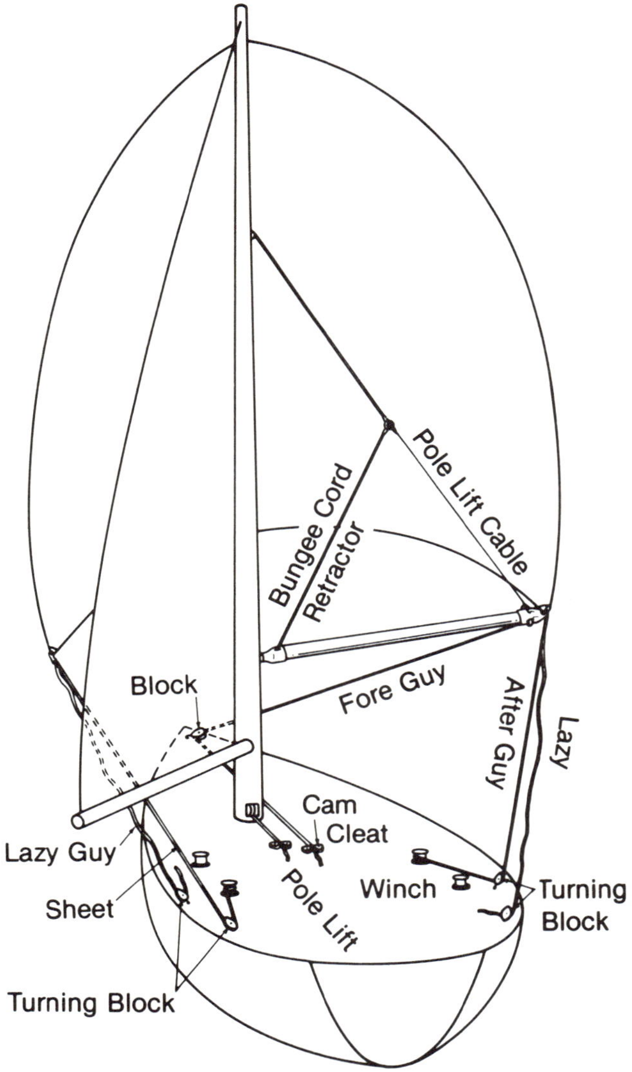

The setup for dip-pole jibing takes more lines and more crew, but is very fast for racing. (The Australians use the term brace *for the American* guy.*)*

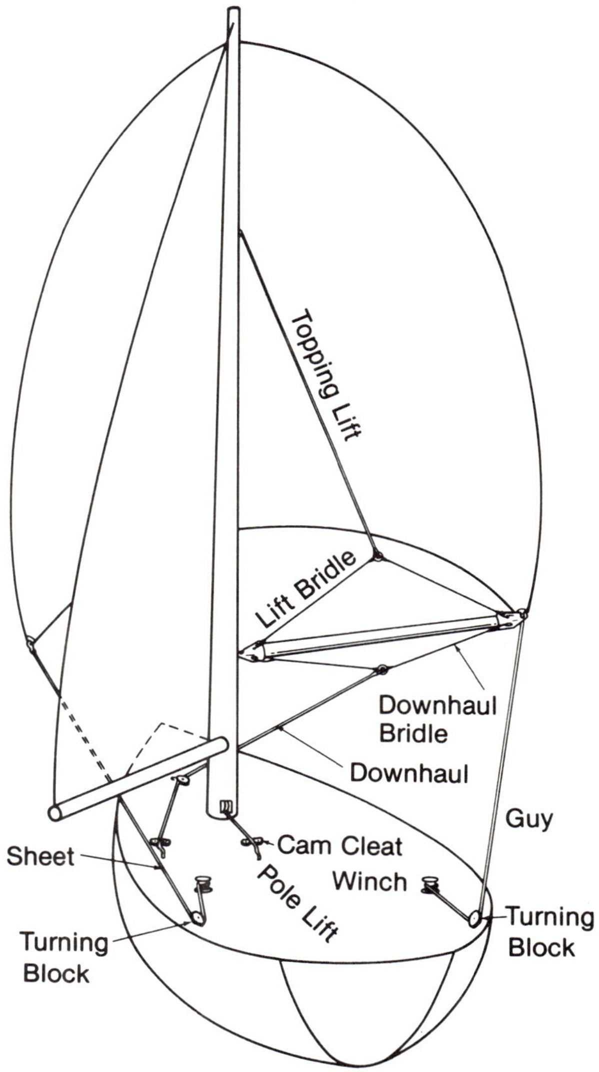

In the older, end-for-end jibe, the guy becomes the sheet, the sheet becomes the guy. The pole comes off the mast fitting as the jibe is executed.

Foredeck takedown procedure:

- ▲ Hoist jib.
- ▲ Ease pole forward.
- ▲ Take short sheet to foredeck cleat or take downhaul line through forehatch.
- ▲ Trip the guy or let it run.
- ▲ Let off halyard and sheet.
- ▲ Pull in spinnaker and stuff down forehatch.

Middeck takedown procedure:

- ▲ Hoist jib.
- ▲ Ease pole forward.
- ▲ Take lazy guy or short sheet to middeck cleat.
- ▲ Either trip the guy or let it run.
- ▲ Let off spinnaker halyard.
- ▲ Gather spinnaker in lee of mainsail and stuff it below.
- ▲ Trim main and jib for new course.

Aft takedown procedure:

- ▲ As above, but wind the sheet into the quarter block rather than bringing the lazy guy forward, and then ease the halyard out slowly and take the sail in on the lee quarter.

WRINKLES

A table for jib sheet diameters

BOAT LENGTH	
20′	1/4″
25′	5/16″
30′	5/16″
35′	3/8″
40′	7/16″
45′	1/2″
50′	9/16″
55′	5/8″

These are minimums. A larger sheet often handles better.

A center vang, when jibing, keeps the boom from "skying," but in very strong winds it's best to ease the vang a bit before the jibe.

Gary Mull's Law: "If two pieces of running rigging cross, there will inevitably be a foul-up."

◄

A simple sloop rig, easily handled by a small crew under all conditions, uses a big reaching jib, without a pole. This sail was made by Herb Hild.

DUTY CYCLE
SPEE-DEE
PATENTED
10WR

Chapter 12

The Ditty Bag/ Tools

Sailors have always been carrying knives, for working tools and as weapons.

A lot depends on the kind of cruise, the work that may need to be done—but even if you are only going across the harbor, the bare minimum tool aboard a boat is a pocket knife. One of many useful versions is the electrician's knife with an extra blade that is a screwdriver; special knives for boats abound.

The rigging knife, with a lanyard attached, is easily kept in the trouser pocket or in a belt case, but when it is in use, the lanyard, attached to the owner's belt, keeps it from going overboard. The rigging knife has a few variations. One type has a steel fid as the extra blade plus the knife's own shackle that can be used to turn the pin in a rigging shackle. Another version is stainless steel, including the handle and shackle. Outdoorsmen who know knives will tell you that stainless steel blades are hard to sharpen. Other versions of what used to be called clasp knives are often used, of course—even the Swiss Army Knife, with its bevy of mini-tools is favored by some, since there is no Swiss Navy Knife.

The sheath knife, typically carried on the belt in the middle of the back, was once very useful, but in these days of peaceful sailing it isn't needed for self-defense. Often the sheath also holds a separate fid, which should surely be on a lanyard.

In addition to these on-the-person tools, many boatmen like to have a couple of tools in their ditty bag: that electrician's knife, which comes in handy for many small repair jobs, for example.

A sailmaker's or rigger's palm is one of the most useful tools in a personal kit.

◀
The on-board tools for a typical cruising boat include fids, beeswax, a palm, Vise-Grip pliers, rigging knife, and a hot knife.

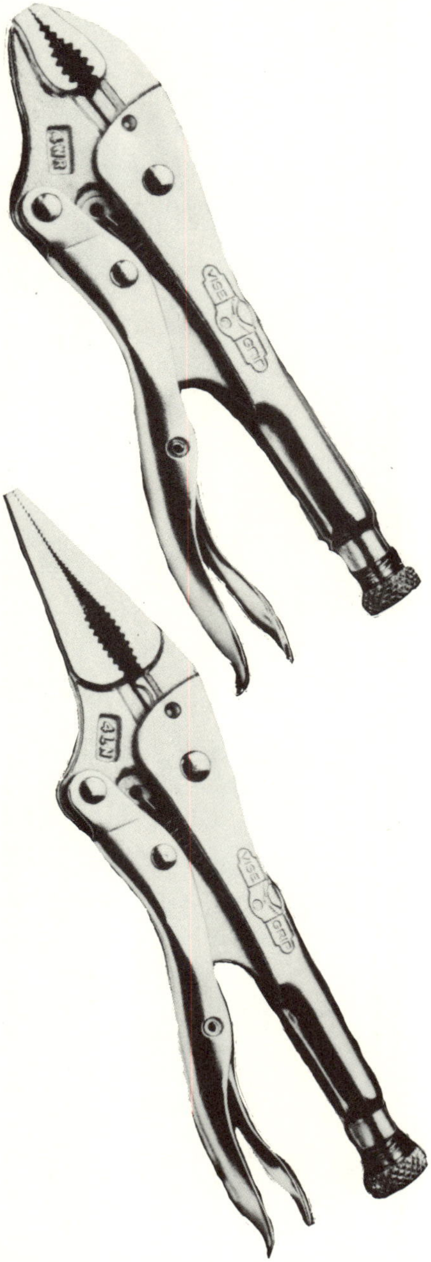

One kind of locking pliers has been enhanced into a clamp. Even the smaller Vise-Grips can substitute for a vise.

Sailmaker's needles, kept in a small bottle or vial, are good for rope work as well as mending sails, awnings, seat cushions, and blue jeans.

A Myers awl is another small tool that finds many uses. For decades one of these little gems cost only a dollar. Nowadays, even by other brand names and with higher prices, it is still a surprisingly good bargain. Essentially, it's a needle with the eye in the point and a handle at the other end and through which sail twine runs, making the Myers a small hand sewing machine with its own pusher so the needle can be worked through canvas and rope. Inside the handle there is room for extra thread and sometimes spare needles.

The ditty bag itself can be any canvas or sailcloth small bag with a drawstring around the throat or perhaps a zipper or Velcro closure. Many chandleries sell them—or you can make one.

In that ditty bag there should be some other items:

Beeswax for waxing **sail twine,** a spool or hank of twine for whipping, perhaps some **marline.** One useful extra is "the office size" of dental floss, if your dentist is the understanding and giving kind. Dental floss, super-strong nylon, is good for whippings on small lines.

A candle. Yes, a candle. Its wax is an acceptable substitute for beeswax when it comes to waxing twine, and its flame is just right for heat-sealing the furry ends of a nylon splice when you don't have an electric hot knife.

A sharpening stone, probably Carborundum, preferably with a rough (coarse) side and a smooth (fine) side, will keep the rigging knife sharp.

A file, also for sharpening knives and other tools, is sometimes needed for small repairs to metal rigging parts.

Fids, traditionally of wood, but now often made of hollow aluminum and of tough, hard plastic, are good for splicing. One of the most useful personal tools of all is Jim McGrew's Fid-O, a hollow fid, for ordinary and special splicing. James McGrew, the inventor and maker, also provides excellent splicing instructions.

Marlinespikes are metal, often steel or stainless steel.

Pliers. Decades ago, Carleton Mitchell gave the author a small pair of pliers with an adjustable wrench as part of one handle. This has proven to be one of those tools with many uses, although there are many varieties. If you must settle for one pair, settle for needle nose pliers . . . probably Vise-Grips. Pliers come in a variety of shapes, and a larger tool box might include several.

The boat's own bosun's locker is supposed to contain some of the extras, but a typical personal ditty bag will often accumulate a few small pieces of sailcloth, a small roll of sail repair tape, and perhaps some Band-Aids for your friends to borrow.

A few additional notes about the tools mentioned: The **palm** is the sailor's equivalent of a thimble, and with it you can push large needles through heavy sailcloth. There are two kinds—those for sailmakers and those for riggers or ropeworkers. The difference is in the size and number of the indentations. Sailmaking needles are finer; roper's needles are larger and fewer. If you find a store with a choice, try one on your hand. (Palms come right-handed and left-handed, unlike shoreside thimbles.) Even with the correct size, some adjusting may be necessary. Neatsfoot oil will help soften the leather and make the palm conform to the hand.

The needles for sail and rope work come in a choice of sizes, of course. Most are three-sided for pushing through canvas and between or through the strands of rope. Since the kind of work to be done may range from making a pretty whipping on a rope's end to repairing a cockpit cushion seam, as well as the more conventional work on sails and awnings, a good assortment of needles, kept safely in Vaseline inside a small bottle or box, is good to have.

Sailmakers' needles take their sizes from standard wire sizes. The largest are #4, the smallest are #18. The sizes are whole sizes except for #14½, which happens to be one of the most useful.

Your ditty bag is the first-aid kit for the boat.

TOOLS FOR THE BOSUN'S LOCKER

The small cruising boat may not have a workshop, but at least a miniature workbench is worth rigging. A drawing board, or a meat and salad cutting board, can be fitted with a small vise, which will make it useful for engine room work, taking to the cockpit for work on rigging, or for rainy day hours in the cabin. The whole "workbench" can be stowed in a canvas bag or a locker when not in use.

Most cruising boats require a toolbox or tool locker. In addition to those for plumbing and engine work, a few of the rigging tools mentioned above should always be aboard, as well as some that are larger than mere personal tools. Several **Vise-Grip** pliers, in several sizes and with several kinds of jaws, including those needle-nose pliers, are exceedingly useful.

Screwdrivers, including short, medium, and long in several blade sizes and types, and particularly including those for Phillips-head screws, are worth choosing with care. **Allen** wrenches, in several sizes, are required for some equipment.

Silicone, Teflon, light oil, and other lubricants, some in spray cans, are needed now and then, although some rigging items can be overlubricated.

A grommet punch and die will come in handy, for repairing or altering an awning or hatch cover. These come in three sizes: 1/4-inch, 5/16-inch, and 3/8-inch. A typical kit also has the brass grommets with it. One is just as likely to find this tool in a small town hardware store as in a chandlery.

With the grommet tools, you need a hammer and a block of wood, to put under the cloth when you make a hole. Sailmakers use a mallet and a small block with the end grain up. A small piece of 2 x 4 or 2 x 6 will also do.

Those who go on long cruises, away from the helpful arms of rigging shops and chandleries, add other tools and supplies to the on-board workbench.

Hacksaw blades

Files

Scotch-brite is often thought of as a good thing for scrubbing pots. However, aboard a boat it: (1) can be used to thoroughly clean stanchions, pulpits, anchors, dinghies, and tracks and other rigging components; (2) makes a good substitute for sandpaper in preparing wood for varnishing.

Vinyl cleaner and vinyl resurfacers are excellent examples of how the inventiveness of man, including his discovery of the spray can and the plastic tube, have made boating easier.

Stove alcohol on sponge, rag, or paper towel is a great cleaner for plastic-covered lifelines.

Wire-cutters, and **compound lever bolt-cutters** are on board most long-range cruising boats.

A hand-swaging press, although no substitute for a hydraulic press, is often carried.

An **electric rope cutter, or hot knife,** when 120-volt electricity is available, is a wonderful tool to have. If you already have an electric soldering iron, get one of the special blades to make it into a rope-cutter.

Ounces of Prevention (in aerosol cans) will clean, remove surface rust, waterproof, and lubricate. Names to look for include WD-40, CRC, LPS, as well as Teflon and silicone sprays and some packaged by rigging manufacturers. On a sticky cabin drawer you can really demonstrate the chemical miracle of the polymer types of lubricant.

A bag of rigging spares: toggles, turnbuckles, cotter pins, circular cotter pins, stainless steel wire, jib hanks, shackles, and perhaps one single and one double block.

THE IDEAL WORKBENCH

The tools for a home workbench for working on rigging and sails are a little more elaborate; the techniques of using them, of course, are pretty much the same. An ideal work place for a boat owner might contain, in addition to the tools already mentioned:

A sailmaker's bench

A sailmaker's hook, almost as good as a third hand

A vise and general workbench or sturdy table

Rope cutter (electric soldering iron with special blade)

Vise-Grip pliers and **C-Clamps**

Prosnips, for cutting sheet metal

Hacksaw blades (a full hacksaw frame is seldom needed)

Lubricants: Teflon and silicone sprays, light oil in both spray cans and conventional oil cans, and waterproof grease, such as **Lubriplate**

Sailmaker's needles in a larger assortment

Small stuff: sail twine, whipping tape, marline, cod line, and electrician tape

Extras: Whip-End dip, rope thimbles, shackles, cotter pins, and cotter rings

Good light above the workspace. Reflector flood or spot bulbs are easily installed.

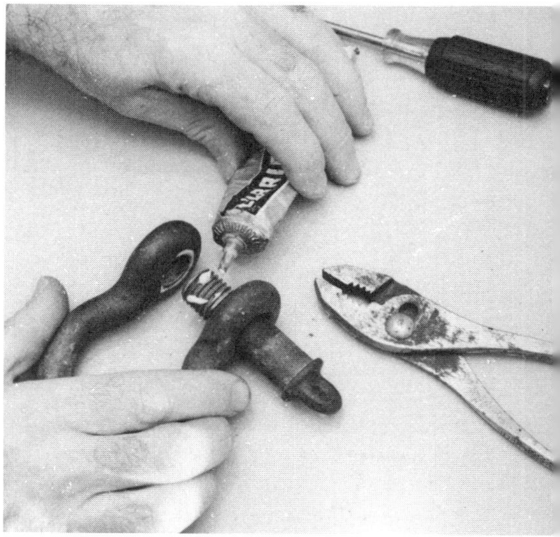

Shackles that will someday require opening should be prelubricated. Unless easily inspectable, wire the pins.

A variety of "small stuff" is handy for whippings, servings, and general repairs.

NOTES ABOUT TOOLS ABOARD AND AT HOME

Not everyone will want to have a sailmaker's bench at home, of course, but it is good to know that these benches also make attractive coffee tables.

Needles, especially, tend to rust in the damp atmosphere of a boat. Keeping them in a tightly stoppered bottle and perhaps adding some oil or Vaseline prevents this.

An awl, pricker, or sharp fid (and perhaps the ice-pick) should

A sailmaker's or rigger's palm is used like a thimble. With sailmaker's needles and twine it is used for making whippings.

have its sharp end protected by a cork. This is partly to keep the point sharp and partly to protect the people.

On-board work on rigging involves both preventive maintenance and repairs, and now and then just making something that is needed. For the long-cruise boatman these are projects involving the available spares, materials, and tools. For the ordinary boat owner the same things can be done in the fitting-out period.

The pleasure of doing these projects easily and the safety factor of being sure they are done well make it worthwhile to pick only top-quality tools. Those that are made of good steel last longer, hold an edge better, and do not break under stress.

There are specialized tools and fittings that the average person may never need but might like to know about. Some of them, invaluable on a long cruise away from ports and workshops, are hard to find, but well worth the trouble.

A serving mallet is an old-time professional tool used by riggers when worming and serving wire splices. It is basically a way to get leverage and thus really tighten a serving. You can improvise one from a hammer.

Temporary seizings and emergency repairs can be made with wire locks. You'll see these used as permanent fittings on tents, children's swings, or farm equipment. They work, but they are hardly smooth looking. Even shock cord now has its own end fittings.

SOURCES OF TOOLS

Although most tools and marine supplies are available if you look long enough, there are a number of sources for hard-to-find tools worth knowing about.

For a catalog of hard-to-find tools of every kind, write to Brookstone Company, 118 Brookstone Building, Peterborough, NH 03458.

Marine Development & Research Corp., Department W, 115 Church Street, Freeport, NY 11520, has a catalog of special marine supplies, from rigging tape to bilge cleaners.

Splicing tools and first-rate instructions can be obtained from Fid-O/McGrew Splicing Tool Co., 8120 Rio Linda Blvd., Elverto, CA 95626.

Samson Ocean Systems, 245 Winter Street, Waltham, MA 02154, has splicing kits for braided rope as well as excellent instruction booklets. These, and many kinds of rope, are obtainable at marine dealers.

Petersen Manufacturing Company, DeWitt, NE 68341, has interesting product literature on the many VISE-GRIP tools, including locking tools of various types, locking C-clamps, and Prosnips.

A sailmaker or marine dealer can get you a hot knife, palm and needles, and special types of twine and tape. (He probably gets them from Howe & Bainbridge, of Boston, Massachusetts, but they do not deal directly with the consumer.)

BOAT/US, a membership organization known more formally as the Boat Owners Association of the United States, is a good source of many tools and supplies for its members. Write BOAT/US, Dept. JW, 880 South Pickett Street, Alexandria, VA 22304 for membership information.

Privacy check? Use a thief knot on your ditty bag. It reveals the fact of someone looking, if not the identity.

WRINKLES

A Thief Knot might be the way to have some old-time foc's'l fun with your ditty bag. Tie it up with a phony square knot, just as a wary AB might have done aboard the clipper ship *Dreadnaught*. The knot looks amazingly like a reef knot, but if anyone goes prying into your kit of tools without telling you, it will be easy to spot it, because in almost every case it will be a reef knot that will be used to tie it up again. You may have to look twice to see the difference in the two knots.

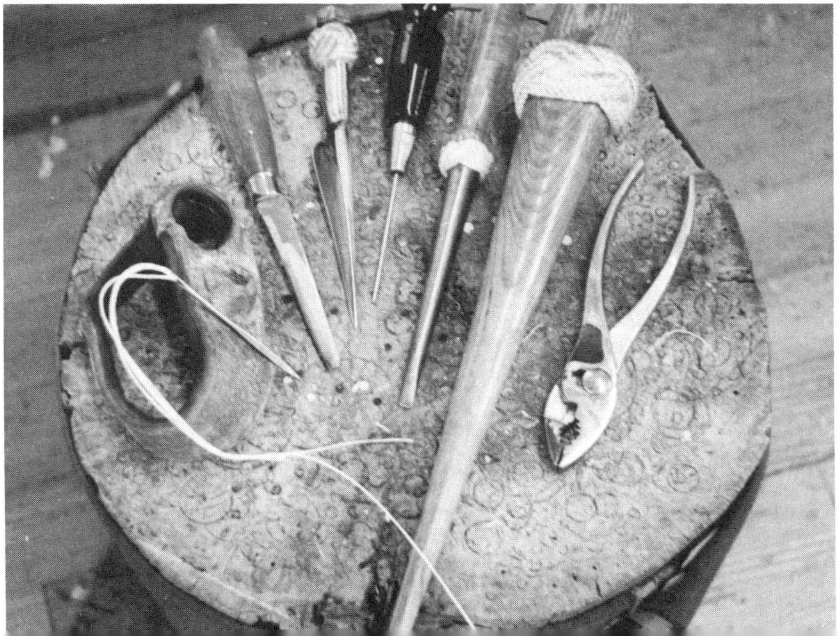

Chapter 13

Marlinespike Workbench

In this chapter, we will look more closely at the types of rope and their actual construction, at the important subject of ways of finishing the ends, and at the various ways that are used to attach rope to fittings or make up lines so they are ready to use. Some of these things, at times, have already been done to rope by the manufacturer or by a rigger, but: (a) some persons prefer to make their own eye splices, for example; and (b) circumstances always arise when you need to make a whipping or reinforce a worn splice.

Start with a coil of new rope. You may never buy a whole coil, but let us look at how it is handled in the back room of a chandlery. If it is laid rope, it will probably be coiled in the traditional way, somewhat the way a ball of twine is made up. Laid rope is always taken from the center, so that it won't start out with an awkward twist.

When we were first looking at rope and a few knots, we saw that the twist in laid rope has to be dealt with, even in making a plain knot. You can feel it with your fingers, and as you tie the knot and pull it tight, you sometimes give the end a small turn to make it all fit better. An old rule, in the days when most rope was right-hand lay, was that half hitches and bights should be made clockwise so that the seaman was working *with* the natural twist in the rope.

When laid rope is manufactured, the first set of twists, to make the strands, is in one direction—and then the three strands are twisted together *in the opposite direction.* With almost all rope, this means to the right. Hold the rope in your hands, going away from you, and you will see the right-hand twist.

◀ *Cutting rope with a hot knife is easier and more effective than using a knife. The heat seals the fibers together.*

Ropemakers call stranded rope Z-twist and S-twist, for reasons easy to see. Most three-strand rope has the Z or right-hand lay.

Because one set of twists balances the other, the rope has "stability," at least to a point. You can unlay the strands for a foot or so and then put them back together. However, if the rope is coiled incorrectly (as in taking it off the original coil) or used incorrectly, as might happen with repeated stressing on a winch, it can develop a tendency to kink, and when a kinked rope is put under a strain, it gets a hockle—a permanent kink that weakens the rope. This twist, or built-in torque-loading, exists in all three- and four-stranded rope whether it is made from natural fibers, synthetic fibers with a little elasticity (nylon), or the lower-stretch fibers of polyester (Dacron), polypropylene, and polyethylene. Even the new mixtures have the same tendency, although they are mostly used with braided construction.

Modern braided rope, which does not have a built-in twist to it, is sold from a free-turning reel. In this case, the problem of adding a set to the rope or a tendency to kink does not arise. Braided rope, except when misused, just does not have this problem. Again, this is true whether it is braid-on-braid, hollow braid, or plaited, and no matter what the basic fiber material is.

When you buy it, rope is measured, often by a measuring machine, and sometimes weighed, for the very good reason that it is more accurate to determine the amount of rope by weight than any other way. A length of rope necessarily has a certain give, a looseness, so that neither its diameter nor its length is a permanent or absolute dimension. The weight, however, is an accurate measure of the amount of material.

CUTTING ROPE

Aboard your boat or on your home workbench, getting ready to make up a dock line or a new jib sheet, you will face the problem of cutting the rope. If it were old-style manila you would have to use a knife, but with the modern synthetics you have a choice. Indeed, it is a better choice: heat.

Cutting with a knife, if that is the only method available, should start with taping the rope on each side of the place marked for the cut. Try cutting rope without taping it and you will see that the yarns and strands of many kinds of rope seem to pop open before your eyes when they are cut. For this kind of temporary work almost any kind of tape will do: black electrical tape, sail-mending

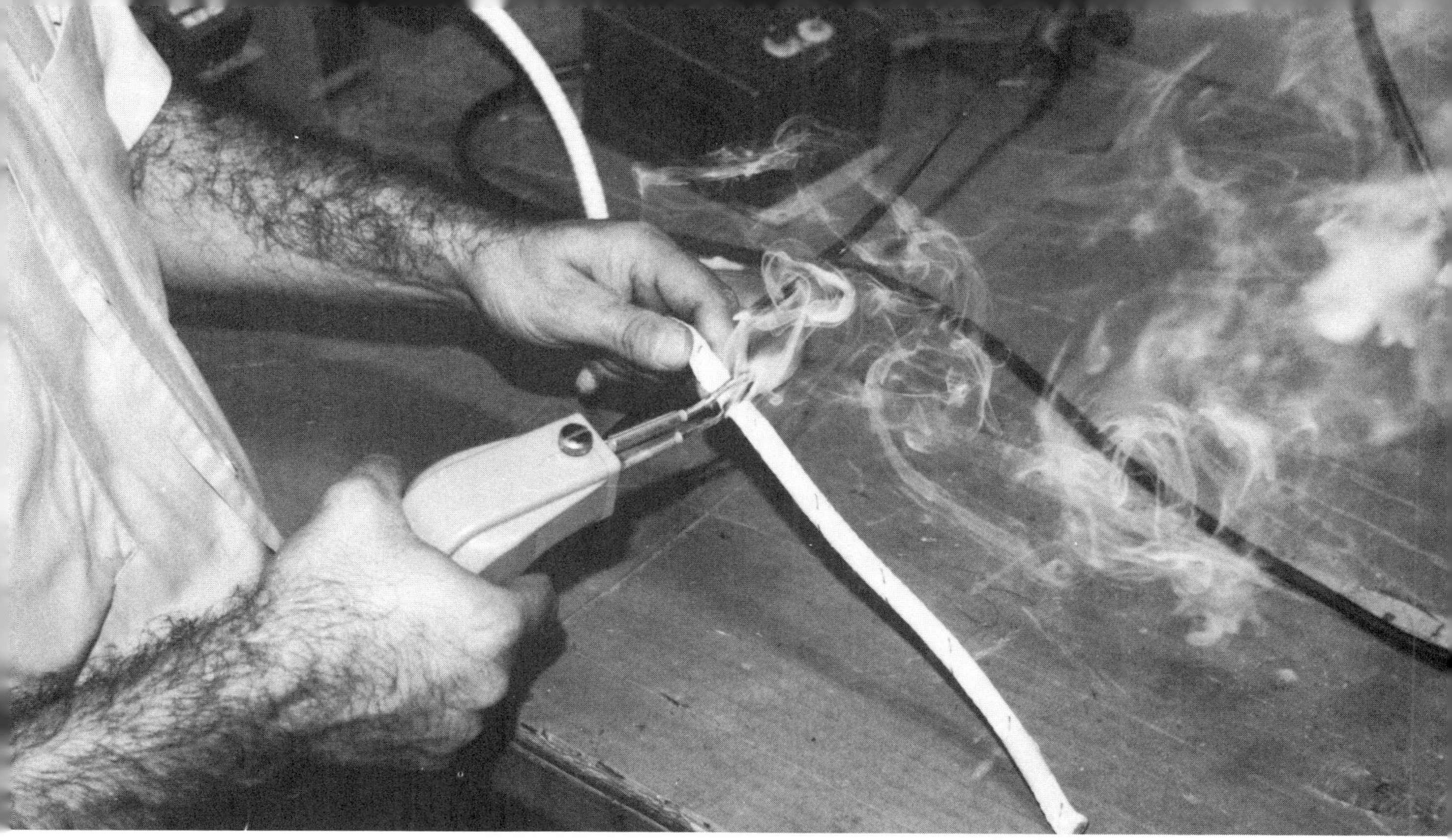

Using hot knife to demonstrate cutting synthetic rope at Florida Wire and Rigging Works. You can get a special cutting tip for an electric soldering iron.

tape, package sealer. Later in this chapter you will look at what to do with the taped ends.

Using an electric rope cutter is a better way to cut rope. A large rope cutter is a common tool in the workshops of riggers and sailmakers; it is base-mounted, has a hot crossbar, and you can bring the rope down to the bar and watch as it melts away.

A hot knife, a special "blade" in an electric soldering iron, is the usual rope-cutting tool of do-it-yourselfers, although professional riggers use them too. There are a number of types of blades, ranging from one about like a miniature spatula to a heavy cross-blade for cutting large rope.

Pretaping is not necessary, although there will be times when it has advantages, especially with laid rope.

If you have a small wooden breadboard for a mini-bench, put the rope across it and bring the hot blade down with a steady pressure. Either laid rope or braided "melts apart" before your eyes. There is an extra use for the hot knife, or even an ordinary tip on an electric soldering iron: After you make splices, you can smooth down the furry leftovers, sealing them, with the hot blade or tip.

If you cut synthetic rope with an ordinary knife, in the absence of a hot knife, or are working with an end that was cut previously and want to get the strength and neatness of heat sealing, here is the low-tech way: Use a flame. If you have nothing else, even matches or a candle will do. Otherwise, a low burner on a gas stove (or an alcohol stove in the galley) can be used to seal the end of rope or the rough edges of an eye splice in three-strand rope. Put the end in and out of the flame, melting it, rather than holding it in too long and letting it catch on fire. Another way that works is to use an old kitchen knife that can afford to have its temper drawn and heat it in the flame every minute or so while cutting rope.

Nylon, polyester, Kevlar, and the various polypropylenes and polyethylenes, as well as mixtures and combinations such as XLS-900, are ideal materials for hot cutting and sealing. Each of the synthetics cuts or fuses in a slightly different way because the melting temperature of each is different. Most of the whipping twines available can also be used with heat. Natural fibers, of course, cannot be handled this way. They merely burn.

FINISHING ROPE ENDS

The finish of any rigging item, dock line, or other line to be put into service is important. The end may already have a temporary finish of black electrician's tape that will keep it from unlaying or unraveling. This isn't good enough, or good looking enough, for a boat, although tree climbers and even balloonists seem satisfied with this finish.

A more secure end finish than tape, though hardly much better from an appearance standpoint, can be provided by using the hot knife to "weld" the fibers together. Similar strength and appearance, even with a bright color, can be obtained with one of the "dip-it" products available on the market.

A whipping is the ideal finish for a rope end, whether it is three-strand laid rope or double braid. Three kinds of whippings are shown in step-by-step fashion in the illustrations. A whipping holds, can be inspected, can be renewed in a few minutes, even at sea or in the rain, and has a seamanlike appearance. A whipping over a sealed end is especially strong.

Materials for whipping: Sail twine, nylon dental floss, nylon or Dacron whipping twine or whipping tape, and possibly a piece of

Halyards that are changed often can have a loop made of part of a strand, or of whipping twine, as these rigger's mini-splices show.

beeswax are the materials used. Although whipping twine is usually prewaxed, you can also pull the twine or tape over the beeswax or even an old candle stub to make it stickier.

The **common whipping** can be made without tools, except for a knife to cut the whipping twine. It can be improvised with heavy sewing thread (button thread) or dental floss if regular nylon whipping twine is not available. A good whipping is about as long as the diameter of the rope or a little more. It takes practice with different sizes of rope to know how long a piece of twine to start with. Try two feet the first time, planning to throw away any excess inchage.

First put a stopper, a figure-eight knot, in the end of the twine. This makes it easy to pull and helps keep it in place, just as if you were using it to sew. Make a loop of whipping twine and lay it along the line. Then wrap the twine tightly around the rope, in smooth, even turns. When the last turn is almost up to the end of the loop, put the free end of the twine through the loop. When you pull on the other end of the loop, you bury the loop-in-a-loop you have just made. Trim the ends.

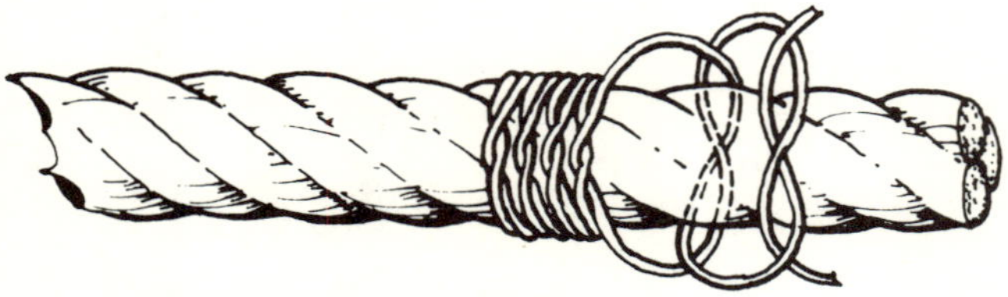

A West Country whipping, from Britain, holds tight while you are making it.

A whipping binds strands of either braided or laid rope, making handling easier.

The sailmaker's whipping, strengthened by stitching through the rope with a needle, is best of all.

Using sail twine or whipping tape, a useful and fancy ending for a line is easy.

The **West Country whipping** is more secure and not much harder to make.

Cut a length of waxed whipping twine just as when you start any whipping. Start with the middle of this piece and make an overhand knot around the rope. You are actually making the first half of a reef knot. Pull it tight (with wax it will hold). Then take both ends of the twine around the rope and tie another overhand knot on the exact opposite side. Pull it tight. Then repeat it so that the third knot is next to the first, the fourth knot is next to the second, and so on. Line up both rows of knots, which of course are on opposite sides of the rope, and keep all turns close together, as with any whipping, and keep it all tight. When your whipping is long enough, as you almost run out of twine, make the final knot a reef knot and trim the ends neatly.

The advantage of the West Country whipping is that each turn is tightened and locked, compared to the common whipping. If the common whipping is too loose, it tends to come undone, of course. If it is made too long and extremely tight, it is difficult to pull the underloop through.

French whipping, sometimes called half-hitch whipping, is in some ways a combination. You start in the same way as the common whipping, with the doubled loop laid along the rope. Each turn is made as a half hitch, and as you work along in the direction of the lay, the half-hitch crossings follow the lay in a spiral fashion. The French whipping is easy to keep taut as it is being made and tends to hold together even if chafed.

The **sailmaker's whipping** is one of the strongest, has a fancy look, and can be made by anyone who is willing to take ten minutes to learn. A sailmaker's needle is required, and it will be easier if you also have a palm. Start with the loop around one of the strand ends. You are essentially putting decorative/reinforcing turns at an angle and using the needle to get the whipping twine around the strands of rope. Another variation, a snaking whipping, is made by going back and forth from the two end turns of twine on a common whipping. You can add a variation by making a half hitch at each crossing.

Using a needle while making a whipping may require a palm as well, to push the needle through. With stiff synthetic line it is sometimes easier to put the twine around the strands, instead of through them.

There are several ways of handling the twine ends with almost any whipping. They can be knotted together, buried under the coils, or buried (using a needle) inside a strand. One end can start with an eye, a knotted loop, over a strand.

Frills and colored markers: Some people use another color twine or a heavier twine to add a decorative touch to a whipping or to identify a particular line (such as a spinnaker guy). You can also add a second whipping a few inches from the end whipping for added security on a line that gets rough usage.

A **quick whipping,** for a temporary hold, can be made with a bag knot, such as the magnus or Ashley's constrictor knot (which is also good for the neck of a bag). All you do is take three turns with the whipping twine, in clove hitch fashion; then you bring up each end on the *inside* of each of the turns and pull very tight; finally, you cut off the loose ends.

Another time-saving trick that still ends up with a good whipping is doubling the twine before you start.

Any whipping must be tight or it isn't worth making.

There are other uses for a whipping not at a rope's end: strengthening an eye splice at the throat, whether the splice is in three-strand or braided rope, and marking distance on a line. An anchor line, a dock line, a halyard, a sheet, or downhaul is often handier to use if predetermined points have been marked.

A French whipping on a tiller or the outer rim of a "destroyer"-type steering wheel is not only ornamental but makes a good handhold.

To join two lines, such as when reeving a new halyard, put a whipping on the end of each, then connect the two ends by temporary zig-zag stitches of whipping twine. This will keep the "joint" small enough to go through a block. Properly done, using a needle and making diagonal stitches that go through the strands, this is a secure way.

Some racing sailors, to reduce windage aloft, use a thin messenger over the spinnaker halyard block when the spinnaker is not flying and replace it with the regular halyard when needed. In this case, either a whipping with a strong eye made of several parts of twine or a miniature eye splice, made with a little less than one strand of the halyard, provides a place to attach the messenger.

A back splice, which is done by starting with a crown knot and then interweaving the three strands back into the lay, is another finish for a rope end. Although it keeps the rope from unlaying and looks "nautical," it is often impractical, because any line finished this way is difficult or impossible to reeve through a block. Or, if it has been put on a main sheet after it is rove through the blocks, it cannot be removed without cutting the line.

There are times when an **eye splice** is the practical way to finish the end of a line such as a dinghy painter or dock line.

WORM, PARCEL, AND SERVE

Similar in construction to a whipping, a seizing, or a serving is a method of adding to rope for a particular purpose.

A serving is made by wrapping "small stuff" such as marline or cod line around a rope in a place where chafe would otherwise weaken the rope. The serving absorbs the wear. On certain types of boats, a serving that has been varnished or painted black or white can lend a shippy air.

Seizing is putting the wrapping around two lines or a doubled line to hold them together. There are a number of different seizings, for different purposes. Hanks and slides are often attached to sails, on the luff rope or the bolt rope, with seizings, although sailmakers today use other methods in many cases. You can make repairs the old way.

A flat seizing is a single layer of turns secured with a clove hitch.

A round seizing is more secure, being two layers of turns.

A racking seizing is made by putting figure eights around the two parts or two lines.

A throat seizing is made by putting a loop (circle) in a line, then making a round seizing to hold it, ending with a clove hitch.

Making either a seizing or a serving takes some practice, some strength in the hands, and often a tool or two. Aboard larger ships, many servings are made by a two-man team.

The usual way to start a serving is to make an eye in the end of the marline or whatever small stuff is being used. A quick eye splice can be made by tucking the end between the strands and "braiding" the line.

Work against the lay when seizing. To make the turns tight, you probably need a tool to apply leverage. A serving mallet is the traditional tool, but a marlinespike, screw driver, tack hammer, short length of wood, or knife handle will also do. Make a marlinespike hitch to get sufficient leverage to pull the turns tight.

Worm, parcel, and serve means to put a heavy chafe guard on a stranded line by first wrapping the line with small stuff to fill in the space between the strands, then applying tape (in the old days it was strips of canvas) spirally, and finally serving. In the old days

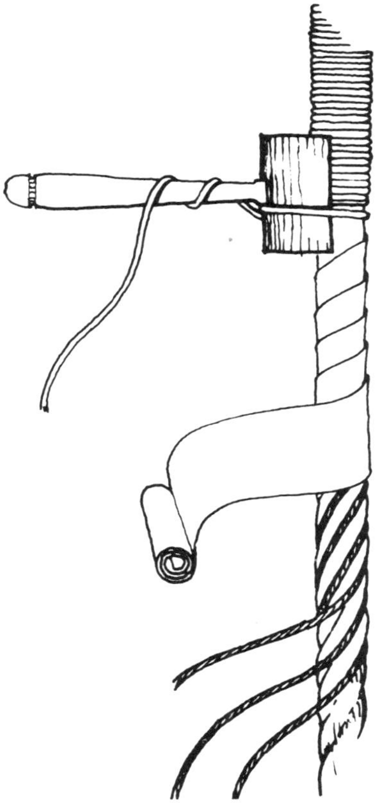

Serve, worm, and parcel in the old-fashioned way.

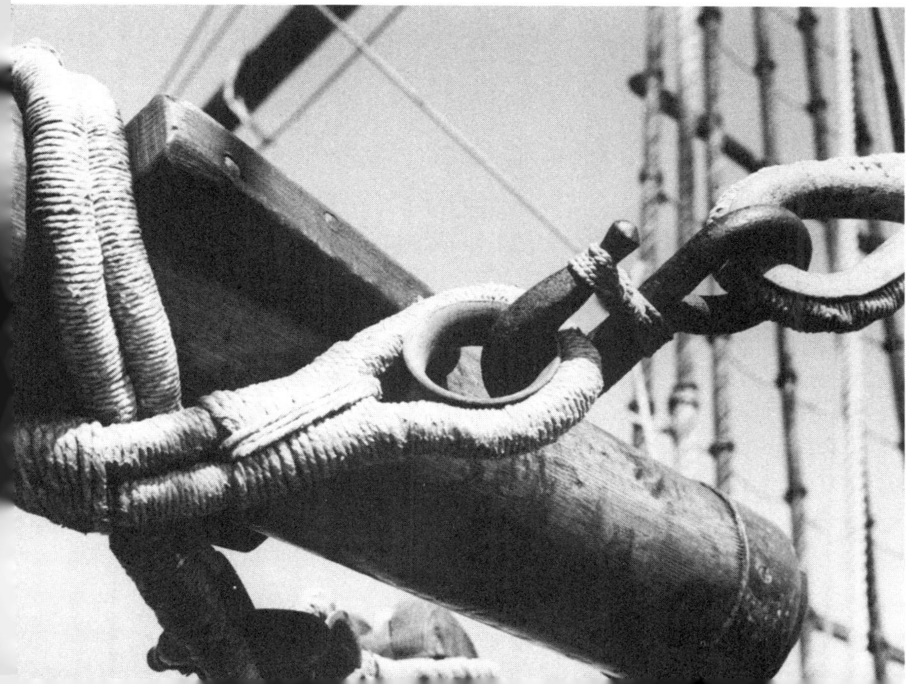

A pressed cringle, made with a tool, is faster and stronger (if less pretty) than the sewn cringle.

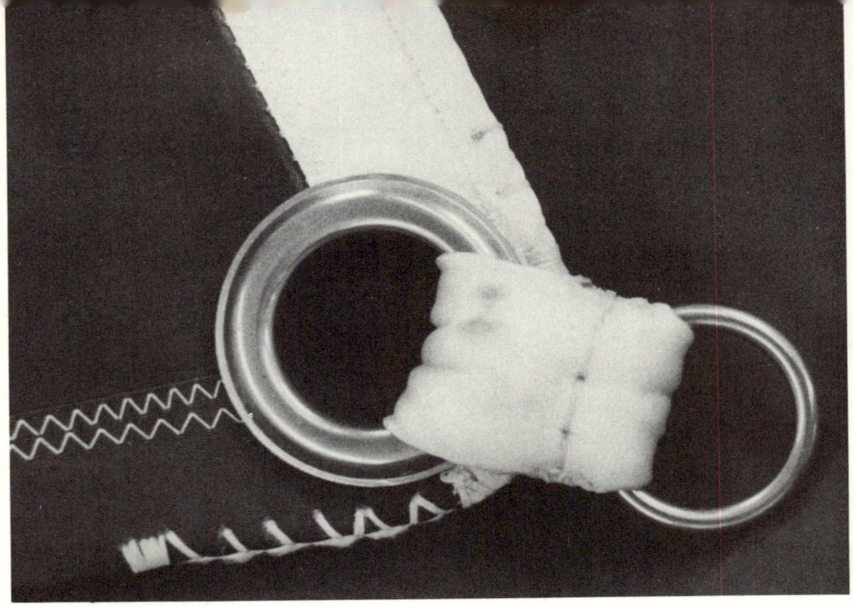

Mousing a hook to keep a line from coming out, or to hold a lifeline gate closed, is a simple process.

tarring, to waterproof and prevent rot, was part of the parcel-and-serve process.

A cringle is an eyelet, a metal or rope grommet (loop) worked into or attached to the corner or edge of a sail. Pressed steel rings today often replace cringles and grommets, and if they are not as pretty to some observer's eyes, they are undoubtedly stronger when made properly.

A rope grommet is a circle of three-strand rope made by taking a single strand from a piece of rope and reworking the lay.

Mousing is making a seizing across a hook to keep a line or shackle from jumping out. A pelican hook in a lifeline, for example, can open accidentally unless moused.

SMALL STUFF

Small stuff is the variety of cordage used for such purposes as lacings, whippings, servings, making batten ties, working cringles, and tying up small items. It is not always possible to find all the varieties of small stuff, some of it traditional and some of it definitely a product of the new technology. Fortunately, one kind of light line can often be substituted for another.

Marline was two-strand natural fiber, impregnated (usually with tar) and used chiefly for seizings and servings, although a large rope or wire rope might have a whipping made of marline. You can buy synthetic marline, made of polyester filament and coated with tar. It looks like "the real thing," but it is better.

Spun yarn can be two, three, or four yarns. It was used chiefly for servings, as was an even less expensive material called rope yarn, made by unlaying condemned, tarred hemp cordage. "Foxes" were two yarns twisted by hand and used to make neat seizings.

Hambro line is three-stranded, really a thin rope made of combed, tarred hemp. It is used on shipboard for larger seizings (where wire is also used).

Sail twine used to be made of hemp, flax, or linen, and the thickest was called roping twine. Today it is most usually nylon or polyester. It is available in white and colors.

Seine twine is three-strand, as is cod line.

Sennet is small braided line made up by separating stranded rope and then plaiting it. Today eight-strand plaited line is similar.

Waxed lacing tape is made of continuous filament polyester. It lays flatter than regular sail twine. It should be in your ditty bag.

Stainless steel seizing wire (3/64-inch diameter) is used for seizing shackles. It is nonmagnetic.

Monel seizing wire is noncorrosive but magnetic and should not be used near a compass.

Ratline stuff and seizing stuff were laid up lines of tarred hemp used for making ratlines and for seizings on larger hawsers.

Brief descriptions of the types of rope commonly used on pleasure boats were given in the introductory chapters. The chapters on deck seamanship and anchoring looked more closely at the types of rope involved with this work, and the chapters on sail handling dealt with sailboat running rigging.

SPLICING

You can buy prespliced dock lines. Your sailmaker or your rigger will make up splices when they are needed. You no longer need to repair rigging shot away by cannon, as you might have done two hundred years ago. A good knot will usually work in almost any powerboat or sailboat situation. Indeed, there is probably a swing to using knots by the top sailors. They are strong.

But what would sailing be without some knowledge of splicing? What about the beauty, the fingertip art, and the pride of craftsmanship? What about the few splices you should know? Suppose you want to make splicing a wintertime hobby?

The principles are easy to grasp. In three-strand ropes, you interweave the strands. It's something like braiding. With double braid, you ignore the braiding . . . you just take the rope apart so you have two hollow braids, and you fit one inside the other in the manner of the famous Chinese handcuffs.

If you are splicing the ends of two stranded lines together, making a short splice, you end up with a thicker piece of rope where the splice is. It may be strong enough, but it won't go through a block. A long splice is the solution. It takes up no more space than the original rope, and it handles perfectly. It isn't as strong, however.

If you want an eye, as you often do, the alternative to making a large one with a bowline or a small, tight one with a buntline hitch is a splice. The splice will be slightly stronger than any knot. There may be two disadvantages: (1) an eye splice, as used on a dock line, can be pulled apart at the throat; it can "deteriorate"; (2) the eye splice on a shackle, such as on the end of a spinnaker halyard, will have just enough size to it so it either jams in the swallow of the halyard block or won't let the sail reach its full height.

The perfect use for an eye splice is over a thimble, as is usually done when making up an anchor line.

THREE-STRAND SPLICES

A short splice is the easiest to learn. Unlay the strands of both rope ends for about ten turns of the lay. Tape, whip, or fuse the ends to prevent unlaying and to make your work easier. You may also want to make a seizing, or use tape, around the main body of the rope to help it hold its shape. Holding the three strands in your fingers, separate them, and do the same with the other end in the other hand. Now "marry them," so they fit together. At this point, tie a light line or tape around the three strands of one rope, not too tightly, to hold it together while you work on the splice. (When you get more expert, you may decide to skip this step.)

Next, start tucking the three free strands over and under, against the lay of the rope. You are merely putting three strands into three strands, and it should end up symetrically. Smooth it down, then make a couple of additional tucks.

Now turn your attention to the other three free ends and repeat the tucking operation, again against the lay of the rope. Smooth it

The fingertip art of splicing starts with getting the feel of rope. Unlay it, try the twist.

Making an eye splice starts this way . . .

out now and then, pull on the ends, and you have a short splice. Trim off the loose ends, but not too short. If convenient, use a flame or a hot knife to smooth down the furry ends.

You could make the short splice look better by tapering it, gradually reducing the thickness of each of the six strands you are working with, each time you make a couple of tucks.

An eye splice is a trifle harder to do perfectly, but since you are more likely to need one, it's worth the practice. The principle is the same.

Start by unlaying the strands, perhaps eight inches in average size rope. Tape or heat seal the ends.

Now form a loop in the rope by laying the end back along the standing part. Hold the standing part away from you in your left hand. The loop should be toward you. Use your right hand to work with the stranded end.

The size of the loop is decided now, when and where you start tucking the strands in. If you are working on a thimble, you need to make everything tight from the beginning. You might even tape it to the thimble to help.

Lay the three open strands across the rope. You are going to tuck each of the three free strands into the three closed strands. Look at the pictures. The trick is to start with the middle one and to tuck it under the topmost strand of the rope, going from right to left against the lay. Haul it up tight, but not enough to distort it. Now take the leftmost of the strands and tuck it under the strand that is to the left of your first tuck. Take the remaining strand and tuck it under the third strand, which of course is to the right. Again, from right to left, and against the lay.

Make three additional tucks, one tuck at a time, one strand at a time. Look at your splice and compare it to the pictures. Turn your splice over and see how it looks. Just as in the short splice, all the tucks are under and over, under and over.

You work the splice, using your fingers, so that the tucks are even. You pull, roll, pull. You may even put it on the floor and roll it with your foot.

As with the short splice, a tapered eye splice looks better and for some kinds of rigging work is better.

A long splice is so easy that all you have to do is follow the drawings.

A back splice requires only that you get all three strands going correctly; it's sort of like tying a simple knot to begin with. It can be tapered just as easily.

SPLICING DOUBLE-BRAID ROPE

Special tools are needed to splice double-braid rope. A hollow fid, a pusher, a marker, and sometimes other little gadgets are needed. In some cases various sizes of tools are recommended. You can buy the tools in nested form, in "one-size-fits-all" form, and even adapt tools. There are a number of techniques, worked out by specialists. Some are easier to learn, some are faster to do, but correctly done splices are a great deal stronger. In some cases, learning to make double-braid splices leads you into more elaborate configurations. It looks so difficult that when you find you can do it, you try other splices.

Lock-stitching, right through the splice, and special whippings, add to the strength and the appearance of the final splices.

Measuring and marking is the trick that you have to learn to make a good braided rope splice. All the rest is following the step-by-step instructions furnished by rope manufacturers and working with your fingers. You can taper the splices as you go. You can learn to make them beautifully.

Seven tools are needed to make this professional eye splice in double braid (or "braid-on-brad") whether it is polyester or nylon:

A pusher, a hollow tubular fid, a wire fid, knife and scissors (a hot knife in addition will make the work look neater), a marking pen, and a roll of tape.

The length of the fid depends on the size of the rope. Rope that is a half-inch in diameter, for example, needs a fid that is a little over ten inches in length.

More measuring, taping, and hand work, such as tapering, are required than in making the familiar quick splice, but the principle is the same: The core become the cover or jacket and the jacket becomes the core. These photographs and instructions are from The Splicing Book *of Wellington Puritan, Inc., Madison, Georgia. Copyright Wellington Puritan, Inc.*

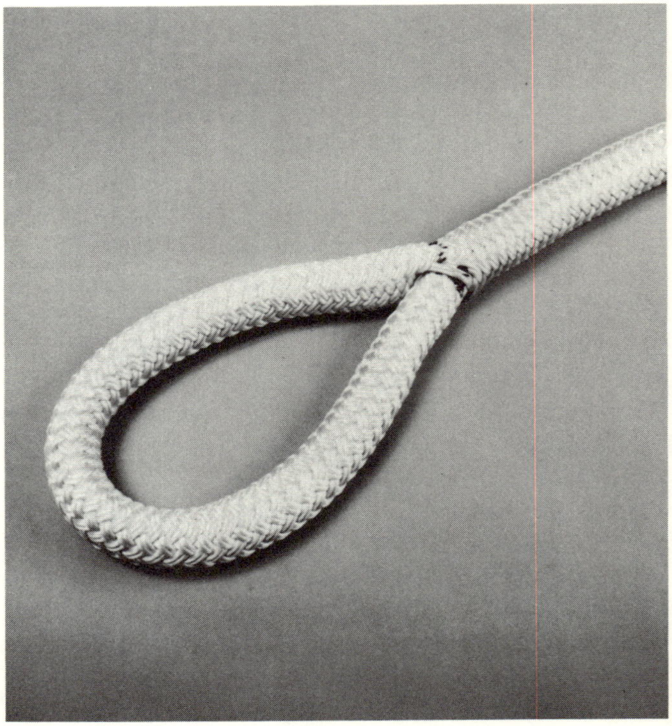

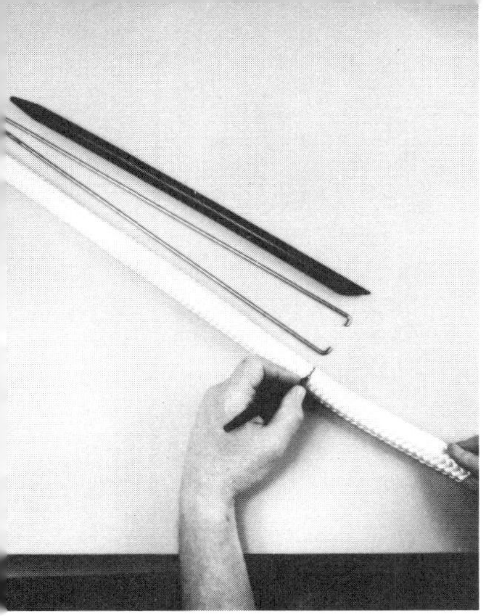

'tep One: Lay out the line, without wists or kinks, on a flat work area. 'ape the end to be spliced. Make he Initial Measurement (IM) by neasuring one fid length from the ope end. Mark around the entire ircumference of the jacket.

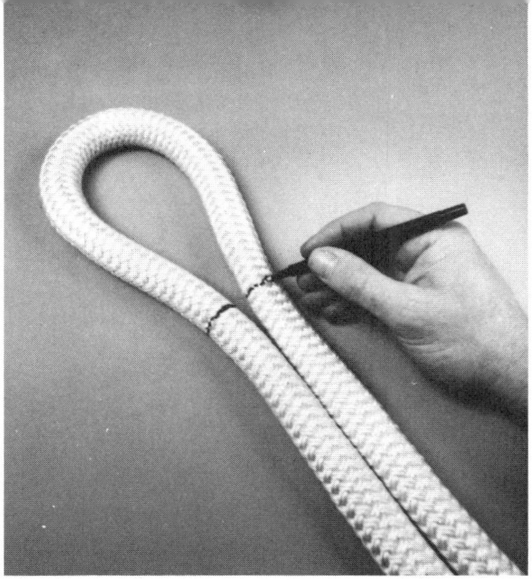

Step Two: Form a loop the size of the desired eye and mark that distance from the Initial Measurement mark toward the standing part of the line. Make an Eye Allowance mark around the entire circumference of the jacket.

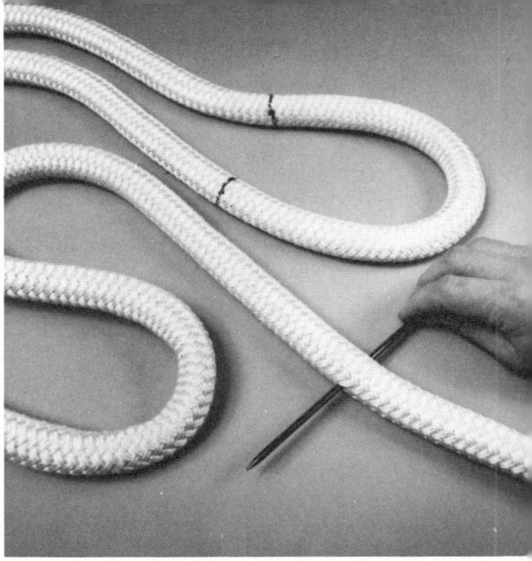

Step Three: Measure a distance approximately four times the Initial Measurement (four fid lengths) from the Eye Allowance mark. Insert a pin through the jacket and core at this point. In small-diameter lines an overhand knot may be tied, instead of a pin.

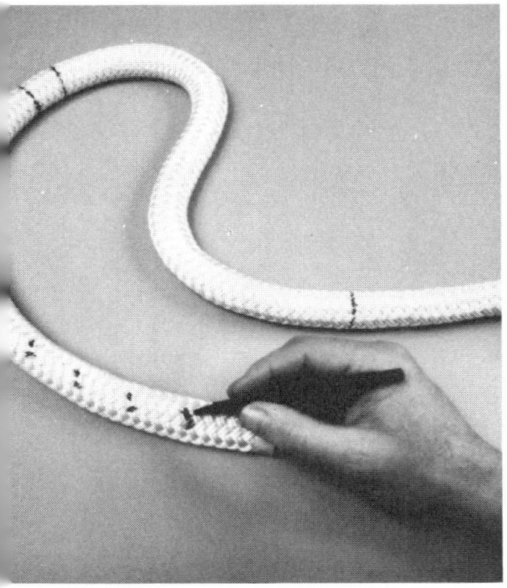

'tep Four: From the IM mark, ount four pics (pairs of strands) oward the bitter end and make a nark around the entire circumference. From this mark, count and nark every fifth pic until you reach he end. Go back and mark the pics rossing these marked strands.

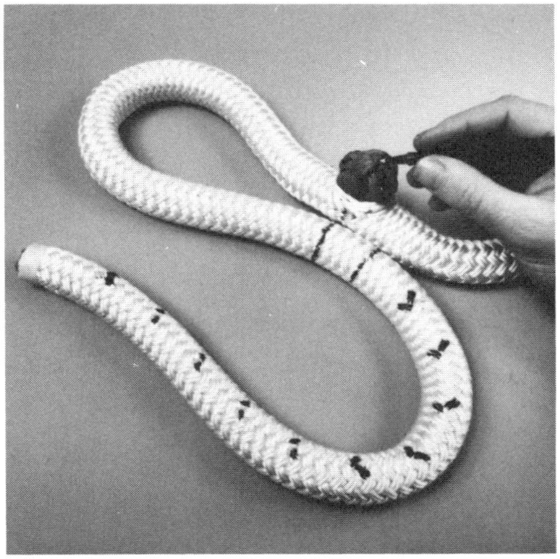

Step Five: Separate the jacket strands at the Eye Allowance mark and put a mark on the core. This is the Core Mark (CM 1). (Note about marking those pics: Five pic taper works with sixteen-, twenty-four-, and thirty-two-strand line. Seven pic taper should be used on twenty-strand line.)

Step Six: After marking, extract the core from the jacket, then tape the end of the core. Expose more core by grasping it with one hand and pushing the jacket back toward the pin with your other hand. (The pin, as you'll see, helps control all this.)

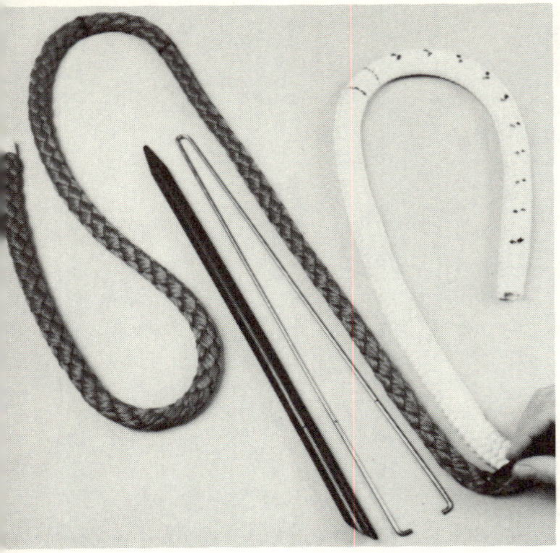

Step Seven: From CM 1, measure toward the standing part of the line one short fid section or about a third of a fid and mark the core CM 2. From this mark measure one short section plus one full fid length and mark the core CM 3.

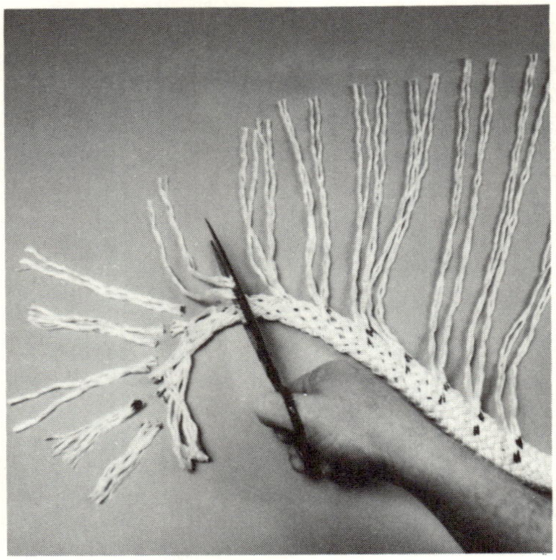

Step Eight: Taper the jacket by extracting the strands marked in Step Four, starting near the bitter end. Using scissors, cut off the strands at the marks and discard. You can seal the loose strands with a hot knife.

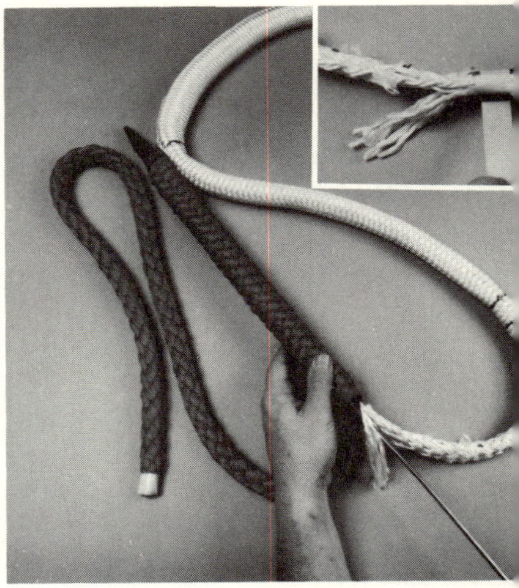

Step Nine: Insert jacket into core. First, fold over end of jacket and insert into hollow end of tubular fid. Insert photo shows how to tape jacket to wire fid. Being careful not to twist the jacket, insert fid into core at CM 2. Using a pusher, push fid through core and out at CM 3 until jacket exits.

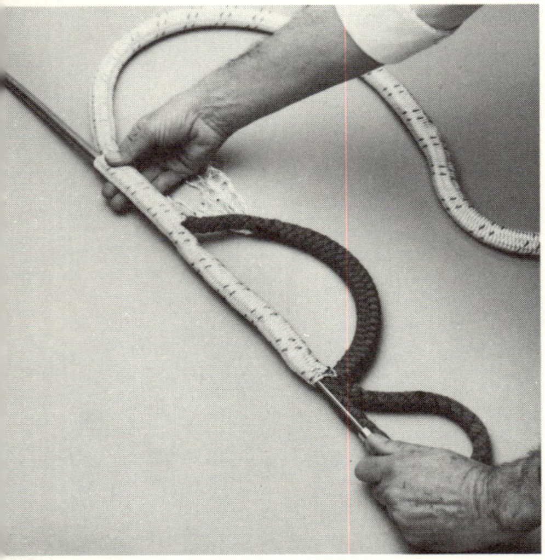

Step Ten: Pull through until first mark on jacket meets Core Mark 2. Remove tape from jacket. Using the fid, insert taped end of core into jacket at this first mark and out of the jacket at a point one third of the fid length beyond the point of extraction.

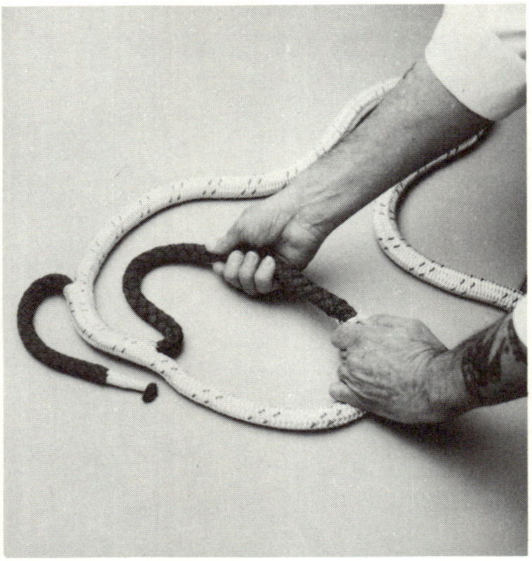

Step Eleven: Pull core through jacket until marks on core and jacket meet at crossover. Remove all slack from the core with your right hand while holding jacket near crossover with your left. This will cause the jacket yarns to retreat back into the core center.

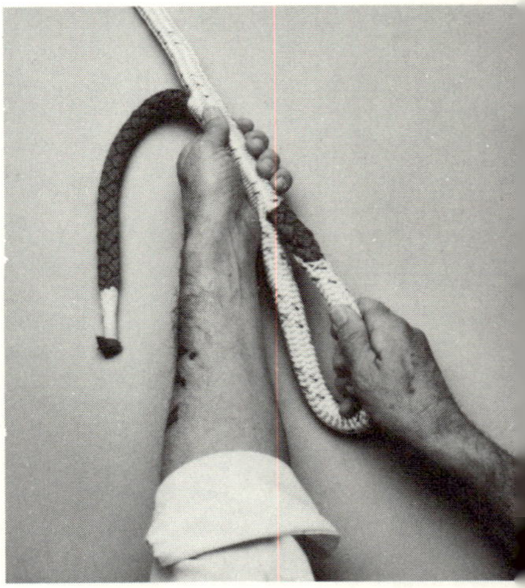

Step Twelve: Holding crossover firmly with your right hand, milk the slack out of the jacket toward the vertex until core retreats into the jacket as far as possible.

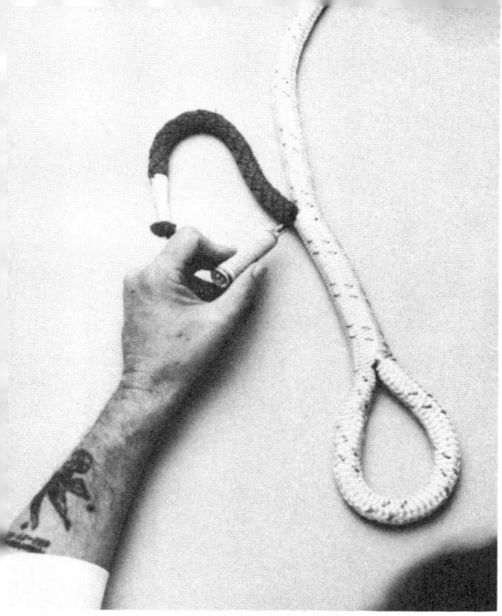

Step Thirteen: Remove all slack from the jacket beginning at the point of the eye where it emerges from the cover (Eye Allowance mark) and past the point where the core comes out of the cover. Make a mark on the core where it comes out of the cover.

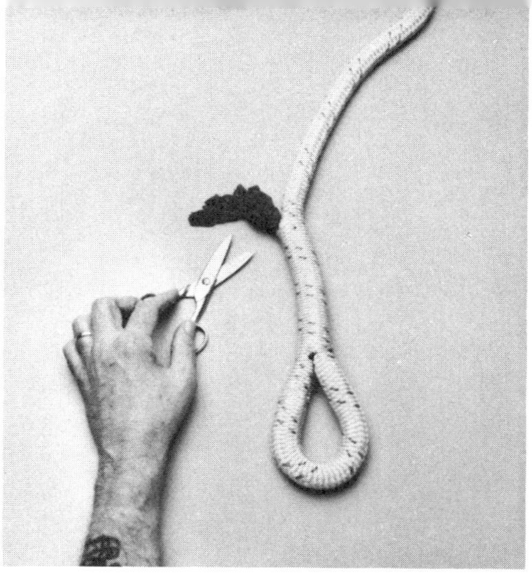

Step Fourteen: Now you're finishing off. Grasp the core and pull it out of the jacket one sixth of the fid length. At this point cut the core at a forty-five-degree angle ending at the mark made where the core emerged from the cover.

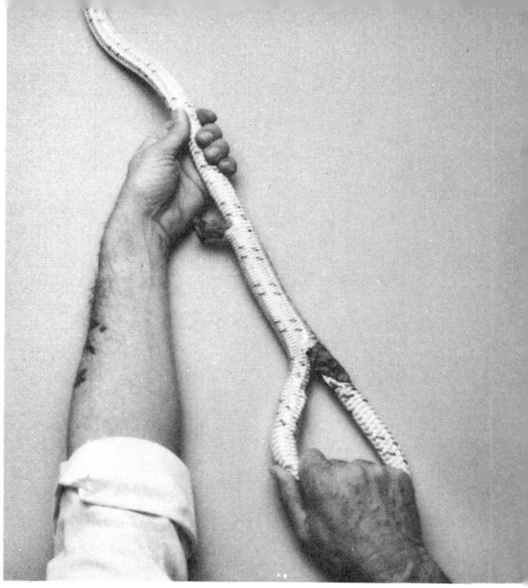

Step Fifteen: Tie off the line near the point where the pin is inserted. Tie to a stationary object. Reset the exposed angled core back inside the jacket by placing a light strain on the rope (pulling the eye against the tie-off point) and removing all slack.

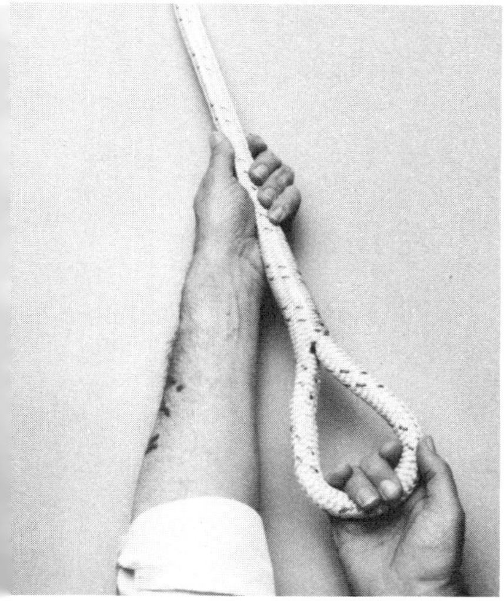

Last step: Pull out the pin at the tie-off point and, starting as close to this point as possible, remove all slack from the jacket or cover. Milk the cover with your hands. For an even longer-lasting eye splice, stitch or whip the throat.

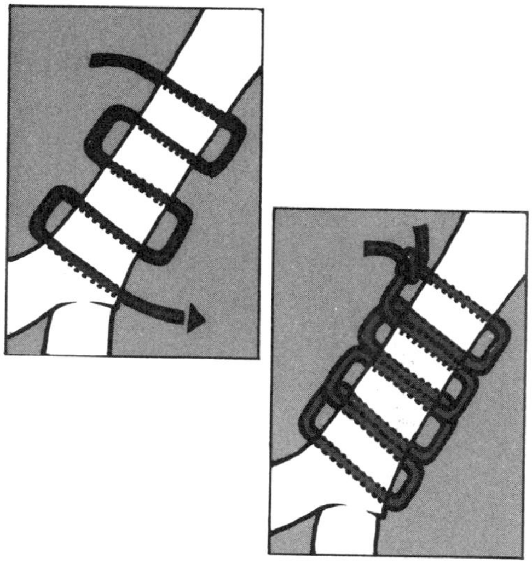

Lock-Stitching: Use heavy nylon twine. With a sail needle, stitch through the splice—snug, but not too tight. Reverse direction back to the starting point. Tie the twine ends together and bury in the line for a neat appearance.

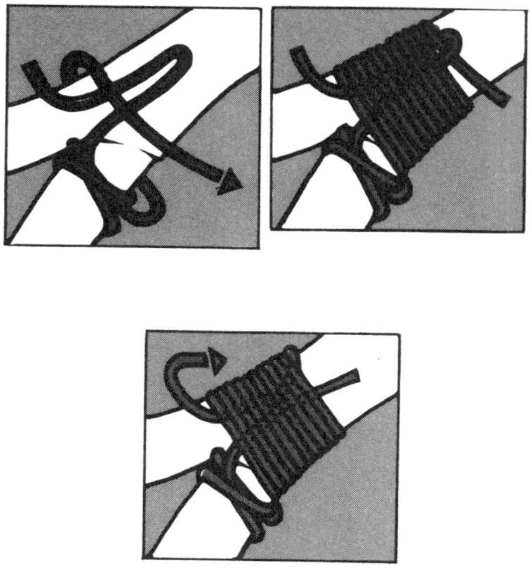

Whipping: Tie a clove hitch to the eye where it enters the line and lay a loop along the spliced area. Tightly whip (wrap) twine around loop and line. On last wrap, insert end through loop and pull it about midway through whipped area. Clip off the twine ends.

The photographs and captions show one good form of braided rope eye splice. It is from Wellington Puritan's small but excellent publication *The Splicing Book.*

For complete details of how to make others, including a hollow-braid hitch, for special tools, write to one of the specialists in braided and laid rope splices, such as the McGrew Splicing Tool Co., 8120 Rio Linda Boulevard, Elverta, CA 95626.

Various rope manufacturers also furnish booklets, tools, and specialized braid-splicing methods, with small variations but all using the same principles. Samson's Red Book on splicing shows professional tricks and techniques, including a variation for old rope.

WRINKLES

The Balloonists' Daisy Chain is a knot configuration you may never need—unless you have occasion to throw half a dozen or more very long lines into the back of a station wagon and plan to retrieve them without fighting a tangled mass of chaos. The seamanlike way would be to coil all the lines and tie all the coils. The balloonists, who also know a thing or two, would tell you to do it this quick and easy way: Double the line. Start from the middle and make a half hitch every eighteen inches. When you get to the last half hitch, make two so that the "daisy chain" won't come unraveled. The "line" is now less than a quarter of its original length, will not tangle even when thrown in with many other daisy chains, and can be ready to use (to tie down your balloon at a height of a mere three hundred feet) on short notice by merely undoing the last half hitch and then pulling. All the "stitches" unravel and your long line is ready to use.

Baggywrinkle was made by twisting old marline or broken up old rope to create a pad to prevent sails chafing on the rigging. If you ever need a quick baggywrinkle for a special purpose, try a paint roller.

The Splicing Book, from Wellington Puritan, Inc., Madison, GA 30650, is a well-illustrated booklet, printed in full color. It is also available with a training kit that includes practice lengths of braid-on-braid rope, a splicing fid, and a pusher. These are generally available from marine dealers.

Splicing Manual, from Samson Ocean Systems, 245 Winter Street, Waltham, MA 02154, is another clear instruction manual.

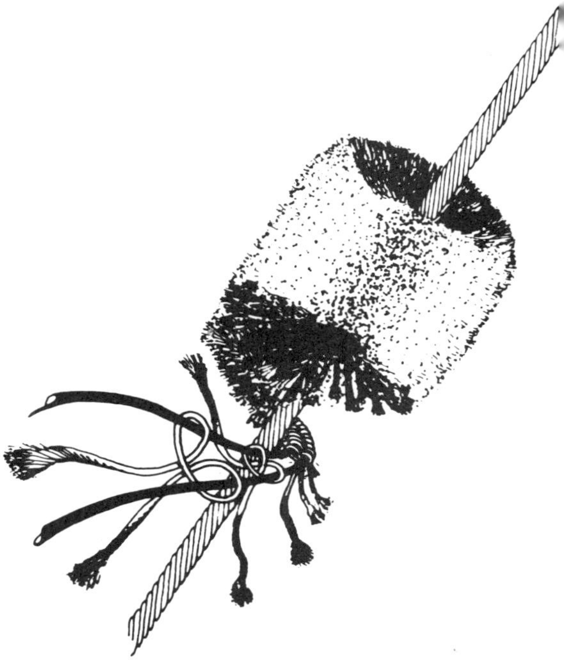

◀ *The lover's knot is fun to make and useful in the cabin or even on deck as a pad to take a "lazy block."*

Chapter 14

Inspection/ Maintenance

Sam Barclay stood next to the rigging shed at Yacht Haven, in Stamford, Connecticut, shaking his head. He pointed to the mast and rigging, just out of a sailboat. The wire rope shrouds had a corkscrew set to them.

"Either that boat has been sailed very hard or that's cheap wire rope. In any case, it's been strained."

Old riggers know a thing or two. They look for early streaks of rust on stainless steel fittings—another sign of strain and warning of eventual breakage. They look for corkscrew sets to the wire. They have learned.

Old riggers, old sailors, young sailors—cruising sailors, racers, skippers, and crew—have to learn how to constantly inspect, maintain, and adjust every part of a boat's rigging.

Start with an attitude. Every time you pass a boat, look at her rigging. You may get a new idea, you may see a spreader about to come loose or a mooring line out of its chock and causing abrasion. Every time you board a boat, keep your eyes sharp. As you sail, watch the little things—especially the ones that build up into big troubles if they're not caught. At the beginning of the season, work through a checklist. At haul-out time, alternate between the boat and the list.

For a hundred details taken care of in this way you'll enjoy several hundred hours of worry-free sailing.

Intersections of mast, hull, and rigging are places to keep an eye on. A wedge out of place under a mast coat can lead to extra, and damaging, flexing at the partners. A collision with another boat

Careful! Careful! The best way to do good work in a bosun's chair is to follow safe procedures, as Gary Jobson demonstrates for Sebago Docksiders.

(even when your boat was in dock and you were absent) can result in a twisted fitting.

Once or twice a year, inspect your mast or have a competent rigger do it. Welds, sheaves, track, and tangs are places where trouble starts.

KEEP A RIGGING NOTEBOOK

Three main things should be in a good rigging notebook:

1) The list of sizes and part numbers, with whatever specs and manufacturers' maintenance notes go with them.
2) The write-ins: the mini-memos to yourself about a small fix or change that should be made in the off season, the inquiries to be made, the possible good idea seen on another boat.
3) The check-off, the date and details of things accomplished.

RIGGING DO'S AND DON'TS

Starting with the standing rigging, here are do's and don'ts suggested by the Florida Wire & Rigging Works and the MacWhyte Wire Rope Company. They involve simultaneous maintenance and inspection.

DO rinse standing rigging regularly with fresh water.

DO use a water-soluble detergent.

DON'T use a cleaner containing chlorine. It is destructive to stainless steel.

DO inspect all unusual stains and corrosion spots.

DON'T use steel wool or steel wool scrubbing pads to remove stains. Minute particles left as residue cause rust.

DO scrub with a nylon or brass scrubbing pad.

DON'T wrap rigging or terminals with tape or other adhesive materials.

DO check your tang/swage fitting for a fairlead. Bad angular alignment puts a bending load on the end of the fitting.

DON'T drag a mast and fittings around a boatyard with cable and fittings trailing on the pavement or left where they might be run over by car, truck, or trailer.

DO unfasten all but minimum standing rigging before unstepping the mast.

DO avoid any kinking or bending at any fitting when unstepping.

DON'T coil rigging too tightly for storage.

DON'T clean plastic-coated cable with chemical cleansers unless you are sure they won't cause damage. Automotive prewax cleaners are best.

DO ask your local rigging shop or rigger about any unusual problems.

The twice-a-year inspection, looking for small troubles, is particularly important in the high-tech sailing world. Sails that don't blow out, stronger rope, hydraulic tensioning devices, vangs, and super-sheeting put increasing strains on all the basic rigging.

Even when your boat is idle, sitting at the mooring, wear is taking its toll. When you sail hard, the slatting of the slack leeward rigging is wearing it out. It's the cycling loads that do it. Not even the largest boats really have a completely taut rigging setup. Many of the smaller boats, with movable rigs, rotating masts, and the like, suffer severe cyclic loading.

"Fatigue failures begin at what is called a 'stress riser' point,"

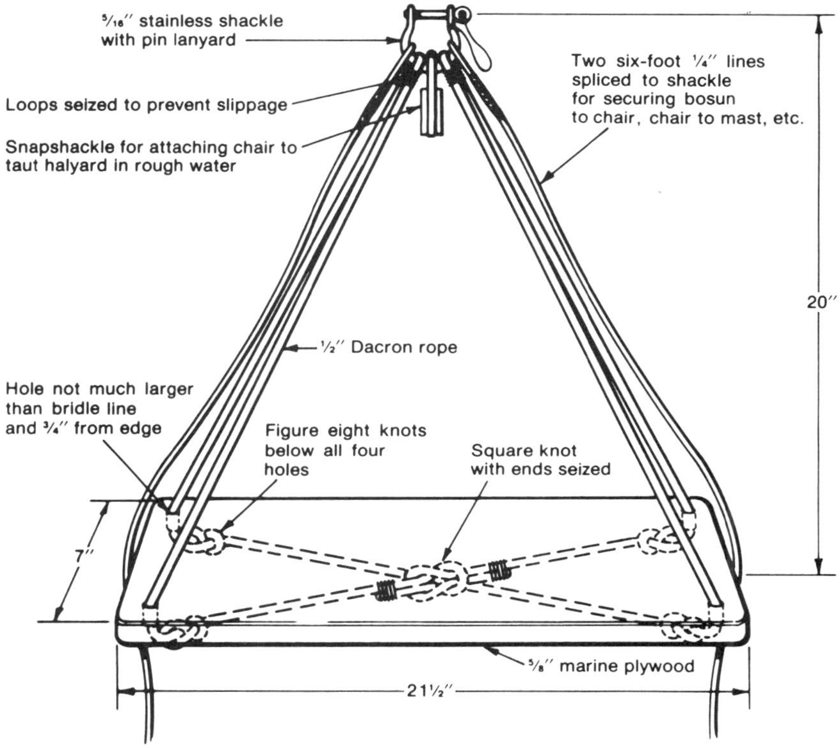

A well-made bosun's chair, as recommended by Rod Stephens, Jr. Other kinds, with canvas for support and pockets for tools, have not had as much testing.

says MacWhyte in its instruction leaflet. "This point could be anywhere in a component system—cable, terminals, turnbuckles, or hull attachments. The stress riser may be an imperfection in the surface of the component, such as a nick, file mark, corrosion pit, or sharp thread root. Under a cycling load, a small crack begins at this imperfection. This crack increases in size as the load cycles until the uncracked portion of the cross-section can no longer support the load, and the whole component fails.

"The warning sign is the small crack. Frequent careful inspection of cables and fittings—especially any threaded portions—should reveal trouble in time for replacement.

"Fatigue in cable is indicated by broken wires. But be careful; they do not always stick out. In good pre-formed stainless wire rope, broken wires can lie in position with the rope break difficult to detect. For this reason, if you are coiling shrouds and stays when unstepping or putting the boat in storage, it is an excellent time to inspect cable—hand over hand—as the likelihood of small breaks sticking out is increased.

"In solid rod rigging, any crack requires instant replacement. In stainless wire rope, you can have an occasional single broken wire and still keep the component in temporary service.

"To determine the strength lost from broken wires divide the number of broken wires by the total number of wires in the cable. Two broken wires in a 1 x 19 strand represent about a 10% (2/19) reduction in strength; two broken wires in a 7 x 19 cable represent only a 1.5% (2/133) reduction. It would be well to replace the 1 x 19 as soon as possible, while the 7 x 19 could still give some useful service. In either case, anytime you find two broken wires, particularly if broken in the same place, look for any unusual cause or determine if the cable is too light for the work it performs."

WEAR, WEAR, AND WEAR

Cycling loads cause wear. Pins wear. Holes are enlarged. Metal components chafe and stretch. These various types of wear can reduce the cross-sectional area, destroy the fit between components, and encourage the creation of surface cracks. This reduces the nominal strength of the component and can lead to failure.

The warning signs to look for are elongated holes, sloppy fit between components, and peening or mushrooming of metal at contact points. Always look for surface cracks.

Any fitting or component showing excessive wear must be replaced.

If wear has extended to chainplates and mast tangs, consult your rigger or a surveyor.

DISCOLORATION

Corrosion in so-called stainless steel is generally the result of the interaction of salt, chemicals in the air and water, and *stress.* "When fittings are swaged to marine cable," says MacWhyte, in the pamphlet, "work hardening of the metal can occur. Salt water acting on the work-hardened fitting causes corrosion to propagate along the metallic grain boundaries leading to cracking and ultimate failure. The discoloration comes first, then the cracks."

DO'S AND DON'TS—SMALL BOATS

More rigging is damaged during unstepping than during regular usage. Set up proper procedures. Here are some MacWhyte do's and don'ts, mainly for smaller sailboats.

DO, if possible, hold up the mast by hand and release all shrouds and stays. This will avoid kinking, bending, crushing, and nicking.

DON'T drag a mast around the yard with terminals trailing.

DO make up pads of old carpet and shock cord to wrap around the mast before securing halyards and standing rigging.

DO plan a routine program to secure rigging and to keep some tension on it while trailering.

DO hose off with fresh water.

DO'S AND DON'TS—LARGE BOATS

For larger boats, a similar routine is necessary. "Plan ahead; don't have a mad scramble when the stick comes down."

DO unfasten all but the minimum standing rigging. Substitute softer halyards for stays wherever and whenever possible. Disconnect lowers, baby stays, and any rigging not required, and tie it out of harm's way.

DO remember that most chainplate tangs do not let turnbuckles lay flat parallel to the deck. Thus, when the mast is set down, if there is tension on the cable, either a sharp bend is forced at the worst place or a stud can be bent at the threaded part of the terminal barrel. Plan to ease off tension as you bring the mast down.

DO have one person whose sole job is to stand off and watch what's happening to rigging and to items on deck as the mast comes down.

DO release all standing rigging as soon as possible after unstepping.

DO label any rigging removed from the mast immediately or before releasing. Get rigging tags before you start.

Make loose coils. Twine and light line are better than tape. Tape collects moisture, leading to corrosion. Tape leaves a residue that attracts dirt, rubs off on sails, and invites trouble spots. Don't wire tags on.

Some other bits of advice are these: If the mast is stored outside, especially near salt water, the place for your rigging is at home in a dry basement or attic. Beware of storing rigging and mast where the temperature will go below freezing. Water will work its way, by capillary action, into terminals, freeze, and thus split them.

Don't coil cable rigging too tightly. If terminals or turnbuckles are heavy, tie them so that bending of their own weight won't damage the swaging points.

Flexible wire ropes, aside from standing rigging, need better care than they usually get. Flapping while trailering, sloppy coils, extra flexing at terminals—all are bad. Wire-to-rope splices must be inspected regularly.

Rod rigging adds to the racing capabilities of a rig—but it has its own maintenance problems. On-board inspection by an expert or disassembly and examination for signs of stress, corrosion, cracking, or cold work crystallization are required.

Dis-assembly of winches, with cleaning and sparing lubrication, is usually needed several times a sailing season. Reel-type halyard winches should not be lubricated (they are brakes, depending on friction to work).

CHECKING MAJOR HARDWARE

Winches, outhauls, travelers, furling gear, and other major components need to be cleaned, lubricated properly (sometimes this means very little, but correctly), disassembled to look for worn parts, and kept free of abrasives or other elements that lead to wear and damage.

Travelers, for example, can get a salt build-up on the ball-bearing races, which will scratch the anodized aluminum rack and cause corrosion. Fresh water rinsing, not greasing, is the correct preventive.

Spinnaker poles, whisker poles, struts and spreaders, sail track on masts and booms, hydraulic gear—any one of these may have a bit of wear that is starting, a couple of loose screws, a dent that keeps slides from running smoothly. Inspect in time; fix in time.

The holes in the plates of modern blocks are not only to reduce weight. They also enable you to rinse the blocks with fresh water. Keeping the blocks clean prevents rust from starting.

Many rigging fittings, such as blocks, winches, cam cleats, and others, are made so that parts can be replaced. Manufacturers even keep parts for "obsolete" rigging components. Factory refits are often available.

TESTING MARINE METAL

If you're in world-class competition or going around the world, you might want some rigging parts checked professionally by X ray. Obviously, testing to destruction is something for manufacturers or testing laboratories. Otherwise, specialized metal testing can be added to the visual-inspection methods suggested earlier in this chapter.

There are two types available: magnetic particle inspection, which is commonly called by a trade name, Magnaflux, and a dye-penetrant method, which is less sensitive but a good deal easier to apply, as it can be done in the field.

The Magnaflux method is used for ferrous alloys. A magnetic field is induced in the rigging part to be tested and this is then exposed to fine magnetic particles. A crack or flaw shows up as a build-up of the iron filings. There is also a fluorescent version, called Magnaglo.

The dye penetrant method, marketed by one of the same companies, uses a penetrating dye and a "developer," to draw out the penetrant and indicate imperfections. There is also a fluorescent version of this.

Visual inspection, especially after severe strains, will reveal excessive wear and deformation, especially if you look at the inside (wearing) surfaces, not the exterior.

LITTLE THINGS TO CHECK AND DO

Halyards should be rigged so the bitter end can be secured with a figure-eight knot as a stopper. Internal halyards, with an exit

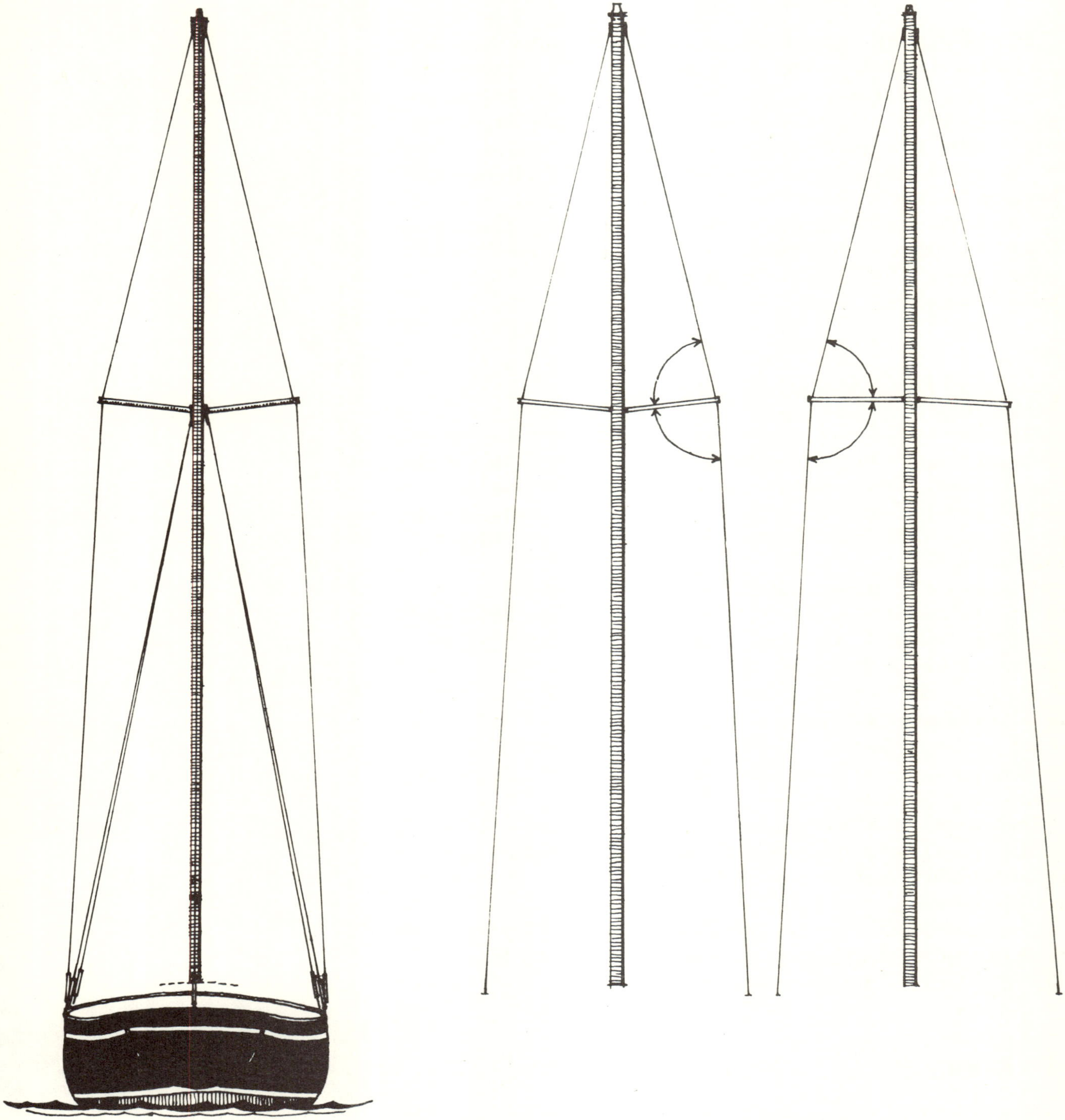

block on the mast, are easily fixed with a stopper so they won't come unrove.

If you use cotter pins, they probably need to be reduced in size—cut off with a wire nipper. Round and smooth the cut ends with a file. When in use, don't bend them back all the way—just open them enough to hold. Better than taping the rough ends, use silicone rubber.

When you have a choice, choose fittings and gear that are inspectable. Turnbuckles and rod rigging fittings are often closed, so you can't see the threads. Internal outhauls on booms, if wire, are impossible to inspect and need a professional and a shop to repair.

Cable steering gear must not only be inspectable (you may need a flashlight), it should be carefully gone over periodically and adjusted, lubricated, or repaired where needed. An emergency tiller should be available and accessible and the crew should try it once a year.

Frayed rope and a line with an unnoticed knot in it are two of the situations that lead to trouble. When an anchor line or a dock line parts, it is at a worn section. A knot reduces the strength of a line by 50 percent, besides making a nuisance of itself when the line is used.

Screw pin shackles—whether part of the anchor rode or in a sailboat's rigging—need to be checked that they are wired or moused, lest the pins work loose.

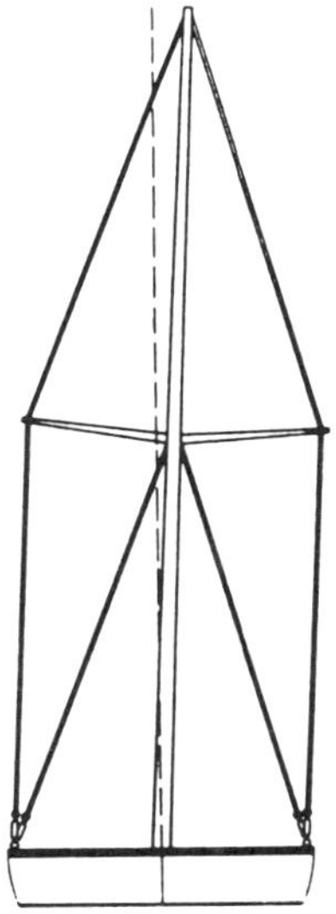

Check the mast at the dock, to make sure it is both straight and vertical. You can swing an arc with a halyard, from port to starboard, to verify that the mast is vertical, and then adjust turnbuckles.

WORKING LOADS

There are a number of definitions that deal with the strength of wire rope, fiber line, and rigging fittings. They should be understood.

Ultimate load is the average load or force (using a number of tests) at which the item no longer supports a load.

Shock load is a force resulting from a rapid change or movement, such as jerking or impacting. It is higher than a static load, but not a "test situation." It is a general term.

Static load results from a constantly applied force.

Proof load is the average force to which a part may be subjected before permanent deformation occurs; it may be a force applied during a proof test.

Proof test is a term designating the tensile strength applied for the purpose of detecting injurious defects.

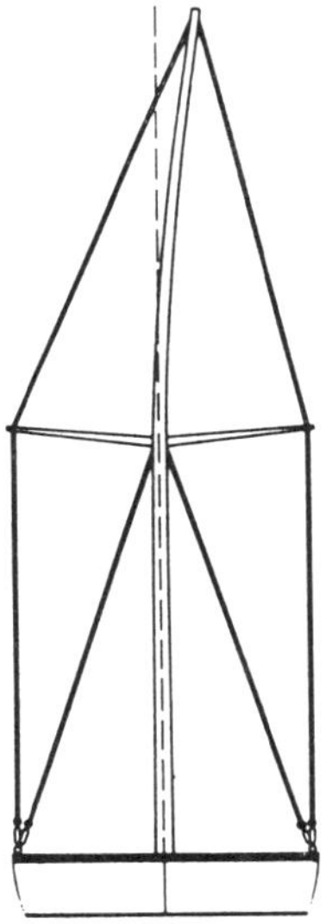

Here the lower shrouds are fine, the uppers are the problem. Ease one, tighten the opposite one, and check again.

If there is too much compression the mast shows it with one hook, or even a double hook;

Working load (sometimes "safe working load," or "rated load," or "SWL," or "Working Load Limit") is the maximum working load that an item should be subjected to.

Safety factor is an industry term denoting theoretical reserve capacity. One manufacturer may state: "Working load should not exceed 40 percent of tensile strength," while another specifies 50 percent.

INSPECTING FIBER ROPE

Manila rope can be inspected by opening the strands and looking for inner abrasion and deterioration. Fibers, sampled by hand from the interior of the rope, may be compared in strength to similar fibers in new rope. The ratio of broken strands to unbroken strands is a further indication of strength loss. Mildew and rot also affect manila rope adversely.

Synthetic ropes, when of the three-strand geometry, can also suffer a loss in strength due to strands breaking. Because of the rope's construction, all strands have an intermittent exposure to surface damage.

Double-braided rope, however, has an independent inner core,

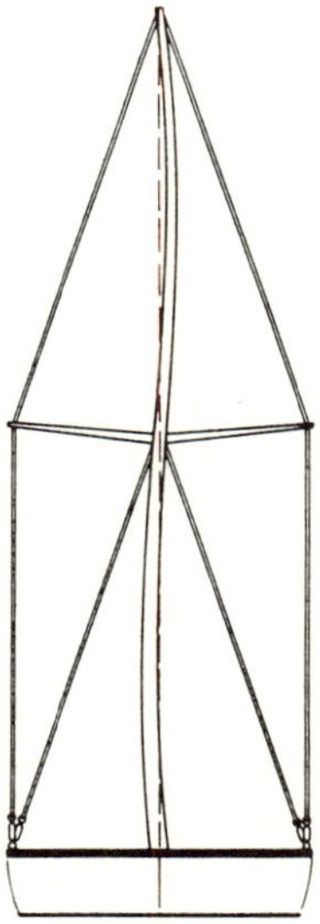

Often several adjustments of upper and lower shrouds are needed to correct double hook in a mast.

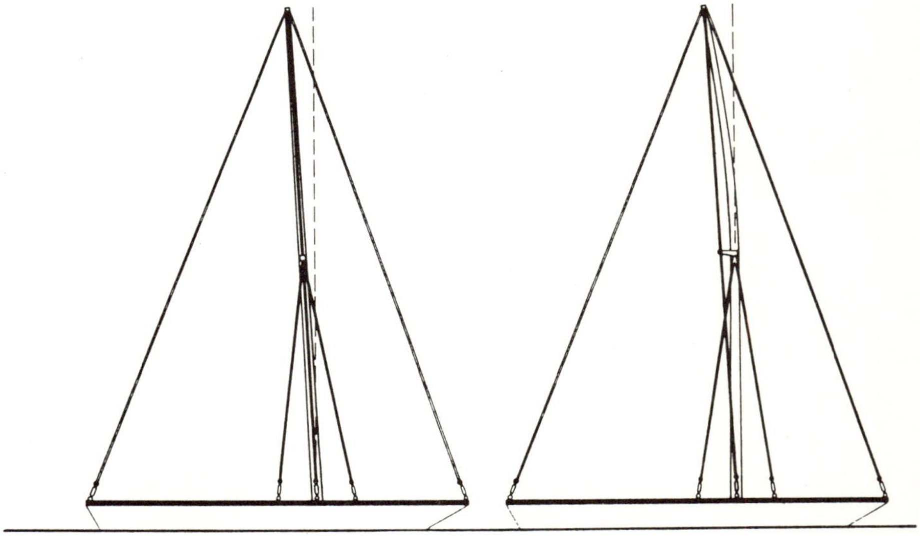

The rake, as well as any bend in the mast, is adjusted with both backstays and the headstays or forestays.

which makes up about 50 percent of the rope's strength. The core, therefore, is likely to stay strong longer, except in certain exceptions to be noted.

Visual inspection of rope is important. Cuts, abrasion, damage by chemicals, and friction burns are the main things to look for in the rope itself. Friction, as on bitts and capstans, can generate serious heat and melting damage. If the melted or fused length is more than four diameters of the rope, the rope should be downgraded, discarded or, under some circumstances, saved by turning end-for-end.

Splices, particularly eye splices in double-braid rope, require careful inspection. The throat, the female side of the eye, is the critical area. Abrasion, cuts, improper splicing, and improper use—like stretching the throat—are all potential problems. The apex of the eye, where the load bears, is the other critical point.

Wear on the cover strand is the most critical for most kinds of synthetic braided ropes. However, certain new synthetics, such as Kevlar, can deteriorate from flexing inside the cover if used on too small a sheave. The breakdown of fibers can weaken an otherwise "strong" rope.

Hardness, in heavily used rope, will indicate reduced strength.

Pulled or cut strands are hazards. A pulled strand may snag on a foreign object during use, leading to further damage. It is often possible to work a pulled strand back into the rope by hand manipulation. A tight whipping will also protect the rope.

If the core is visible through the cover, the rope must be respliced or discarded.

If more than 50 percent of the surface strands are damaged, discard the rope.

If there are more than four consecutive pulled strands, not fixable, discard the rope.

If the core is damaged, pulled, cut, or melted, downgrade or discard the rope.

If burns or melting is visible for more than four diameters, downgrade the rope.

If the rope has been heavily shock-loaded, discard it.

If there is abrasion on the inside radius of the eye or damage to the female side of the eye, resplice.

If there is extensive rust on nylon rope, from contact with bare iron surfaces, severe loss in breaking strength can result.

However, rust does not chemically attack polyester or polypropylene rope.

The recommended working load for synthetic rope is between 11 and 20 percent of the breaking strength of new rope. This applies to static loads, not to dynamic or shock loads.

WRINKLES

"**The tools of the inspector** are tacking hammer, flashlight, awl, and checkoff list. If it won't stand a little tapping, it won't stand up in heavy seas."—U.S. Coast Guard pamphlet on Commercial Vessel Safety.

To wash synthetic rope: put in a mesh bag and put it in an ordinary household washer. Use a mild detergent. Rinse well, but dry in the air, not in the clothes dryer. At other times, a rinse with a hose to take out sand or a dip in the lake can be beneficial.

Compass Check. Although stainless steel, in most alloys, is nonmagnetic, two things that can still affect your compass are: (1) cold working, as hammering, on stainless, which magnetizes it; and (2) a few alloys that are already mildly magnetic. To check, use a magnet on metal within five feet of your compass. If the magnet sticks, the integrity of the compass may be a problem.

The National Association of Marine Surveyors is a recognized professional organization. Its members work with some, but not all, of the safety organizations. Their address is 86 Windsor Gate Drive, North Hills, NY 11040.

The American Boat and Yacht Council is a membership organization that includes manufacturers, naval architects and engineers, other recognized safety organizations, and members of the boating public. Its technical work, done by committees of experts in their field, working with professional staff personnel, includes the drawing up of standards for boat construction and installations, with many closely related to deck seamanship. Their most valuable publication is a book called *Standards and Recommended Practices for Small Craft.* It is updated frequently. The address of ABYC is P.O. Box 806, 190 Ketcham Avenue, Amityville, NY 11701.

Before anyone goes aloft for an inspection trip in a bosun's chair, make sure the halyard, chair, and fittings have been carefully inspected.

◀
Every time you furl a sail, inspect it and nearby fittings for wear or incorrect adjustment.

40569
RI 3929 AA

Chapter 15

Emergency! Emergency!

If a towline breaks in the middle—in a clear, straight segment of the line—it will snap back directly toward the fixed ends and any persons in the way. If the breakage occurs around a curved surface (a bollard or the drum on a winch), the recoiling line sweeps sideways as well, endangering a wide area.

If a line breaks when you're in the way, there's no way you can use this information to keep from being decapitated by the recoil. The snapback is faster than your reactions.

But there is prevention, which is why the U.S. Coast Guard Research and Development Center made tests of rope stretching and breaking to establish the facts about the direction of the recoil. Numerous accidents had already shown the power that builds up in a rope under tension.

The danger of a rope breaking might be anywhere—even if you were standing on a dock just watching someone else bring a boat in on a windy day.

You can write your own rules for preventing snapback. Never stand directly in line with a rope that is under great tension. Use correct operating procedures. Don't use frayed or damaged rope for critical hauling or hoisting. Be careful not to subject lines to the extra strain of shock loads. For many other sometime hazards there are similar rules, based on experience as well as common sense.

In this chapter on emergencies, their prevention, and cure, you will find a number of practical solutions that enable seamen to keep a problem from developing into a crisis. There's more here

◀
A canvas around the hull (tarpaulin, sail, or awning) doesn't seal a big leak, but it slows it up enough to save a boat after a collision.

The Coast Guard lashes the damaged boat alongside and moves slowly into shallow water. (This picture was made before the PFD rule.)

than any one boatperson will ever need, of course. The trans-ocean sailor doesn't run the same risks as the crew of a power cruiser crossing Chesapeake Bay or the skipper of an outboard towing another outboard whose motor has just conked out.

The summary of how to avoid dire emergencies is:

▲ Have your own prevention-and-avoidance program.
▲ Have the right gear for the potential situations you may encounter.
▲ Be sure you—or your crew—have the special skills that may be necessary.

PREVENTION AND AVOIDANCE

Safe operation, considering that the weather and other hazards are always with us, means avoiding things that turn small problems into big ones.

Just as you glance occasionally at your instruments—water temperature gauge, oil pressure gauge, tachometer—to make sure everything is operating smoothly, it is a good idea to look over the whole boat.

When first coming on board: Look aloft, look forward, look aft. A shackle pin half out, a loose line, another boat that has been

The damaged boat is run to shore and the Coast Guard at Block Island starts pumping it out. This was a harbor accident—the easy kind.

dragging its anchor . . . the hazards can be quite small or they can loom out of the fog twice as big as life.

A TON AND A HALF STRONG

Since not every hazard of the sea can be controlled, one aspect of safety is having the proper gear—and the knowledge of how to use it—on board for every situation that might reasonably be expected. You might think that the minimum for a small boat that doesn't go far might be measured as a pound of cure—not counting fire extinguishers, Personal Flotation Devices, and the other safety equipment required by law. But you would be forgetting one item: Although U.S. law does not require a boat to have an anchor aboard, it is an essential of safe operation. An anchor, of course, is not just a parking device for a fishing stop or a cruising overnight. There is the phrase from the mother tongue to remind us: "An anchor to windward."

A knife, several miscellaneous lengths of rope, and a minimum first-aid kit are the basic extras beyond the boat's own equipment that should always be aboard, or even part of your personal gear on someone else's boat. These minimums should apply on anything larger than a canoe on an inland pond.

One other thing is required: an attitude of mind.

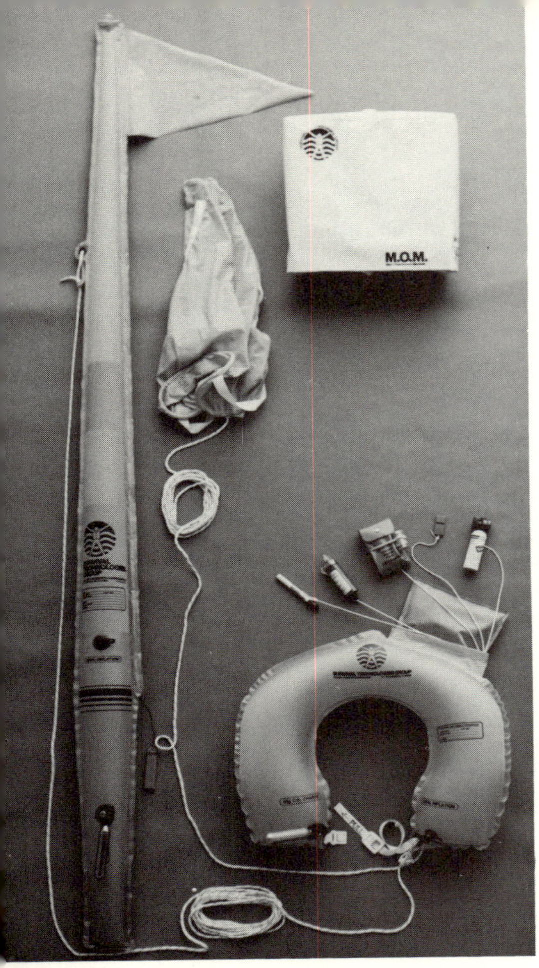

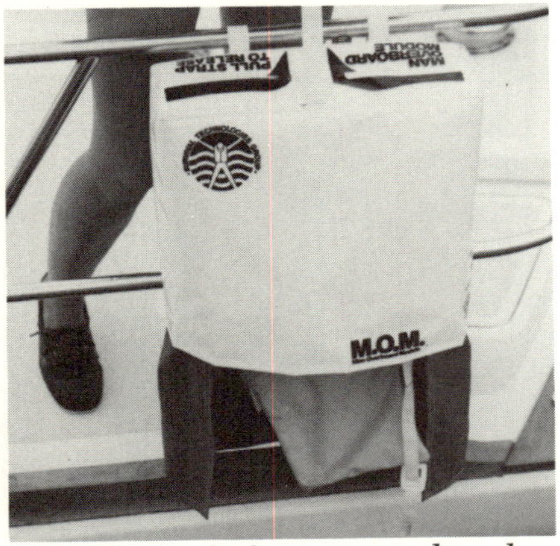

M.O.M. stands for man-overboard module. This one, from Survival Technologies, has lights, whistle, a buoy with a pennant, and even sea marker dye.

Now that we have your attention, let's turn to the sport of survival, and seven ways to keep the crew's attention.

Whether it's family cruising or a crew of agile sailors, there's a way to get it all together. There are seven emergency drills, and they have been tried, one way or another, by capable seamen.

In some cases, a little preparation is desirable. In others, only one person does the preparation.

WALDO HOWLAND'S MAN OVERBOARD DRILL

You can talk about the right procedure, and you should. The first thing to do if a voice cries "Person overboard!" is to get a life preserver ready—but don't throw it until you know where the victim is. If you're sailing, the quickest way to get to the person in the water is to jibe—but that's assuming a complete crew that is capable of jibing in a hurry. There could be circumstances when starting the motor and coming about might save time.

The best way to hold a man overboard drill is the way Waldo Howland, of Concordia Boats, tells about in his autobiography: The well-prepared crew knows the drill will be held. The weather is pleasant. An orange Personal Flotation Device (PFD) is thrown into the water and someone yells "Man overboard!" The crew starts to do its thing—and then they notice what has really happened: One crew member, primed for the job and wearing a PFD, has actually gone into the water! Now it's a real scramble!

- ▲ The crew of a small boat may have nothing more to throw to him than a floating cushion.
- ▲ On any size boat, one person should watch the floating victim. The best plan is for the skipper to be ready to point and say, "You watch him!"
- ▲ A rough-water cruising boat or an ocean racer will have a man-overboard pole ready. A horseshoe buoy, a strobe light, possibly a line ready to trail, or a Throw Bag, complete with line and a plastic float, are the handy things that should be there, ready.

Prevention:

Small children on any boat should wear PFDs, be watched, and know enough not to ride the bow, walk around in rough weather, or break the rules. Netting under the lifelines is a good kind of safety measure.

Rugged men, sailing in rough weather, should know that lifelines, safety harnesses that clip on, and the wearing of PFDs are sensible. Personnel of the U.S. Coast Guard wear PFDs at work, not only to set a good example, but because some of their work could involve personal danger.

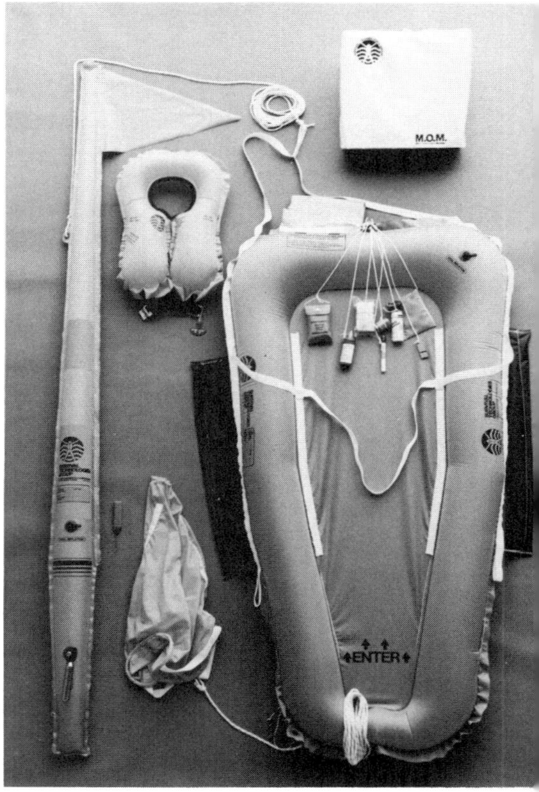

THE MOTOR CONKS OUT DRILL

This one can be a half-hour quiz session instead of playing Trivial Pursuit. "If the motor died right now . . . what would we do?"

The answers will range from "Get the anchor ready!" or "Get the mainsail up, there's a breeze" to "We can drift out here in the middle of the Sound for hours," depending on whether the situation is one with a narrow channel, a fog bank rolling in, or "it was time to get the sails up anyway."

THE SQUALL DRILL

This might as well be a real sail drill. Recognizing severe squalls before they hit, knowing what ought to be done, and having the crew skilled enough to drop and furl the sails are all part of good seamanship.

"WE'RE AGROUND!" DRILL

This one will happen to the crew of almost any boat. A small sailboat can come about in a hurry and get away, in many cases. A small outboard boat can let some of the people get into the water (keeping away from the propeller blades!). Turn off the motor!

Knowing how to use the anchor to kedge off, how to lighten the boat, how to wait for the tide to turn—all are possible solutions.

If it is the direst emergency of all, having a keel boat driven on the beach, a couple of points should be known—but not practiced until the real thing requires it.

1) You can get some weight on the mast, or pull it down with a line, and the boat will be afloat again, where it can be moved out to deeper water.
2) If this, or any other drill like it, actually comes up, remember that the halyard fittings aren't made to take that kind of strain. If there's time and proper gear at hand, rig a separate line to the masthead and use that to get the boat afloat.

You can hold on to a small inflatable raft even if you aren't agile enough to climb aboard.

MINOR PROBLEM DRILL

One of the best preventives is to have all persons aboard take part, at least once a season, in a safety inspection. Look for chafe on the rigging that might become a major problem later. Inspect the steering gear; have a plan of what to do if it should break. If the crew members have been careless about stowing things below, let them find their own ways to protect their property. Make sure everyone knows where the fire extinguishers are, how to get them out of their brackets, and how to use them.

ANOTHER BOAT IN TROUBLE DRILL

Not everyone on the water is a good citizen. Learn how to keep an eye out for real problems, like people trying to signal that they are in distress or people lost in hazy visibility who could use some tactful help.

See what you would do if a tow were necessary.

HELICOPTER RESCUE DRILL

Richard Hiscock's valuable newsletter *Safety Notes for Fishermen* presents good advice, which we paraphrase, for helicopter evacuation from a vessel of someone needing medical attention. Save this for a real emergency.

Remember that helo operations can be hazardous to both your patient and the helicopter crew. Make preparations carefully. Follow the helo's instructions.

Preparations Prior to the Helicopter's Arrival

1) Provide continuous radio guard on 156.8 MHZ (Channel 16 VHF-FM), 2182 KHZ; or other specified voice frequency.
2) Select and clear the most suitable hoist area. Secure loose gear, awnings, and antenna wires. Trice up running rigging and booms. The stern is preferred for the hoist area.
3) If hoist is at night, light the pick-up area as well as possible. DO NOT SHINE ANY LIGHTS ON THE HELICOPTER BECAUSE THEY WILL BLIND THE PILOT. Put a light on any obstructions in the vicinity so the pilot will be aware of their positions.

▶ *Helicopter rescue may be minutes away (or you may not need it for years). Procedures, including communications, should be known in advance.*

U.S. Coast Guardsmen, to set an example and because they stand into danger on short notice, wear their orange PFDs whenever they are afloat and on duty.

4) Because high noise level under the helicopter makes any voice communication virtually impossible, arrange for the crew to use hand signals.

Hoist Operations

1) If possible, move the patient as close to the hoist area as possible.
2) Make sure patient is tagged to indicate what and when medication has been given. Patient should have appropriate documentation: passport, visa, hospital insurance card, etc.
3) Have the patient in a life jacket if conditions permit.
4) Change course to permit the vessel to ride as easily as possible, preferably with the wind on the port bow.
5) Reduce speed but maintain steerageway.
6) When ready, signal the helo that you are ready for the hoist. If you do not have radio contact, signal the helo with a "come on" with your hand.

7) To avoid static shock, allow the basket or stretcher to touch deck prior to handling.
8) If a trail line is dropped by the helo, guide the basket or litter to the deck with the line. Keep the line clear. The line will not cause shock.
9) If a litter is required, it will be necessary to move the patient to the special litter, which will be lowered by the helo. Be prepared to do this quickly. Be sure the patient is strapped in, face up, with a life jacket on if conditions permit.
10) If it is necessary to take the litter away from the hoist point, unhook the hoist cable and keep it free for the helo to haul in. DO NOT SECURE THE CABLE TO THE VESSEL OR ATTEMPT TO MOVE THE STRETCHER WITHOUT UNHOOKING IT.
11) When the patient is strapped in the litter, signal the helo to lower the cable. Allow the hook to touch the deck before handling it, to avoid static shock. Hook up and signal hoist (thumbs up). Steady the stretcher from swinging or turning.
12) If basket is used, place the patient, with a life jacket on, in the basket with hands clear of the sides. Signal for hoist when ready (thumbs up).
13) If a trail line is attached, use it to steady the basket or stretcher.

    Note: The international signal for an aircraft that wants to direct a surface craft to a distress location is: circling the surface craft while opening and closing the throttle or changing propeller pitch (noticeable by change of sound) while crossing ahead of the surface craft and proceeding in the direction of the distress. You should follow the aircraft if you receive such a signal. Additionally, attempt to communicate with the aircraft on 156.8 MHZ (Channel 16 VHF-FM). When your assistance is no longer needed, the aircraft will cross your wake, opening and closing the throttle or changing propeller pitch.

USING A BOSUN'S CHAIR

If rigging breaks and it is necessary to put a crew member up the mast, using a bosun's chair, remember:

▲ If the weather is bad, delay the operation.
▲ Inspect the bosun's chair and all gear and lines used *before* sending anyone aloft.
▲ Use a line circling the crew member and the mast, to prevent swinging, at the least, and as a safety device in case of a mishap.
▲ The number-one choice for a bosun's chair is a plywood bottom, criss-crossed underneath with synthetic rope, such as 1/2″ Dacron, making a backup as well as a hoist. The top of the hoist should be a 5/11″ by 2″ outside diameter ring or an equivalent bow shackle, with the lines seized tightly. The length of the line should be kept to a minimum.

The four holes in the chair's bottom are for the lifting lines. There should be figure-eight knots in the bridle, immediately below each of the corner holes, to prevent sliding and tipping.

Besides the main lines of the chair itself, and the rigging as described, there should also be:

1) A snap shackle on the same bow or ring, for attaching to an extra halyard in rough weather. If this halyard is kept taut against the mast, it keeps the chair from swinging.
2) Two 1/4″ lines, perhaps six feet long, to secure the person in the chair and to fasten the chair in a working position when it is aloft.
3) Two lines, one from each side of the chair bottom, which can be tended from below, to keep the chair from swinging.

Going aloft in a bosun's chair, wearing only shorts and a short-sleeve shirt, exposes the worker to chafes and other injuries.

Pockets for tools, attached to the chair, are fair to good. A canvas bucket with outside pockets for small tools is one of the best ways to carry needed items aloft. Larger tools should be pre-attached, with adequate lines, so they can be used with no fear of dropping them.

The canvas sling type of bosun's chair is comfortable for some persons, but not all of the different varieties are secure or workable.

If there is an adequate crew for the hoisting and helping, getting the worker up the mast is no problem. A winch, if it can be rigged, works well, but it is important that someone tend the line carefully. It is also possible to use the halyard to hoist a block so that a tackle can be used. Reel winches are not considered safe for hoisting personnel.

A flag halyard can sometimes be used to hoist extra tools or fittings to the workman on the bosun's chair. The old-time name for this, or a similar hoisting line rove through a block, was a *gantline.* A *gantline hitch* is a most useful knot if you are going to hoist yourself, single-handed, up the mast. It is tied clear around your body.

Anyone going aloft in a bosun's chair is likely to remember that one of the basic rules of seamanship is: "One hand for yourself, one hand for the ship."

Safety harness, for wear on deck in rough weather (and always at sea at night) . . .

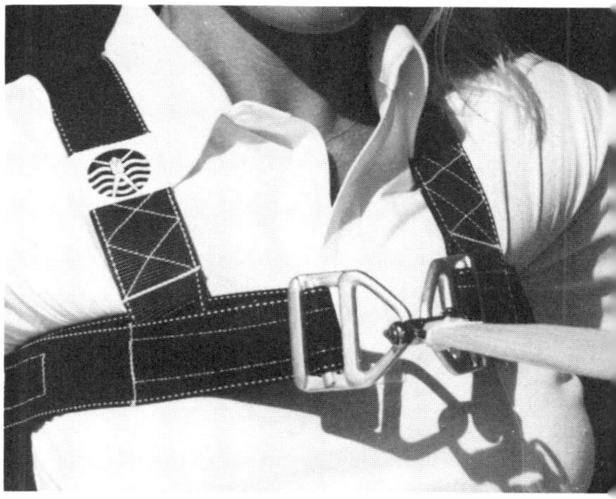

. . . is adjustable for most sizes and for either sex.

SAFETY HARNESSES

Sailing in rough weather or at night, even when you are not in a race that requires safety harnesses, may very well remind you that in addition to the "one hand for yourself" way of holding on, a secure harness that can be clipped to a strong center lifeline, a jackstay, is a way to stay alive.

You have to have a strong hook at the harness end of the tether, and one that can be released. In recent months, two sailors were lost in an Australian race when they could not release their harnesses as the boat sank.

Regular examination of all such gear is important, as is practice in putting it on.

The newest, and one of the most ingenious, improvements in the lifeline/harness systems is the free-running harness system. Instead of hooking and unhooking oneself while moving around the deck, you traverse the stanchions and other supports. The Latchway passes through U-shaped hangers on the lifeline, so you stay attached at all times.

"MAYDAY! MAYDAY! MAYDAY!"

Distress communications procedures should be understood by several persons on board. Even those not regularly using radiotelephone equipment on a boat should have a rudimentary knowledge of how to turn a transmitter on and how to use it.

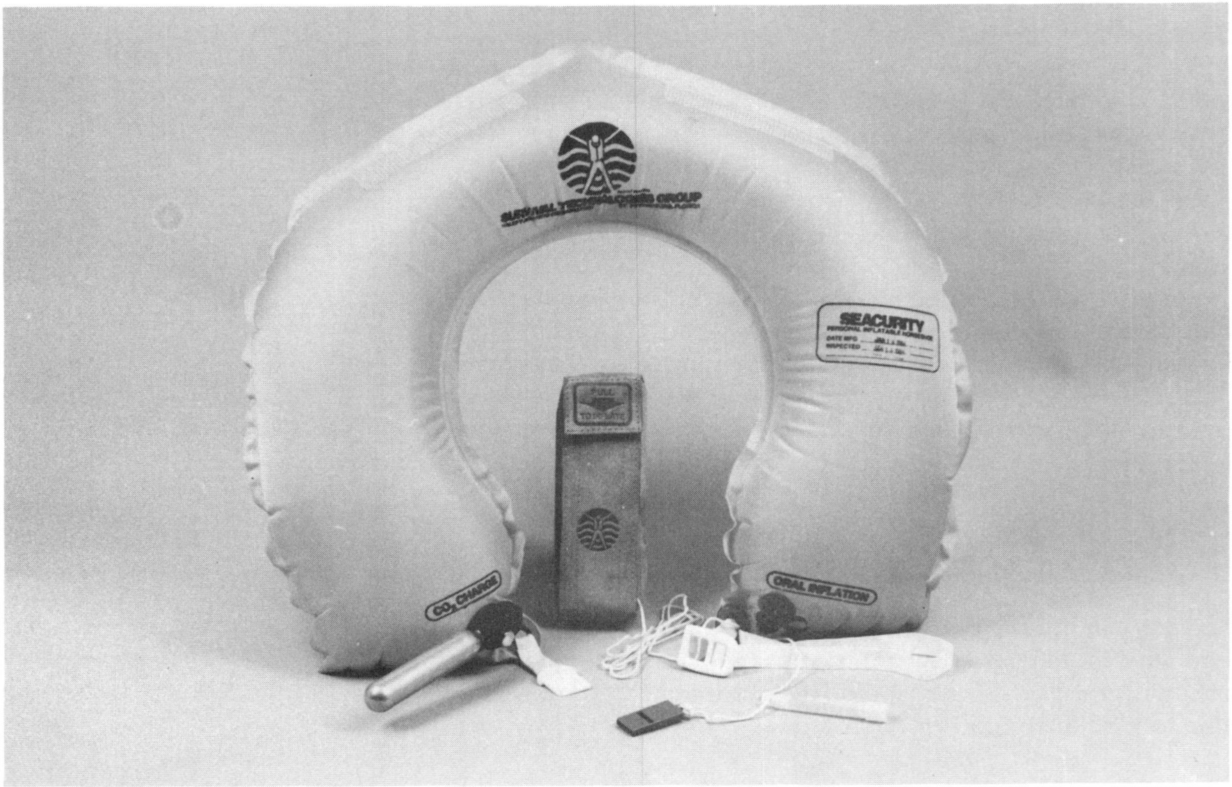
SEACURITY
CHARGE
ORAL INFLATION

The U.S. Coast Guard says the following procedures should be followed:

◀ *Try the floating test yourself.*

1) Speak slowly and clearly.
2) Make sure the radio is turned on.
3) Turn to the distress frequency, Channel 16 for VHF (FM), 2182 kHz, or Channel 9 for Citizens Band.
4) Press microphone button and transmit, "Mayday! Mayday! Mayday!" If available, use the radiotelephone alarm signal, two alternate tones to attract the attention of persons on radio watch.
5) Identify yourself by saying "This is *Boatname, Boatname, Boatname,* CALL sign."
6) Give your position. Identify landmarks that are near, give distances to known geographical positions.
7) Tell what is wrong.
8) Tell what kind of assistance is required.
9) Give the number of people aboard, if any are injured, etc.
10) Give the estimated seaworthiness of your boat.
11) Give a description of your boat, length, type, color of hull, number of masts.
12) Tell which frequency or channel you will be listening on.
13) End your message with, "This is *Boatname Call Sign*, over."
14) Wait for a response. If no answer, repeat your call. If still no answer, try another channel or frequency.

If you hear the phonetically pronounced words *Seelonce Mayday* on the air or *Seelonce Distress,* you should know that all boats not involved in the rescue are being asked to keep off the air.

WRINKLES

Safety Notes for Fishermen is a newsletter published by Richard C. Hiscock, 545 Old Harbor Road, North Chatham, MA 02650. Telephone: (617) 945-9098.

◀ *A horsehoe, with whistle and light, is the minimum for a person overboard. In ocean situations a complete man-overboard module is required.*

Survival suits would be available for more offshore sailors and fishermen if they studied the effects of hypothermia. In 32° water, you will probably be unconscious in fifteen minutes. In water from

40° to 50°, you may stay awake as long as an hour and you can survive up to three hours. In water that is 60° to 70°, you might last 40 hours. Above 70° and 80°, your survival time is a great deal longer.

A ton-and-a-half strong is the requirement for safety harnesses and for a secure lifeline for an ocean racing crew, running the whole length of the boat. There are many kinds and brands on the market and they keep changing (sometimes in response to well-informed criticism and evaluations). Here are some basic points about safety harnesses, based on the Ocean Racing Club and the Transpac:

Every critical part of the harness, including the hook, should exceed the recommended safety limit of 3,000 pounds' yield strength. That's a ton and a half.

The safety hook should have a positive lock—but a way to get it open in a hurry.

Since they have to be worn under working conditions, the harnesses should be the correct size and fully adjustable; the straps should not be constantly slipping off the shoulders. The harnesses with cross straps in the back meet this requirement.

◀ *One kind of prevention is safety netting. It is good when children are aboard—but also helps keep sails from getting adrift.*

Mooring whips protect boats from wakes and wind.

Glossary

NAUTICAL LANGUAGE

If you think salty language is sometimes overdone, consider the following:

"Pintle nozzle" . . . "integrated stage" . . . "pulse motor" . . . and still one more in the age of acronyms: "SLEEC." Fortunately, for all except those who use "advanced solid fuel rocket motor technology," these are space-age words and not in this nautical glossary. Boating persons know, in any case, that a pintle is the fitting on the rudder that slides into the gudgeon on the stern.

The language of sailing and the sea, like most special languages is rich and colorful. It is not ambiguous, but in many cases there is more than one way to say almost the same thing. Often the short way is used as a command, as in "Jibe-O." (For a guest who isn't helping to sail, "Jibe-O" can also be considered as a warning, meaning, "Keep your head down when the boom swings over!") A sophisticated racing sailor, perhaps bored with the short way of saying "Ready about!" may say: "Guess it's time to flop her." This isn't part of nautical language; it's another way of being preppy.

Ground tackle means the anchor, the shackles, the short piece of chain, if there is one, and the anchor line or rode (the rode may also be chain). So if the skipper asks "Is the ground tackle in order?" he means all the parts necessary to anchor.

This glossary, like the book, concentrates on the words relating to cordage, rigging, and knots, and the skills of seamanship dealing with them. In a broad sense, therefore, it is a glossary of "marlinespike seamanship."

Some nautical words have two meanings: A *bend* is a particular kind of knot, and to *bend on* a sail means to insert the slides into the groove, fasten the tack and clew, attach the halyard, and (unless the sail is to be kept furled) hoist the sail. Originally, *bending on a sail* meant using line and bends (the appropriate knots) to attach the sail, before slides, hanks, luff grooves, and other devices were developed. To *bend* means to attach.

Similarly, some nautical words have more than one commonly used spelling. *Marline* and *marlin*, *marlinespike* and *marlinspike*—and there is also a way of attaching canvas to a spar or line with a series of hitches called *marling*. Clifford W. Ashley, author of the noted and scholarly *Ashley Book of Knots*, called all work with cordage "marlingspike" seamanship. Rather than swing back and forth from one expert to another, this book uses the *Merriam-Webster Dictionary* as the spelling style authority, although hundreds of these words and meanings are not to be found in Webster or any other standard dictionary.

The pronunciation of nautical words is often interrelated with the spelling, of course. Boatswain is pronounced bosun and in consequence most writers use some form of aural spelling. You can find bos'n, bo's'n, bosun, or bo'sun for the "petty officer in charge of gear and maintenance." This book's only references are to the bosun's locker and the bosun's chair, and in this case we don't use the Webster spelling. *Boatswain* is literary and historical, but you never pronounce it with the "swain," of course.

Many nautical words have shades of meaning. Some of them are obsolete and/or "literary" or are taken from other fields of knowledge. Others are as modern as the airplane.

One will often hear someone on a sailboat or powerboat referring to an approaching boat in terms of the dial of a clock: "Bandit at three o'clock" instead of "There's a boat on our starboard beam." This, as everyone knows, is aviation "slanguage." Some of that, and even a few mountaineering words, such as *carabiner*, have drifted into the language of the sea.

Almost everyone knows that many words of the sea have worked their way into common speech. *Scuttlebutt*, or gossip, comes from the name of the drinking water cask around which sailors would exchange small talk and rumors. *POSH*, once the initials written on the ticket of an important British personage bound for the East on the Peninsula and Oriental Steamship Line, stood for "Port Out, Starboard Home" and was supposed to designate a stateroom on the shady side of the steamer. Now *posh* means "luxurious" and "smart" even on land. *Cut and run, figurehead, three sheets to the wind*—all are colorful words with added colorful meanings, even for landsmen who may never go near the water.

For those who are on the water a great deal, the special language comes naturally. They know that *mainsail* is pronounced "mains'l" and there's a *jib*, the sail, and a *jibe*, the sailing maneuver, as well as a *gybe*, the same maneuver when the British spell it. They can spell words like *forecastle* and *studdingsail*, but they know to pronounce them in the elided way. Many sailors know that an American *turnbuckle* is a British *rigging screw*, or that what is called *Dacron* in the United States is called *Terylene* by the Brits, just as they know the word *Brits* is preppy language for people whose home is Great Britain. Both *Dacron* (U.S.) and *Terylene* (UK) are proprietary brand names for polyester, used in making rope and sails. The same fiber has half a dozen other brand names when made by various companies, and still more names in Germany, France, Sweden, and other countries.

As a general proposition, most sailors and boatmen don't overdo the salty talk—except perhaps jokingly, or in the wintertime, when they get homesick for the water and nostalgic about the boats. This brings up another point: There are many old, old words in the "sea language." In some cases this glossary includes words that are no longer essential in the operation of small boats. There are reasons for the inclusions: In some cases, an old way of keeping a topping lift out of the leech of the sail makes a comeback when an old-time rigger figures a way to use a block that runs up and down the backstay (it's called a monkey). At other times you may be reading a book, perhaps *Captain Hornblower*, and want to figure out just what braces were on a square-rigger. So a few dozen of the words from the days of wooden ships and iron men are included here.

There is a new/old word in this book and in this glossary. Here is the story: Rod Stephens Jr., the expert sailor and naval architect of the noted firm of Sparkman & Stephens, has for a long time been urging the rediscovery of an old knot, the buntline hitch, which goes back to the days of square-riggers. Samson Cordage Company's Gale P. Foster, himself a sailor, put the knot in a leaflet and has been encouraging its use. The modern uses of the buntline hitch, however, have not been shown in a book until now.

Here is Mr. Stephens in a letter to the author: "My first introduction to the knot was in the 1928 Bermuda Race on Graham Bigelow's Alden schooner, *Teal.* The Captain was a Nova Scotian whose name escapes me, but he asked us to use this particular knot when attaching the halyards to the fisherman staysail or the big balloon main top staysail. The halyards were double-ended and there was no hardware on them to begin with.

"He called the knot 'inside half hitches.' The knot was easy to tie and took up virtually no length—perhaps that was its biggest virtue—and was not too hard to untie.

"The next use of this knot was in Royal Ocean Racing Club competition, where there was a limit to the foot length of the genoas. This made it advantageous to have the shortest possible attachment from the clew to the necessary deck lead block. Most of the aggressive sailors used this knot as it does pull absolutely tight and permits one to bring the clew of the jib right against the block. To make the most out of the limited foot length, it was obviously desirable for the clew to be as low as possible; hence the need for a short knot.

"Next time it came up was when the German sailmaker Hans Beilken took me to the Gleistein rope factory in Bremen to show me the very low-stretch rope they were manufacturing. He thought this would be of interest and value for many yacht applications.

"This low-stretch rope proved a big step ahead and it almost necessitated the use of the buntline hitch where you wanted maximum hoist on all halyards and, at the same time, a good stopper to prevent jamming in the block. (This can happen with a splice and some other kinds of hardware, particularly a sort of carrot-shaped metal piece which Gleistein was recommending but which I never thought much of.)

"Next step was at the London Boat Show in 1974 or 1975, when Marlow was showing me their pre-stretched rope which they thought was better than Gleistein's because you could splice it. My reaction to this was that I was sorry you could splice it because I thought splices made a lot of trouble by sometimes jamming in the blocks. They also made it difficult to end-for-end a halyard or sheet, so, all in all, the ability to splice was not an advantage. Marlow's next point was that the splice would be stronger than a knot, so I suggested they make a little test, since they had the necessary equipment.

"Marlow came back very quickly with the astonishing information that 'my knot' actually was very nearly the same strength as a good splice and measurably better than a bowline and a great deal stronger than a square knot.

"Next step was to try to find the right name, because for a while someone wanted to call it the 'Rod Knot.' I did not want that. In *Ashley's Book of Knots,* I found the knot was called a *buntline hitch* in that authoritative source. Let's keep that name.

"For the reasons outlined above, I think it is probably the best knot for attaching a halyard to a shackle or a snap shackle, for its economy in length, and for its reluctance to jam in the block."

Here is the buntline hitch:

A Alfa. White and blue swallow-tailed flag in the International Signal Code. As a single letter, signal Alfa means "Diver down; keep clear," usually in reference to a salvage diving operation.

A-900 Working name for a high-strength, low-stretch, and lightweight fiber for rope and sailcloth, developed by Allied Corporation, later renamed Spectra-900.

abrasion The wearing away of surface fibers of rope, usually from incorrect leads (sharp angles), and rough surfaces on chocks and fairleads. Rope can also suffer from internal abrasion caused by sand. Friction, as on winch drums, can damage rope through excessive heat.

A.C.E. Trade name for Allied's polyester fiber.

acetal Generic name for a hard, strong plastic used for some marine rigging parts, particularly sheaves. Trade name: Delrin.

adjuster, shroud One of several devices for controlling the tension of standing rigging on a sailboat, using rows of precisely spaced holes and pins. *Deadeyes* were an early form of adjustment device, supplanted by *turnbuckles* (British: *rigging screws*).

advantage, mechanical Ratio of output force to input force, in a purchase, using blocks and rope, or gearing, as a worm gear in a mechanical outhaul or other gear systems in a winch. Thus a *block-and-tackle* using a double block and a single block might have a theoretical mechanical advantage of 1:3; the input rope moves three feet with a force of one pound, and the output rope moves one foot but with the force to lift three pounds (ignoring friction).

after guy A line running from the outboard end of a spinnaker to a block on the quarter, used to control the angle of the pole and thus the sail. The foreguy is eased as the after guy is taken in.

anchor Mechanical device whose weight and shape cause it to dig into the bottom, holding the vessel by means of the *rode.* See *Bruce, Danforth, stockless, yachtsman.* The parts of an anchor are the flukes, the shank, the stock, and the eye, although these may vary with the anchor's geometry.

anchor bend One of several knots that may be used to attach a rope to an anchor or part of the an-

chor system. Often the end of the line is further secured by a seizing.

anchor buoy A float temporarily attached to the end of an anchor line so that a vessel may return to the same anchorage. When used in a permanent anchoring system, it would be called a mooring buoy.

anchor, sea An in-the-water device (*drogue*), usually conical, to which a boat or ship is secured during storms at sea. The sea anchor holds the vessel's bow or stern to the wind, unlike the situation of lying ahull, when the boat is usually broadside to wind and waves.

anodize To treat the surface of a metal (usually aluminum) so that further oxidation and pitting do not occur. Anodizing is an electrolytic process.

answering pennant The signal flag (code flag) flown to indicate that a vessel sees the visual signals being transmitted.

Antron One of many trade names for polyester fiber. See *Dacron.*

aramid A high-strength, low-stretch fiber more generally known by one of its trade names, Kevlar.

arm the lead To coat the bottom of a sounding lead with tallow or waterproof grease in order to pick up bottom samples, as a means of determining position or making a judgment on an anchorage.

Ashley's stopper knot One of several choices of a knot to be tied into the end or other part of a line, to

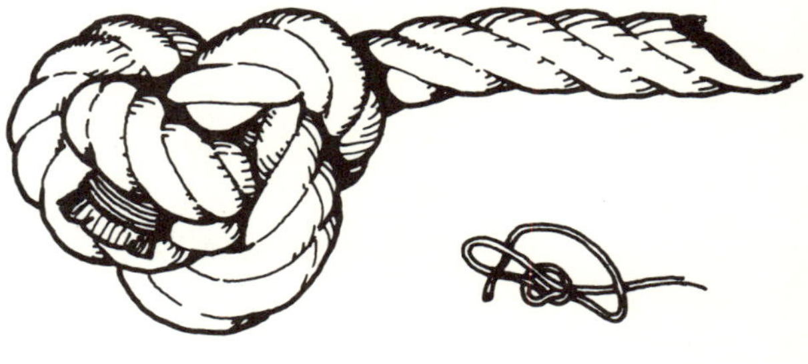

prevent the line inadvertently going through a block or fairlead. See *figure eight*.

aspect ratio The proportion (relationship) between the height of a sail and its width. Thus, a tall narrow sail might have an aspect ratio of 5, while a sail that is wider might have a ratio of 3 or 4. The term is also used to describe the relationship between the length and width of an airplane wing.

aweigh An anchor that has been raised just clear of the bottom is said to be aweigh.

B Bravo. Swallow-tailed red code flag, letter *B*. As a single-letter signal, it means, "I am loading, discharging, or carrying dangerous cargo," such as explosives. Flying this flag when racing is a special signal meaning, "I intend to make a protest," so it is often called a "protest flag."

backsplice A method of finishing the end of a laid rope so that it will not unravel. Each *strand* in turn is tucked under, after starting by unlaying the strands and making a *crown knot*.

backstay The part of the *standing rigging* that supports the mast from aft. Double backstays, one on each side of the boat, are called runners or running backstays (one is usually slacked off while the other is in use). Often the single backstay is used as an antenna for a radio-telephone, and it may have other functions, such as holding the adjustment line for the *topping lift* or even the sheeting arrangement for the mainsail in certain boomless rigs.

baggywrinkle The padding, usually made from discarded rope yarns, wound around rigging, such as shrouds, lazyjacks, or backstays (or the ends of spreaders) to protect the sails from chafe.

bail A fitting, typically a wide U-shape like a flanged strap, on a spar. A sheet or vang is fastened to the bail. Also, the handle of a bucket.

Barber haul Control line, used in racing, to adjust the angle of lead in a jib sheet. Usually, the Barber haul or hauler is attached to the sheet by a ring or a block.

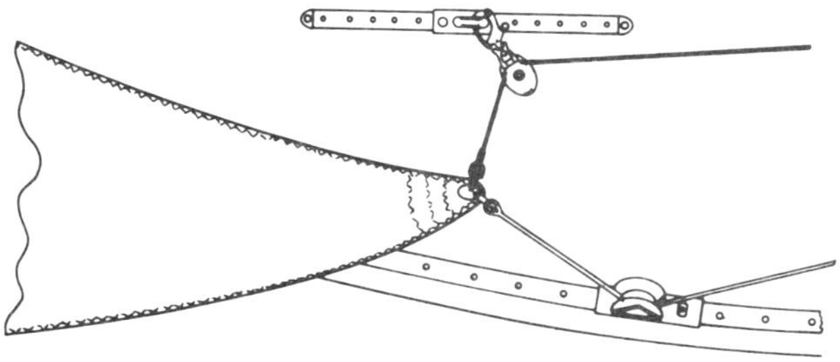

batten A flexible strip (wood, plastic, or reinforced wood) to help shape (keep flat) the *roach* of a sail. The normal mainsail has four battens. A full-length batten, as on a multihull sailboat, helps shape the entire sail. Battens are also used in awnings and to hold hatch tarps.

batten pocket A pocket sewn into the leech of a sail, holding the batten. It is normally at right angles to the *leech*, except the lowest batten, which is often parallel to the boom, for easy reefing. Batten pockets are either closed with a tie or so made that the battens are held in place by the shape of the pockets.

batten knot A special knot (*surgeon's knot in reverse*) to hold a batten in its pocket.

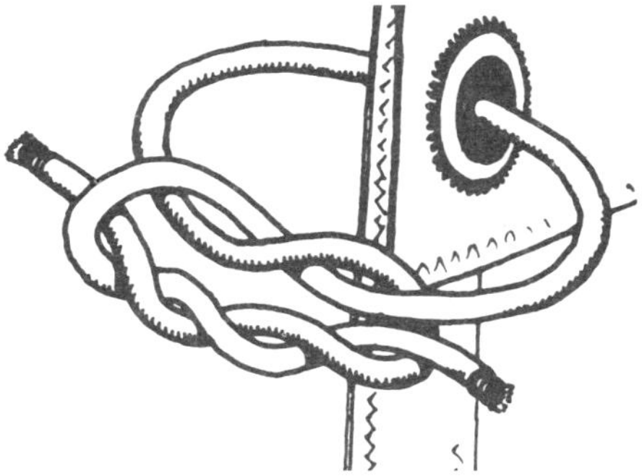

becket A rope handle, a permanent loop made in the end of a rope or wire, or a fitting on a *block* to which the end of a rope may be fastened.

becket bend A simple knot, similar to a *sheet bend*, for attaching a rope to a loop in the end of another rope.

bee-block A fitting on the side of a boom through which a reefing pendant is rove.

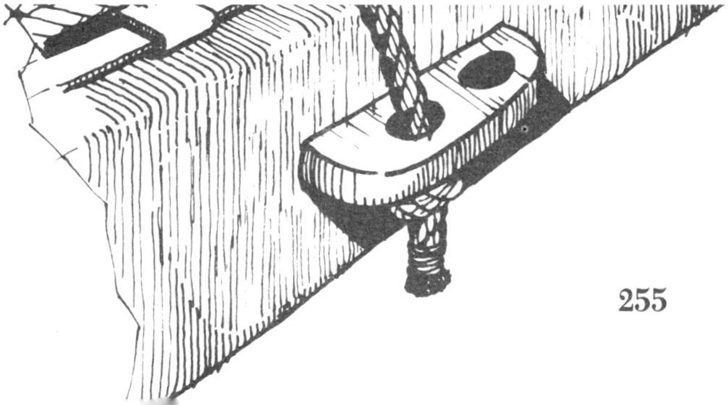

beeswax The lubricant used on sail thread and whipping twine to make it easier to sew or to pull the twine through a rope. The wax helps waterproof the twine.

belay To make a line fast by taking turns around a *cleat, belaying pin, samson post,* or *bollard.*

belaying pin A vertical pin in a *fiferail* to which lines such as *halyards* are fastened, usually on a larger vessel.

bell A bell-shaped fitting, usually on a vertical *track* on the forward side of the mast, into which the end of a spinnaker pole is set.

bell rope The short line, usually ornamental fancy work, by which the clapper of a ship's bell is operated.

bend To connect two ropes with a knot; to prepare a sail for hoisting; to fasten a line to a spar or fitting; a knot used for this purpose. See *knot, hitch.*

bendy mast A flexible mast, in a type of rig designed to attain maximum racing speed through changes in the draft (shape) of the mainsail by controlling the mast's curvature through the backstay and other rigging adjustments. Bendy masts are outlawed by many racing classes, allowed by a few.

bight A loop in a rope or line; the middle part of a slack rope.

bitter end The inboard end of a rope or line (such as an anchor line), which may be made fast, as to the *bitts*; the end opposite to the one in use.

bitts A pair of vertical fittings on deck to which an anchor line, towline, or dock line is made fast. The bitts are strong timbers that extend through the deck, usually to the keel. A bitt may or may not have a cross bar (norman). See also *samson post.*

black band Painted marking (stripe) on mast and boom indicating the limits (position) that the sail should reach when hoisted or fully hauled out, while still conforming to the racing measurements.

blackwall hitch A quick way of attaching a rope to a hook; does not hold unless pressure is continuous.

blend A combination (mix) of different synthetic fibers used in some types of rope.

block A pulley, a rigging fitting consisting of one or more sheaves (grooved wheels) revolving inside a metal or wooden case. Rope (sometimes wire or chain) runs on the sheaves. Strictly, a pulley is the sheave. There are many kinds of blocks: single, double, snatch, cheek, etc.

block, snatch A block, open or latched on the side, used in sailboat *running rigging.* Example: on *genoa track,* to take the genoa sheet, or on a pad-eye for a working jib sheet or spinnaker guy or sheet.

block-and-tackle Any of several arrangements of blocks (pulleys) and line to make a *purchase* and thus gain mechanical advantage. A block-and-tackle may be rigged temporarily for a special purpose, as lifting a heavy weight, or it may be part of the normal running rigging, as in a *downhaul, vang,* or *main sheet.*

blooper A very full sail, technically a headsail like a larger genoa, set opposite a spinnaker to balance its pull and give extra power on a run or very broad reach.

blue peter Sailor's slang for the code flag **P**, blue with a white square in the center, flown to indicate that the vessel is about to sail.

boardboat A surfboard with a sail handled by one person, who stands up and steers partly by turning the boardboat by applying foot pressure, partly by controlling the sail. One kind is called a Windsurfer.

boarding ladder A series of steps temporarily attached to the rail of a vessel. Some are rope, some are folding.

boat boom A spar rigged to hold a tender (dinghy) away from the mother vessel until needed.

boat chocks Fixtures or a cradle on deck or cabin top to hold a dinghy, tender, whaleboat, or lifeboat.

"boat your oars" Command given to oarsmen, as a pulling boat (rowboat) approaches a dock, float, or larger vessel, to get the oars inside the boat and out of the way.

boathook A device, on a pole or stick, to catch a ring bolt or grab a line, such as on a mooring buoy.

bobstay The part of the standing rigging (on a sailboat equipped with a *bowsprit*) that runs from the end of the bowsprit to the vessel's stem.

bollard Vertical iron or wooden fixtures on a pier, float, dock, or (on a larger ship) on deck to which mooring and towing lines are made fast.

boltrope The rope, sewn to or inside one edge of a sail to give it strength and help it hold its shape; a fine quality of rope used for this purpose.

bonnet A small sail fixed to the bottom of another sail to increase its area in light airs.

boom A spar to which the foot or the clew of a fore-and-aft sail is fastened; a spar used for lifting such as a cargo boom or as a boat boom.

boom crotch The removable support for a boom, similar in function to a permanent boom cradle or *gallows frame.* Also called a boom crutch.

boom vang See *vang.*

boomkin A spar, or structure on the stern of a sailboat, to which the *backstay* and sometimes some running rigging may be attached; also bumpkin.

bosun Boatswain—a petty officer in charge of hull, rigging, and sail maintenance as well as deck operations. Other phonetic spellings are bos'n, bo's'n, bo'sun, etc.

bosun's chair A seat, sometimes rigid, sometimes made of canvas, for hoisting a person aloft to repair rigging. A pocket or bag for tools and a safety strap are usually part of the chair; also bosun's seat.

bosun's locker The stowage space and contents for spare rigging gear, tools, and other ship's stores.

bottle screw Another British term for a rigging screw or *turnbuckle.*

bouse To haul down on a rope or tackle; also bowse.

bowknot The square knot with the second part made as two slippery hitches, used for sail *gaskets,* shoelaces, and to tie gift parcels.

bowline A knot in the end of a line, forming a loop that will not slip or jam. It is easily untied. A running bowline forms a noose by forming the knot

around the *standing part*; a bowline on a bight is made with a doubled line and makes a temporary bosun's chair; it is sometimes called a French or Portuguese bowline.

bowse See *bouse.*

bowsprit The permanent spar (as distinguished from a movable jib boom) on the bow of some sailboats to which headstays and jibstays are fastened. The bowsprit may also be used to hold an anchor line roller and to hold the anchor itself when under way.

box haul To tack or wear ship, in a square-rigger, by backing some of the yards to force the bow over while the ship has sternway; sometimes used in heavy weather, sometimes in confined waters; the term is sometimes used loosely when a fore-and-aft rigged sailboat is in irons, to indicate backing the jib or fore staysail in a similar maneuver in order to complete an otherwise difficult tack.

brace A line controlling the yard of a square-rigged vessel; the braces lead aft from the ends of the yards and control the horizontal angle of the spars; as the windward braces are taken in, the leeward braces must be eased. "Splice the main brace" means to have a drink. Australians call a spinnaker guy a "brace."

braid A tubular or flat fabric produced by intertwining a set of yarns according to a definite pattern, by a Maypole process.

braid-on-braid A type of rope, one braided line inside another, used in sailboat running rigging (Dacron) and for anchor lines and dock lines (nylon). Also called double braid.

braided line Several configurations of braided line are made: solid braid, plaited, braid-on-braid. Most of them can be spliced.

brail A rope from the leech (edge) of a fore-and-aft sail to a block on the mast and then down, used for a quick, temporary furl; a line used to assist in getting the sail past the mast when tacking.

breaking strength One standardized measure of the tensile strength of rope, chain, or wire. A rope should never be subjected to more than 20 percent of its known breaking strength; the recommended working load is often 11 percent.

breast line A dock line leading directly abeam from a cleat or chock to the wharf, pier, or float.

breeches buoy A life-saving device carrying a person in a sling seat or chair on a wire or line from a vessel in distress, either to the shore or to a rescue vessel. Similar devices are used in helicopter rescues, lowering a sling or basket stretcher, then hoisting it back aboard the aircraft.

bridle A length of wire or rope fastened at each end to a spar (or to either end of a dinghy). A balanced weight can thus be lifted. Also, a line to each end of a *spinnaker* pole, to which the pole lift is attached.

Bristol fashion Shipshape, neat, orderly, spick-and-span.

Bruce anchor A modern configuration of a holding device for a mooring; a sort of cross between a *plow*, a wishbone anchor, and a bent tablespoon.

Brummel hook A slotted ring or eye, with a matching sister hook, for attaching rigging (spinnaker) lines together.

bulldog grip A temporary U-bolt clamp for wire rigging emergency repairs; used to make a temporary eye or instead of a splice to join two wires.

bullet block A small rigging block.

bull rope An extra line, rigged from the bowsprit to a mooring buoy to prevent the vessel riding up on the buoy.

bullseye A round fairlead, made of metal lined with plastic or *lignum vitae*; an eye that serves to guide a line or change its *lead*.

buntline A rope attached to the foot of a squaresail, then through a block on the yard, to gather in the sail and spill the wind during reefing, or to get the sail in position for furling.

buntline hitch A handy knot for securing a halyard to its shackle on modern boats. Sometimes called the "inside clove hitch." Originally, on a square-rigger, this hitch was used to fasten a buntline

to a cringle or to eyelet holes in the foot of a sail. It is small, secure, and has a number of modern applications.

buoy an anchor To temporarily fasten an anchor rode to a buoy in the water, so that the vessel may return to the anchor at a later time without the trouble of raising the anchor and later reanchoring.

burgee A pennant or flag; a yacht club burgee is usually triangular; a club officer's burgee is swallow-tailed.

burton, Spanish A purchase of single blocks, used for fast work such as lifting fish baskets or barrels.

C Charlie. Blue-white-red-white-blue code flag. As a single-letter signal, it signifies "Affirmative."

cable A large rope (10 inches or more in circumference), wire, or chain; an anchor line; a cable's length is 100 fathoms or 600 feet.

cable lay The particular lay of heavy rope or hawser used for cables, tripling three-strand rope, using left-hand twist.

cam cleat A quick-acting cleat not requiring turns or hitches, used primarily on racing sailboats. Usually, two swivels, with teeth, are used. See *sheet-stopper, jam cleat.*

camber The curve of a sail; a sail closehauled has a flat camber while a sail while running has a full, rounded camber.

canvas Any of several kinds of cloth used for sails, awnings, sail covers, etc. Originally, canvas was cotton; now most sailcloth is polyester or nylon. The word *canvas* is also a general term for sails.

capsize To turn over a coil of rope, to make it ready for running, as a halyard when lowering sail. Some knots, under strain, are said to capsize (change shape).

capstan An anchor winch or windlass; aboard old sailing ships the capstan was turned by men walking in a circle on deck, pushing capstan bars.

car The slide, on a track or bar, used for an outhaul, a main sheet or genoa sheet block, or other movable rigging.

carabiner An oblong mountaineering ring, opening with a snap, protected from accidental opening by a spring-loaded sleeve, used aboard a sailboat for control of a halyard hauling a crew member aloft in a bosun's chair and sometimes for other rigging situations. (British: carbine hook).

carbon fibers A strong reinforcing material (extruded threads or filaments) used with plastic in making structural parts of boats such as rudders.

carrick bend A special knot for attaching two ropes to each other; when made, the carrick bend has an ornamental look, but in use it tightens up, cap-

sizes, and is hard to recognize or untie. A double carrick bend or a seized carrick bend is most often used with large hawsers.

cast off To let go or unfasten a line; to undo dock lines so that a boat may depart.

cat's paw A hitch made in the bight of a line, often attached to a hook and also called a hook hitch.

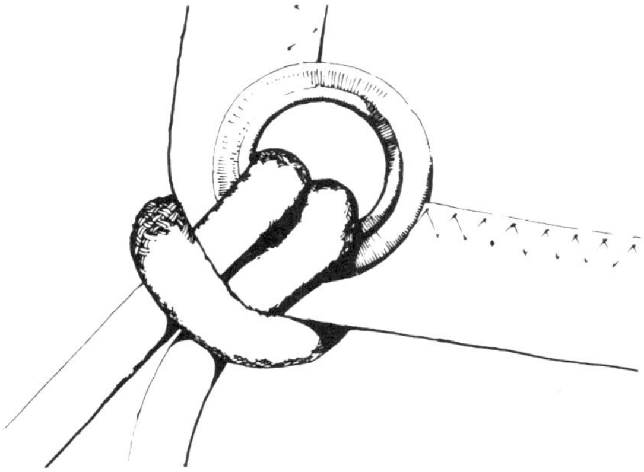

cat the anchor To haul an anchor up to the projecting timber (cat-head) that holds it under way; in modern boats, to haul the anchor to a secure position on the bowsprit.

catboat A sailboat rig with a single mast and a single sail. A British term is *Una-rig*.

catamaran A twin-hulled sailboat, usually with special fully battened sails.

catenary The curve in a line hanging between two points. A towing line or an anchor line has a catenary.

center vang A permanently attached vang helping control the lift of a main boom. The *downhaul* is on the boom at the mast, while the vang is attached toward mid-boom and runs to the base of the mast; the older type of vang may attach to a fitting at the rail and requires changing when tacking or jibing. The modern center vang can stay in place, requiring only minor adjustment, perhaps as the boat is sailed closer to the wind.

chafing gear Canvas, rubber, leather, or other material put on areas of lines, spars, or other parts of a boat to absorb abrasive friction, thus preventing damage to the rigging or the vessel.

chain Linked metal (stud link or open link) used for certain rigging parts, such as *bobstays*, and for anchor lines.

chain locker The storage place, in the bow, for a chain anchor cable.

chain pipe The deck opening (also called the navel) through which anchor chain or anchor rope passes.

chainplates The fittings, once including chain, to which shrouds are attached at the sides of a boat; also the general area of the hull where the shrouds are attached.

chains See *chainplates*.

chandlery A marine store, selling rigging, fittings, rope, paint, and other nautical supplies.

cheek block A single block, attached on its side, usually to a boom or mast.

chip log An obsolete but simple device for measuring a vessel's speed through the water. The chip was attached to a log line, and as the vessel moved ahead, the line, with knots tied in it, spaced evenly every 47.25 feet, ran out in such a way that counting the knots gave an indication of the vessel's speed. Hence, *knots* is a measure of speed: nautical miles per hour.

chock A metal or plastic guide through which lines such as dock lines, towing lines, and anchor lines are led. A roller chock reduces friction and thus chafe or abrasion. Also, a block or fitting supporting a small boat or an anchor.

chockablock Full up, tight—as when two blocks of a tackle come together and no more movement is possible. When a cask or hold is full to the top, it is said to be chockablock.

clap on To add on to an existing part or system, as to clap on more sail, to clap on a purchase when additional power is needed; to lend a hand when help is needed.

claw A fitting encircling the boom, with rollers at the top, to which is attached a vang or the main sheet; also called a boom claw, reefing claw, or claw ring; see also *devil's claw*.

cleat A horned fitting, of metal, wood, or both, to which lines are fastened, using half hitches.

cleat hitches The series of turns, half hitches, made with a line around a cleat.

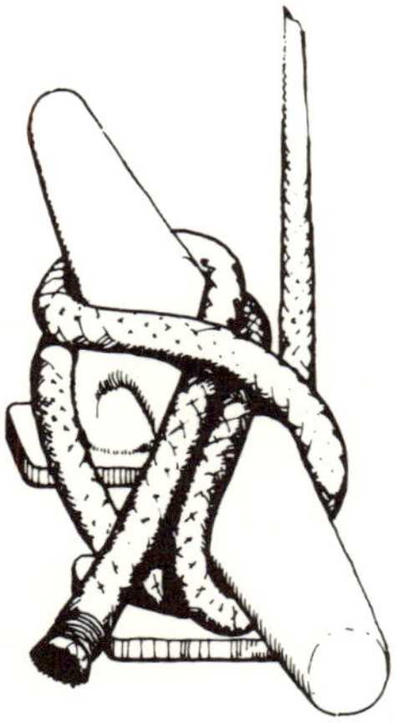

clevis pin A locking pin, used in rigging, as to fasten shroud adjusters to chainplates, with a head at one end and an eye at the other; a split ring or cotter pin keeps the clevis in place.

clew On a fore-and-aft sail the lower, aft corner; on a square sail or a spinnaker the lower, outer corners; a clew eye or grommet, reinforced by patches called *tabling*, takes the load of the *outhaul* or the sheet.

clew garnet The line or tackle hauling the clew of the *course* up to the *yard* when the sail is to be furled.

clew outhaul The line, tackle, or worm-geared mechanism used on a boom to haul a sail taut along the foot or to adjust its *camber*.

clockwise The direction of coiling for right-hand lay rope; the direction in which U.S. sheet winches turn.

clove hitch An easy-to-tie hitch, useful for attaching a line to a piling or spar in some situations;

easily adjustable, but prone to loosen unless a half hitch is added for security.

club A short spar, a jib boom, used for the foot of a self-tending jib or staysail.

club hauling A square-rigger's desperate maneuver to go on the opposite tack under adverse wind and current conditions by using a kedge (anchor) to the lee quarter, at the same time backing the head yards as in *box-hauling*.

code flag The answering pennant in the International Signal Code, with alternating red and white vertical stripes.

codline Three-stranded small cordage, used for whippings and servings when marline is not large enough; largely replaced by synthetic small lines.

coffee grinder A powerful sheet winch used on large modern racing sailboats, named for the large handles on a pedestal. Usually, the two-man grinder is geared so that the winch drums can be efficiently placed while the husky sailors at the pedestal are out of the way—sometimes even below deck.

coiling Arranging a line in overlapping circles to

prevent snarling and to make it easy to run out. Three-strand rope, with a right-hand lay, is coiled clockwise, preventing kinking. Braided rope coils differently, usually ending up as figure eights.

Colregs International Regulations for the Prevention of Collision at Sea (a term used by the U.S. Coast Guard).

cone A black cloth, plastic or metal signal shape, hoisted in the rigging to indicate that a sailing vessel is using her auxiliary engine, for example.

constrictor knot A tight fastening for the neck of a bag, such as a sailbag, or for a temporary whipping, developed from the miller's knot; the constrictor

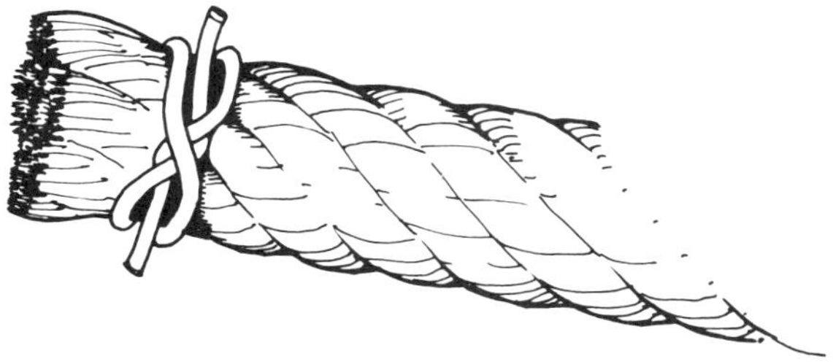

knot is easier to untie if made with a slip hitch to finish off; invented or rediscovered by Clifford Ashley (see also *Ashley's stopper knot*).

cordage The general term for rope, line, whipping, and serving line such as marline, whether stranded or braided, made from natural fibers or synthetic fibers.

Cordage Institute The industry trade association that sets standards for testing, dimensions, and other characteristics of rope in the U.S.

core The center strands of braid-on-braid rope or of some configurations of wire rope. The outer part is the cover.

cotter pin A bronze or steel split pin used as an end fastening on some items of rigging and some mechanisms. A circular ring, performing the same function, is less likely to break or to foul lines and sails.

cotton Once the premier material for sails, cotton canvas was soft and easy to handle when dry, although difficult in wet or cold weather. Sails have been made of flax, linen, and jute. Today they are made largely from polyester (Dacron) and nylon fibers. Sea Island cotton and Egyptian cotton were once considered the best.

course The sail set from a lower yard on a square-rigged vessel; the largest of the square sails. See *ship*.

cover The outer "layer" of braid-on-braid rope.

CQR anchor A patent anchor, also called a plow anchor.

crane The short bracket at the masthead to which stays and sometimes blocks such as the spinnaker halyard block are fastened.

cringle A rope loop or circular eye made on a metal or plastic thimble on a lower corner of a sail or along the luff and leech for the corner hold-downs in reefing.

cross trees The thwartship timbers supporting the topmast above a lower mast; *spreaders*.

crowfoot A multiple bridle with a central eye used to hold up an awning by means of a topping lift or a halyard.

crown knot A knot made in the end of three-strand rope to prevent it from unlaying or as a stopper; often the crown is used as the start of a backsplice or combined with a wall knot.

crutch See *boom crotch*.

Cunningham A rigging arrangement based on the Cunningham eye or cringle, in the luff of a mainsail above the tack. When the eye is pulled down, this alters the *camber* of the sail, flattening it.

cutter A single-masted sailboat with mainsail and more than one headsail, usually a forestaysail and jib. This divided rig is moderately popular for cruising boats because it enables several sizes and combinations of sails to be set, varying with the strength of the wind.

Cycolac A plastic, also called ABS or Acrylonitric Butadene Styrene, used in making boat parts. It can be molded to accurate shapes, resists water and most solvents, and does not shatter, mar, or deform under moderate impact. It can be chrome-plated.

cylinder A cloth device, hoisted aloft as a signal. A black cylinder indicates a vessel whose maneuverability is limited because of her draft. Red, blue, and white cylinders are used by regatta and race committees to signal warning times before the start of a race.

D Delta. Yellow-blue-yellow code flag. As a single letter, it means "Keep clear, maneuvering with difficulty."

D-shackle A straight-sided shackle shaped like a *D*, used in rigging.

Dacron Trade name, generally used for *polyester* fibers in sailcloth and rope. Dacron 77 has shorter fibers, and rope made from it is fuzzy, easy on the hands, and has sufficient surface friction to work well on winches.

dan buoy A buoy with a short spar or pole, with flag attached, used to mark the position of a person who has fallen overboard; a similar buoy used to temporarily mark the end of a race starting line or a turning mark.

Danforth A patent anchor, originally developed in World War II for landing ships, now popular for cruising boats. The anchor was invented by William Danforth and Robert Ogg and is now made in high tensile steel as well as the original heavier-gauge steel. The Danforth anchor uses its shape or geometry rather than its weight to give good holding power. A short length of chain and a long *scope* are considered advisable to make it dig in at the proper angle.

davits Small cranes, used (usually in pairs) to hoist and lower boats. Single davits are used for handling anchors.

deadeye A circular wooden (lignum vitae) block, usually with three holes to take a lanyard, spliced to a shroud and used to take up (tighten) the rigging before the development of turnbuckles or rigging screws.

deck pipe The fitting and opening through which an anchor line or chain passes.

Delrin A hard, strong, smooth plastic (DuPont's trade name for acetal) used for sheaves and other rigging parts requiring strength and resistance to sun, salt water, chemicals, and oil.

devil's claw A chain hook with two prongs, dropped over a chain link to hold an anchor cable.

dhow Originally, a lateen-rigged Arab vessel; a popular brand of rowing and sailing dinghies designed and made by Dyer in Rhode Island.

diameter One of the measurements for rope, as 5/8-inch rope in the U.S.; British and other European rope measurements are usually by circumference; rope manufacturers point out that weight is a better standard for cost, because any given rope will change its diameter and circumference when stretched.

dinghy A small boat used as a tender by a cruising boat or yacht; a type of small racing sailboat.

dip A flag is at the dip when partially lowered (six feet on a ship) as a salute or acknowledgment.

dip-pole jibe In this maneuver, developed in the U.S., the inboard end of the spinnaker pole is kept attached to the mast while the outboard end is lowered (after the original guys have been detached) and dipped beneath the headstay to the other side. Then the new guy (the former sheet) is attached to the pole as the boat jibes and the spinnaker is reset. Other types of spinnaker jibes include *end-for-end* and *twin-pole.*

distress signals Under international regulations fourteen methods, some improvised, for calling for help are recognized: firing a gun or explosive; continuous fog horn sounding; rockets or shells; SOS (. . . – – – . . .) by radio or light; the radio call "Mayday"; International Signal Code flags N over C; hoisting a square flag plus a ball; flames (as burning tar in a bucket); parachute red flare or hand flare, smoke signal (orange); slowly and repeatedly raising and lowering outstretched arms; radio-telegraph alarm signal; signals transmitted by Emergency Position Indicating Radio Beacon (EPIRB); a piece of orange-colored canvas with a black square or circle; a dye marker.

ditty bag A small canvas bag for personal tools and belongings.

dock, docks An enclosed water area; all the port installations; a place where vessels can moor, as a pier, wharf, or floating dock.

docking The procedure of bringing a vessel up to a pier or float or into a slip, making fast with dock lines, and protecting the vessel with fenders and fender boards.

dodger A weather cloth; a canvas hood over the companionway.

dolphin A post, piling, or group of pilings used for a mooring or to hold a daymark in a channel.

dolphin striker A downward-projecting short spar on a bowsprit. The *bobstay* leads to its base; the martingale extends from the boat's stem to the end of the striker, then to the end of the bowsprit; the dolphin striker acts like a spreader, to strengthen and stiffen the bowsprit structure.

double braid A configuration of braided rope, with a core inside a cover, sometimes called braid-on-braid, yacht braid, etc.

double up To increase the number of mooring or dock lines, as when heavy weather is expected. See *single up*.

downhaul A line or tackle used to adjust or pull down a sail, boom, or other spar.

dress a mast A rigger's term for preparing the mast by attaching stays, shrouds, halyards, topping lifts, and other lines before stepping it.

drogue A sea anchor; a canvas cone, held open by a metal ring, attached to a line, used in heavy

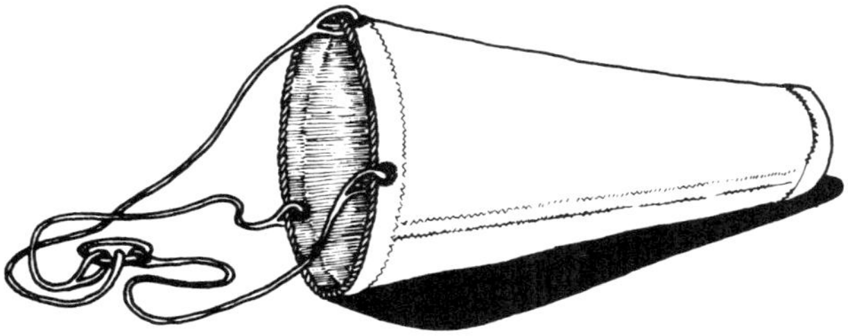

weather to keep a boat's bow into the wind and waves.

drum winch A sail-control mechanism, often geared, used to haul in sheets.

Duron Trade name for polyester fibers used in rope made by Samson Ocean Systems.

E Echo. Blue-red code flag for the letter *E*. As a single-letter signal, it means "I am altering my course to starboard."

earing A short line attached to a *cringle*, as to *luff* and *leech* cringles, for reefing; on square-riggers, a similar line spliced to a cringle at the corner of a sail.

ease To let out a rope with full control, gradually.

electrician's knot A knot made in wire to strengthen the wire's attachment to some object.

elongation The stretching of rope.

end-for-end To reverse a line so that the wear comes in different places.

end-for-end jibe A standard method of jibing a spinnaker, in which the pole is reversed, used especially when there is a mid-stay, which would make a *dip-pole jibe* impossible.

Enkalin A trade name for nylon manufactured in Germany.

ensign A national flag or a recognized identification flag, such as that of the U.S. Power Squadrons or the U.S. Coast Guard Auxiliary.

epoxy An adhesive material, made with a resin and a hardener, used for marine repairs, for some reinforced fiber glass construction, and for paint.

Esterlon Trade name for polyester fiber used in rope.

eye A loop or eye splice; a hole in a sail reinforced with a pressed or sewn grommet.

eyebolt A metal fitting, with an eye at one end and a threaded bolt at the other; used, preferably with a large washer or a backing plate, for towing and lifting eyes on a dinghy or as a rigging fitting when put through a structure, as a deck.

eye splice A permanent eye or loop, made by splicing the end of a rope back into the standing part. Often, an eye splice is made over a *thimble*. With wire rope, a swaged eye, or one made with a *Nicopress* (U.S.) or *Talurit* (British) fitting is now more generally used.

eyelet A small reinforced hole in canvas (sailbag, awning, sail) usually made with a brass *grommet*, for lacing or otherwise attaching small lines.

F Foxtrot. White code flag with a red diamond; the letter *F* in the International Signal Code of signals. As a single flag, Foxtrot means "I am disabled, communicate with me."

fairlead A rigging fitting, essentially an eye, through which a line is rove to alter its lead; a bull's eye; some fairleads rotate or are on slides, adjustable on a track.

fake (Or flake) One turn in a coil of rope. Faking down is coiling a line so that the running end will be on top. See *capsize, coil.*

fall A line passing through blocks of a tackle to which the power is applied in hoisting; the line in the tackle for a davit used to hoist or lower a boat.

fathom A nautical distance; six feet. One hundred fathoms is a cable's length.

fender A resilient shock-absorbing device, made of rubber, sometimes inflated, or multi-plaited rope, used between a vessel and a pier or float to prevent chafe.

fender board A board, often padded on one side, used to supplement fenders and provide greater protection between a docked vessel and the pier or float.

fiber The slender element of natural or synthetic material from which cordage and sailcloth is made. Fibers are spun into yarns; yarns are twisted into strands; strands are plaited or twisted (laid) into rope.

fiber glass Thin filaments of glass, used with various plastics in marine construction. Other terms are FRP, fiberglass reinforced plastics, and GRP, glass reinforced plastic.

fid A wooden or plastic tool, sharp at one end, rounded at the other, used in rope-working and sailmaking. Some fids, used in working with hollow-braid rope, are themselves hollow, such as the Fid-O Splicer. Smaller, similar metal tools are marlinspikes; spikes used for wire have different points.

fiddle block A block with two sheaves, one smaller than the other and one above the other, occasionally used for main sheets.

fiferail A pinrail, holding belaying pins, in a semicircle around the base of a mast.

figure-eight knot By adding one extra turn in an overhand knot, one makes a figure eight. This is a good knot to stop a line before it runs out through a block or fairlead. The general term for such a knot is *stopper knot.*

filament Extrusion of synthetic material, as in a monofilament fishline or the basic fiber used for fabrics and rope.

fish To repair a broken spar by binding or lashing reinforcing pieces to it with tape or line. Also, to attempt to catch and therefore secure a line, as to fish a line through the throat of a block.

fisherman Another name for the yachtsman type of anchor; also a reaching staysail set between the masts of a ketch or schooner, sometimes called a gollywobbler.

fisherman's bend A secure knot, used for bending a line to an anchor. Pass two turns around the ring, then make a half hitch through the turns and another half hitch around the line. Added neatness, if not security, is given by *stopping* the end to the *standing part,* using a serving of light line. Also called an anchor bend.

fishhook A sharp, projecting strand of (loose or broken) wire in a wire rope, posing a danger when handling the line.

flag halyard A line on a flagstaff, to a spreader or to the masthead serving to hoist an ensign, signal flags, or other flags.

flake down To coil a line, or lay it on deck in figure eights, ready for running; an anchor line or towline may be flaked down, or faked down, so that it is ready for instant use.

Flemish coil An ornamental coil made on deck, with each coil close to the next and the end of the line in the center.

float A platform rising and falling with the tide that serves as a landing stage or in lieu of a pier; a small buoy used to mark an anchor or mooring.

fly The long side of a flag, as compared to the *hoist*, the side on the halyard or flagstaff.

foot The lower edge of a sail.

footrope A rope slung under a yard or bowsprit for sailors to stand on while furling sails.

foreguy A line running forward from the end of a boom or spinnaker pole controlling how far aft the spar can swing.

foremast The first mast abaft the bow, except in a ketch or yawl, where the first mast is the mainmast.

forepeak The compartment in the bow of a boat, often used for stowage of the anchor rode.

forestay In strict U.S. usage, a wire stay from the deck to a point on the mast—in contrast to a headstay, which runs from the stem or the end of the bowsprit to the masthead and is thus the outermost stay.

foretriangle The area between the mast, the headstay or forestay, and the deck, used in rating racing sailboats.

Fortrel Trade name, one of several, for plastic used in making fibers for rope and sailcloth.

fothering Covering a hole or structural damage to a hull with canvas as a temporary repair to prevent sinking.

foul Tangled or jammed, unable to run free, as a line in a vessel's running rigging or an anchor line.

four-strand rope A special-purpose type of rope. Shrouds, when made of rope on square-riggers, were made of four-strand or "shroud laid" rope, as were many boat falls.

frapping A tight binding to take up slack, as in tying halyards away from the mast to keep them from slatting noisily, or in a seizing to help hold the ropes more tightly.

free To clear a fouled line.

French bowline A double bowline, useful as an improvised bosun's chair. Also called Portuguese bowline.

French whipping A type of whipping in which each turn of twine is locked with a half hitch.

freshen the nip To readjust a line slightly by hauling or veering so that a fresh place takes the surface abrasion.

furling Rolling, gathering, or folding a sail on its boom or yard and fastening it with *gaskets* or tyers, or *shock cord.*

G Golf. Yellow-blue-yellow-blue-yellow code flag. The single-letter signal means "I want a pilot."

gaff A spar, used in some fore-and-aft rigs, holding the sail up and out; a spar on which flags are hoisted.

gallows frame An inverted U-shaped frame to support a boom when its sail is lowered. A gallows frame is permanent; a crutch is removable.

gamming chair A chair hoisted from one whaling ship to another, or by way of a whaleboat, so that the captains' wives could visit and have a "gam."

gammon, gammoning The fastenings used to hold a bowsprit in place.

gantline A line rove through a block fixed aloft used for hoisting spars during the rigging of a ship, or for such shipboard needs as a utility line for hanging clothing to dry. A gantline hitch was used by riggers in a bosun's chair.

garnet A clew line on a square sail.

gasket A sewn canvas or webbing strap used to tie a furled sail. May also be made of shock cord or rope. (British: tyer or tier)

gate A section of a lifeline, fitted at one end with a *pelican hook* for easy opening and closing, through which crew members and dunnage may come aboard a boat; a switch in a mast track, to permit a storm sail to be readied for hoisting or to otherwise ease the work of bending sails.

genoa An overlapping headsail (jib) used on fore-and-aft rigged sailboats.

genoa track The track, usually on the toerail of a sailboat, on which slides or cars for snatch blocks can be adjusted to trim the genoa sheets.

geometry Ropemakers' word for the configurations of various kinds of rope: three-strand laid, four strand, plaited, double braid, etc.

gilguy A line or shock cord used to tie halyards away from the mast, to prevent noisy slatting.

gooseneck A jointed or hinged fitting attaching a boom to a mast or to the deck in the case of a jibboom. A gooseneck can slide up or down the mast on a track or incorporate roller reefing gear.

goosewing Setting the sails, downwind, so that the mainsail is on one side and the jib is opposite. Thus the jib is not blanketed. Often the jib is held out with a *whisker pole* or Forespar. An accidental or incorrectly done jibe can also result in a goosewing involving just the twisted mainsail, with battens caught on the spreaders.

granny An awkward knot that is often made, out

of ignorance or inadvertence, instead of a square knot. It is not dependable and is sometimes hard to untie.

grapnel A type of anchor, with multiple flukes, sometimes used to recover objects from the bottom.

gripe A tie-down line or strap, such as one used to hold a dinghy in its chocks on deck or on a cabin top.

grommet A ring. A rope grommet is a circle made by unlaying the rope, then using one strand spirally to twist onto itself, replacing the original strands. A metal ring grommet is put in place in a hole in canvas with a grommet punch.

groove A slot in a mast or boom into which the bolt rope or special slides can be inserted, instead of using a track and slides.

ground tackle The general term for the anchor, shackles, chain, and anchor line. In describing a permanent mooring, this would include the float, pickup line, and any other parts of the anchoring system.

gun tackle purchase A prepared tackle consisting of two single blocks. If the lower block is the one that moves, double force is gained. If the upper block moves, triple force is gained.

guy A control or steadying line attached to the end of a movable spar, such as a spinnaker pole.

gypsy A sprocketed drum to take chain links on an anchor winch. In the U.S., also called a wildcat.

H Hotel. White and red code flag. As a single-letter signal, it means "Pilot on board."

half hitch The simplest knot, sometimes used by itself as in fastening a line to a cleat, but generally part of another knot, as two half hitches or fisherman's bend.

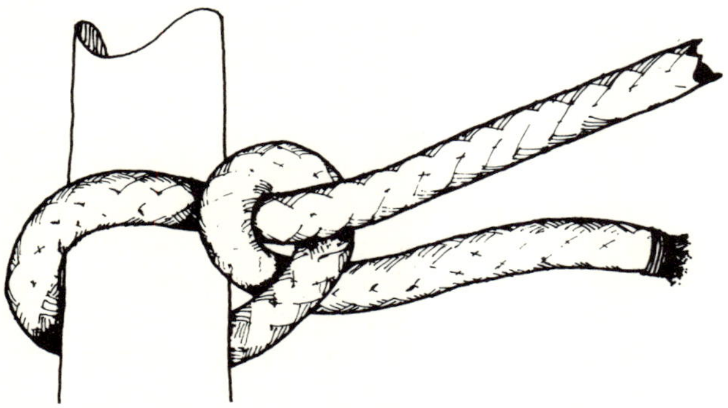

halyard A line (rope or wire) used to hoist a sail, flag, or (on a square-rigger) a spar (hence the name—to haul a yard).

halyard winch A winch, usually on the mast, to haul a halyard.

handsomely Slowly, carefully, at a steady rate without jerking, as: "Hoist that boat handsomely."

handy billy A ready-to-use tackle with one single and one double block and a tail or hook on each block for attaching.

hank A fitting, metal, or plastic, attached to a sail to hold the luff to a stay. Some hanks are hook-shaped, some have spring-loaded openings.

harness, safety A system of webbing and snaphooks worn by sailors on deck in rough weather; the harness is attached by a snaphook and a line to a fore-and-aft jackline so that the crew member can move about with relative freedom.

hauling part The part of a tackle (as a boat fall) to which power is applied.

hawser Strong, heavy rope 4½″ or larger in circumference (or wire rope) used by towboats and larger ships for towing and mooring.

hawser laid A normal configuration of three-strand rope, usually made by right-hand twisting of the strands together. Shroud-laid ropes are four-stranded.

head The upper end (corner) of a triangular sail; the upper side of a four-sided sail, as on a gaff-rigged boat. The heads were projecting timbers, over the water, used by sailors as a toilet area.

headboard The built-in fitting in the upper corner of a sail to which the halyard is attached.

headfoil A grooved rod or fitting on a headstay into which headsail luffs slide. Usually, twin headfoils are used, to aid in quick sail changes. Headfoils may reduce wind resistance and increase sail efficiency.

headstay A stay from the extreme bow to the masthead; the foremost stay on a boat.

heaving line A small line, weighted at one end with a *monkey's fist* and attached to a heavier dock line or hawser. The heaving line is thrown to a pier or another vessel and is then used to haul the heavier line ashore or aboard.

heaving line bend A quickly made bend for fastening a messenger or heaving line to a larger rope.

hemp Cordage made from fibers of the hemp plant; now largely supplanted by synthetic fibers.

Herculon A trade name for polypropylene.

hitch A type of knot whose parts jamb each other when in use yet are easily untied.

hockle A kink in laid rope that has become permanent, deforming and weakening the rope.

hoist The height of a sail; the side of a flag next to the staff or halyard; the vertical measurement of a flag.

hollow braid A form of braided rope without a core.

hoops Wooden rings around the mast to which the luff of a sail is fastened, now largely made obsolete by slides and tracks or grooves.

horn The projecting arm of a cleat or bitt; one of the two projections on the mast end of a gaff that form the jaw.

horse A transverse bar, rail, or wire on which the main sheet lower block or that of a self-tending jib or forestaysail travels. A track with a sliding car is more generally used in modern rigging.

horseshoe buoy A lifebuoy or emergency Personal Flotation Device shaped like an inverted U and mounted in a ready-for-use bracket at the rail, intended for man-overboard situations.

hounds The part of the mast where shrouds and stays are attached; originally, wooden shoulders supporting eyes of rigging and *cross trees.*

Hyfield lever A toggle device for quickly loosening or tightening running backstays.

I India. Yellow code flag with a black ball. The International Signal Code flag for the letter *F.* As a single flag, it means "I am altering my course to port."

Iceline A strong, lightweight rope, developed in Norway, sold in the U.S. by Tubbs Cordage.

in stops Stopping twine or other light stuff is used to wrap a sail loosely before it is hoisted; when the sheets are hardened, the sail fills and the twine or elastic bands break, letting the sail be set quickly.

International Signal Code The set of 40 flags (including letters of the alphabet, answering pennants, numerals, and three repeaters) by which vessels of any nationality can communicate with each other as well as with the shore; the same letters, names, and special meanings are also used in radio and visual communications, such as signal lights.

Irish pennants Ragged, frayed ends of rope.

J Juliett. Blue-white-blue code flag. "On fire, keep clear," when used as a one-flag signal.

jackline An adjustable line in the clew area of a mainsail, so arranged through cringles that roller reefing will not unduly distort the sail; a similar line on the forestaysail; a line running from bow to stern to which crew members can snap their safety harnesses when moving on deck in bad weather; a taut rope or wire on which a breeches buoy operates (also called a jackstay).

jackstaff The staff at the bow of some vessels from which special flags are flown.

Jacob's ladder A rope ladder with wooden or metal rungs (sometimes double) lowered over the side of a vessel, as for the pilot to climb aboard.

jam cleat A quick-acting form of line-stopper in which a tapering slot pinches the line. Jam cleats can damage rope.

jeers Heavy tackle, with double and triple blocks, used in square-rigged ships to hoist the yards.

jib A triangular headsail (although a few quadrilateral jibs have been tried) set on a stay forward of the mast. When a boat's sail inventory includes several jibs, the #1 is the largest, #2 next largest, and so on. A spitfire jib is a storm jib. A genoa jib is an overlapping sail, sometimes with an area as large as the mainsail.

jib-boom A movable extension of a bowsprit; a spar on which a jib is set, similar to a staysail boom.

jib sheet The control line from the clew of a jib, used to adjust or trim it.

jiffy reefing A method of quickly reefing a fore-and-aft sail, such as a mainsail, using a hook and a pendant. The bunt may be left free or gathered with *reef points.* Also called slab reefing.

jigger Mizzenmast or mizzensail (U.S.); a light tackle with one single block and one double block, a luff tackle.

jury rig A temporary fix for broken or missing rigging (or other parts of a vessel).

K Kilo. Yellow and blue code flag in international code. "I wish to communicate with you."

kedge A type of anchor; to run an anchor out from a vessel that is aground, in a dinghy for example, and then to haul in the line and "kedge off."

kellet A sentinel, a weight hung onto a midpoint of an anchor line to change the *catenary* and provide a more nearly horizontal force on the anchor.

ketch A two-masted sailboat with the mizzenmast proportionately larger than a *yawl*'s, usually identifiable because the ketch's mizzenmast is stepped forward of the rudder post.

Kevlar A high-strength, low-stretch synthetic (aramid) fiber used in high-technology sailboat rigging for sails and line.

kicking strap A control (line, tackle, or mechanism) to haul down on the boom and prevent it lifting on a reach or run (British). In the U.S., it is usually called a *boom vang*.

kingposts Double derrick-masts for handling cargo.

knot A bend, hitch, or splice. Although the distinction between these terms is not precise, knot is: (1) an inclusive term; (2) strictly, a tucking of strands to form an ornamental or useful enlargement of a rope, as in a *manrope* knot; (3) more permanent, compared to a *bend* or *hitch*.

Kodel Trade name for Eastman's polyester fiber.

L Lima. Black and yellow checkered code flag in the international signals. As a single-letter signal, it means "Stop instantly."

lacing line A thin line or cord used to attach a sail, instead of using track and slides (as on a jibboom), or for an awning, weather cloth, dodger, or other canvas.

laid Twisted, as the strands of a laid rope.

lanyard A short line to hold a knife, bosun's whistle, etc.; a temporary replacement for a *turnbuckle* or *shroud adjuster*, rove through a shackle or thimble and the eye of the *chainplate* in the same way as on square-riggers of the early nineteenth century, when *deadeyes* were used.

lashing Securing by tying down with cordage.

Lavsan Polyester fiber in the USSR.

lazy block The one block of a pair that is not in use at a given time, such as a genoa sheet block.

lazy guy A guy that is not in use at a particular time but is rigged and ready.

lazy jacks Lines for controlling a sail while it is being lowered. Lazy jacks are on each side of the sail, usually made in an inverted Y.

lead The angle or direction of a line, as the lead of a jib sheet, which controls its shape and efficiency. A jib sheet lead can be changed by moving a block or bullseye on a track, by switching the place the block is attached, or with a *Barber haul*.

lead line The line used with a sounding lead, usually marked in fathoms.

leader A fairlead.

leech The after edge of a sail (the outer sides of a square sail).

leech line A drawstring built into the leech of a sail, for making small adjustments in the shape of the sail.

left-hand lay Rope made by twisting the strands to the left is said to have a left-hand lay. Most rope is right-hand lay.

lifelines Protective lines on the sides of a boat, similar to guardrails. They are secured by stanchions and run from the bow pulpit to the stern pulpit. Tension is adjusted with *turnbuckles*. A gate, a length of lifeline between two stanchions equipped with a *pelican hook*, enables crew members to board the boat without climbing over the lifeline. Lifeline heights are frequently governed by racing regulations. The *jackline* rigged from bow to stern for the attachment of safety harness is sometimes called the lifeline, as is the short line between the harness and the jackline.

lift A line supporting a spar or part of the rigging, as a topping lift or a spinnaker pole lift.

lignum vitae The hard, smooth wood used for the *sheaves* for blocks, *deadeyes*, liners for fairleads, and (until modern metallic packings were developed) for engine shaft bearings.

line Rope, as soon as it is put to use on a boat, is called line, or by its specific name, as a halyard or a sheet, in the U.S. There are very few "ropes" on an American boat. But in the UK, the word *line* refers to cordage, or "small stuff," and the word *rope* is used for larger cordage.

linen Linen rope, made from flax, was often used for running rigging on yachts before the development of synthetic fibers.

lizard A short length of line with a thimble spliced into the end, used like a fairlead to control the angle of another line or at the end of a boat boom to make a hitch for small boats.

long splice A way of joining the ends of two lines, interweaving the strands in such a way that the splice is no thicker than the original rope. A long splice goes readily through blocks or other fittings but is not as strong as a thicker short splice.

loose-footed A mainsail that does not fasten to a boom with slides, lacing, or by the bolt-rope in a groove but is held at tack and clew only, is said to be loose-footed. In some new rigs a loose-footed mainsail does not have a boom but is sheeted to a beefed-up backstay. A trysail or standing lug sail is also loose-footed.

lover's knot An ornamental configuration of rope sometimes used as a pad for a *lazy block*.

luff The leading edge of a fore-and-aft sail. To luff up is to temporarily head a sailboat into the wind, usually so she will lose headway or momentarily point higher to get around a mark.

luff groove The groove in a rod stay in which the slides are held when the sail is hoisted.

luff rope A sailmaker's bolt-rope sewn onto the luff of a sail. In some cases, the luff rope fits in a groove in the mast or in a headfoil or luff groove device.

luff spar A flat spar, usually wood, with a groove for the luff of a headsail. Typically a luff spar, used mainly on catamarans, is larger than a headfoil.

luff tackle A common arrangement of blocks, with one single and one double; the standing part is attached to the single block.

M Mike. Blue flag with a white cross in the International Signal Code. As a single-flag signal: "I am stopped."

macrame Sailors' ornamental knot work and fancy work, such as the fringe on an admiral's barge.

magic box A tackle or purchase system in a housing. A typical magic box has two triple blocks, one with a becket. Because the entire system is housed, the line does not need to be kept free and clear. The line has a limited travel, but used for such purposes as a downhaul, vang, or outhaul, the system can be organized in advance. Ball bearings in the special sheave arrangement reduce friction.

magnus hitch The rolling hitch when used to close a bag.

mainsail The principal sail in a fore-and-aft rigged vessel; in a square-rigger, the *course*, the principal sail on the mainmast.

main sheet The line controlling the mainsail. On most fore-and-aft rigged vessels, the main sheet is rigged as a tackle to the boom, except on boats with a boomless rig, when it is rigged to the clew of the mainsail.

mallet A serving mallet is a device for tightening a serving, sometimes with a reel for the marline.

manila A rope fiber once used extensively, now supplanted by the stronger and more adaptable synthetics.

manrope A line rigged on an accommodation ladder or gangplank as a handrail.

manrope knot A stopper knot in a manrope, to prevent it unreeving through the eye of the stanchion.

Marconi rig A fore-and-aft rigging system without a gaff, sometimes called Bermuda rig.

Marinium Trade name for an alloy of aluminum that is hard, strong, and resistant to corrosion; used for cleats and deck fittings.

marline Light two-stranded line, formerly made from hemp and either tarred or untarred, used for lacings, servings, and seizings. Also spelled marlin and marling.

marlinespike A sharp pointed steel spike used by riggers, sailmakers, and sailors for opening the strands in rope, as for splicing.

marling hitch A series of half hitches spaced out to lace a weather cloth, hold a furled sail, or hold a sail to a spar.

marry To join the butt ends of two ropes together, using a seizing, so that (for example) a new line can be rove through a high block.

mast coat A taped sleeve or boot around a mast at the partners, to make the opening watertight.

mast hoops Wooden rings circling a mast to which the sail is seized, usually on gaff-rigged sailboats. A similar fitting, a line with wooden or plastic beads, is called a parrel. Both have been largely supplanted by slides and track or grooves, or by a boltrope in a slot, in smaller boats.

Matthew Walker knot A simple but beautiful stopper knot, tied near the end of a manrope, used on beckets and for such objects as the rope handles for buckets.

mechanical advantage The ratio of output force to input force, as a measure of a tackle, gearing system, or other mechanism.

Mediterranean moor A method of mooring a vessel in close quarters, with the bow anchored and the stern tied up at a pier. This is used in crowded harbors in Europe.

messenger A light line attached to a line that must be rove through a block. One use: The messenger is used in place of a spinnaker halyard to reduce wind resistance, then replaced with the halyard when the sail is to be used. The messenger carries the halyard aloft. Another: as a heaving line, attached to a heavier dock line or hawser.

midshipman's hitch A rolling hitch made around its own standing part, making an adjustable loop.

miller's knot Tied around the neck of a bag, such as a sailbag, the miller's knot is easily opened. See *constrictor knot.*

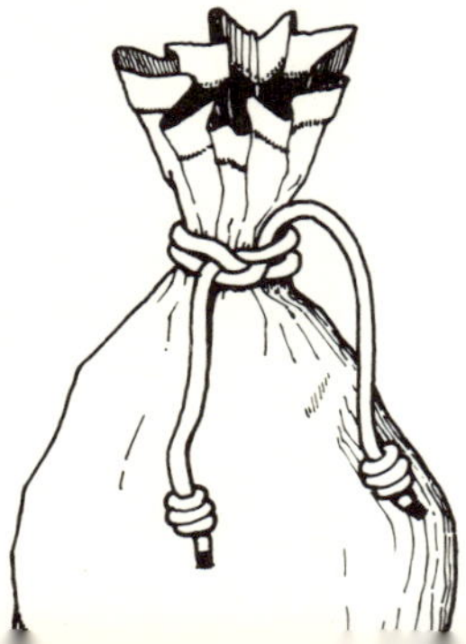

Monel metal A strong, corrosion-resistant alloy of nickel, copper, and other metals useful for some marine applications. Unlike many stainless steel alloys, however, Monel is magnetic and its use is usually avoided in locations where it might affect the compass.

monkey block A block, such as on a backstay, that moves up and down to adjust another line (a topping lift, for example).

monkey's fist A complex knot, usually around a small weight, used at the end of a heaving line.

monkey's tail A single throat seizing put in a rope to act as a stopper, also called a pigtail.

monofilament Single extruded synthetic line, used by fishermen; useful for servings. Multifilaments, finer, are used in ropemaking.

mooring A system of heavy anchor, shackles, chain, pick-up line or pendant and buoy used for permanent anchoring; the general term for an anchorage area, often used in the plural.

mousing Seizing the open ends of a hook (such as a *pelican hook* on a lifeline) to prevent disengaging.

multifilament A fine diameter extrusion, such as polyester, polyamide, or polypropylene, used as continuous fibers to make rope.

mushroom anchor A permanent type of mooring anchor, which needs both weight and settling in to hold efficiently.

Mylar A sheet plastic; in its transparent form it makes a good window in a sail, to allow the helmsman to keep a good lookout forward.

N November. Blue and white checkered flag in the international code. As a single-flag signal, it means "Negative."

naval bronze A hard, strong alloy used for many rigging fittings.

navel pipe Deck pipe through which an anchor line is led.

needle A sailmaker's needle is triangular, to help make a hole when it is used in heavy sailcloth, which may be doubled or tripled.

Nicopress A compression fitting on the end of wire rope, to hold a toggle, turnbuckle, eye, etc.

nip A section of rope that is under stress or subject to abrasion. To "freshen the nip" is to make a small adjustment so that the chafe comes on another point.

norman The crossbar on a bitt or a rudder.

Northill A patent anchor with two flukes and, in most versions, a removable stock.

nylon Polyamide synthetic material with a long-chain molecule. Fibers are used for sailcloth and rope. Nylon has considerable elasticity, making it suitable for spinnakers, anchor lines, and dock lines. A hard nylon plastic is used for some rigging parts, such as sheaves in small blocks.

O Oscar. Red and yellow flag in the international code. Used alone, it means "Man overboard."

oar An implement, usually wood, whose parts are the blade, the loom, and the handle.

o'clock An alternate system of indicating directions from a vessel, as "twelve o'clock" is "dead ahead," "three o'clock" is on the "starboard beam," etc. Originally used by aircraft pilots and crew.

olefin Any of a class of unsaturated hydrocarbons such as ethylenes used in making fibers. Polypropylene and polyethylene are both olefins.

outhaul A line, tackle, or geared mechanism for tensioning or adjusting the foot of a sail on a boom when attached to the clew.

overhand knot The simplest of all knots, except

for the half hitch, which derives from it. One use for the overhand knot is in the end of sewing thread, as a stopper.

overhaul To ready a line for running, making sure there are no snarls, kinks, or knots, usually by going the length of it hand over hand and coiling it or faking it down in figure eights.

override Too many turns on a sheet winch, or a turn that gets caught under another turn, resulting in jamming the line so it cannot be taken up or eased.

P Papa. Blue code flag with a white rectangle, also called the Blue Peter. When flown alone: "About to sail."

padeye A rigging fixture, with a half loop and a base to be bolted to the deck or a spar, to hold blocks, shackles, or a line such as an awning tie-down.

painter A small boat's towline or tie-up line, fastened to the bow.

palm A sailmaker's or rigger's device, worn on the hand for pushing needles through sailcloth or rope strands.

parbuckle A simple purchase for raising a round object. A line is made fast at one end, then looped around the object so that hauling on the free end raises the object. Usually, as in lifting a spar, the parbuckle is set up doubled.

parcel To wrap tape or canvas strips around a rope or part of it, protecting it from the weather.

parrel A loop of rope around a mast, often with parrel beads, that slides up and down a mast, to carry a gaff or yard, or the luff of a sail, like a mast hoop.

partners The heavy reinforcing timbers at the deck opening through which a mast passes; the general area of the opening for the mast.

patch A cloth reinforcement of a sail, put on to protect against chafe or to strengthen the sail where the strain is greatest.

patent log A device for determining a vessel's speed through the water and distance run; a rotor towed on a line affixed to a mechanism that counts and records rotations.

pawl A hinged lug, dropping against a toothed wheel to prevent it running back, as on a trailer haul-out winch, an anchor windlass, etc.

pay out To let a line out, under control and not running free; the opposite of "letting fly."

peak halyard With a gaff rig, the halyard that raises the peak or outer end of the gaff, as opposed to the throat halyard.

pedestal A deck fitting to hold the gooseneck of a staysail boom.

pelican hook A hook, secured by a sliding ring, used for the gate in a lifeline.

pendant A short length of rope or wire, attached to a mooring buoy, a spar, or a cringle, as a reefing cringle on a sail; a tapering flag.

pennant Another spelling of *pendant.*

Perlon German brand of polyamide or nylon.

PFD The acronym for Personal Flotation Device, generally called a life preserver or life jacket.

pier A structure (wood, concrete, or stone), often built on piles, to which vessels can moor and on which stores can be transported to the vessel.

pile, piling A timber or post driven into the bottom to which boats can moor, which often support piers and wharves or to which floats are secured.

pinrail A rail holding belaying pins, usually along the rail of a vessel, similar to a *fiferail* which encircles the mast.

plaited rope One of several types of braided or interlaced configurations, as distinguished from twisted (laid) rope.

plow anchor A type of stockless anchor, also called CQR, which resembles an agricultural plow.

polyamide The synthetic elastic material used for fibers in both nylon sailcloth (spinnakers) and rope (usually dock lines and anchor lines).

polyester The synthetic material (one trade name: Dacron), with much less elasticity than polyamide (nylon), used for rope or sails when stretch is not desired.

polyethylene Lightweight synthetic material, used for sheet plastic and some low-cost rope fibers.

polypropylene Lightweight synthetic material used for rope fibers; because this rope floats, it is used for ski tow ropes, dinghy painters, etc. Lightweight fibers are sometimes combined with stronger, heavier fibers for special-purpose rigging lines.

Polyvinylchloride A plastic used for some marine parts not requiring great strength.

pram Dinghy, small rowing boat used as a tender, with a blunt bow, named for its fancied resemblance to a perambulator.

preventer A vang, a line rigged to prevent the boom rising; a running backstay; any line rigged in heavy weather to supplement existing rigging.

pricker A sailmaker's tool, usually with a handle, used for piercing holes, smaller than a marlinespike.

pulley A sheave, also the landsman's term for a block.

punch A tool for making holes, as a grommet punch, used with a die set to insert a metal or plastic grommet in canvas.

pulpit An enclosure on the foredeck made of metal railings and stanchions. Often the *lifeline* is secured to it.

purchase A mechanical means of increasing an applied force, such as a tackle or levers.

PVC Polyvinylchloride plastic.

Q Quebec. Yellow code flag in international signals. Means: "My vessel is healthy and I request free practique." Also referred to as the quarantine flag.

quarter The side of the hull, from amidships to the stern, or the equivalent general deck and rail area where rigging fittings such as quarter blocks are fastened; the term is also used to indicate direction from a boat, as "broad on the quarter."

quarter block A block located on the quarter, as a spinnaker sheet's turning block.

quay A masonry structure at the water's edge to which vessels can tie up and where cargo can be loaded and unloaded.

R Romeo. Red code flag with a yellow cross in the International Signal Code. No single-flag meaning.

radar reflector A metal reflector, sometimes encased in plastic to lessen wind resistance, hoisted aloft on a light halyard to be a "target" for the radar of an approaching ship. The octahedral shape makes a better reflector of radar signals than the curved parts of a vessel.

ramp A sloping launching area, usually paved,

for trailered boats; a similar slip for repairing or launching ships and boats.

rafting An informal and temporary side-by-side mooring scheme used by boats for sociability and to save space in a crowded anchorage.

ratchet block, ratchet winch Rigging devices with teeth to grip the line, allowing it to go only one way. A ratchet winch is also called a snubbing winch.

ratlines Cross lines seized to the shrouds, making the steps of a rope ladder.

rawhide Untanned leather, used for *palms,* as chafe guards on oars and, in strips, as lacings.

reaching strut A light spar with a sheave in the end used with a spinnaker pole to keep the spinnaker guy clear of the shrouds, thus avoiding chafe. British: jockey pole.

reef To reduce the area of a sail by using reef pendants and reef points or a reefing line to take in a fold of the sail or by means of a rotating boom (roller reefing).

reef knot A square knot, also made with one end slipped for easier untying.

reef pendant A strong line used to hold the luff or leech cringle to the boom when reefing.

reef points Short lines that pass through reinforcing patches or a reef band, used to reef the sail by being tied (in a reef knot) around the foot of the sail.

reel winch A special winch on the mast used for wire halyards. The wire is coiled on the drum, which is held or released by a brake.

reeve To pass a line through one or more blocks or fairleads in order to make a rigging arrangement (tackle, halyard, sheets, guys, etc.) ready for use.

reeving line bend One of several ways of attaching two ropes that must be rove through a fairlead.

relieving tackles Tackles used on the rudder to take some of the strain in heavy seas.

rig To organize and set up the rigging; to put to use by getting everything set and working, as to rig an awning; the arrangement of sails in use on a particular boat, as fore-and-aft rig.

rigging screw A turnbuckle (British usage).

right-hand lay Rope twisted to the right is said to have a right-hand lay; also called Z-twist.

roach The part of a fore-and-aft sail extending beyond a straight line between clew and head, a semicircular strip of "unmeasured" sail area.

rod rigging Stainless steel rods used in place of wire rope in sailboats; may be round or shaped to reduce wind resistance; sometimes grooved for the luff rope or slides of the headsail.

rode The anchor cable, whether rope, chain, or wire rope.

roller furling A system of reducing sail area (the equivalent of reefing) or housing the sail when not in use by rolling the sail on its luff or forward edge.

roller reefing A method of temporarily cutting down a sail's working area by rolling it up on the boom, usually by means of a mechanism attached to the boom.

rolling hitch A hitch used for attaching a line to a spar or a larger rope. When made upon its own standing part, it is a *midshipman's hitch.*

rope A strong, flexible cord made by twisting or braiding strands of natural or synthetic fibers or wire, used to transmit power or as a fastening.

rope walk The main manufacturing area where rope is made.

round turn A complete turn of a line around an object, which may be to belay the line or as the start of a knot.

round turn and two half hitches An alternate way of attaching a line to a ring or shackle, with the line circling the object and the first hitch made through one of the turns.

runners, running backstays Backstays rigged, one on each side of the boat, so that one can be in use and the other slacked off on a given tack.

running bowline A useful way to make a noose, particularly for throwing over a piling or recovering an object, as it can be tightened easily.

running rigging The sailboat rigging that controls sails and spars, as opposed to the more permanent *standing rigging.*

S Sierra. White flag with a blue rectangle, in the international code. Used alone, it means "My engines are going astern."

safety harness Straps at waist and shoulders worn by crew members working on deck in heavy weather. A line with a snap is attachable to a jackline and to various suitable rigging fixtures.

sail slides Fittings, attached to the luff of a sail, which slide up and down on a track as the sail is hoisted or lowered.

sail stops Cloth or webbing straps used to tie furled sails, also called *gaskets* or *tyers.*

sailmaker's needles Large needles, mostly triangular in section, used for hand sewing and repairs on sails and other canvas and for some ropework.

sailmaker's whipping An elaborate, secure whipping for the end of a piece of rope.

samson post A fitting, used for fastening anchor lines and towlines, similar to *bitts,* which are double.

schooner A fore-and-aft sailboat rig in which the foremast is shorter than the mainmast. A schooner may have two, three, or more masts.

scope The ratio of anchor line in use to the depth of the water; adequate scope ensures that the load on the anchor will be more nearly horizontal, thus making it bury deeper instead of pulling out.

scowing an anchor Fastening the anchor line at the crown, then stopping it at the eye of the anchor so that if it becomes fouled (as under a cable or rock), it can be raised by breaking the stop with a heavy pull and getting the anchor out by the crown. An alternative to using a separate trip line to the crown.

Scuba flag A special flag, not the international code flag, to indicate that the underwater diver, who may be using a **S**elf **C**ontained **U**nderwater **B**reathing **A**pparatus, is in the area. Other boats should take heed.

seizing A binding, as of two ropes together or a rope to a spar, using light line.

self-tailing winch A winch that takes the jib sheet in a V-shaped slot, so that another crew member is not needed to haul on the tail or cleat it.

self-tending A sail whose sheet is rigged so that it will take care of itself when the boat comes about is said to be "self-tending," as compared to a jib with a double sheet, one part of which must be slacked and the other hauled in at every tack.

sennet, sennit Small stuff, plaited to make a mat or chafing gear.

sentinel A weight, run down an anchor line to a point perhaps midway on the catenary and retrievable by a light line, to change the pull of the vessel to more nearly horizontal, thus relieving the strain on the anchor.

serving A protective line wound around a rope or part of a rope, to absorb chafe.

shackle A rigging fitting, basically U-shaped with a pin, bolt, or toggle fitted across it. A shackle may be a D-shape, a bow or harp shape, or twisted at 90° for special uses. Often used at the end of a halyard to fasten onto the headboard of a sail. A snap shackle has a spring-loaded pin.

sheave A grooved wheel, turning in a block, to carry line in a tackle, at the masthead, or as a way of changing the lead.

sheepshank A knot, more useful for shortening a tent guy on land than it is on shipboard.

sheer legs Spars or timbers forming an inverted V with a tackle rigged from the top, used for hoisting heavy objects, such as in stepping a mast.

sheet A line, attached to the clew or to a boom, to control a sail. Often rigged with tackles of various kinds, as in main sheets; jib sheets (unless self-tending) are in pairs. When a spinnaker is jibed, the sheet becomes the guy (on the pole) and the original guy becomes the sheet.

sheet bend A knot used to fasten two ropes together or to fasten a rope to an eye.

sheet stopper A mechanical contrivance, used on racing sailboats, to quickly belay a sheet without the necessity of cleating it. It also releases the winch for other uses.

sheet winch Any of several winches used to take in on and control the sheets (and sometimes guys) of a sailing vessel. Chiefly, main sheet winches and jib sheet winches are used, but in some cases they are multipurpose.

ship A large vessel; a full-rigged sailing vessel, square-rigged on all three masts.

shock cord A highly elastic line, useful for tie-downs, gilguys, or for holding a topping lift out of the leach of a sail. Shock cord has a rubber core with a braided synthetic cover or jacket.

short splice The strongest way to attach two lines to each other, by interweaving the strands.

shrouds The lateral supports of a mast, port and starboard, usually wire rope. The upper shrouds lead from the chainplates, usually over spreaders, to the masthead. The lower shrouds run from the chainplates to the base of the spreaders. Shroud tension is adjusted by tightening or loosening turnbuckles or by means of shroud adjusters, which have variable hole and pin combinations.

signal halyard A line for hoisting signals, as the international code flags.

silicone A polymeric organic silicone compound used for waterproof lubricants. Silicone rubber is frequently used in sealing deck fittings to prevent leaks.

single up To reduce the number of dock lines to a bare minimum, preparatory to departure.

single whip A single block with a line rove through it.

sisal An inexpensive, comparatively weak fiber used for some twine and rope; it is more suitable to packages than to any shipboard use.

slab reefing Another name for *jiffy reefing.*

sling A rope or chain used to hoist an object.

slip A berth between two piers or sets of pilings in which a boat or ship is docked.

slip knot A knot that can be untied by a quick pull, as one half of a bowknot.

slippery hitch A slip knot.

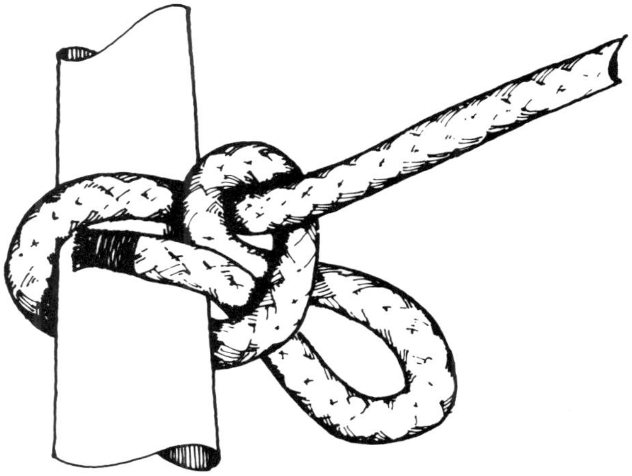

small stuff Light line, marline, codline, waxed twine, etc., used for whippings, seizings, and servings.

snap A hook to hold the luff of a headsail to the stay, a hank.

snap shackle A rigging shackle with a spring-loaded closure.

snatch block A deck block used for quick work, as setting new sheets or guys, without reeving the line. The block opens and closes with a latch.

snotter A ring or strop holding the heel of a sprit close to the mast; a rope loop used to prevent any object from slipping.

snubbing winch A winch used for quick sail-handling, with neither gearing nor a handle for leverage.

solid braid A rope construction of 9, 12, or 18 strands of fiber. It holds its shape under pressure or load but is not as strong as some other braided configurations. It is not spliceable, although plaited line (8 plaits) is.

Spanish burton A standard purchase on work boats and fishing boats, convenient and fast in use, using two single blocks, each with a becket.

Spanish windlass A method of tightening a seizing, using a roller and handspike. The marlinspike, with a bight of the seizing, is used as a lever to turn the bar; turns of the seizing around the bar make it possible to get maximum tautness. It is similar to an improvised serving mallet.

Spectra-900 A new fiber from Allied, strong, light, and abrasion resistant. It is used for rope and sailcloth.

spinnaker A three-cornered sail of light, stretchy sailcloth, usually nylon, used in running before the wind. Usually set with a pole, most spinnakers today have two leeches and two clews and are thus conveniently jibed. Often called a 'chute or a parachute spinnaker because some of the design technology, particularly the multiple panels of light nylon cloth, was an aviation development.

spinnaker chute A tubular device of canvas, netting, or plastic on the foredeck or in some versions on the halyard. Used on smaller racing boats, usually not at sea. The spinnaker is lowered into it, using downhaul lines; the sail can be raised again by merely hoisting.

spinnaker guy The line aft from the pole clew of a spinnaker is the after guy. The line forward and down, used as a downhaul on the pole, is called the foreguy.

spinnaker net The netting sometimes used in dowsing the spinnaker so it won't get overboard when being lowered.

spinnaker sheet The principal sail control line, from the free clew aft.

splice A method of interweaving the ends of two ropes or a rope into its own standing part; also, a method of splicing fiber rope to wire rope.

spreacher blocks Blocks used for both the spinnaker guys and sheets and for jib sheets when reaching.

spreader boots Rubber, leather, or canvas padding attached to the tips of spreaders to reduce chafe on a genoa jib when sailing closehauled.

spreaders On a sailboat, short wood or metal spars used to spread the upper shrouds, adding strength to the rigging.

spring line A dock line leading forward or aft whose primary purpose is to keep the vessel from moving aft or foward along the pier or float.

spun fibers Synthetic fibers that have been texturized by spinning before being twisted into yarn. Spun fibers are used for running rigging, partly for efficiency on sheet winches, partly for the feeling on the hands.

spun yarn Two- or three-strand small stuff, twisted loosely, usually tarred, used for servings and small lashings.

square knot One of the most useful (and sometimes overused) of all knots. Also called the reef knot, good for tying around something, inadequate for tying two lines together.

staghorn bollard A bollard with two horizontal arms.

stainless steel Any of many formulations or alloys of iron that resist rust. Some are nonmagnetic unless cold-worked. If not kept clean, surface corrosion can lead to superficial rust and eventually pit the metal.

stanchion An upright pillar support. On pleasure boats, stanchions are mainly used with lifelines for guard rails or the hold awnings.

standing rigging The permanent rigging of a sailboat or ship, usually wire rope and fittings, as distinguished from the running rigging, which controls the sails, booms, and movable spars.

standing part The fixed or inactive part of a line; the hauling part, in contrast, is the active portion of the line in a tackle.

start sheets To ease sheets just slightly, after sailing closehauled, thus adding speed to the boat, although she will not point quite as high into the wind.

stays The portion of the standing rigging on a sailboat supporting the masts in a fore-and-aft direction. There are backstays, headstays (to the masthead), and forestays.

staysail boom A boom, for either a forestaysail or

a sail set on a stay to another mast. The sail may be laced to its boom, use slides and a track, or have only the tack and the clew made fast. The sheet usually works on a fixed deck block or a traveler on a track and thus is *self-tending*.

stemhead The top of the stem (the furthest foward part of a vessel); stemhead fittings are designed for the attachment of headstays, jib downhauls, and other rigging.

step The base on which a mast sets; to put a mast into place (in its step) in a vessel.

stock The crossbar of a standard anchor, at right angles to the flukes, whose purpose is to turn the anchor so the flukes dig into the bottom.

stockless anchor An anchor of nontraditional geometry, using shapes such as the plow, or with the equivalent of a stock at the crown end so arranged that it turns the anchor to a dig-in position.

stop A limiting device, on a track, traveler, rudder, or other part; a gasket, sail stop, or tyer; a method of securing the end of a line, after a knot is tied, to the standing part, as by seizing it, for added security; to tie a light twine around a sail (particularly a spinnaker) so that it can be hoisted, then broken out by breaking the light line.

stopper Something that holds a line; a stopper knot; a *sheet stopper*, which works by jamming the line; a chain stopper like the devil's claw; a line put on another to haul it.

stopping twine Light string, sometimes called "rotten twine," used to tie a bundled spinnaker so it can be hoisted "in stops."

strand The yarns, twisted together, that are twisted or laid in the opposite direction to form laid rope or plaited to form braided rope.

strop A ring of rope around a block or a spar, with a ring or becket in it to take a shackle; a short line to add to the length of a headsail luff.

strut A small projecting support or bracket, as a jumper strut, usually part of the rigging; a similar support for a propeller shaft.

studding sail (Pronounced stuns'l) Extension sails, for light airs, set outside squaresails.

S-twist Rope made in a left-hand lay configuration, so named because the strands appear to slant

from left to right as in the letter *S*. Right-hand rope has a Z-twist.

sausage A long sail cover/bag for a preflaked headsail, usually a genoa, using Velcro strip or a plastic zipper in such a way that the jib can be ready to hoist rapidly.

surgeon's knot A square knot with one extra twist in the first part of it to keep it from coming undone while it is being tied; useful for package tying. Done in reverse, with the extra twist on the outside, it is good for tying in battens because it rarely shakes out like a square knot.

swage, swaging Any of several pressure-fitting processes, for the end of a wire rope, in which a metal sleeve or other compression arrangement fastens a terminal to the wire when put in a swaging press.

swageless terminal A wire rope terminal using a screw compression over a specially shaped core.

swallow The opening in a block through which the rope enters to run over the sheave.

swallow-tail pennant A pennant with a V-shape at the end.

switch A track device, also called a gate, enabling either of two sails to be run onto the same track, as when setting a storm trysail.

synthetic Man-made plastics used in hard form

(nylon, Duron, Delrin, Tufnol) or as fibers, as in rope and sailcloth (nylon, polyester, Dacron, Terylene, polypropylene, polyethylene).

T Tango. Red, white, and blue code flag. In U.S. harbors a large T-flag is often used to indicate: "Send shore boat or launch."

tabling Double or triple reinforcement hems in a sail.

tack The forward bottom corner of a fore-and-aft sail or either bottom corner of a square-sail.

tackle A purchase to increase power, using line (the fall) and one or more blocks. See *mechanical advantage*; the total parts used for a special purpose, as *ground tackle.*

tackline The attachment line, used between signal flags.

tagline Control lines, to adjust a mainsheet traveler.

Talurite British compression fitting, usually for terminals of wire rope, although occasionally used on special synthetic double-braid line.

tang A metal fitting by which shrouds and stays are attached to a mast; a rigging fitting on a spar.

Tanzaloy An aluminum alloy used in rigging fittings.

taper To gradually reduce the numbers of yarns in a strand, to make a splice smaller.

tarring Coating rope, light line such as marlin, or a serving with tar to preserve and waterproof the natural fibers.

Teflon A synthetic fluorine used to prevent sticking; a typical marine use is as a spray lubricant.

tell-tale A feather, yarn, or vane to indicate apparent wind direction while sailing.

tender A small boat, such as a dinghy, used for transporting crew and supplies to and from a larger boat.

Tergal French polyester, used in rope and sailcloth.

Terital Polyester fiber manufactured in Italy.

Terlenka Polyester fiber manufactured in The Netherlands.

tensile strength The resistance of rope to a force tending to break it; also called breaking strength.

terminals The end fittings of wire rigging, shrouds, stays, lifelines, and sometimes rope rigging such as halyards, etc.

Terylene Polyester fibers (made in Britain) used for rope and sailcloth.

Tetoron Trade name, Japanese, for polyester.

thief knot A simple but tricky knot resembling a square knot.

thimble An eye or ring used inside a rope eye splice, reducing chafe and enabling a shackle to be attached. The line fits into the concave outside; the inside is convex and bears the strain and wear. Some newer design thimbles have ears added.

three-strand rope Laid rope, the oldest form known, is made by twisting three strands, which themselves are formed by twisting the yarns in the opposite direction.

throat halyard A gaff-rigged halyard used at the throat of the gaff, the end nearest the mast, in conjunction with the peak halyard.

tide rode A vessel at anchor swinging with the current is said to be "tide rode," as opposed to "wind rode."

tie-downs Light line, shock cord, straps, or webbing used to secure objects on deck.

tiers Variation of British *tyers*; short straps used to hold a furled sail (in U.S., *gaskets* or *stops*).

timber hitch A quick knot for fastening a line to a round object, such as a spar.

titanium A silvery gray metal, light and strong, used in alloys for high-tech spars and rigging.

toggle A universal joint, a U-shaped link with a pin, used between a *chainplate* and a *turnbuckle.*

tophamper The parts of a boat (cabin top, masts and spars, rigging, objects stowed on deck) above the deck, which affect both the stability and the windage of a vessel.

topping lift A line used to support or adjust a boom or other spar; when a sail is lowered, the topping lift holds the boom; a spinnaker pole's topping lift controls the horizontal angle of the pole and thus the set of the sail.

torque Rotational force; the tendency of a (laid) rope to rotate under a load.

towboat hitch An excellent, if specialized, knot,

quickly tied and always easy to unfasten, even under strain.

track Steel, light alloy, or plastic fitting on deck or on a spar, on which slides are used to hold the luff or foot of a sail, or cars (travelers) for rigging fittings such as blocks for sheets or a spinnaker pole socket.

trampoline The netting or canvas between the hulls of a catamaran.

trapeze A sling-seat or harness, attached to a wire from the mast, used by small-boat racing sailors to get their weight outboard to windward.

traveler A slide or car used on a track in the adjustment of rigging.

Trevira Polyester manufactured in Germany.

triatic stay A stay from one masthead to the other in a fore-and-aft rigged boat such as a ketch, yawl, or schooner.

trice To haul up or to lash an object with a line.

trip line A line to the crown of an anchor (or the outboard end of a sea anchor) so that it can be pulled free if the flukes get caught under a rock or cable.

truck The top of a mast or the circular block of wood at the masthead with a sheave for a burgee halyard.

trunnion A double pivot, used for cannons, shackles, and other mechanisms.

Tufnol A tough plastic used for small rigging parts.

tune To adjust the rigging for maximum performance on a sailboat. Hydraulic backstay adjusters, mast jacks, shroud adjusters, tension gauges, and other devices are used on advanced racing boats.

turk's head A fancy knot used for ornamentation.

turnbuckle A screw-type shroud adjuster (U.S.), also called a rigging screw and a bottle screw.

turtle A cloth device, a circular bag closed at one end with Velcro or an elastic strip at one end, to hold a spinnaker before hoisting.

twine Small stuff used for whippings, often waxed.

twin foil headstay A double headstay, used on racing sailboats so that one jib can be hoisted before the other is lowered.

twin-pole jibe A method of jibing spinnakers, using two poles, as compared with *dip pole* or *end-for-end jibing.*

two half hitches A knot formed by making a basic clove hitch around its own standing part.

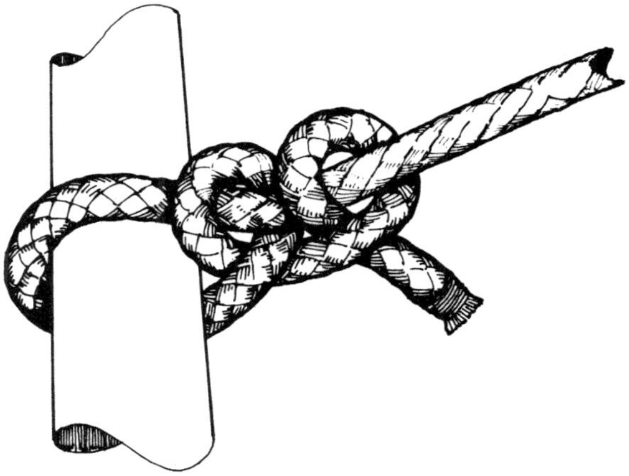

two-blocked Drawn up as far as possible, a line is chockablock or two-blocked.

U Uniform. Red and white checkered code flag. Used alone, it means "You are running into danger."

ultraviolet light Invisible rays at one end of the spectrum that cause weakening of many fibers, particularly polyethylene.

Una-rig One British way of saying catboat, for an early model, named *Una,* with a single sail on one mast.

V Victor. White code flag with a red cross. Flown alone, it means "I require assistance."

vane Light metal or plastic sheet on a pivot, to show the direction of the apparent wind.

vang A line, tackle, or hydraulic strut to hold the boom down and thus increase the mainsail's efficiency or prevent slatting. Modern racing rigs have center vangs, which don't need adjusting when tacking. A vang rigged from mid-boom to a shackle on the rail is often rigged on ocean-sailing yachts, whether racing or cruising.

veer To pay out an anchor line, to increase scope, or to pay out a line at a dock to change the angle of the vessel. The wind is also said to veer when it changes direction clockwise.

Velcro Trade name for a plastic tape fastener with thousands of tiny hooks; useful for closures, for securing coils of rope, curtains, dodgers, etc.

vernier stay adjuster A mechanism, with graduated scale adjustments, for tensioning shrouds and stays.

Vise-Grip Trade name for compound levers, pliers and other tools, including C-clamps.

W Whisky. Blue, white, and red code flag. As a single-flag signal, it means "I require medical assistance."

wall and crown A wall knot forms a knob that prevents a line passing through an eye or aperture. A crown knot added to the wall makes it more ornamental as well as increasing the diameter and helping keep the wall knot from coming undone.

warp A line, such as a hawser, used in towing, kedging, or mooring; to move a vessel by hauling on a warp.

weather cloth A canvas strip fastened to the lifelines, protecting the cockpit or deck from spray, a *dodger*.

webbing Comparatively heavy woven straps, used as sail *gaskets*, dinghy *gripes*, and for tie-downs such as for boats on trailers.

weighing Raising the anchor.

West Country whipping A knotted whipping, made by tying overhand knots on alternate sides of the rope.

wharf Shore structure, built on piles, parallel to the water's edge, unlike a *pier*, which juts out.

whip A single line rove through a single block aloft and used for hoisting (no mechanical advantage). Another block can be added, in any of several ways.

whipping Binding twine or marline about the ends of a line to prevent unlaying or fraying. Common whipping, sailmaker's whipping, and West Country whippings are the most commonly used.

whisker pole A light spar used to wing out a jib on the side opposite the mainsail when sailing downwind.

wildcat A wheel or narrow drum on one side of an anchor windlass, shaped so it will accept chain links (U.S.); in Britain, a gypsy, although this term is also used in the U.S. for a windlass drum used for anchor line.

winch A revolving drum, operated by hand power or electricity, for hauling anchor lines and halyards and for controlling sheets; usually geared, a winch may be either horizontal or vertical. See *windlass*.

wind-rode A vessel at anchor may lie to the wind if its force is greater than any currents present; she is then said to be wind-rode, as opposed to *tide-rode*.

windlass A winch mounted on deck for hoisting an anchor.

windsail An air scoop used to force fresh air into the cabin of a boat at anchor.

wire rope Rope made from twisted wires, but in more elaborate configurations than laid rope; used for standing rigging, some running rigging, for lifelines (often plastic-covered), and occasionally for anchor lines. Two numbers indicate the geometry; the first is for the number of strands and the second for the number of wires in each strand. Examples: 7 x 19, 7 x 7, 1 x 19.

wishbone A double spar, with each side bow-shaped; the sail is in the center and can take a cambered shape somewhat differently than a sail held at the foot on a track. Most sailboards have wishbone rigs.

wishbone anchor A lightweight anchor with a single broad fluke enclosed in a "wishbone shank."

worm-and-parcel To wrap a line first with tarred marline then with canvas, thus making a chafe guard. The worming fills the space between the strands. Worming can also be done before serving.

X X-ray. White code flag with a blue cross. As a single-letter signal, it means "Stop carrying out your intention; watch for my signals."

xebec A three-masted Mediterranean sailing ship with long overhangs at bow and stern.

XLS-900 A composite double-braid rope, made by Samson, with a polyester cover and a Spectra-900 core.

Y Yankee. A yellow and red diagonally striped flag in the international code. Used alone: "I am dragging my anchor."

yacht Originally, a state vessel, as a monarch's personal boat; a pleasure craft (excluding canoes and dinghies); in British usage, *yacht* usually means "sailboat," while in the U.S. there is a connotation of luxury, sail or power.

yacht braid A spliceable double braid or braid inside another braid used for running rigging on a sailboat.

yachtsman anchor A modification of the old-fashioned anchor, with a stock that in use is held in place with a key but can be folded for easier deck stowage.

yard A horizontal spar on which a square-sail can be set; the term is also used for the spar on which a lateen sail or lugsail is set. "The sun is over the yardarm," is an invitation to have a drink.

yarn When fibers or filaments are spun, they become yarn. Yarns are twisted into strands, and the strands are braided or laid into rope.

yawl A two-masted vessel in which the after mast is comparatively short (compared to a ketch). A yawl's mast is stepped aft of the rudder post, a ketch's forward.

Z Zulu. Black, yellow, blue, and red code flag. As a single-letter signal, it means "I require a tug."

zipper In sailmaking, a device to take out or add fullness at the foot of a sail or to make a sleeve luff around a spar or stay. Zippers are also used for sailcovers, *sausages*, and many miscellaneous items.

Z-twist Right-hand lay.

Index